FREDERICK DOUGLASS

SELECTED WORKS COLLECTION

Narrative of the Life of Frederick Douglass
My Bondage and My Freedom

Frederick Douglass

C L A S S Y
PUBLISHING

FREDERICK DOUGLASS SELECTED WORKS COLLECTION
by Frederick Douglass
Published by Classy Publishing, 2024

www.classypublishing.com
info@classypublishing.com

ISBN: 978-93-5522-790-4

Cover Design by Classy Publishing

For more books
Please visit *classypublishing.com*

FREDERICK DOUGLASS

Frederick Douglass was born in slavery as Frederick Augustus Washington Bailey near Easton in Talbot County, Maryland. He was not sure of the exact year of his birth, but he knew that it was 1817 or 1818. As a young boy he was sent to Baltimore, to be a house servant, where he learned to read and write, with the assistance of his master's wife. In 1838 he escaped from slavery and went to New York City, where he married Anna Murray, a free colored woman whom he had met in Baltimore. Soon thereafter he changed his name to Frederick Douglass. In 1841 he addressed a convention of the Massachusetts Anti-Slavery Society in Nantucket and so greatly impressed the group that they immediately employed him as an agent. He was such an impressive orator that numerous persons doubted if he had ever been a slave, so he wrote *Narrative Of The Life Of Frederick Douglass*. During the Civil War he assisted in the recruiting of colored men for the 54th and 55th Massachusetts Regiments and consistently argued for the emancipation of slaves. After the war he was active in securing and protecting the rights of the freemen. In his later years, at different times, he was secretary of the Santo Domingo Commission, marshall and recorder of deeds of the District of Columbia, and United States Minister to Haiti. His other autobiographical works are *My Bondage And My Freedom* and *Life And Times Of Frederick Douglass*, published in 1855 and 1881 respectively. He died in 1895.

CONTENTS

NARRATIVE OF THE LIFE OF FREDERICK DOUGLASS

AN AMERICAN SLAVE

PREFACE

In the month of August, 1841, I attended an anti-slavery convention in Nantucket, at which it was my happiness to become acquainted with *Frederick Douglass*, the writer of the following Narrative. He was a stranger to nearly every member of that body; but, having recently made his escape from the southern prison-house of bondage, and feeling his curiosity excited to ascertain the principles and measures of the abolitionists,—of whom he had heard a somewhat vague description while he was a slave,—he was induced to give his attendance, on the occasion alluded to, though at that time a resident in New Bedford.

Fortunate, most fortunate occurrence!—fortunate for the millions of his manacled brethren, yet panting for deliverance from their awful thraldom!—fortunate for the cause of negro emancipation, and of universal liberty!—fortunate for the land of his birth, which he has already done so much to save and bless!—fortunate for a large circle of friends and acquaintances, whose sympathy and affection he has strongly secured by the many sufferings he has endured, by his virtuous traits of character, by his ever-abiding remembrance of those who are in bonds, as being bound with them!—fortunate for the multitudes, in various parts of our republic, whose minds he has enlightened on the subject of slavery, and who have been melted to tears by his pathos, or roused to virtuous indignation by his stirring eloquence against the enslavers of men!—fortunate for himself, as it at once brought him into the field of public usefulness, "gave the world assurance of a MAN," quickened the slumbering energies of his soul, and consecrated him to the great work of breaking the rod of the oppressor, and letting the oppressed go free!

I shall never forget his first speech at the convention—the extraordinary emotion it excited in my own mind—the powerful impression it created upon a crowded auditory, completely taken by surprise—the applause which followed from the beginning to the end of his felicitous remarks. I think I never hated slavery so intensely as at that moment; certainly, my perception of the enormous outrage which is inflicted by it, on the godlike nature of its victims, was rendered far more clear than ever. There stood one, in physical proportion and stature commanding and exact—in intellect richly endowed—in natural eloquence a prodigy—in soul manifestly "created but a little lower than the angels"—yet a slave, ay, a fugitive slave,—trembling for his safety, hardly daring to believe that on the American soil, a single white person could be found who would befriend him at all hazards, for the love of God and humanity! Capable of high attainments as an intellectual and moral being—needing nothing but a comparatively small amount of cultivation to make him an ornament to society and a blessing to his race—by the law of the land, by the voice of the people, by the terms of the slave code, he was only a piece of property, a beast of burden, a chattel personal, nevertheless!

A beloved friend from New Bedford prevailed on Mr. DOUGLASS to address the convention. He came forward to the platform with a hesitancy and embarrassment, necessarily the attendants of a sensitive mind in such a novel position. After apologizing for his ignorance, and reminding the audience that slavery was a poor school for the human intellect and heart, he proceeded to narrate some of the facts in his own history as a slave, and in the course of his speech gave utterance to many noble thoughts and thrilling reflections. As soon as he had taken his seat, filled with hope and admiration, I rose, and declared that PATRICK HENRY, of revolutionary fame, never made a speech more eloquent in the cause of liberty, than the one we had just listened to from the lips of that hunted fugitive. So I believed at that time—such is my belief now. I reminded the audience of the peril which surrounded this self-emancipated young man at the North,—even in Massachusetts, on the soil of the Pilgrim Fathers, among the descendants of revolutionary sires; and I appealed to them, whether they would ever allow him to be carried back into slavery,—law or no law, constitution or no constitution. The response was unanimous and in thunder-tones—"NO!" "Will you succor and protect him as a brother-man—a resident of the old Bay State?" "YES!" shouted the whole mass, with an energy so startling, that the ruthless tyrants south of Mason and Dixon's line might almost have heard the mighty burst of feeling, and recognized it as the pledge of an invincible determination, on the part of those who gave it, never to betray him that wanders, but to hide the outcast, and firmly to abide the consequences.

It was at once deeply impressed upon my mind, that, if Mr. DOUGLASS could be persuaded to consecrate his time and talents to the promotion of the anti-slavery enterprise, a powerful impetus would be given to it, and a stunning blow at the same time inflicted on northern prejudice against a colored complexion. I therefore endeavored to instil hope and courage into his mind, in order that he might dare to engage in a vocation so anomalous and responsible for a person in his situation; and I was seconded in this effort by warm-hearted friends, especially by the late General Agent of the Massachusetts Anti-Slavery Society, Mr. JOHN A. COLLINS, whose judgment in this instance entirely coincided with my own. At first, he could give no encouragement; with unfeigned diffidence, he expressed his conviction that he was not adequate to the performance of so great a task; the path marked out was wholly an untrodden one; he was sincerely apprehensive that he should do more harm than good. After much deliberation, however, he consented to make a trial; and ever since that period, he has acted as a lecturing agent, under the auspices either of the American or the Massachusetts Anti-Slavery Society. In labors he has been most abundant; and his success in combating prejudice, in gaining proselytes, in agitating the public mind, has far surpassed the most sanguine expectations that were raised at the commencement of his brilliant career. He has borne himself with gentleness and meekness, yet with true manliness of character. As a public speaker, he excels in pathos, wit, comparison, imitation, strength of reasoning, and fluency of language. There is in him that union of head and heart, which is indispensable to an enlightenment of the heads and a winning of the hearts of others. May his strength continue to be equal to his day! May he continue to "grow in grace, and in the knowledge of God," that he may be increasingly serviceable in the cause of bleeding humanity, whether at home or abroad!

It is certainly a very remarkable fact, that one of the most efficient advocates of the slave population, now before the public, is a fugitive slave, in the person of *Frederick Douglass*; and that the free colored population of the United States are as ably represented by one of their own number, in the person of *Charles Lenox Remond*, whose eloquent appeals have extorted the highest applause of multitudes on both sides of the Atlantic. Let the calumniators of the colored race despise themselves for their baseness and illiberality of spirit, and henceforth cease to talk of the natural inferiority of those who require nothing but time and opportunity to attain to the highest point of human excellence.

It may, perhaps, be fairly questioned, whether any other portion of the population of the earth could have endured the privations, sufferings and horrors of slavery, without having become more degraded in the scale of humanity than the slaves of African descent. Nothing has been left undone to cripple their intellects, darken their minds, debase their moral nature, obliterate all traces of their relationship to mankind; and yet how wonderfully they have sustained the mighty load of a most frightful bondage, under which they have been groaning for centuries! To illustrate the effect of slavery on the white man,—to show that he has no powers of endurance, in such a condition, superior to those of his black brother,—*Daniel O'Connell*, the distinguished advocate of universal emancipation, and the mightiest champion of prostrate but not conquered Ireland, relates the following anecdote in a speech delivered by him in the Conciliation Hall, Dublin, before the Loyal National Repeal Association, March 31, 1845. "No matter," said *Mr. O'Connell*, "under what specious term it may disguise itself, slavery is still hideous. *It has a natural, an inevitable tendency to brutalize every noble faculty of man.* An American sailor, who was cast away on the shore of Africa, where he was kept in slavery for three years, was, at the expiration of that period, found to be imbruted and stultified—he had lost all reasoning power; and having forgotten his native language, could only utter some savage gibberish between Arabic and English, which nobody could understand, and which even he himself found difficulty in pronouncing. So much for the humanizing influence of *The Domestic Institution!*" Admitting this to have been an extraordinary case of mental deterioration, it proves at least that the white slave can sink as low in the scale of humanity as the black one.

Mr. Douglass has very properly chosen to write his own Narrative, in his own style, and according to the best of his ability, rather than to employ some one else. It is, therefore, entirely his own production; and, considering how long and dark was the career he had to run as a slave,—how few have been his opportunities to improve his mind since he broke his iron fetters,—it is, in my judgment, highly creditable to his head and heart. He who can peruse it without a tearful eye, a heaving breast, an afflicted spirit,—without being filled with an unutterable abhorrence of slavery and all its abettors, and animated with a determination to seek the immediate overthrow of that execrable system,—without trembling for the fate of this country in the hands of a righteous God, who is ever on the side of the oppressed, and whose arm is not shortened that it cannot save,—must have a flinty heart, and be qualified to act the part of a trafficker "in slaves and the souls of men." I am confident that it is essentially true in all its statements; that nothing has been set down in malice, nothing exaggerated, nothing drawn from the imagination; that it comes short of the reality, rather than overstates a single fact in regard to *slavery as it is*. The experience of *Frederick Douglass*, as a slave, was not a peculiar one; his lot was not especially a hard one; his case may be regarded as a very fair specimen of the treatment of slaves in Maryland, in which State it is conceded that they are better fed and less cruelly treated than in Georgia, Alabama, or Louisiana. Many have suffered incomparably more, while very few on the plantations have suffered less, than himself. Yet how deplorable was his situation! what terrible chastisements were inflicted upon his person! what still more shocking outrages were perpetrated upon his mind! with all his noble powers and sublime aspirations, how like a brute was he treated, even by those professing to have the same mind in them that was in Christ Jesus! to what dreadful liabilities was he continually subjected! how destitute of friendly counsel and aid, even in his greatest extremities! how heavy was the midnight of woe which shrouded in blackness the last ray of hope, and filled the future with terror and gloom! what longings after freedom took possession of his breast, and how his misery augmented, in proportion as he grew reflective and intelligent,—thus demonstrating that a happy slave is an extinct man! how he thought, reasoned, felt, under the lash of the driver, with the chains upon his limbs! what perils he encountered in his endeavors to escape from his horrible doom! and how signal have been his deliverance and preservation in the midst of a nation of pitiless enemies!

This Narrative contains many affecting incidents, many passages of great eloquence and power; but I think the most thrilling one of them all is the description *Douglass* gives of his feelings, as he stood soliloquizing respecting his fate, and the chances of his one day being a freeman, on the banks of the Chesapeake Bay—viewing the receding vessels as they flew with their white wings before the breeze, and apostrophizing them as animated by the living spirit of freedom. Who can read that passage, and be insensible to its pathos and sublimity? Compressed into it is a whole Alexandrian library of thought, feeling, and sentiment—all that can, all that need be urged, in the form of expostulation, entreaty, rebuke, against that crime of crimes,—making man the property of his fellow-man! O, how accursed is that system, which entombs the godlike mind of man, defaces the divine image, reduces those who by creation were crowned with glory and honor to a level with four-footed beasts, and exalts the dealer in human flesh above all that is called God! Why should its existence be prolonged one hour? Is it not evil, only evil, and that continually? What does its presence imply but the absence of all fear of God, all regard for man, on the part of the people of the United States? Heaven speed its eternal overthrow!

So profoundly ignorant of the nature of slavery are many persons, that they are stubbornly incredulous whenever they read or listen to any recital of the cruelties which are daily inflicted on its victims. They do not deny that the slaves are held as property; but that terrible fact seems to convey to their minds no idea of injustice, exposure to outrage, or savage barbarity. Tell them of cruel scourgings, of mutilations and brandings, of scenes of pollution and blood, of the banishment of all light and knowledge, and they affect to be greatly indignant at such enormous exaggerations, such wholesale misstatements, such abominable libels on the character of the southern planters! As if all these direful outrages were not the natural results of slavery! As if it were less cruel to reduce a human being to the condition of a thing, than to give him a severe flagellation, or to deprive him of necessary food and clothing! As if whips, chains, thumb-screws, paddles, blood-hounds, overseers, drivers, patrols, were not all indispensable to keep the slaves down, and to give protection to their ruthless oppressors! As if, when the marriage institution is abolished, concubinage, adultery, and incest, must not necessarily abound; when all the rights of humanity are annihilated, any barrier remains to protect the victim from the fury of the spoiler; when absolute power is assumed over life and liberty, it will not be wielded with destructive sway! Skeptics of this character abound in society. In some few instances, their incredulity arises from a want of reflection; but, generally, it indicates a hatred of the light, a desire to shield slavery from the assaults of its foes, a contempt of the colored race, whether bond or free. Such will try to discredit the shocking tales of slaveholding cruelty which are recorded in this truthful Narrative; but they will labor in vain. *Mr. Douglass* has frankly disclosed the place of his birth, the names of those who claimed ownership in his body and soul, and the names also of those who committed the crimes which he has alleged against them. His statements, therefore, may easily be disproved, if they are untrue.

In the course of his Narrative, he relates two instances of murderous cruelty,—in one of which a planter deliberately shot a slave belonging to a neighboring plantation, who had unintentionally gotten within his lordly domain in quest of fish; and in the other, an overseer blew out the brains of a slave who had fled to a stream of water to escape a bloody scourging. *Mr. Douglass* states that in neither of these instances was any thing done by way of legal arrest or judicial investigation. The Baltimore American, of March 17, 1845, relates a similar case of atrocity, perpetrated with similar impunity—as follows:—"*Shooting a slave.*—We learn, upon the authority of a letter from Charles county, Maryland, received by a gentleman of this city, that a young man, named Matthews, a nephew of General Matthews, and whose father, it is believed, holds an office at Washington, killed one of the slaves upon his father's farm by shooting him. The letter states that young Matthews had been left in charge of the farm; that he gave an order to the servant, which was disobeyed, when he proceeded to the house, *obtained a gun, and, returning, shot the servant.* He immediately, the letter continues, fled to his father's residence, where he still remains unmolested."—Let it never be forgotten, that no slaveholder or overseer can be convicted of any outrage perpetrated on the person of a slave, however diabolical it may be, on the testimony of colored witnesses, whether bond or free. By the slave code, they are adjudged to be as incompetent to testify against a white man, as though they were indeed a part of the brute creation. Hence, there is no legal protection in fact, whatever there may be in form, for the slave population; and any amount of cruelty may be inflicted on them with impunity. Is it possible for the human mind to conceive of a more horrible state of society?

The effect of a religious profession on the conduct of southern masters is vividly described in the following Narrative, and shown to be any thing but salutary. In the nature of the case, it must be in the highest degree pernicious. The testimony of *Mr. Douglass*, on this point, is sustained by a cloud of witnesses, whose veracity is unimpeachable. "A slaveholder's profession of Christianity is a palpable imposture. He is a felon of the highest grade. He is a man-stealer. It is of no importance what you put in the other scale."

Reader! are you with the man-stealers in sympathy and purpose, or on the side of their down-trodden victims? If with the former, then are you the foe of God and man. If with the latter, what are you prepared to do and dare in their behalf? Be faithful, be vigilant, be untiring in your efforts to break every yoke, and let the oppressed go free. Come what may—cost what it may—inscribe on the banner which you unfurl to the breeze, as your religious and political motto—"NO COMPROMISE WITH SLAVERY! NO UNION WITH SLAVEHOLDERS!"

WM. LLOYD GARRISON BOSTON,
May 1, 1845.

LETTER FROM WENDELL PHILLIPS, ESQ.

BOSTON, *April* 22, 1845.

My Dear Friend:

You remember the old fable of "The Man and the Lion," where the lion complained that he should not be so misrepresented "when the lions wrote history."

I am glad the time has come when the "lions write history." We have been left long enough to gather the character of slavery from the involuntary evidence of the masters. One might, indeed, rest sufficiently satisfied with what, it is evident, must be, in general, the results of such a relation, without seeking farther to find whether they have followed in every instance. Indeed, those who stare at the half-peck of corn a week, and love to count the lashes on the slave's back, are seldom the "stuff" out of which reformers and abolitionists are to be made. I remember that, in 1838, many were waiting for the results of the West India experiment, before they could come into our ranks. Those "results" have come long ago; but, alas! few of that number have come with them, as converts. A man must be disposed to judge of emancipation by other tests than whether it has increased the produce of sugar,—and to hate slavery for other reasons than because it starves men and whips women,—before he is ready to lay the first stone of his anti-slavery life.

I was glad to learn, in your story, how early the most neglected of God's children waken to a sense of their rights, and of the injustice done them. Experience is a keen teacher; and long before you had mastered your A B C, or knew where the "white sails" of the Chesapeake were bound, you began, I see, to gauge the wretchedness of the slave, not by his hunger and want, not by his lashes and toil, but by the cruel and blighting death which gathers over his soul.

In connection with this, there is one circumstance which makes your recollections peculiarly valuable, and renders your early insight the more remarkable. You come from that part of the country where we are told slavery appears with its fairest features. Let us hear, then, what it is at its best estate—

gaze on its bright side, if it has one; and then imagination may task her powers to add dark lines to the picture, as she travels southward to that (for the colored man) Valley of the Shadow of Death, where the Mississippi sweeps along.

Again, we have known you long, and can put the most entire confidence in your truth, candor, and sincerity. Every one who has heard you speak has felt, and, I am confident, every one who reads your book will feel, persuaded that you give them a fair specimen of the whole truth. No one-sided portrait,—no wholesale complaints,—but strict justice done, whenever individual kindliness has neutralized, for a moment, the deadly system with which it was strangely allied. You have been with us, too, some years, and can fairly compare the twilight of rights, which your race enjoy at the North, with that "noon of night" under which they labor south of Mason and Dixon's line. Tell us whether, after all, the half-free colored man of Massachusetts is worse off than the pampered slave of the rice swamps!

In reading your life, no one can say that we have unfairly picked out some rare specimens of cruelty. We know that the bitter drops, which even you have drained from the cup, are no incidental aggravations, no individual ills, but such as must mingle always and necessarily in the lot of every slave. They are the essential ingredients, not the occasional results, of the system.

After all, I shall read your book with trembling for you. Some years ago, when you were beginning to tell me your real name and birthplace, you may remember I stopped you, and preferred to remain ignorant of all. With the exception of a vague description, so I continued, till the other day, when you read me your memoirs. I hardly knew, at the time, whether to thank you or not for the sight of them, when I reflected that it was still dangerous, in Massachusetts, for honest men to tell their names! They say the fathers, in 1776, signed the Declaration of Independence with the halter about their necks. You, too, publish your declaration of freedom with danger compassing you around. In all the broad lands which the Constitution of the United States overshadows, there is no single spot,—however narrow or desolate,—where a fugitive slave can plant himself and say, "I am safe." The whole armory of Northern Law has no shield for you. I am free to say that, in your place, I should throw the MS. into the fire.

You, perhaps, may tell your story in safety, endeared as you are to so many warm hearts by rare gifts, and a still rarer devotion of them to the service of others. But it will be owing only to your labors, and the fearless efforts of those who, trampling the laws and Constitution of the country under their feet, are determined that they will "hide the outcast," and that their hearths shall be, spite of the law, an asylum for the oppressed, if, some time or other, the humblest may stand in our streets, and bear witness in safety against the cruelties of which he has been the victim.

Yet it is sad to think, that these very throbbing hearts which welcome your story, and form your best safeguard in telling it, are all beating contrary to the "statute in such case made and provided." Go on, my dear friend, till you, and those who, like you, have been saved, so as by fire, from the dark prison-house, shall stereotype these free, illegal pulses into statutes; and New England, cutting loose from a blood-stained Union, shall glory in being the house of refuge for the oppressed,—till we no longer merely "*hide* the outcast," or make a merit of standing idly by while he is hunted in our midst; but, consecrating anew the soil of the Pilgrims as an asylum for the oppressed, proclaim our *welcome* to the slave so loudly, that the tones shall reach every hut in the Carolinas, and make the broken-hearted bondman leap up at the thought of old Massachusetts.

God speed the day!
Till then, and ever,
Yours truly,
WENDELL PHILLIPS

CHAPTER I

I was born in Tuckahoe, near Hillsborough, and about twelve miles from Easton, in Talbot county, Maryland. I have no accurate knowledge of my age, never having seen any authentic record containing it. By far the larger part of the slaves know as little of their ages as horses know of theirs, and it is the wish of most masters within my knowledge to keep their slaves thus ignorant. I do not remember to have ever met a slave who could tell of his birthday. They seldom come nearer to it than planting-time, harvest-time, cherry-time, spring-time, or fall-time. A want of information concerning my own was a source of unhappiness to me even during childhood. The white children could tell their ages. I could not tell why I ought to be deprived of the same privilege. I was not allowed to make any inquiries of my master concerning it. He deemed all such inquiries on the part of a slave improper and impertinent, and evidence of a restless spirit. The nearest estimate I can give makes me now between twenty-seven and twenty-eight years of age. I come to this, from hearing my master say, some time during 1835, I was about seventeen years old.

My mother was named Harriet Bailey. She was the daughter of Isaac and Betsey Bailey, both colored, and quite dark. My mother was of a darker complexion than either my grandmother or grandfather.

My father was a white man. He was admitted to be such by all I ever heard speak of my parentage. The opinion was also whispered that my master was my father; but of the correctness of this opinion, I know nothing; the means of knowing was withheld from me. My mother and I were separated when I was but an infant—before I knew her as my mother. It is a common custom, in the part of Maryland from which I ran away, to part children from their mothers at a very early age. Frequently, before the child has reached its twelfth month, its mother is taken from it, and hired out on some farm a considerable distance off, and the child is placed under the care of an old woman, too old for field labor. For what this separation is done, I do not know, unless it be to hinder the development of the child's affection toward its mother, and to blunt and destroy the natural affection of the mother for the child. This is the inevitable result.

I never saw my mother, to know her as such, more than four or five times in my life; and each of these times was very short in duration, and at night. She was hired by a Mr. Stewart, who lived about twelve miles from my home. She made her journeys to see me in the night, travelling the whole distance on foot, after the performance of her day's work. She was a field hand, and a whipping is the penalty of not being in the field at sunrise, unless a slave has special permission from his or her master to the contrary—a permission which they seldom get, and one that gives to him that gives it the proud name of being a kind master. I do not recollect of ever seeing my mother by the light of day. She was with me in the night. She would lie down with me, and get me to sleep, but long before I waked she was gone. Very little communication ever took place between us. Death soon ended what little we could have while she lived, and with it her hardships and suffering. She died when I was about seven years old, on one of my master's farms, near Lee's Mill. I was not allowed to be present during her illness, at her death, or burial. She was gone long before I knew any thing about it. Never having enjoyed, to any considerable extent, her soothing presence, her tender and watchful care, I received the tidings of her death with much the same emotions I should have probably felt at the death of a stranger.

Called thus suddenly away, she left me without the slightest intimation of who my father was. The whisper that my master was my father, may or may not be true; and, true or false, it is of but little consequence to my purpose whilst the fact remains, in all its glaring odiousness, that slaveholders have ordained, and by law established, that the children of slave women shall in all cases follow the condition of their mothers; and this is done too obviously to administer to their own lusts, and make a gratification of their wicked desires profitable as well as pleasurable; for by this cunning arrangement, the slaveholder, in cases not a few, sustains to his slaves the double relation of master and father.

I know of such cases; and it is worthy of remark that such slaves invariably suffer greater hardships, and have more to contend with, than others. They are, in the first place, a constant offence to their mistress. She is ever disposed to find fault with them; they can seldom do any thing to please her; she is never better pleased than when she sees them under the lash, especially when she suspects her husband of showing to his mulatto children favors which he withholds from his black slaves. The master is frequently compelled to sell this class of his slaves, out of deference to the feelings of his white wife; and, cruel as the deed may strike any one to be, for a man to sell his own children to human flesh-mongers, it is often the dictate of humanity for him to do so; for, unless he does this, he must not only whip them himself, but must stand by and see one white son tie up his brother, of but few shades darker complexion than himself, and ply the gory lash to his naked back; and if he lisp one word of disapproval, it is set down to his parental partiality, and only makes a bad matter worse, both for himself and the slave whom he would protect and defend.

Every year brings with it multitudes of this class of slaves. It was doubtless in consequence of a knowledge of this fact, that one great statesman of the south predicted the downfall of slavery by the inevitable laws of population. Whether this prophecy is ever fulfilled or not, it is nevertheless plain that a very different-looking class of people are springing up at the south, and are now held in slavery, from those originally brought to this country from Africa; and if their increase do no other good, it will do away the force of the argument, that God cursed Ham, and therefore American slavery is right. If the lineal descendants of Ham are alone to be scripturally enslaved, it is certain that slavery at the south must soon become unscriptural; for thousands are ushered into the world, annually, who, like myself, owe their existence to white fathers, and those fathers most frequently their own masters.

I have had two masters. My first master's name was Anthony. I do not remember his first name. He was generally called Captain Anthony—a title which, I presume, he acquired by sailing a craft on the Chesapeake Bay. He was not considered a rich slaveholder. He owned two or three farms, and about thirty slaves. His farms and slaves were under the care of an overseer. The overseer's name was Plummer. Mr. Plummer was a miserable drunkard, a profane swearer, and a savage monster. He always went armed with a cowskin and a heavy cudgel. I have known him to cut and slash the women's heads so horribly, that even master would be enraged at his cruelty, and would threaten to whip him if he did not mind himself. Master, however, was not a humane slaveholder. It required extraordinary barbarity on the part of an overseer to affect him. He was a cruel man, hardened by a long life of slaveholding. He would at times seem to take great pleasure in whipping a slave. I have often been awakened at the dawn of day by the most heart-rending shrieks of an own aunt of mine, whom he used to tie up to a joist, and whip upon her naked back till she was literally covered with blood. No words, no tears, no prayers, from his gory victim, seemed to move his iron heart from its bloody purpose. The louder she screamed, the harder he whipped; and where the blood ran fastest, there he whipped longest. He would whip her to make her scream, and whip her to make her hush; and not until overcome by fatigue, would he cease to swing the blood-clotted cowskin. I remember the first time I ever witnessed this horrible exhibition. I was quite a child, but I well remember it. I never shall forget it whilst I remember any thing. It was the first of a long series of such outrages, of which I was doomed to be a witness and a participant. It struck me with awful force. It was the blood-stained gate, the entrance to the hell of slavery, through which I was about to pass. It was a most terrible spectacle. I wish I could commit to paper the feelings with which I beheld it.

This occurrence took place very soon after I went to live with my old master, and under the following circumstances. Aunt Hester went out one night,—where or for what I do not know,—and happened to be absent when my master desired her presence. He had ordered her not to go out evenings, and warned her that she must never let him catch her in company with a young man, who was paying attention to her belonging to Colonel Lloyd. The young man's name was Ned Roberts, generally called Lloyd's Ned. Why master was so careful of her, may be safely left to conjecture. She was a woman of noble form, and of graceful proportions, having very few equals, and fewer superiors, in personal appearance, among the colored or white women of our neighborhood.

Aunt Hester had not only disobeyed his orders in going out, but had been found in company with Lloyd's Ned; which circumstance, I found, from what he said while whipping her, was the chief offence. Had he been a man of pure morals himself, he might have been thought interested in protecting the innocence of my aunt; but those who knew him will not suspect him of any such virtue. Before he commenced whipping Aunt Hester, he took her into the kitchen, and stripped her from neck to waist, leaving her neck, shoulders, and back, entirely naked. He then told her to cross her hands, calling her at the same time a d——d b—-h. After crossing her hands, he tied them with a strong rope, and led her to a stool under a large hook in the joist, put in for the purpose. He made her get upon the stool, and tied her hands to the hook. She now stood fair for his infernal purpose. Her arms were stretched up at their full length, so that she stood upon the ends of her toes. He then said to her, "Now, you d——d b—-h, I'll learn you how to disobey my orders!" and after rolling up his sleeves, he commenced to lay on the heavy cowskin, and soon the warm, red blood (amid heart-rending shrieks from her, and horrid oaths from him) came dripping to the floor. I was so terrified and horror-stricken at the sight, that I hid myself in a closet, and dared not venture out till long after the bloody transaction was over. I expected it would be my turn next. It was all new to me. I had never seen any thing like it before. I had always lived with my grandmother on the outskirts of the plantation, where she was put to raise the children of the younger women. I had therefore been, until now, out of the way of the bloody scenes that often occurred on the plantation.

CHAPTER II

My master's family consisted of two sons, Andrew and Richard; one daughter, Lucretia, and her husband, Captain Thomas Auld. They lived in one house, upon the home plantation of Colonel Edward Lloyd. My master was Colonel Lloyd's clerk and superintendent. He was what might be called the overseer of the overseers. I spent two years of childhood on this plantation in my old master's family. It was here that I witnessed the bloody transaction recorded in the first chapter; and as I received my first impressions of slavery on this plantation, I will give some description of it, and of slavery as it there existed. The plantation is about twelve miles north of Easton, in Talbot county, and is situated on the border of Miles River. The principal products raised upon it were tobacco, corn, and wheat. These were raised in great abundance; so that, with the products of this and the other farms belonging to him, he was able to keep in almost constant employment a large sloop, in carrying them to market at Baltimore. This sloop was named Sally Lloyd, in honor of one of the colonel's daughters. My master's son-in-law, Captain Auld, was master of the vessel; she was otherwise manned by the colonel's own slaves. Their names were Peter, Isaac, Rich, and Jake. These were esteemed very highly by the other slaves, and looked upon as the privileged ones of the plantation; for it was no small affair, in the eyes of the slaves, to be allowed to see Baltimore.

Colonel Lloyd kept from three to four hundred slaves on his home plantation, and owned a large number more on the neighboring farms belonging to him. The names of the farms nearest to the home plantation were Wye Town and New Design. "Wye Town" was under the overseership of a man named Noah Willis. New Design was under the overseership of a Mr. Townsend. The overseers of these, and all the rest of the farms, numbering over twenty, received advice and direction from the managers of the home plantation. This was the great business place. It was the seat of government for the whole twenty farms. All disputes among the overseers were settled here. If a slave was convicted of any high misdemeanor, became unmanageable, or evinced a determination to run away, he was brought immediately here, severely whipped, put on board the sloop, carried to Baltimore, and sold to Austin Woolfolk, or some other slave-trader, as a warning to the slaves remaining.

Here, too, the slaves of all the other farms received their monthly allowance of food, and their yearly clothing. The men and women slaves received, as their monthly allowance of food, eight pounds of pork, or its equivalent in fish, and one bushel of corn meal. Their yearly clothing consisted of two coarse linen shirts, one pair of linen trousers, like the shirts, one jacket, one pair of trousers for winter, made of coarse negro cloth, one pair of stockings, and one pair of shoes; the whole of which could not have cost more than seven dollars. The allowance of the slave children was given to their mothers, or the old women having the care of them. The children unable to work in the field had neither shoes, stockings, jackets, nor trousers, given to them; their clothing consisted of two coarse linen shirts per year. When these failed them, they went naked until the next allowance-day. Children from seven to ten years old, of both sexes, almost naked, might be seen at all seasons of the year.

There were no beds given the slaves, unless one coarse blanket be considered such, and none but the men and women had these. This, however, is not considered a very great privation. They find less difficulty from the want of beds, than from the want of time to sleep; for when their day's work in the field is done, the most of them having their washing, mending, and cooking to do, and having few or none of the ordinary facilities for doing either of these, very many of their sleeping hours are consumed in preparing for the field the coming day; and when this is done, old and young, male and female, married and single, drop down side by side, on one common bed,—the cold, damp floor,—each covering himself or herself with their miserable blankets; and here they sleep till they are summoned to the field by the driver's horn. At the sound of this, all must rise, and be off to the field. There must be no halting; every one must be at his or her post; and woe betides them who hear not this morning summons to the field; for if they are not awakened by the sense of hearing, they are by the sense of feeling: no age nor sex finds any favor. Mr. Severe, the overseer, used to stand by the door of the quarter, armed with a large hickory stick and heavy cowskin, ready to whip any one who was so unfortunate as not to hear, or, from any other cause, was prevented from being ready to start for the field at the sound of the horn.

Mr. Severe was rightly named: he was a cruel man. I have seen him whip a woman, causing the blood to run half an hour at the time; and this, too, in the midst of her crying children, pleading for their mother's release. He seemed to take pleasure in manifesting his fiendish barbarity. Added to his cruelty, he was a profane swearer. It was enough to chill the blood and stiffen the hair of an ordinary man to hear him talk. Scarce a sentence escaped him but that was commenced or concluded by some horrid oath. The field was the place to witness his cruelty and profanity. His presence made it both the field of blood and of blasphemy. From the rising till the going down of the sun, he was cursing, raving, cutting, and slashing among the slaves of the field, in the most frightful manner. His career was short. He died very soon after I went to Colonel Lloyd's; and he died as he lived, uttering, with his dying groans, bitter curses and horrid oaths. His death was regarded by the slaves as the result of a merciful providence.

Mr. Severe's place was filled by a Mr. Hopkins. He was a very different man. He was less cruel, less profane, and made less noise, than Mr. Severe. His course was characterized by no extraordinary demonstrations of cruelty. He whipped, but seemed to take no pleasure in it. He was called by the slaves a good overseer.

The home plantation of Colonel Lloyd wore the appearance of a country village. All the mechanical operations for all the farms were performed here. The shoemaking and mending, the blacksmithing, cartwrighting, coopering, weaving, and grain-grinding, were all performed by the slaves on the home plantation. The whole place wore a business-like aspect very unlike the neighboring farms. The number of houses, too, conspired to give it advantage over the neighboring farms. It was called by the slaves the *Great House Farm*. Few privileges were esteemed higher, by the slaves of the out-farms, than that of being selected to do errands at the Great House Farm. It was associated in their minds with greatness. A representative could not be prouder of his election to a seat in the American Congress, than a slave on one of the out-farms would be of his election to do errands at the Great House Farm. They regarded it as evidence of great confidence reposed in them by their overseers; and it was on this account, as well as a constant desire to be out of the field from under the driver's lash, that they esteemed it a high privilege, one worth careful living for. He was called the smartest and most trusty fellow, who had this honor conferred upon him the most frequently. The competitors for this office sought as diligently to please their overseers, as the office-seekers in the political parties seek to please and deceive the people. The same traits of character might be seen in Colonel Lloyd's slaves, as are seen in the slaves of the political parties.

The slaves selected to go to the Great House Farm, for the monthly allowance for themselves and their fellow-slaves, were peculiarly enthusiastic. While on their way, they would make the dense old woods, for miles around, reverberate with their wild songs, revealing at once the highest joy and the deepest sadness. They would compose and sing as they went along, consulting neither time nor tune. The thought that came up, came out—if not in the word, in the sound;— and as frequently in the one as in the other. They would sometimes sing the most pathetic sentiment in the most rapturous tone, and the most rapturous sentiment in the most pathetic tone. Into all of their songs they would manage to weave something of the Great House Farm. Especially would they do this, when leaving home. They would then sing most exultingly the following words:—

> "I am going away to the Great House Farm!
> O, yea! O, yea! O!"

This they would sing, as a chorus, to words which to many would seem unmeaning jargon, but which, nevertheless, were full of meaning to themselves. I have sometimes thought that the mere hearing of those songs would do more to impress some minds with the horrible character of slavery, than the reading of whole volumes of philosophy on the subject could do.

I did not, when a slave, understand the deep meaning of those rude and apparently incoherent songs. I was myself within the circle; so that I neither saw nor heard as those without might see and hear. They told a tale of woe which was then altogether beyond my feeble comprehension; they were tones loud, long, and deep; they breathed the prayer and complaint of souls boiling over with the bitterest anguish. Every tone was a testimony against slavery, and a prayer to God for deliverance from chains. The hearing of those wild notes always depressed my spirit, and filled me with ineffable sadness. I have frequently found myself in tears while hearing them. The mere recurrence to those songs, even now, afflicts me; and while I am writing these lines, an expression of feeling has already found its way down my cheek. To those songs I trace my first glimmering conception of the dehumanizing character of slavery. I can never get rid of that conception. Those songs still follow me, to deepen my hatred of slavery, and quicken my sympathies for my brethren in bonds. If any one wishes to be impressed with the soul-killing effects of slavery, let him go to Colonel Lloyd's plantation, and, on allowance-day, place himself in the deep pine woods, and there let him, in silence, analyze the sounds that shall pass through the chambers of his soul,—and if he is not thus impressed, it will only be because "there is no flesh in his obdurate heart."

I have often been utterly astonished, since I came to the north, to find persons who could speak of the singing, among slaves, as evidence of their contentment and happiness. It is impossible to conceive of a greater mistake. Slaves sing most when they are most unhappy. The songs of the slave represent the sorrows of his heart; and he is relieved by them, only as an aching heart is relieved by its tears. At least, such is my experience. I have often sung to drown my sorrow, but seldom to express my happiness. Crying for joy, and singing for joy, were alike uncommon to me while in the jaws of slavery. The singing of a man cast away upon a desolate island might be as appropriately considered as evidence of contentment and happiness, as the singing of a slave; the songs of the one and of the other are prompted by the same emotion.

CHAPTER III

Colonel Lloyd kept a large and finely cultivated garden, which afforded almost constant employment for four men, besides the chief gardener, (Mr. M'Durmond.) This garden was probably the greatest attraction of the place. During the summer months, people came from far and near—from Baltimore, Easton, and Annapolis—to see it. It abounded in fruits of almost every description, from the hardy apple of the north to the delicate orange of the south. This garden was not the least source of trouble on the plantation. Its excellent fruit was quite a temptation to the hungry swarms of boys, as well as the older slaves, belonging to the colonel, few of whom had the virtue or the vice to resist it. Scarcely a day passed, during the summer, but that some slave had to take the lash for stealing fruit. The colonel had to resort to all kinds of stratagems to keep his slaves out of the garden. The last and most successful one was that of tarring his fence all around; after which, if a slave was caught with any tar upon his person, it was deemed sufficient proof that he had either been into the garden, or had tried to get in. In either case, he was severely whipped by the chief gardener. This plan worked well; the slaves became as fearful of tar as of the lash. They seemed to realize the impossibility of touching *tar* without being defiled.

The colonel also kept a splendid riding equipage. His stable and carriage-house presented the appearance of some of our large city livery establishments. His horses were of the finest form and noblest blood. His carriage-house contained three splendid coaches, three or four gigs, besides dearborns and barouches of the most fashionable style.

This establishment was under the care of two slaves—old Barney and young Barney—father and son. To attend to this establishment was their sole work. But it was by no means an easy employment; for in nothing was Colonel Lloyd more particular than in the management of his horses. The slightest inattention to these was unpardonable, and was visited upon those, under whose care they were placed, with the severest punishment; no excuse could shield them, if the colonel only suspected any want of attention to his horses—a supposition which he frequently indulged, and one which, of course, made the office of old and young Barney a very trying one. They never knew when they were safe from punishment. They were frequently whipped when least deserving, and escaped whipping when most deserving it. Every thing depended upon the looks of the horses, and the state of Colonel Lloyd's own mind when his horses were brought to him for use. If a horse did not move fast enough, or hold his head high enough, it was owing to some fault of his keepers. It was painful to stand near the stable-door, and hear the various complaints against the keepers when a horse was taken out for use. "This horse has not had proper attention. He has not been sufficiently rubbed and curried, or he has not been properly fed; his food was too wet or too dry; he got it too soon or too late; he was too hot or too cold; he had too much hay, and not enough of grain; or he had too much grain, and not enough of hay; instead of old Barney's attending to the horse, he had very improperly left it to his son." To all these complaints, no matter how unjust, the slave must answer never a word. Colonel Lloyd could not brook any contradiction from a slave. When he spoke, a slave must stand, listen, and tremble; and such was literally the case. I have seen Colonel Lloyd make old Barney, a man between fifty and sixty years of age, uncover his bald head, kneel down upon the cold, damp ground, and receive upon his naked and toil-worn shoulders more than thirty lashes at the time. Colonel Lloyd had three sons—Edward, Murray, and Daniel,—and three sons-in-law, Mr. Winder, Mr. Nicholson, and Mr. Lowndes. All of these lived at the Great House Farm, and enjoyed the luxury of whipping the servants when they pleased, from old Barney down to William Wilkes, the coach-driver. I have seen Winder make one of the house-servants stand off from him a suitable distance to be touched with the end of his whip, and at every stroke raise great ridges upon his back.

To describe the wealth of Colonel Lloyd would be almost equal to describing the riches of Job. He kept from ten to fifteen house-servants. He was said to own a thousand slaves, and I think this estimate quite within the truth. Colonel Lloyd owned so many that he did not know them when he saw them; nor did all the slaves of the out-farms know him. It is reported of him, that, while riding along the road one day, he met a colored man, and addressed him in the usual manner of speaking to colored people on the public highways of the south: "Well, boy, whom do you belong to?" "To Colonel Lloyd," replied the slave. "Well, does the colonel treat you well?" "No, sir," was the ready reply. "What, does he work you too hard?" "Yes, sir." "Well, don't he give you enough to eat?" "Yes, sir, he gives me enough, such as it is."

The colonel, after ascertaining where the slave belonged, rode on; the man also went on about his business, not dreaming that he had been conversing with his master. He thought, said, and heard nothing more of the matter, until two or three weeks afterwards. The poor man was then informed by his overseer that, for having found fault with his master, he was now to be sold to a Georgia trader.

He was immediately chained and handcuffed; and thus, without a moment's warning, he was snatched away, and forever sundered, from his family and friends, by a hand more unrelenting than death. This is the penalty of telling the truth, of telling the simple truth, in answer to a series of plain questions.

It is partly in consequence of such facts, that slaves, when inquired of as to their condition and the character of their masters, almost universally say they are contented, and that their masters are kind. The slaveholders have been known to send in spies among their slaves, to ascertain their views and feelings in regard to their condition. The frequency of this has had the effect to establish among the slaves the maxim, that a still tongue makes a wise head. They suppress the truth rather than take the consequences of telling it, and in so doing prove themselves a part of the human family. If they have any thing to say of their masters, it is generally in their masters' favor, especially when speaking to an untried man. I have been frequently asked, when a slave, if I had a kind master, and do not remember ever to have given a negative answer; nor did I, in pursuing this course, consider myself as uttering what was absolutely false; for I always measured the kindness of my master by the standard of kindness set up among slaveholders around us. Moreover, slaves are like other people, and imbibe prejudices quite common to others. They think their own better than that of others. Many, under the influence of this prejudice, think their own masters are better than the masters of other slaves; and this, too, in some cases, when the very reverse is true. Indeed, it is not uncommon for slaves even to fall out and quarrel among themselves about the relative goodness of their masters, each contending for the superior goodness of his own over that of the others. At the very same time, they mutually execrate their masters when viewed separately. It was so on our plantation. When Colonel Lloyd's slaves met the slaves of Jacob Jepson, they seldom parted without a quarrel about their masters; Colonel Lloyd's slaves contending that he was the richest, and Mr. Jepson's slaves that he was the smartest, and most of a man. Colonel Lloyd's slaves would boast his ability to buy and sell Jacob Jepson. Mr. Jepson's slaves would boast his ability to whip Colonel Lloyd. These quarrels would almost always end in a fight between the parties, and those that whipped were supposed to have gained the point at issue. They seemed to think that the greatness of their masters was transferable to themselves. It was considered as being bad enough to be a slave; but to be a poor man's slave was deemed a disgrace indeed!

CHAPTER IV

Mr. Hopkins remained but a short time in the office of overseer. Why his career was so short, I do not know, but suppose he lacked the necessary severity to suit Colonel Lloyd. Mr. Hopkins was succeeded by Mr. Austin Gore, a man possessing, in an eminent degree, all those traits of character indispensable to what is called a first-rate overseer. Mr. Gore had served Colonel Lloyd, in the capacity of overseer, upon one of the out-farms, and had shown himself worthy of the high station of overseer upon the home or Great House Farm.

Mr. Gore was proud, ambitious, and persevering. He was artful, cruel, and obdurate. He was just the man for such a place, and it was just the place for such a man. It afforded scope for the full exercise of all his powers, and he seemed to be perfectly at home in it. He was one of those who could torture the slightest look, word, or gesture, on the part of the slave, into impudence, and would treat it accordingly. There must be no answering back to him; no explanation was allowed a slave, showing himself to have been wrongfully accused. Mr. Gore acted fully up to the maxim laid down by slaveholders,—"It is better that a dozen slaves should suffer under the lash, than that the overseer should be convicted, in the presence of the slaves, of having been at fault." No matter how innocent a slave might be—it availed him nothing, when accused by Mr. Gore of any misdemeanor. To be accused was to be convicted, and to be convicted was to be punished; the one always following the other with immutable certainty. To escape punishment was to escape accusation; and few slaves had the fortune to do either, under the overseership of Mr. Gore. He was just proud enough to demand the most debasing homage of the slave, and quite servile enough to crouch, himself, at the feet of the master. He was ambitious enough to be contented with nothing short of the highest rank of overseers, and persevering enough to reach the height of his ambition. He was cruel enough to inflict the severest punishment, artful enough to descend to the lowest trickery, and obdurate enough to be insensible to the voice of a reproving conscience. He was, of all the overseers, the most dreaded by the slaves. His presence was painful; his eye flashed confusion; and seldom was his sharp, shrill voice heard, without producing horror and trembling in their ranks.

Mr. Gore was a grave man, and, though a young man, he indulged in no jokes, said no funny words, seldom smiled. His words were in perfect keeping with his looks, and his looks were in perfect keeping with his words. Overseers will sometimes indulge in a witty word, even with the slaves; not so with Mr. Gore. He spoke but to command, and commanded but to be obeyed; he dealt sparingly with his words, and bountifully with his whip, never using the former where the latter would answer as well. When he whipped, he seemed to do so from a sense of duty, and feared no consequences. He did nothing reluctantly, no matter how disagreeable; always at his post, never inconsistent. He never promised but to fulfil. He was, in a word, a man of the most inflexible firmness and stone-like coolness.

His savage barbarity was equalled only by the consummate coolness with which he committed the grossest and most savage deeds upon the slaves under his charge. Mr. Gore once undertook to whip one of Colonel Lloyd's slaves, by the name of Demby. He had given Demby but few stripes, when, to get rid of the scourging, he ran and plunged himself into a creek, and stood there at the depth of his shoulders, refusing to come out. Mr. Gore told him that he would give him three calls, and that, if he did not come out at the third call, he would shoot him. The first call was given. Demby made no response, but stood his ground. The second and third calls were given with the same result. Mr. Gore then, without consultation or deliberation with any one, not even giving Demby an additional call, raised his musket to his face, taking deadly aim at his standing victim, and in an instant poor Demby was no more. His mangled body sank out of sight, and blood and brains marked the water where he had stood.

A thrill of horror flashed through every soul upon the plantation, excepting Mr. Gore. He alone seemed cool and collected. He was asked by Colonel Lloyd and my old master, why he resorted to this extraordinary expedient. His reply was, (as well as I can remember,) that Demby had become unmanageable. He was setting a dangerous example to the other slaves,—one which, if suffered to pass without some such demonstration on his part, would finally lead to the total subversion of all rule and order upon the plantation. He argued that if one slave refused to be corrected, and escaped with his life, the other slaves would soon copy the example; the result of which would be, the freedom of the slaves, and the enslavement of the whites. Mr. Gore's defence was satisfactory. He was continued in his station as overseer upon the home plantation. His fame as an overseer went abroad. His horrid crime was not even submitted to judicial investigation. It was committed in the presence of slaves, and they of course could neither institute a suit, nor testify against him; and thus the guilty perpetrator of one of the bloodiest and most foul murders goes unwhipped of justice, and uncensured by the community in which he lives. Mr. Gore lived in St. Michael's, Talbot county, Maryland, when I left there; and if he is still alive, he very probably lives there now; and if so, he is now, as he was then, as highly esteemed and as much respected as though his guilty soul had not been stained with his brother's blood.

I speak advisedly when I say this,—that killing a slave, or any colored person, in Talbot county, Maryland, is not treated as a crime, either by the courts or the community. Mr. Thomas Lanman, of St. Michael's, killed two slaves, one of whom he killed with a hatchet, by knocking his brains out. He used to boast of the commission of the awful and bloody deed. I have heard him do so laughingly, saying, among other things, that he was the only benefactor of his country in the company, and that when others would do as much as he had done, we should be relieved of "the d——d niggers."

The wife of Mr. Giles Hicks, living but a short distance from where I used to live, murdered my wife's cousin, a young girl between fifteen and sixteen years of age, mangling her person in the most horrible manner, breaking her nose and breastbone with a stick, so that the poor girl expired in a few hours afterward. She was immediately buried, but had not been in her untimely grave but a few hours before she was taken up and examined by the coroner, who decided that she had come to her death by severe beating. The offence for which this girl was thus murdered was this:—She had been set that night to mind Mrs. Hicks's baby, and during the night she fell asleep, and the baby cried. She, having lost her rest for several nights previous, did not hear the crying. They were both in the room with Mrs. Hicks. Mrs. Hicks, finding the girl slow to move, jumped from her bed, seized an oak stick of wood by the fireplace, and with it broke the girl's nose and breastbone, and thus ended her life. I will not say that this most horrid murder produced no sensation in the community. It did produce sensation, but not enough to bring the murderess to punishment. There was a warrant issued for her arrest, but it was never served. Thus she escaped not only punishment, but even the pain of being arraigned before a court for her horrid crime.

Whilst I am detailing bloody deeds which took place during my stay on Colonel Lloyd's plantation, I will briefly narrate another, which occurred about the same time as the murder of Demby by Mr. Gore.

Colonel Lloyd's slaves were in the habit of spending a part of their nights and Sundays in fishing for oysters, and in this way made up the deficiency of their scanty allowance. An old man belonging to Colonel Lloyd, while thus engaged, happened to get beyond the limits of Colonel Lloyd's, and on the premises of Mr. Beal Bondly. At this trespass, Mr. Bondly took offence, and with his musket came down to the shore, and blew its deadly contents into the poor old man.

Mr. Bondly came over to see Colonel Lloyd the next day, whether to pay him for his property, or to justify himself in what he had done, I know not. At any rate, this whole fiendish transaction was soon hushed up. There was very little said about it at all, and nothing done. It was a common saying, even among little white boys, that it was worth a half-cent to kill a "nigger," and a half-cent to bury one.

CHAPTER V

As to my own treatment while I lived on Colonel Lloyd's plantation, it was very similar to that of the other slave children. I was not old enough to work in the field, and there being little else than field work to do, I had a great deal of leisure time. The most I had to do was to drive up the cows at evening, keep the fowls out of the garden, keep the front yard clean, and run of errands for my old master's daughter, Mrs. Lucretia Auld. The most of my leisure time I spent in helping Master Daniel Lloyd in finding his birds, after he had shot them. My connection with Master Daniel was of some advantage to me. He became quite attached to me, and was a sort of protector of me. He would not allow the older boys to impose upon me, and would divide his cakes with me.

I was seldom whipped by my old master, and suffered little from any thing else than hunger and cold. I suffered much from hunger, but much more from cold. In hottest summer and coldest winter, I was kept almost naked—no shoes, no stockings, no jacket, no trousers, nothing on but a coarse tow linen shirt, reaching only to my knees. I had no bed. I must have perished with cold, but that, the coldest nights, I used to steal a bag which was used for carrying corn to the mill. I would crawl into this bag, and there sleep on the cold, damp, clay floor, with my head in and feet out. My feet have been so cracked with the frost, that the pen with which I am writing might be laid in the gashes.

We were not regularly allowanced. Our food was coarse corn meal boiled. This was called *mush*. It was put into a large wooden tray or trough, and set down upon the ground. The children were then called, like so many pigs, and like so many pigs they would come and devour the mush; some with oyster-shells, others with pieces of shingle, some with naked hands, and none with spoons. He that ate fastest got most; he that was strongest secured the best place; and few left the trough satisfied.

I was probably between seven and eight years old when I left Colonel Lloyd's plantation. I left it with joy. I shall never forget the ecstasy with which I received the intelligence that my old master (Anthony) had determined to let me go to Baltimore, to live with Mr. Hugh Auld, brother to my old master's son-in-law,

Captain Thomas Auld. I received this information about three days before my departure. They were three of the happiest days I ever enjoyed. I spent the most part of all these three days in the creek, washing off the plantation scurf, and preparing myself for my departure.

The pride of appearance which this would indicate was not my own. I spent the time in washing, not so much because I wished to, but because Mrs. Lucretia had told me I must get all the dead skin off my feet and knees before I could go to Baltimore; for the people in Baltimore were very cleanly, and would laugh at me if I looked dirty. Besides, she was going to give me a pair of trousers, which I should not put on unless I got all the dirt off me. The thought of owning a pair of trousers was great indeed! It was almost a sufficient motive, not only to make me take off what would be called by pig-drovers the mange, but the skin itself. I went at it in good earnest, working for the first time with the hope of reward.

The ties that ordinarily bind children to their homes were all suspended in my case. I found no severe trial in my departure. My home was charmless; it was not home to me; on parting from it, I could not feel that I was leaving any thing which I could have enjoyed by staying. My mother was dead, my grandmother lived far off, so that I seldom saw her. I had two sisters and one brother, that lived in the same house with me; but the early separation of us from our mother had well nigh blotted the fact of our relationship from our memories. I looked for home elsewhere, and was confident of finding none which I should relish less than the one which I was leaving. If, however, I found in my new home hardship, hunger, whipping, and nakedness, I had the consolation that I should not have escaped any one of them by staying. Having already had more than a taste of them in the house of my old master, and having endured them there, I very naturally inferred my ability to endure them elsewhere, and especially at Baltimore; for I had something of the feeling about Baltimore that is expressed in the proverb, that "being hanged in England is preferable to dying a natural death in Ireland." I had the strongest desire to see Baltimore. Cousin Tom, though not fluent in speech, had inspired me with that desire by his eloquent description of the place. I could never point out any thing at the Great House, no matter how beautiful or powerful, but that he had seen something at Baltimore far exceeding, both in beauty and strength, the object which I pointed out to him. Even the Great House itself, with all its pictures, was far inferior to many buildings in Baltimore. So strong was my desire, that I thought a gratification of it would fully compensate for whatever loss of comforts I should sustain by the exchange. I left without a regret, and with the highest hopes of future happiness.

We sailed out of Miles River for Baltimore on a Saturday morning. I remember only the day of the week, for at that time I had no knowledge of the days of the month, nor the months of the year. On setting sail, I walked aft, and gave to Colonel Lloyd's plantation what I hoped would be the last look. I then placed myself in the bows of the sloop, and there spent the remainder of the day in looking ahead, interesting myself in what was in the distance rather than in things near by or behind.

In the afternoon of that day, we reached Annapolis, the capital of the State. We stopped but a few moments, so that I had no time to go on shore. It was the first large town that I had ever seen, and though it would look small compared with some of our New England factory villages, I thought it a wonderful place for its size—more imposing even than the Great House Farm!

We arrived at Baltimore early on Sunday morning, landing at Smith's Wharf, not far from Bowley's Wharf. We had on board the sloop a large flock of sheep; and after aiding in driving them to the slaughterhouse of Mr. Curtis on Louden Slater's Hill, I was conducted by Rich, one of the hands belonging on board of the sloop, to my new home in Alliciana Street, near Mr. Gardner's ship-yard, on Fells Point.

Mr. and Mrs. Auld were both at home, and met me at the door with their little son Thomas, to take care of whom I had been given. And here I saw what I had never seen before; it was a white face beaming with the most kindly emotions; it was the face of my new mistress, Sophia Auld. I wish I could describe the rapture that flashed through my soul as I beheld it. It was a new and strange sight to me, brightening up my pathway with the light of happiness. Little Thomas was told, there was his Freddy,—and I was told to take care of little Thomas; and thus I entered upon the duties of my new home with the most cheering prospect ahead.

I look upon my departure from Colonel Lloyd's plantation as one of the most interesting events of my life. It is possible, and even quite probable, that but for the mere circumstance of being removed from that plantation to Baltimore, I should have to-day, instead of being here seated by my own table, in the enjoyment of freedom and the happiness of home, writing this Narrative, been confined in the galling chains of slavery. Going to live at Baltimore laid the foundation, and opened the gateway, to all my subsequent prosperity. I have ever regarded it as the first plain manifestation of that kind providence which has ever since attended me, and marked my life with so many favors. I regarded the selection of myself as being somewhat remarkable. There were a number of slave children that might have been sent from the plantation to Baltimore. There were those younger, those older, and those of the same age. I was chosen from among them all, and was the first, last, and only choice.

I may be deemed superstitious, and even egotistical, in regarding this event as a special interposition of divine Providence in my favor. But I should be false to the earliest sentiments of my soul, if I suppressed the opinion. I prefer to be true to myself, even at the hazard of incurring the ridicule of others, rather than to be false, and incur my own abhorrence. From my earliest recollection, I date the entertainment of a deep conviction that slavery would not always be able to hold me within its foul embrace; and in the darkest hours of my career in slavery, this living word of faith and spirit of hope departed not from me, but remained like ministering angels to cheer me through the gloom. This good spirit was from God, and to him I offer thanksgiving and praise.

CHAPTER VI

My new mistress proved to be all she appeared when I first met her at the door,—a woman of the kindest heart and finest feelings. She had never had a slave under her control previously to myself, and prior to her marriage she had been dependent upon her own industry for a living. She was by trade a weaver; and by constant application to her business, she had been in a good degree preserved from the blighting and dehumanizing effects of slavery. I was utterly astonished at her goodness. I scarcely knew how to behave towards her. She was entirely unlike any other white woman I had ever seen. I could not approach her as I was accustomed to approach other white ladies. My early instruction was all out of place. The crouching servility, usually so acceptable a quality in a slave, did not answer when manifested toward her. Her favor was not gained by it; she seemed to be disturbed by it. She did not deem it impudent or unmannerly for a slave to look her in the face. The meanest slave was put fully at ease in her presence, and none left without feeling better for having seen her. Her face was made of heavenly smiles, and her voice of tranquil music.

But, alas! this kind heart had but a short time to remain such. The fatal poison of irresponsible power was already in her hands, and soon commenced its infernal work. That cheerful eye, under the influence of slavery, soon became red with rage; that voice, made all of sweet accord, changed to one of harsh and horrid discord; and that angelic face gave place to that of a demon.

Very soon after I went to live with Mr. and Mrs. Auld, she very kindly commenced to teach me the A, B, C. After I had learned this, she assisted me in learning to spell words of three or four letters. Just at this point of my progress, Mr. Auld found out what was going on, and at once forbade Mrs. Auld to instruct me further, telling her, among other things, that it was unlawful, as well as unsafe, to teach a slave to read. To use his own words, further, he said, "If you give a nigger an inch, he will take an ell. A nigger should know nothing but to obey his master—to do as he is told to do. Learning would *spoil* the best nigger in the world. Now," said he, "if you teach that nigger (speaking of myself) how to read, there would be no keeping him. It would forever unfit him to be a slave. He would at once become unmanageable, and of no value to his master.

As to himself, it could do him no good, but a great deal of harm. It would make him discontented and unhappy." These words sank deep into my heart, stirred up sentiments within that lay slumbering, and called into existence an entirely new train of thought. It was a new and special revelation, explaining dark and mysterious things, with which my youthful understanding had struggled, but struggled in vain. I now understood what had been to me a most perplexing difficulty—to wit, the white man's power to enslave the black man. It was a grand achievement, and I prized it highly. From that moment, I understood the pathway from slavery to freedom. It was just what I wanted, and I got it at a time when I the least expected it. Whilst I was saddened by the thought of losing the aid of my kind mistress, I was gladdened by the invaluable instruction which, by the merest accident, I had gained from my master. Though conscious of the difficulty of learning without a teacher, I set out with high hope, and a fixed purpose, at whatever cost of trouble, to learn how to read. The very decided manner with which he spoke, and strove to impress his wife with the evil consequences of giving me instruction, served to convince me that he was deeply sensible of the truths he was uttering. It gave me the best assurance that I might rely with the utmost confidence on the results which, he said, would flow from teaching me to read. What he most dreaded, that I most desired. What he most loved, that I most hated. That which to him was a great evil, to be carefully shunned, was to me a great good, to be diligently sought; and the argument which he so warmly urged, against my learning to read, only served to inspire me with a desire and determination to learn. In learning to read, I owe almost as much to the bitter opposition of my master, as to the kindly aid of my mistress. I acknowledge the benefit of both.

I had resided but a short time in Baltimore before I observed a marked difference, in the treatment of slaves, from that which I had witnessed in the country. A city slave is almost a freeman, compared with a slave on the plantation. He is much better fed and clothed, and enjoys privileges altogether unknown to the slave on the plantation. There is a vestige of decency, a sense of shame, that does much to curb and check those outbreaks of atrocious cruelty so commonly enacted upon the plantation. He is a desperate slaveholder, who will shock the humanity of his non-slaveholding neighbors with the cries of his lacerated slave. Few are willing to incur the odium attaching to the reputation of being a cruel master; and above all things, they would not be known as not giving a slave enough to eat. Every city slaveholder is anxious to have it known of him, that he feeds his slaves well; and it is due to them to say, that most of them do give their slaves enough to eat. There are, however, some painful exceptions to this rule. Directly opposite to us, on Philpot Street, lived Mr. Thomas Hamilton. He owned two slaves. Their names were Henrietta and Mary. Henrietta was about twenty-two years of age, Mary was about fourteen; and of all the mangled and emaciated creatures I ever looked upon, these two were the most so. His heart must be harder than stone, that could look upon these unmoved. The head, neck, and shoulders of Mary were literally cut to pieces. I have frequently felt her head, and found it nearly covered with festering sores, caused by the lash of her cruel mistress. I do not know that her master ever whipped her, but I have been an eye-witness to the cruelty of Mrs. Hamilton. I used to be in Mr. Hamilton's house nearly every day. Mrs. Hamilton used to sit in a large chair in the middle of the room, with a heavy cowskin always by her side, and scarce an hour passed during the day but was marked by the blood of one of these slaves. The girls seldom passed her without her saying, "Move faster, you *black gip!*" at the same time giving them a blow with the cowskin over the head or shoulders, often drawing the blood. She would then say, "Take that, you *black gip!*" continuing, "If you don't move faster, I'll move you!" Added to the cruel lashings to which these slaves were subjected, they were kept nearly half-starved. They seldom knew what it was to eat a full meal. I have seen Mary contending with the pigs for the offal thrown into the street. So much was Mary kicked and cut to pieces, that she was oftener called "*pecked*" than by her name.

CHAPTER VII

I lived in Master Hugh's family about seven years. During this time, I succeeded in learning to read and write. In accomplishing this, I was compelled to resort to various stratagems. I had no regular teacher. My mistress, who had kindly commenced to instruct me, had, in compliance with the advice and direction of her husband, not only ceased to instruct, but had set her face against my being instructed by any one else. It is due, however, to my mistress to say of her, that she did not adopt this course of treatment immediately. She at first lacked the depravity indispensable to shutting me up in mental darkness. It was at least necessary for her to have some training in the exercise of irresponsible power, to make her equal to the task of treating me as though I were a brute.

My mistress was, as I have said, a kind and tender-hearted woman; and in the simplicity of her soul she commenced, when I first went to live with her, to treat me as she supposed one human being ought to treat another. In entering upon the duties of a slaveholder, she did not seem to perceive that I sustained to her the relation of a mere chattel, and that for her to treat me as a human being was not only wrong, but dangerously so. Slavery proved as injurious to her as it did to me. When I went there, she was a pious, warm, and tender-hearted woman. There was no sorrow or suffering for which she had not a tear. She had bread for the hungry, clothes for the naked, and comfort for every mourner that came within her reach. Slavery soon proved its ability to divest her of these heavenly qualities. Under its influence, the tender heart became stone, and the lamblike disposition gave way to one of tiger-like fierceness. The first step in her downward course was in her ceasing to instruct me. She now commenced to practise her husband's precepts. She finally became even more violent in her opposition than her husband himself. She was not satisfied with simply doing as well as he had commanded; she seemed anxious to do better. Nothing seemed to make her more angry than to see me with a newspaper. She seemed to think that here lay the danger. I have had her rush at me with a face made all up of fury, and snatch from me a newspaper, in a manner that fully revealed her apprehension. She was an apt woman; and a little experience soon demonstrated, to her satisfaction, that education and slavery were incompatible with each other.

From this time I was most narrowly watched. If I was in a separate room any considerable length of time, I was sure to be suspected of having a book, and was at once called to give an account of myself. All this, however, was too late. The first step had been taken. Mistress, in teaching me the alphabet, had given me the *inch,* and no precaution could prevent me from taking the *ell.*

The plan which I adopted, and the one by which I was most successful, was that of making friends of all the little white boys whom I met in the street. As many of these as I could, I converted into teachers. With their kindly aid, obtained at different times and in different places, I finally succeeded in learning to read. When I was sent of errands, I always took my book with me, and by going one part of my errand quickly, I found time to get a lesson before my return. I used also to carry bread with me, enough of which was always in the house, and to which I was always welcome; for I was much better off in this regard than many of the poor white children in our neighborhood. This bread I used to bestow upon the hungry little urchins, who, in return, would give me that more valuable bread of knowledge. I am strongly tempted to give the names of two or three of those little boys, as a testimonial of the gratitude and affection I bear them; but prudence forbids;—not that it would injure me, but it might embarrass them; for it is almost an unpardonable offence to teach slaves to read in this Christian country. It is enough to say of the dear little fellows, that they lived on Philpot Street, very near Durgin and Bailey's ship-yard. I used to talk this matter of slavery over with them. I would sometimes say to them, I wished I could be as free as they would be when they got to be men. "You will be free as soon as you are twenty-one, *but I am a slave for life!* Have not I as good a right to be free as you have?" These words used to trouble them; they would express for me the liveliest sympathy, and console me with the hope that something would occur by which I might be free.

I was now about twelve years old, and the thought of being *a slave for life* began to bear heavily upon my heart. Just about this time, I got hold of a book entitled "The Columbian Orator." Every opportunity I got, I used to read this book. Among much of other interesting matter, I found in it a dialogue between a master and his slave. The slave was represented as having run away from his master three times. The dialogue represented the conversation which took place between them, when the slave was retaken the third time. In this dialogue, the whole argument in behalf of slavery was brought forward by the master, all of which was disposed of by the slave. The slave was made to say some very smart as well as impressive things in reply to his master—things which had the desired though unexpected effect; for the conversation resulted in the voluntary emancipation of the slave on the part of the master.

In the same book, I met with one of Sheridan's mighty speeches on and in behalf of Catholic emancipation. These were choice documents to me. I read them over and over again with unabated interest. They gave tongue to interesting thoughts of my own soul, which had frequently flashed through my mind, and died away for want of utterance. The moral which I gained from the dialogue was the power of truth over the conscience of even a slaveholder. What I got from Sheridan was a bold denunciation of slavery, and a powerful vindication of human rights. The reading of these documents enabled me to utter my thoughts, and to meet the arguments brought forward to sustain slavery; but while they relieved me of one difficulty, they brought on another even more painful than the one of which I was relieved. The more I read, the more I was led to abhor and detest my enslavers. I could regard them in no other light than a band of successful robbers, who had left their homes, and gone to Africa, and stolen us from our homes, and in a strange land reduced us to slavery. I loathed them as being the meanest as well as the most wicked of men. As I read and contemplated the subject, behold! that very discontentment which Master Hugh had predicted would follow my learning to read had already come, to torment and sting my soul to unutterable anguish. As I writhed under it, I would at times feel that learning to read had been a curse rather than a blessing. It had given me a view of my wretched condition, without the remedy. It opened my eyes to the horrible pit, but to no ladder upon which to get out. In moments of agony, I envied my fellow-slaves for their stupidity. I have often wished myself a beast. I preferred the condition of the meanest reptile to my own. Any thing, no matter what, to get rid of thinking! It was this everlasting thinking of my condition that tormented me. There was no getting rid of it. It was pressed upon me by every object within sight or hearing, animate or inanimate. The silver trump of freedom had roused my soul to eternal wakefulness. Freedom now appeared, to disappear no more forever. It was heard in every sound, and seen in every thing. It was ever present to torment me with a sense of my wretched condition. I saw nothing without seeing it, I heard nothing without hearing it, and felt nothing without feeling it. It looked from every star, it smiled in every calm, breathed in every wind, and moved in every storm.

I often found myself regretting my own existence, and wishing myself dead; and but for the hope of being free, I have no doubt but that I should have killed myself, or done something for which I should have been killed. While in this state of mind, I was eager to hear any one speak of slavery. I was a ready listener. Every little while, I could hear something about the abolitionists. It was some time before I found what the word meant. It was always used in such connections as to make it an interesting word to me. If a slave ran away and succeeded in getting clear, or if a slave killed his master, set fire to a barn, or did any thing very wrong in the mind of a slaveholder, it was spoken of as the fruit of *abolition.* Hearing the word in this connection very often, I set about learning what it meant. The dictionary afforded me little or no help. I found it was "the act of abolishing;" but then I did not know what was to be abolished. Here I was perplexed. I did not dare to ask any one about its meaning, for I was satisfied that it was something they wanted me to know very little about. After a patient waiting, I got one of our city papers, containing an account of the number of petitions from the north, praying for the abolition of slavery in the District of Columbia, and of the slave trade between the States. From this time I understood the words *abolition* and *abolitionist,* and always drew near when that word was spoken, expecting to hear something of importance to myself and fellow-slaves. The light broke in upon me by degrees. I went one day down on the wharf of Mr. Waters; and seeing two Irishmen unloading a scow of stone, I went, unasked, and helped them. When we had finished, one of them came to me and asked me if I were a slave. I told him I was. He asked, "Are ye a slave for life?" I told him that I was. The good Irishman seemed to be deeply affected by the statement. He said to the other that it was a pity so fine a little fellow as myself should be a slave for life. He said it was a shame to hold me. They both advised me to run away to the north; that I should find friends there, and that I should be free. I pretended not to be interested in what they said, and treated them as if I did not understand them; for I feared they might be treacherous. White men have been known to encourage slaves to escape, and then, to get the reward, catch them and return them to their masters. I was afraid that these seemingly good men might use me so; but I nevertheless remembered their advice, and from that time I resolved to run away. I looked forward to a time at which it would be safe for me to escape. I was too young to think of doing so immediately; besides, I wished to learn how to write, as I might have occasion to write my own pass. I consoled myself with the hope that I should one day find a good chance. Meanwhile, I would learn to write.

The idea as to how I might learn to write was suggested to me by being in Durgin and Bailey's ship-yard, and frequently seeing the ship carpenters, after hewing, and getting a piece of timber ready for use, write on the timber the name of that part of the ship for which it was intended. When a piece of timber was intended for the larboard side, it would be marked thus—"L." When a piece was for the starboard side, it would be marked thus—"S." A piece for the larboard side forward, would be marked thus—"L. F." When a piece was for starboard side forward, it would be marked thus—"S. F." For larboard aft, it would be marked thus—"L. A." For starboard aft, it would be marked thus—"S. A." I soon learned the names of these letters, and for what they were intended when placed upon a piece of timber in the ship-yard. I immediately commenced copying them, and in a short time was able to make the four letters named. After that, when I met with any boy who I knew could write, I would tell him I could write as well as he. The next word would be, "I don't believe you. Let me see you try it." I would then make the letters which I had been so fortunate as to learn, and ask him to beat that. In this way I got a good many lessons in writing, which it is quite possible I should never have gotten in any other way. During this time, my copy-book was the board fence, brick wall, and pavement; my pen and ink was a lump of chalk. With these, I learned mainly how to write. I then commenced and continued copying the Italics in Webster's Spelling Book, until I could make them all without looking on the book. By this time, my little Master Thomas had gone to school, and learned how to write, and had written over a number of copy-books. These had been brought home, and shown to some of our near neighbors, and then laid aside. My mistress used to go to class meeting at the Wilk Street meetinghouse every Monday afternoon, and leave me to take care of the house. When left thus, I used to spend the time in writing in the spaces left in Master Thomas's copy-book, copying what he had written. I continued to do this until I could write a hand very similar to that of Master Thomas. Thus, after a long, tedious effort for years, I finally succeeded in learning how to write.

CHAPTER VIII

In a very short time after I went to live at Baltimore, my old master's youngest son Richard died; and in about three years and six months after his death, my old master, Captain Anthony, died, leaving only his son, Andrew, and daughter, Lucretia, to share his estate. He died while on a visit to see his daughter at Hillsborough. Cut off thus unexpectedly, he left no will as to the disposal of his property. It was therefore necessary to have a valuation of the property, that it might be equally divided between Mrs. Lucretia and Master Andrew. I was immediately sent for, to be valued with the other property. Here again my feelings rose up in detestation of slavery. I had now a new conception of my degraded condition. Prior to this, I had become, if not insensible to my lot, at least partly so. I left Baltimore with a young heart overborne with sadness, and a soul full of apprehension. I took passage with Captain Rowe, in the schooner Wild Cat, and, after a sail of about twenty-four hours, I found myself near the place of my birth. I had now been absent from it almost, if not quite, five years. I, however, remembered the place very well. I was only about five years old when I left it, to go and live with my old master on Colonel Lloyd's plantation; so that I was now between ten and eleven years old.

We were all ranked together at the valuation. Men and women, old and young, married and single, were ranked with horses, sheep, and swine. There were horses and men, cattle and women, pigs and children, all holding the same rank in the scale of being, and were all subjected to the same narrow examination. Silvery-headed age and sprightly youth, maids and matrons, had to undergo the same indelicate inspection. At this moment, I saw more clearly than ever the brutalizing effects of slavery upon both slave and slaveholder.

After the valuation, then came the division. I have no language to express the high excitement and deep anxiety which were felt among us poor slaves during this time. Our fate for life was now to be decided. We had no more voice in that decision than the brutes among whom we were ranked. A single word from the white men was enough—against all our wishes, prayers, and entreaties—to sunder forever the dearest friends, dearest kindred, and strongest ties known to human beings. In addition to the pain of separation, there was the horrid dread of falling into the hands of Master Andrew. He was known to us all as being a most cruel wretch,—a common drunkard, who had, by his reckless mismanagement and profligate dissipation, already wasted a large portion of his father's property. We all felt that we might as well be sold at once to the Georgia traders, as to pass into his hands; for we knew that that would be our inevitable condition,—a condition held by us all in the utmost horror and dread.

I suffered more anxiety than most of my fellow-slaves. I had known what it was to be kindly treated; they had known nothing of the kind. They had seen little or nothing of the world. They were in very deed men and women of sorrow, and acquainted with grief. Their backs had been made familiar with the bloody lash, so that they had become callous; mine was yet tender; for while at Baltimore I got few whippings, and few slaves could boast of a kinder master and mistress than myself; and the thought of passing out of their hands into those of Master Andrew—a man who, but a few days before, to give me a sample of his bloody disposition, took my little brother by the throat, threw him on the ground, and with the heel of his boot stamped upon his head till the blood gushed from his nose and ears—was well calculated to make me anxious as to my fate. After he had committed this savage outrage upon my brother, he turned to me, and said that was the way he meant to serve me one of these days,—meaning, I suppose, when I came into his possession.

Thanks to a kind Providence, I fell to the portion of Mrs. Lucretia, and was sent immediately back to Baltimore, to live again in the family of Master Hugh. Their joy at my return equalled their sorrow at my departure. It was a glad day to me. I had escaped a worse than lion's jaws. I was absent from Baltimore, for the purpose of valuation and division, just about one month, and it seemed to have been six.

Very soon after my return to Baltimore, my mistress, Lucretia, died, leaving her husband and one child, Amanda; and in a very short time after her death, Master Andrew died. Now all the property of my old master, slaves included, was in the hands of strangers,—strangers who had had nothing to do with accumulating it. Not a slave was left free. All remained slaves, from the youngest to the oldest. If any one thing in my experience, more than another, served to deepen my conviction of the infernal character of slavery, and to fill me with unutterable loathing of slaveholders, it was their base ingratitude to my poor old grandmother. She had served my old master faithfully from youth to old age. She had been the source of all his wealth; she had peopled his plantation with slaves; she had become a great grandmother in his service. She had rocked him in infancy, attended him in childhood, served him through life, and at his death wiped from his icy brow the cold death-sweat, and closed his eyes forever. She was nevertheless left a slave—a slave for life—a slave in the hands of strangers; and in their hands she saw her children, her grandchildren, and her great-grandchildren, divided, like so many sheep, without being gratified with the small privilege of a single word, as to their or her own destiny. And, to cap the climax of their base ingratitude and fiendish barbarity, my grandmother, who was now very old, having outlived my old master and all his children, having seen the beginning and end of all of them, and her present owners finding she was of but little value, her frame already racked with the pains of old age, and complete helplessness fast stealing over her once active limbs, they took her to the woods, built her a little hut, put up a little mud-chimney, and then made her welcome to the privilege of supporting herself there in perfect loneliness; thus virtually turning her out to die! If my poor old grandmother now lives, she lives to suffer in utter loneliness; she lives to remember and mourn over the loss of children, the loss of grandchildren, and the loss of great-grandchildren. They are, in the language of the slave's poet, Whittier,—

> "Gone, gone, sold and gone
> To the rice swamp dank and lone,
> Where the slave-whip ceaseless swings,
> Where the noisome insect stings,
> Where the fever-demon strews
> Poison with the falling dews,
> Where the sickly sunbeams glare
> Through the hot and misty air:—
> Gone, gone, sold and gone
> To the rice swamp dank and lone,
> From Virginia hills and waters—
> Woe is me, my stolen daughters!"

The hearth is desolate. The children, the unconscious children, who once sang and danced in her presence, are gone. She gropes her way, in the darkness of age, for a drink of water. Instead of the voices of her children, she hears by day the moans of the dove, and by night the screams of the hideous owl. All is gloom. The grave is at the door. And now, when weighed down by the pains and aches of old age, when the head inclines to the feet, when the beginning and ending of human existence meet, and helpless infancy and painful old age combine together—at this time, this most needful time, the time for the exercise of that tenderness and affection which children only can exercise towards a declining parent—my poor old grandmother, the devoted mother of twelve children, is left all alone, in yonder little hut, before a few dim embers. She stands—she sits—she staggers—she falls—she groans—she dies—and there are none of her children or grandchildren present, to wipe from her wrinkled brow the cold sweat of death, or to place beneath the sod her fallen remains. Will not a righteous God visit for these things?

In about two years after the death of Mrs. Lucretia, Master Thomas married his second wife. Her name was Rowena Hamilton. She was the eldest daughter of Mr. William Hamilton. Master now lived in St. Michael's. Not long after his marriage, a misunderstanding took place between himself and Master Hugh; and as a means of punishing his brother, he took me from him to live with himself at St. Michael's. Here I underwent another most painful separation. It, however, was not so severe as the one I dreaded at the division of property; for, during this interval, a great change had taken place in Master Hugh and his once kind and affectionate wife. The influence of brandy upon him, and of slavery upon her, had effected a disastrous change in the characters of both; so that, as far as they were concerned, I thought I had little to lose by the change. But it was not to them that I was attached. It was to those little Baltimore boys that I felt the strongest attachment. I had received many good lessons from them, and was still receiving them, and the thought of leaving them was painful indeed. I was leaving, too, without the hope of ever being allowed to return. Master Thomas had said he would never let me return again. The barrier betwixt himself and brother he considered impassable.

I then had to regret that I did not at least make the attempt to carry out my resolution to run away; for the chances of success are tenfold greater from the city than from the country.

I sailed from Baltimore for St. Michael's in the sloop Amanda, Captain Edward Dodson. On my passage, I paid particular attention to the direction which the steamboats took to go to Philadelphia. I found, instead of going down, on reaching North Point they went up the bay, in a north-easterly direction. I deemed this knowledge of the utmost importance. My determination to run away was again revived. I resolved to wait only so long as the offering of a favorable opportunity. When that came, I was determined to be off.

CHAPTER IX

I have now reached a period of my life when I can give dates. I left Baltimore, and went to live with Master Thomas Auld, at St. Michael's, in March, 1832. It was now more than seven years since I lived with him in the family of my old master, on Colonel Lloyd's plantation. We of course were now almost entire strangers to each other. He was to me a new master, and I to him a new slave. I was ignorant of his temper and disposition; he was equally so of mine. A very short time, however, brought us into full acquaintance with each other. I was made acquainted with his wife not less than with himself. They were well matched, being equally mean and cruel. I was now, for the first time during a space of more than seven years, made to feel the painful gnawings of hunger—a something which I had not experienced before since I left Colonel Lloyd's plantation. It went hard enough with me then, when I could look back to no period at which I had enjoyed a sufficiency. It was tenfold harder after living in Master Hugh's family, where I had always had enough to eat, and of that which was good. I have said Master Thomas was a mean man. He was so. Not to give a slave enough to eat, is regarded as the most aggravated development of meanness even among slaveholders. The rule is, no matter how coarse the food, only let there be enough of it. This is the theory; and in the part of Maryland from which I came, it is the general practice,—though there are many exceptions. Master Thomas gave us enough of neither coarse nor fine food. There were four slaves of us in the kitchen—my sister Eliza, my aunt Priscilla, Henny, and myself; and we were allowed less than a half of a bushel of corn-meal per week, and very little else, either in the shape of meat or vegetables. It was not enough for us to subsist upon. We were therefore reduced to the wretched necessity of living at the expense of our neighbors. This we did by begging and stealing, whichever came handy in the time of need, the one being considered as legitimate as the other. A great many times have we poor creatures been nearly perishing with hunger, when food in abundance lay mouldering in the safe and smoke-house, and our pious mistress was aware of the fact; and yet that mistress and her husband would kneel every morning, and pray that God would bless them in basket and store!

Bad as all slaveholders are, we seldom meet one destitute of every element of character commanding respect. My master was one of this rare sort. I do not know of one single noble act ever performed by him. The leading trait in his character was meanness; and if there were any other element in his nature, it was made subject to this. He was mean; and, like most other mean men, he lacked the ability to conceal his meanness. Captain Auld was not born a slaveholder. He had been a poor man, master only of a Bay craft. He came into possession of all his slaves by marriage; and of all men, adopted slaveholders are the worst. He was cruel, but cowardly. He commanded without firmness. In the enforcement of his rules, he was at times rigid, and at times lax. At times, he spoke to his slaves with the firmness of Napoleon and the fury of a demon; at other times, he might well be mistaken for an inquirer who had lost his way. He did nothing of himself. He might have passed for a lion, but for his ears. In all things noble which he attempted, his own meanness shone most conspicuous. His airs, words, and actions, were the airs, words, and actions of born slaveholders, and, being assumed, were awkward enough. He was not even a good imitator. He possessed all the disposition to deceive, but wanted the power. Having no resources within himself, he was compelled to be the copyist of many, and being such, he was forever the victim of inconsistency; and of consequence he was an object of contempt, and was held as such even by his slaves. The luxury of having slaves of his own to wait upon him was something new and unprepared for. He was a slaveholder without the ability to hold slaves. He found himself incapable of managing his slaves either by force, fear, or fraud. We seldom called him "master;" we generally called him "Captain Auld," and were hardly disposed to title him at all. I doubt not that our conduct had much to do with making him appear awkward, and of consequence fretful. Our want of reverence for him must have perplexed him greatly. He wished to have us call him master, but lacked the firmness necessary to command us to do so. His wife used to insist upon our calling him so, but to no purpose. In August, 1832, my master attended a Methodist camp-meeting held in the Bay-side, Talbot county, and there experienced religion. I indulged a faint hope that his conversion would lead him to emancipate his slaves, and that, if he did not do this, it would, at any rate, make him more kind and humane. I was disappointed in both these respects. It neither made him to be humane to his slaves, nor to emancipate them. If it had any effect on his character, it made him more cruel and hateful in all his ways; for I believe him to have been a much worse man after his conversion than before. Prior to his conversion, he relied upon his own depravity to shield and sustain him in his savage barbarity; but after his conversion, he found religious sanction and support for his slaveholding cruelty. He made the greatest pretensions to piety. His house was the house of prayer. He prayed morning, noon, and night. He very soon distinguished himself among his brethren, and was soon made a class-leader and exhorter. His activity in revivals was great, and he proved himself an instrument in the hands of the church in converting many souls. His house was the preachers' home. They used to take great pleasure in coming there to put up; for while he starved us, he stuffed them. We have had three or four preachers there at a time. The names of those who used to come most frequently while I lived there, were Mr. Storks, Mr. Ewery, Mr. Humphry, and Mr. Hickey. I have also seen Mr. George Cookman at our house. We slaves loved Mr. Cookman. We believed him to be a good man. We thought him instrumental in getting Mr. Samuel Harrison, a very rich slaveholder, to emancipate his slaves; and by some means got the impression that he was laboring to effect the emancipation of all the slaves. When he was at our house, we were sure to be called in to prayers. When the others were there, we were sometimes called in and sometimes not. Mr. Cookman took more notice of us than either of the other ministers. He could not come among us without betraying his sympathy for us, and, stupid as we were, we had the sagacity to see it.

While I lived with my master in St. Michael's, there was a white young man, a Mr. Wilson, who proposed to keep a Sabbath school for the instruction of such slaves as might be disposed to learn to read the New Testament. We met but three times, when Mr. West and Mr. Fairbanks, both class-leaders, with many others, came upon us with sticks and other missiles, drove us off, and forbade us to meet again. Thus ended our little Sabbath school in the pious town of St. Michael's.

I have said my master found religious sanction for his cruelty. As an example, I will state one of many facts going to prove the charge. I have seen him tie up a lame young woman, and whip her with a heavy cowskin upon her naked shoulders, causing the warm red blood to drip; and, in justification of the bloody deed, he would quote this passage of Scripture—"He that knoweth his master's will, and doeth it not, shall be beaten with many stripes."

Master would keep this lacerated young woman tied up in this horrid situation four or five hours at a time. I have known him to tie her up early in the morning, and whip her before breakfast; leave her, go to his store, return at dinner, and whip her again, cutting her in the places already made raw with his cruel lash. The secret of master's cruelty toward "Henny" is found in the fact of her being almost helpless. When quite a child, she fell into the fire, and burned herself horribly. Her hands were so burnt that she never got the use of them. She could do very little but bear heavy burdens. She was to master a bill of expense; and as he was a mean man, she was a constant offence to him. He seemed desirous of getting the poor girl out of existence. He gave her away once to his sister; but, being a poor gift, she was not disposed to keep her. Finally, my benevolent master, to use his own words, "set her adrift to take care of herself."

Here was a recently-converted man, holding on upon the mother, and at the same time turning out her helpless child, to starve and die! Master Thomas was one of the many pious slaveholders who hold slaves for the very charitable purpose of taking care of them.

My master and myself had quite a number of differences. He found me unsuitable to his purpose. My city life, he said, had had a very pernicious effect upon me. It had almost ruined me for every good purpose, and fitted me for every thing which was bad. One of my greatest faults was that of letting his horse run away, and go down to his father-in-law's farm, which was about five miles from St. Michael's. I would then have to go after it. My reason for this kind of carelessness, or carefulness, was, that I could always get something to eat when I went there. Master William Hamilton, my master's father-in-law, always gave his slaves enough to eat. I never left there hungry, no matter how great the need of my speedy return. Master Thomas at length said he would stand it no longer. I had lived with him nine months, during which time he had given me a number of severe whippings, all to no good purpose. He resolved to put me out, as he said, to be broken; and, for this purpose, he let me for one year to a man named Edward Covey. Mr. Covey was a poor man, a farm-renter. He rented the place upon which he lived, as also the hands with which he tilled it. Mr. Covey had acquired a very high reputation for breaking young slaves, and this reputation was of immense value to him. It enabled him to get his farm tilled with much less expense to himself than he could have had it done without such a reputation. Some slaveholders thought it not much loss to allow Mr. Covey to have their slaves one year, for the sake of the training to which they were subjected, without any other compensation. He could hire young help with great ease, in consequence of this reputation. Added to the natural good qualities of Mr. Covey, he was a professor of religion—a pious soul—a member and a class-leader in the Methodist church. All of this added weight to his reputation as a "nigger-breaker." I was aware of all the facts, having been made acquainted with them by a young man who had lived there. I nevertheless made the change gladly; for I was sure of getting enough to eat, which is not the smallest consideration to a hungry man.

CHAPTER X

I had left Master Thomas's house, and went to live with Mr. Covey, on the 1st of January, 1833. I was now, for the first time in my life, a field hand. In my new employment, I found myself even more awkward than a country boy appeared to be in a large city. I had been at my new home but one week before Mr. Covey gave me a very severe whipping, cutting my back, causing the blood to run, and raising ridges on my flesh as large as my little finger. The details of this affair are as follows: Mr. Covey sent me, very early in the morning of one of our coldest days in the month of January, to the woods, to get a load of wood. He gave me a team of unbroken oxen. He told me which was the in-hand ox, and which the off-hand one. He then tied the end of a large rope around the horns of the in-hand ox, and gave me the other end of it, and told me, if the oxen started to run, that I must hold on upon the rope. I had never driven oxen before, and of course I was very awkward. I, however, succeeded in getting to the edge of the woods with little difficulty; but I had got a very few rods into the woods, when the oxen took fright, and started full tilt, carrying the cart against trees, and over stumps, in the most frightful manner. I expected every moment that my brains would be dashed out against the trees. After running thus for a considerable distance, they finally upset the cart, dashing it with great force against a tree, and threw themselves into a dense thicket. How I escaped death, I do not know. There I was, entirely alone, in a thick wood, in a place new to me. My cart was upset and shattered, my oxen were entangled among the young trees, and there was none to help me. After a long spell of effort, I succeeded in getting my cart righted, my oxen disentangled, and again yoked to the cart. I now proceeded with my team to the place where I had, the day before, been chopping wood, and loaded my cart pretty heavily, thinking in this way to tame my oxen. I then proceeded on my way home. I had now consumed one half of the day. I got out of the woods safely, and now felt out of danger. I stopped my oxen to open the woods gate; and just as I did so, before I could get hold of my ox-rope, the oxen again started, rushed through the gate, catching it between the wheel and the body of the cart, tearing it to pieces, and coming within a few inches of crushing me against the gate-post. Thus twice, in one short day, I escaped death by the merest chance.

On my return, I told Mr. Covey what had happened, and how it happened. He ordered me to return to the woods again immediately. I did so, and he followed on after me. Just as I got into the woods, he came up and told me to stop my cart, and that he would teach me how to trifle away my time, and break gates. He then went to a large gum-tree, and with his axe cut three large switches, and, after trimming them up neatly with his pocketknife, he ordered me to take off my clothes. I made him no answer, but stood with my clothes on. He repeated his order. I still made him no answer, nor did I move to strip myself. Upon this he rushed at me with the fierceness of a tiger, tore off my clothes, and lashed me till he had worn out his switches, cutting me so savagely as to leave the marks visible for a long time after. This whipping was the first of a number just like it, and for similar offences.

I lived with Mr. Covey one year. During the first six months, of that year, scarce a week passed without his whipping me. I was seldom free from a sore back. My awkwardness was almost always his excuse for whipping me. We were worked fully up to the point of endurance. Long before day we were up, our horses fed, and by the first approach of day we were off to the field with our hoes and ploughing teams. Mr. Covey gave us enough to eat, but scarce time to eat it. We were often less than five minutes taking our meals. We were often in the field from the first approach of day till its last lingering ray had left us; and at saving-fodder time, midnight often caught us in the field binding blades.

Covey would be out with us. The way he used to stand it, was this. He would spend the most of his afternoons in bed. He would then come out fresh in the evening, ready to urge us on with his words, example, and frequently with the whip. Mr. Covey was one of the few slaveholders who could and did work with his hands. He was a hard-working man. He knew by himself just what a man or a boy could do. There was no deceiving him. His work went on in his absence almost as well as in his presence; and he had the faculty of making us feel that he was ever present with us. This he did by surprising us. He seldom approached the spot where we were at work openly, if he could do it secretly. He always aimed at taking us by surprise. Such was his cunning, that we used to call him, among ourselves, "the snake." When we were at work in the cornfield, he would sometimes crawl on his hands and knees to avoid detection, and all at once he would rise nearly in our midst, and scream out, "Ha, ha! Come, come! Dash on, dash on!" This being his mode of attack, it was never safe to stop a single minute. His comings were like a thief in the night. He appeared to us as being ever at hand. He was under every tree, behind every stump, in every bush, and at every window, on the plantation. He would sometimes mount his horse, as if bound to St. Michael's, a distance of seven miles, and in half an hour afterwards you would see him coiled up in the corner of the wood-fence, watching every motion of the slaves. He would, for this purpose, leave his horse tied up in the woods. Again, he would sometimes walk up to us, and give us orders as though he was upon the point of starting on a long journey, turn his back upon us, and make as though he was going to the house to get ready; and, before he would get half way thither, he would turn short and crawl into a fence-corner, or behind some tree, and there watch us till the going down of the sun.

Mr. Covey's *forte* consisted in his power to deceive. His life was devoted to planning and perpetrating the grossest deceptions. Every thing he possessed in the shape of learning or religion, he made conform to his disposition to deceive. He seemed to think himself equal to deceiving the Almighty. He would make a short prayer in the morning, and a long prayer at night; and, strange as it may seem, few men would at times appear more devotional than he. The exercises of his family devotions were always commenced with singing; and, as he was a very poor singer himself, the duty of raising the hymn generally came upon me. He would read his hymn, and nod at me to commence. I would at times do so; at others, I would not. My non-compliance would almost always produce much confusion. To show himself independent of me, he would start and stagger through with his hymn in the most discordant manner. In this state of mind, he prayed with more than ordinary spirit. Poor man! such was his disposition, and success at deceiving, I do verily believe that he sometimes deceived himself into the solemn belief, that he was a sincere worshipper of the most high God; and this, too, at a time when he may be said to have been guilty of compelling his woman slave to commit the sin of adultery. The facts in the case are these: Mr. Covey was a poor man; he was just commencing in life; he was only able to buy one slave; and, shocking as is the fact, he bought her, as he said, for *a breeder*. This woman was named Caroline. Mr. Covey bought her from Mr. Thomas Lowe, about six miles from St. Michael's. She was a large, able-bodied woman, about twenty years old. She had already given birth to one child, which proved her to be just what he wanted. After buying her, he hired a married man of Mr. Samuel Harrison, to live with him one year; and him he used to fasten up with her every night! The result was, that, at the end of the year, the miserable woman gave birth to twins. At this result Mr. Covey seemed to be highly pleased, both with the man and the wretched woman. Such was his joy, and that of his wife, that nothing they could do for Caroline during her confinement was too good, or too hard, to be done. The children were regarded as being quite an addition to his wealth.

If at any one time of my life more than another, I was made to drink the bitterest dregs of slavery, that time was during the first six months of my stay with Mr. Covey. We were worked in all weathers. It was never too hot or too cold; it could never rain, blow, hail, or snow, too hard for us to work in the field. Work, work, work, was scarcely more the order of the day than of the night. The longest days were too short for him, and the shortest nights too long for him. I was somewhat unmanageable when I first went there, but a few months of this discipline tamed me. Mr. Covey succeeded in breaking me. I was broken in body, soul, and spirit. My natural elasticity was crushed, my intellect languished, the disposition to read departed, the cheerful spark that lingered about my eye died; the dark night of slavery closed in upon me; and behold a man transformed into a brute!

Sunday was my only leisure time. I spent this in a sort of beast-like stupor, between sleep and wake, under some large tree. At times I would rise up, a flash of energetic freedom would dart through my soul, accompanied with a faint beam of hope, that flickered for a moment, and then vanished. I sank down again, mourning over my wretched condition. I was sometimes prompted to take my life, and that of Covey, but was prevented by a combination of hope and fear. My sufferings on this plantation seem now like a dream rather than a stern reality.

Our house stood within a few rods of the Chesapeake Bay, whose broad bosom was ever white with sails from every quarter of the habitable globe. Those beautiful vessels, robed in purest white, so delightful to the eye of freemen, were to me so many shrouded ghosts, to terrify and torment me with thoughts of my wretched condition. I have often, in the deep stillness of a summer's Sabbath, stood all alone upon the lofty banks of that noble bay, and traced, with saddened heart and tearful eye, the countless number of sails moving off to the mighty ocean. The sight of these always affected me powerfully. My thoughts would compel utterance; and there, with no audience but the Almighty, I would pour out my soul's complaint, in my rude way, with an apostrophe to the moving multitude of ships:—

"You are loosed from your moorings, and are free; I am fast in my chains, and am a slave! You move merrily before the gentle gale, and I sadly before the bloody whip! You are freedom's swift-winged angels, that fly round the world; I am confined in bands of iron! O that I were free! O, that I were on one of your gallant decks, and under your protecting wing! Alas! betwixt me and you, the turbid waters roll. Go on, go on. O that I could also go! Could I but swim! If I could fly! O, why was I born a man, of whom to make a brute! The glad ship is gone; she hides in the dim distance. I am left in the hottest hell of unending slavery. O God, save me! God, deliver me! Let me be free! Is there any God? Why am I a slave? I will run away. I will not stand it. Get caught, or get clear, I'll try it. I had as well die with ague as the fever. I have only one life to lose. I had as well be killed running as die standing. Only think of it; one hundred miles straight north, and I am free! Try it? Yes! God helping me, I will. It cannot be that I shall live and die a slave. I will take to the water. This very bay shall yet bear me into freedom. The steamboats steered in a north-east course from North Point. I will do the same; and when I get to the head of the bay, I will turn my canoe adrift, and walk straight through Delaware into Pennsylvania. When I get there, I shall not be required to have a pass; I can travel without being disturbed. Let but the first opportunity offer, and, come what will, I am off. Meanwhile, I will try to bear up under the yoke. I am not the only slave in the world. Why should I fret? I can bear as much as any of them. Besides, I am but a boy, and all boys are bound to some one. It may be that my misery in slavery will only increase my happiness when I get free. There is a better day coming."

Thus I used to think, and thus I used to speak to myself; goaded almost to madness at one moment, and at the next reconciling myself to my wretched lot.

I have already intimated that my condition was much worse, during the first six months of my stay at Mr. Covey's, than in the last six. The circumstances leading to the change in Mr. Covey's course toward me form an epoch in my humble history. You have seen how a man was made a slave; you shall see how a slave was made a man. On one of the hottest days of the month of August, 1833, Bill Smith, William Hughes, a slave named Eli, and myself, were engaged in fanning wheat. Hughes was clearing the fanned wheat from before the fan. Eli was turning, Smith was feeding, and I was carrying wheat to the fan. The work was simple, requiring strength rather than intellect; yet, to one entirely unused to such work, it came very hard. About three o'clock of that day, I broke down; my strength failed me; I was seized with a violent aching of the head, attended with extreme dizziness; I trembled in every limb. Finding what was coming, I nerved myself up, feeling it would never do to stop work. I stood as long as I could stagger to the hopper with grain. When I could stand no longer, I fell, and felt as if held down by an immense weight. The fan of course stopped; every one had his own work to do; and no one could do the work of the other, and have his own go on at the same time.

Mr. Covey was at the house, about one hundred yards from the treading-yard where we were fanning. On hearing the fan stop, he left immediately, and came to the spot where we were. He hastily inquired what the matter was. Bill answered that I was sick, and there was no one to bring wheat to the fan. I had by this time crawled away under the side of the post and rail-fence by which the yard was enclosed, hoping to find relief by getting out of the sun. He then asked where I was. He was told by one of the hands. He came to the spot, and, after looking at me awhile, asked me what was the matter. I told him as well as I could, for I scarce had strength to speak. He then gave me a savage kick in the side, and told me to get up. I tried to do so, but fell back in the attempt. He gave me another kick, and again told me to rise. I again tried, and succeeded in gaining my feet; but, stooping to get the tub with which I was feeding the fan, I again staggered and fell. While down in this situation, Mr. Covey took up the hickory slat with which Hughes had been striking off the half-bushel measure, and with it gave me a heavy blow upon the head, making a large wound, and the blood ran freely; and with this again told me to get up. I made no effort to comply, having now made up my mind to let him do his worst. In a short time after receiving this blow, my head grew better. Mr. Covey had now left me to my fate. At this moment I resolved, for the first time, to go to my master, enter a complaint, and ask his protection. In order to do this, I must that afternoon walk seven miles; and this, under the circumstances, was truly a severe undertaking. I was exceedingly feeble; made so as much by the kicks and blows which I received, as by the severe fit of sickness to which I had been subjected. I, however, watched my chance, while Covey was looking in an opposite direction, and started for St. Michael's. I succeeded in getting a considerable distance on my way to the woods, when Covey discovered me, and called after me to come back, threatening what he would do if I did not come. I disregarded both his calls and his threats, and made my way to the woods as fast as my feeble state would allow; and thinking I might be overhauled by him if I kept the road, I walked through the woods, keeping far enough from the road to avoid detection, and near enough to prevent losing my way. I had not gone far before my little strength again failed me. I could go no farther. I fell down, and lay for a considerable time. The blood was yet oozing from the wound on my head. For a time I thought I should bleed to death; and think now that I should have done so, but that the blood so matted my hair as to stop the wound. After lying there about three quarters of an hour, I nerved myself up again, and started on my way, through bogs and briers, barefooted and bareheaded, tearing my feet sometimes at nearly every step; and after a journey of about seven miles, occupying some five hours to perform it, I arrived at master's store. I then presented an appearance enough to affect any but a heart of iron. From the crown of my head to my feet, I was covered with blood. My hair was all clotted with dust and blood; my shirt was stiff with blood. I suppose I looked like a man who had escaped a den of wild beasts, and barely escaped them. In this state I appeared before my master, humbly entreating him to interpose his authority for my protection. I told him all the circumstances as well as I could, and it seemed, as I spoke, at times to affect him. He would then walk the floor, and seek to justify Covey by saying he expected I deserved it. He asked me what I wanted. I told him, to let me get a new home; that as sure as I lived with Mr. Covey again, I should live with but to die with him; that Covey would surely kill me; he was in a fair way for it. Master Thomas ridiculed the idea that there was any danger of Mr. Covey's killing me, and said that he knew Mr. Covey; that he was a good man, and that he could not think of taking me from him; that, should he do so, he would lose the whole year's wages; that I belonged to Mr. Covey for one year, and that I must go back to him, come what might; and that I must not trouble him with any more stories, or that he would himself *get hold of me*. After threatening me thus, he gave me a very large dose of salts, telling me that I might remain in St. Michael's that night, (it being quite late,) but that I must be off back to Mr. Covey's early in the morning; and that if I did not, he would *get hold of me,* which meant that he would whip me. I remained all night, and, according to his orders, I started off to Covey's in the morning, (Saturday morning,) wearied in body and broken in spirit. I got no supper that night, or breakfast that morning. I reached Covey's about nine o'clock; and just as I was getting over the fence that divided Mrs. Kemp's fields from ours, out ran Covey with his cowskin, to give me another whipping. Before he could reach me, I succeeded in getting to the cornfield; and as the corn was very high, it afforded me the means of hiding. He seemed very angry, and searched for me a long time. My behavior was altogether unaccountable. He finally gave up the chase, thinking, I suppose, that I must come home for something to eat; he would give himself no further trouble in looking for me. I spent that day mostly in the woods, having the alternative before me,—to go home and be whipped to death, or stay in the woods and be starved to death. That night, I fell in with Sandy Jenkins, a slave with whom I was somewhat acquainted. Sandy had a free wife who lived about four miles from Mr. Covey's; and it being Saturday, he was on his way to see her. I told him my circumstances, and he very kindly invited me to go home with him. I went home with him, and talked this whole matter over, and got his advice as to what course it was best for me to pursue. I found Sandy an old adviser. He told me, with great solemnity, I must go back to Covey; but that before I went, I must go with him into another part of the woods, where there was a certain *root,* which, if I would take some of it with me, carrying it *always on my right side,* would render it impossible for Mr. Covey, or any other white man, to whip me. He said he had carried it for years; and since he had done so, he had never received a blow, and never expected to while he carried it. I at first rejected the idea, that the simple carrying of a root in my pocket would have any such effect as he had said, and was not disposed to take it; but Sandy impressed the necessity with much earnestness, telling me it could do no harm, if it did no good. To please him, I at length took the root, and, according to his direction, carried it upon my right side. This was Sunday morning. I immediately started for home; and upon entering the yard gate, out came Mr. Covey on his way to meeting. He spoke to me very kindly, bade me drive the pigs from a lot near by, and passed on towards the church. Now, this singular conduct of Mr. Covey really made me begin to think that there was something in the *root* which Sandy had given me; and had it been on any other day than Sunday, I could have attributed the conduct to no other cause than the influence of that root; and as it was, I was half inclined to think the *root* to be something more than I at first had taken it to be. All went well till Monday morning. On this morning, the virtue of the *root* was fully tested. Long before daylight, I was called to go and rub, curry, and feed, the horses. I obeyed, and was glad to obey. But whilst thus engaged, whilst in the act of throwing down some blades from the loft, Mr. Covey entered the stable with a long rope; and just as I was half out of the loft, he caught hold of my legs, and was about tying me. As soon as I found what he was up to, I gave a sudden spring, and as I did so, he holding to my legs, I was brought sprawling on the stable floor. Mr. Covey seemed now to think he had me, and could do what he pleased; but at this moment—from whence came the spirit I don't know—I resolved to fight; and, suiting my action to the resolution, I seized Covey hard by the throat; and as I did so, I rose. He held on to me, and I to him. My resistance was so entirely unexpected that Covey seemed taken all aback. He trembled like a leaf. This gave me assurance, and I held him uneasy, causing the blood to run where I touched him with the ends of my fingers. Mr. Covey soon called out to Hughes for help. Hughes came, and, while Covey held me, attempted to tie my right hand. While he was in the act of doing so, I watched my chance, and gave him a heavy kick close under the ribs. This kick fairly sickened Hughes, so that he left me in the hands of Mr. Covey. This kick had the effect of not only weakening Hughes, but Covey also. When he saw Hughes bending over with pain, his courage quailed. He asked me if I meant to persist in my resistance. I told him I did, come what might; that he had used me like a brute for six months, and that I was determined to be used so no longer. With that, he strove to drag me to a stick that was lying just out of the stable door. He meant to knock me down. But just as he was leaning over to get the stick, I seized him with both hands by his collar, and brought him by a sudden snatch to the ground. By this time, Bill came. Covey called upon him for assistance. Bill wanted to know what he could do. Covey said, "Take hold of him, take hold of him!" Bill said his master hired him out to work, and not to help to whip me; so he left Covey and myself to fight our own battle out. We were at it for nearly two hours. Covey at length let me go, puffing and blowing at a great rate, saying that if I had not resisted, he would not have whipped me half so much. The truth was, that he had not whipped me at all. I considered him as getting entirely the worst end of the bargain; for he had drawn no blood from me, but I had from him. The whole six months afterwards, that I spent with Mr. Covey, he never laid the weight of his finger upon me in anger. He would occasionally say, he didn't want to get hold of me again. "No," thought I, "you need not; for you will come off worse than you did before."

This battle with Mr. Covey was the turning-point in my career as a slave. It rekindled the few expiring embers of freedom, and revived within me a sense of my own manhood. It recalled the departed self-confidence, and inspired me again with a determination to be free. The gratification afforded by the triumph was a full compensation for whatever else might follow, even death itself. He only can understand the deep satisfaction which I experienced, who has himself repelled by force the bloody arm of slavery. I felt as I never felt before. It was a glorious resurrection, from the tomb of slavery, to the heaven of freedom. My long-crushed spirit rose, cowardice departed, bold defiance took its place; and I now resolved that, however long I might remain a slave in form, the day had passed forever when I could be a slave in fact. I did not hesitate to let it be known of me, that the white man who expected to succeed in whipping, must also succeed in killing me.

From this time I was never again what might be called fairly whipped, though I remained a slave four years afterwards. I had several fights, but was never whipped.

It was for a long time a matter of surprise to me why Mr. Covey did not immediately have me taken by the constable to the whipping-post, and there regularly whipped for the crime of raising my hand against a white man in defence of myself. And the only explanation I can now think of does not entirely satisfy me; but such as it is, I will give it. Mr. Covey enjoyed the most unbounded reputation for being a first-rate overseer and negro-breaker. It was of considerable importance to him. That reputation was at stake; and had he sent me—a boy about sixteen years old—to the public whipping-post, his reputation would have been lost; so, to save his reputation, he suffered me to go unpunished.

My term of actual service to Mr. Edward Covey ended on Christmas day, 1833. The days between Christmas and New Year's day are allowed as holidays; and, accordingly, we were not required to perform any labor, more than to feed and take care of the stock. This time we regarded as our own, by the grace of our masters; and we therefore used or abused it nearly as we pleased. Those of us who had families at a distance, were generally allowed to spend the whole six days in their society. This time, however, was spent in various ways. The staid, sober, thinking and industrious ones of our number would employ themselves in making corn-brooms, mats, horse-collars, and baskets; and another class of us would spend the time in hunting opossums, hares, and coons. But by far the larger part engaged in such sports and merriments as playing ball, wrestling, running foot-races, fiddling, dancing, and drinking whisky; and this latter mode of spending the time was by far the most agreeable to the feelings of our masters. A slave who would work during the holidays was considered by our masters as scarcely deserving them. He was regarded as one who rejected the favor of his master. It was deemed a disgrace not to get drunk at Christmas; and he was regarded as lazy indeed, who had not provided himself with the necessary means, during the year, to get whisky enough to last him through Christmas.

From what I know of the effect of these holidays upon the slave, I believe them to be among the most effective means in the hands of the slaveholder in keeping down the spirit of insurrection. Were the slaveholders at once to abandon this practice, I have not the slightest doubt it would lead to an immediate insurrection among the slaves. These holidays serve as conductors, or safety-valves, to carry off the rebellious spirit of enslaved humanity. But for these, the slave would be forced up to the wildest desperation; and woe betide the slaveholder, the day he ventures to remove or hinder the operation of those conductors! I warn him that, in such an event, a spirit will go forth in their midst, more to be dreaded than the most appalling earthquake.

The holidays are part and parcel of the gross fraud, wrong, and inhumanity of slavery. They are professedly a custom established by the benevolence of the slaveholders; but I undertake to say, it is the result of selfishness, and one of the grossest frauds committed upon the down-trodden slave. They do not give the slaves this time because they would not like to have their work during its continuance, but because they know it would be unsafe to deprive them of it. This will be seen by the fact, that the slaveholders like to have their slaves spend those days just in such a manner as to make them as glad of their ending as of their beginning. Their object seems to be, to disgust their slaves with freedom, by plunging them into the lowest depths of dissipation. For instance, the slaveholders not only like to see the slave drink of his own accord, but will adopt various plans to make him drunk. One plan is, to make bets on their slaves, as to who can drink the most whisky without getting drunk; and in this way they succeed in getting whole multitudes to drink to excess. Thus, when the slave asks for virtuous freedom, the cunning slaveholder, knowing his ignorance, cheats him with a dose of vicious dissipation, artfully labelled with the name of liberty. The most of us used to drink it down, and the result was just what might be supposed; many of us were led to think that there was little to choose between liberty and slavery. We felt, and very properly too, that we had almost as well be slaves to man as to rum. So, when the holidays ended, we staggered up from the filth of our wallowing, took a long breath, and marched to the field,— feeling, upon the whole, rather glad to go, from what our master had deceived us into a belief was freedom, back to the arms of slavery.

I have said that this mode of treatment is a part of the whole system of fraud and inhumanity of slavery. It is so. The mode here adopted to disgust the slave with freedom, by allowing him to see only the abuse of it, is carried out in other things. For instance, a slave loves molasses; he steals some. His master, in many cases, goes off to town, and buys a large quantity; he returns, takes his whip, and commands the slave to eat the molasses, until the poor fellow is made sick at the very mention of it. The same mode is sometimes adopted to make the slaves refrain from asking for more food than their regular allowance. A slave runs through his allowance, and applies for more. His master is enraged at him; but, not willing to send him off without food, gives him more than is necessary, and compels him to eat it within a given time. Then, if he complains that he cannot eat it, he is said to be satisfied neither full nor fasting, and is whipped for being hard to please! I have an abundance of such illustrations of the same principle, drawn from my own observation, but think the cases I have cited sufficient. The practice is a very common one.

On the first of January, 1834, I left Mr. Covey, and went to live with Mr. William Freeland, who lived about three miles from St. Michael's. I soon found Mr. Freeland a very different man from Mr. Covey. Though not rich, he was what would be called an educated southern gentleman. Mr. Covey, as I have shown, was a well-trained negro-breaker and slave-driver. The former (slaveholder though he was) seemed to possess some regard for honor, some reverence for justice, and some respect for humanity. The latter seemed totally insensible to all such sentiments. Mr. Freeland had many of the faults peculiar to slaveholders, such as being very passionate and fretful; but I must do him the justice to say, that he was exceedingly free from those degrading vices to which Mr. Covey was constantly addicted. The one was open and frank, and we always knew where to find him. The other was a most artful deceiver, and could be understood only by such as were skilful enough to detect his cunningly-devised frauds. Another advantage I gained in my new master was, he made no pretensions to, or profession of, religion; and this, in my opinion, was truly a great advantage. I assert most unhesitatingly, that the religion of the south is a mere covering for the most horrid crimes,—a justifier of the most appalling barbarity,—a sanctifier of the most hateful frauds,—and a dark shelter under, which the darkest, foulest, grossest, and most infernal deeds of slaveholders find the strongest protection. Were I to be again reduced to the chains of slavery, next to that enslavement, I should regard being the slave of a religious master the greatest calamity that could befall me. For of all slaveholders with whom I have ever met, religious slaveholders are the worst. I have ever found them the meanest and basest, the most cruel and cowardly, of all others. It was my unhappy lot not only to belong to a religious slaveholder, but to live in a community of such religionists. Very near Mr. Freeland lived the Rev. Daniel Weeden, and in the same neighborhood lived the Rev. Rigby Hopkins. These were members and ministers in the Reformed Methodist Church. Mr. Weeden owned, among others, a woman slave, whose name I have forgotten. This woman's back, for weeks, was kept literally raw, made so by the lash of this merciless, *religious* wretch. He used to hire hands. His maxim was, Behave well or behave ill, it is the duty of a master occasionally to whip a slave, to remind him of his master's authority. Such was his theory, and such his practice.

Mr. Hopkins was even worse than Mr. Weeden. His chief boast was his ability to manage slaves. The peculiar feature of his government was that of whipping slaves in advance of deserving it. He always managed to have one or more of his slaves to whip every Monday morning. He did this to alarm their fears, and strike terror into those who escaped. His plan was to whip for the smallest offences, to prevent the commission of large ones. Mr. Hopkins could always find some excuse for whipping a slave. It would astonish one, unaccustomed to a slaveholding life, to see with what wonderful ease a slaveholder can find things, of which to make occasion to whip a slave. A mere look, word, or motion,—a mistake, accident, or want of power,—are all matters for which a slave may be whipped at any time. Does a slave look dissatisfied? It is said, he has the devil in him, and it must be whipped out. Does he speak loudly when spoken to by his master? Then he is getting high-minded, and should be taken down a button-hole lower. Does he forget to pull off his hat at the approach of a white person? Then he is wanting in reverence, and should be whipped for it. Does he ever venture to vindicate his conduct, when censured for it? Then he is guilty of impudence,—one of the greatest crimes of which a slave can be guilty. Does he ever venture to suggest a different mode of doing things from that pointed out by his master? He is indeed presumptuous, and getting above himself; and nothing less than a flogging will do for him. Does he, while ploughing, break a plough,—or, while hoeing, break a hoe? It is owing to his carelessness, and for it a slave must always be whipped. Mr. Hopkins could always find something of this sort to justify the use of the lash, and he seldom failed to embrace such opportunities. There was not a man in the whole county, with whom the slaves who had the getting their own home, would not prefer to live, rather than with this Rev. Mr. Hopkins. And yet there was not a man any where round, who made higher professions of religion, or was more active in revivals,—more attentive to the class, love-feast, prayer and preaching meetings, or more devotional in his family,—that prayed earlier, later, louder, and longer,—than this same reverend slave-driver, Rigby Hopkins.

But to return to Mr. Freeland, and to my experience while in his employment. He, like Mr. Covey, gave us enough to eat; but, unlike Mr. Covey, he also gave us sufficient time to take our meals. He worked us hard, but always between sunrise and sunset. He required a good deal of work to be done, but gave us good tools with which to work. His farm was large, but he employed hands enough to work it, and with ease, compared with many of his neighbors. My treatment, while in his employment, was heavenly, compared with what I experienced at the hands of Mr. Edward Covey.

Mr. Freeland was himself the owner of but two slaves. Their names were Henry Harris and John Harris. The rest of his hands he hired. These consisted of myself, Sandy Jenkins,* and Handy Caldwell.

---

* This is the same man who gave me the roots to prevent my being whipped by Mr. Covey. He was "a clever soul." We used frequently to talk about the fight with Covey, and as often as we did so, he would claim my success as the result of the roots which he gave me. This superstition is very common among the more ignorant slaves. A slave seldom dies but that his death is attributed to trickery.

Henry and John were quite intelligent, and in a very little while after I went there, I succeeded in creating in them a strong desire to learn how to read. This desire soon sprang up in the others also. They very soon mustered up some old spelling-books, and nothing would do but that I must keep a Sabbath school. I agreed to do so, and accordingly devoted my Sundays to teaching these my loved fellow-slaves how to read. Neither of them knew his letters when I went there. Some of the slaves of the neighboring farms found what was going on, and also availed themselves of this little opportunity to learn to read. It was understood, among all who came, that there must be as little display about it as possible. It was necessary to keep our religious masters at St. Michael's unacquainted with the fact, that, instead of spending the Sabbath in wrestling, boxing, and drinking whisky, we were trying to learn how to read the will of God; for they had much rather see us engaged in those degrading sports, than to see us behaving like intellectual, moral, and accountable beings. My blood boils as I think of the bloody manner in which Messrs. Wright Fairbanks and Garrison West, both class-leaders, in connection with many others, rushed in upon us with sticks and stones, and broke up our virtuous little Sabbath school, at St. Michael's—all calling themselves Christians! humble followers of the Lord Jesus Christ! But I am again digressing.

I held my Sabbath school at the house of a free colored man, whose name I deem it imprudent to mention; for should it be known, it might embarrass him greatly, though the crime of holding the school was committed ten years ago. I had at one time over forty scholars, and those of the right sort, ardently desiring to learn. They were of all ages, though mostly men and women. I look back to those Sundays with an amount of pleasure not to be expressed. They were great days to my soul. The work of instructing my dear fellow-slaves was the sweetest engagement with which I was ever blessed. We loved each other, and to leave them at the close of the Sabbath was a severe cross indeed. When I think that these precious souls are to-day shut up in the prison-house of slavery, my feelings overcome me, and I am almost ready to ask, "Does a righteous God govern the universe? and for what does he hold the thunders in his right hand, if not to smite the oppressor, and deliver the spoiled out of the hand of the spoiler?" These dear souls came not to Sabbath school because it was popular to do so, nor did I teach them because it was reputable to be thus engaged. Every moment they spent in that school, they were liable to be taken up, and given thirty-nine lashes. They came because they wished to learn. Their minds had been starved by their cruel masters. They had been shut up in mental darkness. I taught them, because it was the delight of my soul to be doing something that looked like bettering the condition of my race. I kept up my school nearly the whole year I lived with Mr. Freeland; and, beside my Sabbath school, I devoted three evenings in the week, during the winter, to teaching the slaves at home. And I have the happiness to know, that several of those who came to Sabbath school learned how to read; and that one, at least, is now free through my agency.

The year passed off smoothly. It seemed only about half as long as the year which preceded it. I went through it without receiving a single blow. I will give Mr. Freeland the credit of being the best master I ever had, *till I became my own master*. For the ease with which I passed the year, I was, however, somewhat indebted to the society of my fellow-slaves. They were noble souls; they not only possessed loving hearts, but brave ones. We were linked and interlinked with each other. I loved them with a love stronger than any thing I have experienced since. It is sometimes said that we slaves do not love and confide in each other. In answer to this assertion, I can say, I never loved any or confided in any people more than my fellow-slaves, and especially those with whom I lived at Mr. Freeland's. I believe we would have died for each other. We never undertook to do any thing, of any importance, without a mutual consultation. We never moved separately. We were one; and as much so by our tempers and dispositions, as by the mutual hardships to which we were necessarily subjected by our condition as slaves.

At the close of the year 1834, Mr. Freeland again hired me of my master, for the year 1835. But, by this time, I began to want to live *upon free land* as well as *with Freeland;* and I was no longer content, therefore, to live with him or any other slaveholder. I began, with the commencement of the year, to prepare myself for a final struggle, which should decide my fate one way or the other. My tendency was upward. I was fast approaching manhood, and year after year had passed, and I was still a slave. These thoughts roused me—I must do something. I therefore resolved that 1835 should not pass without witnessing an attempt, on my part, to secure my liberty. But I was not willing to cherish this determination alone. My fellow-slaves were dear to me. I was anxious to have them participate with me in this, my life-giving determination. I therefore, though with great prudence, commenced early to ascertain their views and feelings in regard to their condition, and to imbue their minds with thoughts of freedom. I bent myself to devising ways and means for our escape, and meanwhile strove, on all fitting occasions, to impress them with the gross fraud and inhumanity of slavery. I went first to Henry, next to John, then to the others. I found, in them all, warm hearts and noble spirits. They were ready to hear, and ready to act when a feasible plan should be proposed. This was what I wanted. I talked to them of our want of manhood, if we submitted to our enslavement without at least one noble effort to be free. We met often, and consulted frequently, and told our hopes and fears, recounted the difficulties, real and imagined, which we should be called on to meet. At times we were almost disposed to give up, and try to content ourselves with our wretched lot; at others, we were firm and unbending in our determination to go. Whenever we suggested any plan, there was shrinking—the odds were fearful. Our path was beset with the greatest obstacles; and if we succeeded in gaining the end of it, our right to be free was yet questionable—we were yet liable to be returned to bondage. We could see no spot, this side of the ocean, where we could be free. We knew nothing about Canada. Our knowledge of the north did not extend farther than New York; and to go there, and be forever harassed with the frightful liability of being returned to slavery—with the certainty of being treated tenfold worse than before—the thought was truly a horrible one, and one which it was not easy to overcome. The case sometimes stood thus: At every gate through which we were to pass, we saw a watchman—at every ferry a guard—on every bridge a sentinel—and in every wood a patrol. We were hemmed in upon every side. Here were the difficulties, real or imagined—the good to be sought, and the evil to be shunned. On the one hand, there stood slavery, a stern reality, glaring frightfully upon us,—its robes already crimsoned with the blood of millions, and even now feasting itself greedily upon our own flesh. On the other hand, away back in the dim distance, under the flickering light of the north star, behind some craggy hill or snow-covered mountain, stood a doubtful freedom—half frozen—beckoning us to come and share its hospitality. This in itself was sometimes enough to stagger us; but when we permitted ourselves to survey the road, we were frequently appalled. Upon either side we saw grim death, assuming the most horrid shapes. Now it was starvation, causing us to eat our own flesh;—now we were contending with the waves, and were drowned;—now we were overtaken, and torn to pieces by the fangs of the terrible bloodhound. We were stung by scorpions, chased by wild beasts, bitten by snakes, and finally, after having nearly reached the desired spot,—after swimming rivers, encountering wild beasts, sleeping in the woods, suffering hunger and nakedness,—we were overtaken by our pursuers, and, in our resistance, we were shot dead upon the spot! I say, this picture sometimes appalled us, and made us

"rather bear those ills we had,
Than fly to others, that we knew not of."

In coming to a fixed determination to run away, we did more than Patrick Henry, when he resolved upon liberty or death. With us it was a doubtful liberty at most, and almost certain death if we failed. For my part, I should prefer death to hopeless bondage.

Sandy, one of our number, gave up the notion, but still encouraged us. Our company then consisted of Henry Harris, John Harris, Henry Bailey, Charles Roberts, and myself. Henry Bailey was my uncle, and belonged to my master. Charles married my aunt: he belonged to my master's father-in-law, Mr. William Hamilton.

The plan we finally concluded upon was, to get a large canoe belonging to Mr. Hamilton, and upon the Saturday night previous to Easter holidays, paddle directly up the Chesapeake Bay. On our arrival at the head of the bay, a distance of seventy or eighty miles from where we lived, it was our purpose to turn our canoe adrift, and follow the guidance of the north star till we got beyond the limits of Maryland. Our reason for taking the water route was, that we were less liable to be suspected as runaways; we hoped to be regarded as fishermen; whereas, if we should take the land route, we should be subjected to interruptions of almost every kind. Any one having a white face, and being so disposed, could stop us, and subject us to examination.

The week before our intended start, I wrote several protections, one for each of us. As well as I can remember, they were in the following words, to wit:—

> "This is to certify that I, the undersigned, have given the bearer, my servant, full liberty to go to Baltimore, and spend the Easter holidays. Written with mine own hand, &c., 1835.
>
> > "WILLIAM HAMILTON,
> > "Near St. Michael's, in Talbot county, Maryland."

We were not going to Baltimore; but, in going up the bay, we went toward Baltimore, and these protections were only intended to protect us while on the bay.

As the time drew near for our departure, our anxiety became more and more intense. It was truly a matter of life and death with us. The strength of our determination was about to be fully tested. At this time, I was very active in explaining every difficulty, removing every doubt, dispelling every fear, and inspiring all with the firmness indispensable to success in our undertaking; assuring them that half was gained the instant we made the move; we had talked long enough; we were now ready to move; if not now, we never should be; and if we did not intend to move now, we had as well fold our arms, sit down, and acknowledge ourselves fit only to be slaves. This, none of us were prepared to acknowledge. Every man stood firm; and at our last meeting, we pledged ourselves afresh, in the most solemn manner, that, at the time appointed, we would certainly start in pursuit of freedom. This was in the middle of the week, at the end of which we were to be off. We went, as usual, to our several fields of labor, but with bosoms highly agitated with thoughts of our truly hazardous undertaking. We tried to conceal our feelings as much as possible; and I think we succeeded very well.

After a painful waiting, the Saturday morning, whose night was to witness our departure, came. I hailed it with joy, bring what of sadness it might. Friday night was a sleepless one for me. I probably felt more anxious than the rest, because I was, by common consent, at the head of the whole affair. The responsibility of success or failure lay heavily upon me. The glory of the one, and the confusion of the other, were alike mine. The first two hours of that morning were such as I never experienced before, and hope never to again. Early in the morning, we went, as usual, to the field. We were spreading manure; and all at once, while thus engaged, I was overwhelmed with an indescribable feeling, in the fulness of which I turned to Sandy, who was near by, and said, "We are betrayed!" "Well," said he, "that thought has this moment struck me." We said no more. I was never more certain of any thing.

The horn was blown as usual, and we went up from the field to the house for breakfast. I went for the form, more than for want of any thing to eat that morning. Just as I got to the house, in looking out at the lane gate, I saw four white men, with two colored men. The white men were on horseback, and the colored ones were walking behind, as if tied. I watched them a few moments till they got up to our lane gate. Here they halted, and tied the colored men to the gate-post. I was not yet certain as to what the matter was. In a few moments, in rode Mr. Hamilton, with a speed betokening great excitement. He came to the door, and inquired if Master William was in. He was told he was at the barn. Mr. Hamilton, without dismounting, rode up to the barn with extraordinary speed. In a few moments, he and Mr. Freeland returned to the house. By this time, the three constables rode up, and in great haste dismounted, tied their horses, and met Master William and Mr. Hamilton returning from the barn; and after talking awhile, they all walked up to the kitchen door. There was no one in the kitchen but myself and John. Henry and Sandy were up at the barn. Mr. Freeland put his head in at the door, and called me by name, saying, there were some gentlemen at the door who wished to see me. I stepped to the door, and inquired what they wanted. They at once seized me, and, without giving me any satisfaction, tied me—lashing my hands closely together. I insisted upon knowing what the matter was. They at length said, that they had learned I had been in a "scrape," and that I was to be examined before my master; and if their information proved false, I should not be hurt.

In a few moments, they succeeded in tying John. They then turned to Henry, who had by this time returned, and commanded him to cross his hands. "I won't!" said Henry, in a firm tone, indicating his readiness to meet the consequences of his refusal. "Won't you?" said Tom Graham, the constable. "No, I won't!" said Henry, in a still stronger tone. With this, two of the constables pulled out their shining pistols, and swore, by their Creator, that they would make him cross his hands or kill him. Each cocked his pistol, and, with fingers on the trigger, walked up to Henry, saying, at the same time, if he did not cross his hands, they would blow his damned heart out. "Shoot me, shoot me!" said Henry; "you can't kill me but once. Shoot, shoot,—and be damned! *I won't be tied!*" This he said in a tone of loud defiance; and at the same time, with a motion as quick as lightning, he with one single stroke dashed the pistols from the hand of each constable. As he did this, all hands fell upon him, and, after beating him some time, they finally overpowered him, and got him tied.

During the scuffle, I managed, I know not how, to get my pass out, and, without being discovered, put it into the fire. We were all now tied; and just as we were to leave for Easton jail, Betsy Freeland, mother of William Freeland, came to the door with her hands full of biscuits, and divided them between Henry and John. She then delivered herself of a speech, to the following effect:—addressing herself to me, she said, "*You devil! You yellow devil!* it was you that put it into the heads of Henry and John to run away. But for you, you long-legged mulatto devil! Henry nor John would never have thought of such a thing." I made no reply, and was immediately hurried off towards St. Michael's. Just a moment previous to the scuffle with Henry, Mr. Hamilton suggested the propriety of making a search for the protections which he had understood Frederick had written for himself and the rest. But, just at the moment he was about carrying his proposal into effect, his aid was needed in helping to tie Henry; and the excitement attending the scuffle caused them either to forget, or to deem it unsafe, under the circumstances, to search. So we were not yet convicted of the intention to run away.

When we got about half way to St. Michael's, while the constables having us in charge were looking ahead, Henry inquired of me what he should do with his pass. I told him to eat it with his biscuit, and own nothing; and we passed the word around, "*Own nothing;*" and "*Own nothing!*" said we all. Our confidence in each other was unshaken. We were resolved to succeed or fail together, after the calamity had befallen us as much as before. We were now prepared for any thing. We were to be dragged that morning fifteen miles behind horses, and then to be placed in the Easton jail. When we reached St. Michael's, we underwent a sort of examination. We all denied that we ever intended to run away. We did this more to bring out the evidence against us, than from any hope of getting clear of being sold; for, as I have said, we were ready for that. The fact was, we cared but little where we went, so we went together. Our greatest concern was about separation. We dreaded that more than any thing this side of death. We found the evidence against us to be the testimony of one person; our master would not tell who it was; but we came to a unanimous decision among ourselves as to who their informant was. We were sent off to the jail at Easton. When we got there, we were delivered up to the sheriff, Mr. Joseph Graham, and by him placed in jail. Henry, John, and myself, were placed in one room together—Charles, and Henry Bailey, in another. Their object in separating us was to hinder concert.

We had been in jail scarcely twenty minutes, when a swarm of slave traders, and agents for slave traders, flocked into jail to look at us, and to ascertain if we were for sale. Such a set of beings I never saw before! I felt myself surrounded by so many fiends from perdition. A band of pirates never looked more like their father, the devil. They laughed and grinned over us, saying, "Ah, my boys! we have got you, haven't we?" And after taunting us in various ways, they one by one went into an examination of us, with intent to ascertain our value. They would impudently ask us if we would not like to have them for our masters. We would make them no answer, and leave them to find out as best they could. Then they would curse and swear at us, telling us that they could take the devil out of us in a very little while, if we were only in their hands.

While in jail, we found ourselves in much more comfortable quarters than we expected when we went there. We did not get much to eat, nor that which was very good; but we had a good clean room, from the windows of which we could see what was going on in the street, which was very much better than though we had been placed in one of the dark, damp cells. Upon the whole, we got along very well, so far as the jail and its keeper were concerned. Immediately after the holidays were over, contrary to all our expectations, Mr. Hamilton and Mr. Freeland came up to Easton, and took Charles, the two Henrys, and John, out of jail, and carried them home, leaving me alone. I regarded this separation as a final one. It caused me more pain than any thing else in the whole transaction. I was ready for any thing rather than separation. I supposed that they had consulted together, and had decided that, as I was the whole cause of the intention of the others to run away, it was hard to make the innocent suffer with the guilty; and that they had, therefore, concluded to take the others home, and sell me, as a warning to the others that remained. It is due to the noble Henry to say, he seemed almost as reluctant at leaving the prison as at leaving home to come to the prison. But we knew we should, in all probability, be separated, if we were sold; and since he was in their hands, he concluded to go peaceably home.

I was now left to my fate. I was all alone, and within the walls of a stone prison. But a few days before, and I was full of hope. I expected to have been safe in a land of freedom; but now I was covered with gloom, sunk down to the utmost despair. I thought the possibility of freedom was gone. I was kept in this way about one week, at the end of which, Captain Auld, my master, to my surprise and utter astonishment, came up, and took me out, with the intention of sending me, with a gentleman of his acquaintance, into Alabama. But, from some cause or other, he did not send me to Alabama, but concluded to send me back to Baltimore, to live again with his brother Hugh, and to learn a trade.

Thus, after an absence of three years and one month, I was once more permitted to return to my old home at Baltimore. My master sent me away, because there existed against me a very great prejudice in the community, and he feared I might be killed.

In a few weeks after I went to Baltimore, Master Hugh hired me to Mr. William Gardner, an extensive ship-builder, on Fell's Point. I was put there to learn how to calk. It, however, proved a very unfavorable place for the accomplishment of this object. Mr. Gardner was engaged that spring in building two large man-of-war brigs, professedly for the Mexican government. The vessels were to be launched in the July of that year, and in failure thereof, Mr. Gardner was to lose a considerable sum; so that when I entered, all was hurry. There was no time to learn any thing. Every man had to do that which he knew how to do. In entering the shipyard, my orders from Mr. Gardner were, to do whatever the carpenters commanded me to do. This was placing me at the beck and call of about seventy-five men. I was to regard all these as masters. Their word was to be my law. My situation was a most trying one. At times I needed a dozen pair of hands. I was called a dozen ways in the space of a single minute. Three or four voices would strike my ear at the same moment. It was—"Fred., come help me to cant this timber here."—"Fred., come carry this timber yonder."—"Fred., bring that roller here."—"Fred., go get a fresh can of water."—"Fred., come help saw off the end of this timber."—"Fred., go quick, and get the crowbar."—"Fred., hold on the end of this fall."—"Fred., go to the blacksmith's shop, and get a new punch."—"Hurra, Fred! run and bring me a cold chisel."—"I say, Fred., bear a hand, and get up a fire as quick as lightning under that steam-box."—"Halloo, nigger! come, turn this grindstone."—"Come, come! move, move! and *bowse* this timber forward."—"I say, darky, blast your eyes, why don't you heat up some pitch?"—"Halloo! halloo! halloo!" (Three voices at the same time.) "Come here!—Go there!—Hold on where you are! Damn you, if you move, I'll knock your brains out!"

This was my school for eight months; and I might have remained there longer, but for a most horrid fight I had with four of the white apprentices, in which my left eye was nearly knocked out, and I was horribly mangled in other respects. The facts in the case were these: Until a very little while after I went there, white and black ship-carpenters worked side by side, and no one seemed to see any impropriety in it. All hands seemed to be very well satisfied. Many of the black carpenters were freemen. Things seemed to be going on very well. All at once, the white carpenters knocked off, and said they would not work with free colored workmen. Their reason for this, as alleged, was, that if free colored carpenters were encouraged, they would soon take the trade into their own hands, and poor white men would be thrown out of employment. They therefore felt called upon at once to put a stop to it. And, taking advantage of Mr. Gardner's necessities, they broke off, swearing they would work no longer, unless he would discharge his black carpenters. Now, though this did not extend to me in form, it did reach me in fact. My fellow-apprentices very soon began to feel it degrading to them to work with me. They began to put on airs, and talk about the "niggers" taking the country, saying we all ought to be killed; and, being encouraged by the journeymen, they commenced making my condition as hard as they could, by hectoring me around, and sometimes striking me. I, of course, kept the vow I made after the fight with Mr. Covey, and struck back again, regardless of consequences; and while I kept them from combining, I succeeded very well; for I could whip the whole of them, taking them separately. They, however, at length combined, and came upon me, armed with sticks, stones, and heavy handspikes. One came in front with a half brick. There was one at each side of me, and one behind me. While I was attending to those in front, and on either side, the one behind ran up with the handspike, and struck me a heavy blow upon the head. It stunned me. I fell, and with this they all ran upon me, and fell to beating me with their fists. I let them lay on for a while, gathering strength. In an instant, I gave a sudden surge, and rose to my hands and knees. Just as I did that, one of their number gave me, with his heavy boot, a powerful kick in the left eye. My eyeball seemed to have burst. When they saw my eye closed, and badly swollen, they left me. With this I seized the handspike, and for a time pursued them. But here the carpenters interfered, and I thought I might as well give it up. It was impossible to stand my hand against so many. All this took place in sight of not less than fifty white ship-carpenters, and not one interposed a friendly word; but some cried, "Kill the damned nigger! Kill him! kill him! He struck a white person." I found my only chance for life was in flight. I succeeded in getting away without an additional blow, and barely so; for to strike a white man is death by Lynch law,—and that was the law in Mr. Gardner's ship-yard; nor is there much of any other out of Mr. Gardner's ship-yard.

I went directly home, and told the story of my wrongs to Master Hugh; and I am happy to say of him, irreligious as he was, his conduct was heavenly, compared with that of his brother Thomas under similar circumstances. He listened attentively to my narration of the circumstances leading to the savage outrage, and gave many proofs of his strong indignation at it. The heart of my once overkind mistress was again melted into pity. My puffed-out eye and blood-covered face moved her to tears. She took a chair by me, washed the blood from my face, and, with a mother's tenderness, bound up my head, covering the wounded eye with a lean piece of fresh beef. It was almost compensation for my suffering to witness, once more, a manifestation of kindness from this, my once affectionate old mistress. Master Hugh was very much enraged. He gave expression to his feelings by pouring out curses upon the heads of those who did the deed. As soon as I got a little the better of my bruises, he took me with him to Esquire Watson's, on Bond Street, to see what could be done about the matter. Mr. Watson inquired who saw the assault committed. Master

Hugh told him it was done in Mr. Gardner's ship-yard at midday, where there were a large company of men at work. "As to that," he said, "the deed was done, and there was no question as to who did it." His answer was, he could do nothing in the case, unless some white man would come forward and testify. He could issue no warrant on my word. If I had been killed in the presence of a thousand colored people, their testimony combined would have been insufficient to have arrested one of the murderers. Master Hugh, for once, was compelled to say this state of things was too bad. Of course, it was impossible to get any white man to volunteer his testimony in my behalf, and against the white young men. Even those who may have sympathized with me were not prepared to do this. It required a degree of courage unknown to them to do so; for just at that time, the slightest manifestation of humanity toward a colored person was denounced as abolitionism, and that name subjected its bearer to frightful liabilities. The watchwords of the bloody-minded in that region, and in those days, were, "Damn the abolitionists!" and "Damn the niggers!" There was nothing done, and probably nothing would have been done if I had been killed. Such was, and such remains, the state of things in the Christian city of Baltimore.

Master Hugh, finding he could get no redress, refused to let me go back again to Mr. Gardner. He kept me himself, and his wife dressed my wound till I was again restored to health. He then took me into the ship-yard of which he was foreman, in the employment of Mr. Walter Price. There I was immediately set to calking, and very soon learned the art of using my mallet and irons. In the course of one year from the time I left Mr. Gardner's, I was able to command the highest wages given to the most experienced calkers. I was now of some importance to my master. I was bringing him from six to seven dollars per week. I sometimes brought him nine dollars per week: my wages were a dollar and a half a day. After learning how to calk, I sought my own employment, made my own contracts, and collected the money which I earned. My pathway became much more smooth than before; my condition was now much more comfortable. When I could get no calking to do, I did nothing. During these leisure times, those old notions about freedom would steal over me again. When in Mr. Gardner's employment, I was kept in such a perpetual whirl of excitement, I could think of nothing, scarcely, but my life; and in thinking of my life, I almost forgot my liberty. I have observed this in my experience of slavery,—that whenever my condition was improved, instead of its increasing my contentment, it only increased my desire to be free, and set me to thinking of plans to gain my freedom. I have found that, to make a contented slave, it is necessary to make a thoughtless one. It is necessary to darken his moral and mental vision, and, as far as possible, to annihilate the power of reason. He must be able to detect no inconsistencies in slavery; he must be made to feel that slavery is right; and he can be brought to that only when he ceases to be a man.

I was now getting, as I have said, one dollar and fifty cents per day. I contracted for it; I earned it; it was paid to me; it was rightfully my own; yet, upon each returning Saturday night, I was compelled to deliver every cent of that money to Master Hugh. And why? Not because he earned it,—not because he had any hand in earning it,—not because I owed it to him,—nor because he possessed the slightest shadow of a right to it; but solely because he had the power to compel me to give it up. The right of the grim-visaged pirate upon the high seas is exactly the same.

CHAPTER XI

I now come to that part of my life during which I planned, and finally succeeded in making, my escape from slavery. But before narrating any of the peculiar circumstances, I deem it proper to make known my intention not to state all the facts connected with the transaction. My reasons for pursuing this course may be understood from the following: First, were I to give a minute statement of all the facts, it is not only possible, but quite probable, that others would thereby be involved in the most embarrassing difficulties. Secondly, such a statement would most undoubtedly induce greater vigilance on the part of slaveholders than has existed heretofore among them; which would, of course, be the means of guarding a door whereby some dear brother bondman might escape his galling chains. I deeply regret the necessity that impels me to suppress any thing of importance connected with my experience in slavery. It would afford me great pleasure indeed, as well as materially add to the interest of my narrative, were I at liberty to gratify a curiosity, which I know exists in the minds of many, by an accurate statement of all the facts pertaining to my most fortunate escape. But I must deprive myself of this pleasure, and the curious of the gratification which such a statement would afford. I would allow myself to suffer under the greatest imputations which evil-minded men might suggest, rather than exculpate myself, and thereby run the hazard of closing the slightest avenue by which a brother slave might clear himself of the chains and fetters of slavery.

I have never approved of the very public manner in which some of our western friends have conducted what they call the *underground railroad*, but which I think, by their open declarations, has been made most emphatically the *upperground railroad.* I honor those good men and women for their noble daring, and applaud them for willingly subjecting themselves to bloody persecution, by openly avowing their participation in the escape of slaves. I, however, can see very little good resulting from such a course, either to themselves or the slaves escaping; while, upon the other hand, I see and feel assured that those open declarations are a positive evil to the slaves remaining, who are seeking to escape. They do nothing towards enlightening the slave, whilst they do much towards enlightening the master. They stimulate him to greater watchfulness, and enhance his power to capture his slave. We owe something to the slave south of the line as well as to those north of it; and in aiding the latter on their way to freedom, we should be careful to do nothing which would be likely to hinder the former from escaping from slavery. I would keep the merciless slaveholder profoundly ignorant of the means of flight adopted by the slave. I would leave him to imagine himself surrounded by myriads of invisible tormentors, ever ready to snatch from his infernal grasp his trembling prey. Let him be left to feel his way in the dark; let darkness commensurate with his crime hover over him; and let him feel that at every step he takes, in pursuit of the flying bondman, he is running the frightful risk of having his hot brains dashed out by an invisible agency. Let us render the tyrant no aid; let us not hold the light by which he can trace the footprints of our flying brother. But enough of this. I will now proceed to the statement of those facts, connected with my escape, for which I am alone responsible, and for which no one can be made to suffer but myself.

In the early part of the year 1838, I became quite restless. I could see no reason why I should, at the end of each week, pour the reward of my toil into the purse of my master. When I carried to him my weekly wages, he would, after counting the money, look me in the face with a robber-like fierceness, and ask, "Is this all?" He was satisfied with nothing less than the last cent. He would, however, when I made him six dollars, sometimes give me six cents, to encourage me. It had the opposite effect. I regarded it as a sort of admission of my right to the whole. The fact that he gave me any part of my wages was proof, to my mind, that he believed me entitled to the whole of them. I always felt worse for having received any thing; for I feared that the giving me a few cents would ease his conscience, and make him feel himself to be a pretty honorable sort of robber. My discontent grew upon me. I was ever on the look-out for means of escape; and, finding no direct means, I determined to try to hire my time, with a view of getting money with which to make my escape. In the spring of 1838, when Master Thomas came to Baltimore to purchase his spring goods, I got an opportunity, and applied to him to allow me to hire my time. He unhesitatingly refused my request, and told me this was another stratagem by which to escape. He told me I could go nowhere but that he could get me; and that, in the event of my running away, he should spare no pains in his efforts to catch me. He exhorted me to content myself, and be obedient. He told me, if I would be happy, I must lay out no plans for the future. He said, if I behaved myself properly, he would take care of me. Indeed, he advised me to complete thoughtlessness of the future, and taught me to depend solely upon him for happiness. He seemed to see fully the pressing necessity of setting aside my intellectual nature, in order to contentment in slavery. But in spite of him, and even in spite of myself, I continued to think, and to think about the injustice of my enslavement, and the means of escape.

About two months after this, I applied to Master Hugh for the privilege of hiring my time. He was not acquainted with the fact that I had applied to Master Thomas, and had been refused. He too, at first, seemed disposed to refuse; but, after some reflection, he granted me the privilege, and proposed the following terms: I was to be allowed all my time, make all contracts with those for whom I worked, and find my own employment; and, in return for this liberty, I was to pay him three dollars at the end of each week; find myself in calking tools, and in board and clothing. My board was two dollars and a half per week. This, with the wear and tear of clothing and calking tools, made my regular expenses about six dollars per week. This amount I was compelled to make up, or relinquish the privilege of hiring my time. Rain or shine, work or no work, at the end of each week the money must be forthcoming, or I must give up my privilege. This arrangement, it will be perceived, was decidedly in my master's favor. It relieved him of all need of looking after me. His money was sure. He received all the benefits of slaveholding without its evils; while I endured all the evils of a slave, and suffered all the care and anxiety of a freeman. I found it a hard bargain. But, hard as it was, I thought it better than the old mode of getting along. It was a step towards freedom to be allowed to bear the responsibilities of a freeman, and I was determined to hold on upon it. I bent myself to the work of making money. I was ready to work at night as well as day, and by the most untiring perseverance and industry, I made enough to meet my expenses, and lay up a little money every week. I went on thus from May till August. Master Hugh then refused to allow me to hire my time longer. The ground for his refusal was a failure on my part, one Saturday night, to pay him for my week's time. This failure was occasioned by my attending a camp meeting about ten miles from Baltimore. During the week, I had entered into an engagement with a number of young friends to start from Baltimore to the camp ground early Saturday evening; and being detained by my employer, I was unable to get down to Master Hugh's without disappointing the company. I knew that Master Hugh was in no special need of the money that night. I therefore decided to go to camp meeting, and upon my return pay him the three dollars. I staid at the camp meeting one day longer than I intended when I left. But as soon as I returned, I called upon him to pay him what he considered his due. I found him very angry; he could scarce restrain his wrath. He said he had a great mind to give me a severe whipping. He wished to know how I dared go out of the city without asking his permission. I told him I hired my time and while I paid him the price which he asked for it, I did not know that I was bound to ask him when and where I should go. This reply troubled him; and, after reflecting a few moments, he turned to me, and said I should hire my time no longer; that the next thing he should know of, I would be running away. Upon the same plea, he told me to bring my tools and clothing home forthwith. I did so; but instead of seeking work, as I had been accustomed to do previously to hiring my time, I spent the whole week without the performance of a single stroke of work. I did this in retaliation. Saturday night, he called upon me as usual for my week's wages. I told him I had no wages; I had done no work that week. Here we were upon the point of coming to blows. He raved, and swore his determination to get hold of me. I did not allow myself a single word; but was resolved, if he laid the weight of his hand upon me, it should be blow for blow. He did not strike me, but told me that he would find me in constant employment in future. I thought the matter over during the next day, Sunday, and finally resolved upon the third day of September, as the day upon which I would make a second attempt to secure my freedom. I now had three weeks during which to prepare for my journey. Early on Monday morning, before Master Hugh had time to make any engagement for me, I went out and got employment of Mr. Butler, at his ship-yard near the drawbridge, upon what is called the City Block, thus making it unnecessary for him to seek employment for me. At the end of the week, I brought him between eight and nine dollars. He seemed very well pleased, and asked why I did not do the same the week before. He little knew what my plans were. My object in working steadily was to remove any suspicion he might entertain of my intent to run away; and in this I succeeded admirably. I suppose he thought I was never better satisfied with my condition than at the very time during which I was planning my escape. The second week passed, and again I carried him my full wages; and so well pleased was he, that he gave me twenty-five cents, (quite a large sum for a slaveholder to give a slave,) and bade me to make a good use of it. I told him I would.

Things went on without very smoothly indeed, but within there was trouble. It is impossible for me to describe my feelings as the time of my contemplated start drew near. I had a number of warmhearted friends in Baltimore,—friends that I loved almost as I did my life,—and the thought of being separated from them forever was painful beyond expression. It is my opinion that thousands would escape from slavery, who now remain, but for the strong cords of affection that bind them to their friends. The thought of leaving my friends was decidedly the most painful thought with which I had to contend. The love of them was my tender point, and shook my decision more than all things else. Besides the pain of separation, the dread and apprehension of a failure exceeded what I had experienced at my first attempt. The appalling defeat I then sustained returned to torment me. I felt assured that, if I failed in this attempt, my case would be a hopeless one—it would seal my fate as a slave forever. I could not hope to get off with any thing less than the severest punishment, and being placed beyond the means of escape. It required no very vivid imagination to depict the most frightful scenes through which I should have to pass, in case I failed. The wretchedness of slavery, and the blessedness of freedom, were perpetually before me. It was life and death with me. But I remained firm, and, according to my resolution, on the third day of September, 1838, I left my chains, and succeeded in reaching New York without the slightest interruption of any kind. How I did so,—what means I adopted,—what direction I travelled, and by what mode of conveyance,—I must leave unexplained, for the reasons before mentioned.

I have been frequently asked how I felt when I found myself in a free State. I have never been able to answer the question with any satisfaction to myself. It was a moment of the highest excitement I ever experienced. I suppose I felt as one may imagine the unarmed mariner to feel when he is rescued by a friendly man-of-war from the pursuit of a pirate. In writing to a dear friend, immediately after my arrival at New York, I said I felt like one who had escaped a den of hungry lions. This state of mind, however, very soon subsided; and I was again seized with a feeling of great insecurity and loneliness. I was yet liable to be taken back, and subjected to all the tortures of slavery. This in itself was enough to damp the ardor of my enthusiasm. But the loneliness overcame me. There I was in the midst of thousands, and yet a perfect stranger; without home and without friends, in the midst of thousands of my own brethren—children of a common Father, and yet I dared not to unfold to any one of them my sad condition. I was afraid to speak to any one for fear of speaking to the wrong one, and thereby falling into the hands of money-loving kidnappers, whose business it was to lie in wait for the panting fugitive, as the ferocious beasts of the forest lie in wait for their prey. The motto which I adopted when I started from slavery was this—"Trust no man!" I saw in every white man an enemy, and in almost every colored man cause for distrust. It was a most painful situation; and, to understand it, one must needs experience it, or imagine himself in similar circumstances. Let him be a fugitive slave in a strange land—a land given up to be the hunting-ground for slaveholders—whose inhabitants are legalized kidnappers—where he is every moment subjected to the terrible liability of being seized upon by his fellowmen, as the hideous crocodile seizes upon his prey!—I say, let him place himself in my situation—without home or friends—without money or credit—wanting shelter, and no one to give it—wanting bread, and no money to buy it,—and at the same time let him feel that he is pursued by merciless men-hunters, and in total darkness as to what to do, where to go, or where to stay,—perfectly helpless both as to the means of defence and means of escape,—in the midst of plenty, yet suffering the terrible gnawings of hunger,—in the midst of houses, yet having no home,—among fellow-men, yet feeling as if in the midst of wild beasts, whose greediness to swallow up the trembling and half-famished fugitive is only equalled by that with which the monsters of the deep swallow up the helpless fish upon which they subsist,—I say, let him be placed in this most trying situation,—the situation in which I was placed,—then, and not till then, will he fully appreciate the hardships of, and know how to sympathize with, the toil-worn and whip-scarred fugitive slave.

Thank Heaven, I remained but a short time in this distressed situation. I was relieved from it by the humane hand of *Mr. David Ruggles*, whose vigilance, kindness, and perseverance, I shall never forget. I am glad of an opportunity to express, as far as words can, the love and gratitude I bear him. Mr. Ruggles is now afflicted with blindness, and is himself in need of the same kind offices which he was once so forward in the performance of toward others. I had been in New York but a few days, when Mr. Ruggles sought me out, and very kindly took me to his boarding-house at the corner of Church and Lespenard Streets. Mr. Ruggles was then very deeply engaged in the memorable *Darg* case, as well as attending to a number of other fugitive slaves, devising ways and means for their successful escape; and, though watched and hemmed in on almost every side, he seemed to be more than a match for his enemies.

Very soon after I went to Mr. Ruggles, he wished to know of me where I wanted to go; as he deemed it unsafe for me to remain in New York. I told him I was a calker, and should like to go where I could get work. I thought of going to Canada; but he decided against it, and in favor of my going to New Bedford, thinking I should be able to get work there at my trade. At this time, Anna,[*] my intended wife, came on; for I wrote to her immediately after my arrival at New York, (notwithstanding my homeless, houseless, and helpless condition,) informing her of my successful flight, and wishing her to come on forthwith. In a few days after her arrival, Mr. Ruggles called in the Rev. J. W. C. Pennington, who, in the presence of Mr. Ruggles, Mrs. Michaels, and two or three others, performed the marriage ceremony, and gave us a certificate, of which the following is an exact copy:—

> "This may certify, that I joined together in holy matrimony Frederick Johnson[†] and Anna Murray, as man and wife, in the presence of Mr. David Ruggles and Mrs. Michaels.
>
> > "JAMES W. C. PENNINGTON
> > "*New York, Sept.* 15, 1838"

Upon receiving this certificate, and a five-dollar bill from Mr. Ruggles, I shouldered one part of our baggage, and Anna took up the other, and we set out forthwith to take passage on board of the steamboat John W. Richmond for Newport, on our way to New Bedford. Mr. Ruggles gave me a letter to a Mr. Shaw in Newport, and told me, in case my money did not serve me to New Bedford, to stop in Newport and obtain further assistance; but upon our arrival

---

[*] She was free.

[†] I had changed my name from Frederick *Bailey* to that of *Johnson*.

at Newport, we were so anxious to get to a place of safety, that, notwithstanding we lacked the necessary money to pay our fare, we decided to take seats in the stage, and promise to pay when we got to New Bedford. We were encouraged to do this by two excellent gentlemen, residents of New Bedford, whose names I afterward ascertained to be Joseph Ricketson and William C. Taber. They seemed at once to understand our circumstances, and gave us such assurance of their friendliness as put us fully at ease in their presence.

It was good indeed to meet with such friends, at such a time. Upon reaching New Bedford, we were directed to the house of Mr. Nathan Johnson, by whom we were kindly received, and hospitably provided for. Both Mr. and Mrs. Johnson took a deep and lively interest in our welfare. They proved themselves quite worthy of the name of abolitionists. When the stage-driver found us unable to pay our fare, he held on upon our baggage as security for the debt. I had but to mention the fact to Mr. Johnson, and he forthwith advanced the money.

We now began to feel a degree of safety, and to prepare ourselves for the duties and responsibilities of a life of freedom. On the morning after our arrival at New Bedford, while at the breakfast-table, the question arose as to what name I should be called by. The name given me by my mother was, "Frederick Augustus Washington Bailey." I, however, had dispensed with the two middle names long before I left Maryland so that I was generally known by the name of "Frederick Bailey." I started from Baltimore bearing the name of "Stanley." When I got to New York, I again changed my name to "Frederick Johnson," and thought that would be the last change. But when I got to New Bedford, I found it necessary again to change my name. The reason of this necessity was, that there were so many Johnsons in New Bedford, it was already quite difficult to distinguish between them. I gave Mr. Johnson the privilege of choosing me a name, but told him he must not take from me the name of "Frederick." I must hold on to that, to preserve a sense of my identity. Mr. Johnson had just been reading the "Lady of the Lake," and at once suggested that my name be "Douglass." From that time until now I have been called "Frederick Douglass;" and as I am more widely known by that name than by either of the others, I shall continue to use it as my own.

I was quite disappointed at the general appearance of things in New Bedford. The impression which I had received respecting the character and condition of the people of the north, I found to be singularly erroneous. I had very strangely supposed, while in slavery, that few of the comforts, and scarcely any of the luxuries, of life were enjoyed at the north, compared with what were enjoyed by the slaveholders of the south. I probably came to this conclusion from the fact that northern people owned no slaves. I supposed that they were about upon a level with the non-slaveholding population of the south. I knew *they* were exceedingly poor, and I had been accustomed to regard their poverty as the necessary consequence of their being non-slaveholders. I had somehow imbibed the opinion that, in the absence of slaves, there could be no wealth, and very little refinement. And upon coming to the north, I expected to meet with a rough, hard-handed, and uncultivated population, living in the most Spartan-like simplicity, knowing nothing of the ease, luxury, pomp, and grandeur of southern slaveholders. Such being my conjectures, any one acquainted with the appearance of New Bedford may very readily infer how palpably I must have seen my mistake.

In the afternoon of the day when I reached New Bedford, I visited the wharves, to take a view of the shipping. Here I found myself surrounded with the strongest proofs of wealth. Lying at the wharves, and riding in the stream, I saw many ships of the finest model, in the best order, and of the largest size. Upon the right and left, I was walled in by granite warehouses of the widest dimensions, stowed to their utmost capacity with the necessaries and comforts of life. Added to this, almost every body seemed to be at work, but noiselessly so, compared with what I had been accustomed to in Baltimore. There were no loud songs heard from those engaged in loading and unloading ships. I heard no deep oaths or horrid curses on the laborer. I saw no whipping of men; but all seemed to go smoothly on. Every man appeared to understand his work, and went at it with a sober, yet cheerful earnestness, which betokened the deep interest which he felt in what he was doing, as well as a sense of his own dignity as a man. To me this looked exceedingly strange. From the wharves I strolled around and over the town, gazing with wonder and admiration at the splendid churches, beautiful dwellings, and finely-cultivated gardens; evincing an amount of wealth, comfort, taste, and refinement, such as I had never seen in any part of slaveholding Maryland.

Every thing looked clean, new, and beautiful. I saw few or no dilapidated houses, with poverty-stricken inmates; no half-naked children and barefooted women, such as I had been accustomed to see in Hillsborough, Easton, St. Michael's, and Baltimore. The people looked more able, stronger, healthier, and happier, than those of Maryland. I was for once made glad by a view of extreme wealth, without being saddened by seeing extreme poverty. But the most astonishing as well as the most interesting thing to me was the condition of the colored people, a great many of whom, like myself, had escaped thither as a refuge from the hunters of men. I found many, who had not been seven years out of their chains, living in finer houses, and evidently enjoying more of the comforts of life, than the average of slaveholders in Maryland. I will venture to assert, that my friend Mr. Nathan Johnson (of whom I can say with a grateful heart, "I was hungry, and he gave me meat; I was thirsty, and he gave me drink; I was a stranger, and he took me in") lived in a neater house; dined at a better table; took, paid for, and read, more newspapers; better understood the moral, religious, and political character of the nation,—than nine tenths of the slaveholders in Talbot county Maryland. Yet Mr. Johnson was a working man. His hands were hardened by toil, and not his alone, but those also of Mrs. Johnson. I found the colored people much more spirited than I had supposed they would be. I found among them a determination to protect each other from the blood-thirsty kidnapper, at all hazards. Soon after my arrival, I was told of a circumstance which illustrated their spirit. A colored man and a fugitive slave were on unfriendly terms. The former was heard to threaten the latter with informing his master of his whereabouts. Straightway a meeting was called among the colored people, under the stereotyped notice, "Business of importance!" The betrayer was invited to attend. The people came at the appointed hour, and organized the meeting by appointing a very religious old gentleman as president, who, I believe, made a prayer, after which he addressed the meeting as follows: "*Friends, we have got him here, and I would recommend that you young men just take him outside the door, and kill him!*" With this, a number of them bolted at him; but they were intercepted by some more timid than themselves, and the betrayer escaped their vengeance, and has not been seen in New Bedford since. I believe there have been no more such threats, and should there be hereafter, I doubt not that death would be the consequence.

I found employment, the third day after my arrival, in stowing a sloop with a load of oil. It was new, dirty, and hard work for me; but I went at it with a glad heart and a willing hand. I was now my own master. It was a happy moment, the rapture of which can be understood only by those who have been slaves. It was the first work, the reward of which was to be entirely my own. There was no Master Hugh standing ready, the moment I earned the money, to rob me of it. I worked that day with a pleasure I had never before experienced. I was at work for myself and newly-married wife. It was to me the starting-point of a new existence. When I got through with that job, I went in pursuit of a job of calking; but such was the strength of prejudice against color, among the white calkers, that they refused to work with me, and of course I could get no employment.[*] Finding my trade of no immediate benefit, I threw off my calking habiliments, and prepared myself to do any kind of work I could get to do. Mr. Johnson kindly let me have his wood-horse and saw, and I very soon found myself a plenty of work. There was no work too hard—none too dirty. I was ready to saw wood, shovel coal, carry wood, sweep the chimney, or roll oil casks,—all of which I did for nearly three years in New Bedford, before I became known to the anti-slavery world.

---

[*] I am told that colored persons can now get employment at calking in New Bedford—a result of anti-slavery effort.

In about four months after I went to New Bedford, there came a young man to me, and inquired if I did not wish to take the "Liberator." I told him I did; but, just having made my escape from slavery, I remarked that I was unable to pay for it then. I, however, finally became a subscriber to it. The paper came, and I read it from week to week with such feelings as it would be quite idle for me to attempt to describe. The paper became my meat and my drink. My soul was set all on fire. Its sympathy for my brethren in bonds—its scathing denunciations of slaveholders—its faithful exposures of slavery—and its powerful attacks upon the upholders of the institution—sent a thrill of joy through my soul, such as I had never felt before!

I had not long been a reader of the "Liberator," before I got a pretty correct idea of the principles, measures and spirit of the anti-slavery reform. I took right hold of the cause. I could do but little; but what I could, I did with a joyful heart, and never felt happier than when in an anti-slavery meeting. I seldom had much to say at the meetings, because what I wanted to say was said so much better by others. But, while attending an anti-slavery convention at Nantucket, on the 11th of August, 1841, I felt strongly moved to speak, and was at the same time much urged to do so by Mr. William C. Coffin, a gentleman who had heard me speak in the colored people's meeting at New Bedford. It was a severe cross, and I took it up reluctantly. The truth was, I felt myself a slave, and the idea of speaking to white people weighed me down. I spoke but a few moments, when I felt a degree of freedom, and said what I desired with considerable ease. From that time until now, I have been engaged in pleading the cause of my brethren— with what success, and with what devotion, I leave those acquainted with my labors to decide.

APPENDIX

I find, since reading over the foregoing Narrative, that I have, in several instances, spoken in such a tone and manner, respecting religion, as may possibly lead those unacquainted with my religious views to suppose me an opponent of all religion. To remove the liability of such misapprehension, I deem it proper to append the following brief explanation. What I have said respecting and against religion, I mean strictly to apply to the *slaveholding religion* of this land, and with no possible reference to Christianity proper; for, between the Christianity of this land, and the Christianity of Christ, I recognize the widest possible difference—so wide, that to receive the one as good, pure, and holy, is of necessity to reject the other as bad, corrupt, and wicked. To be the friend of the one, is of necessity to be the enemy of the other. I love the pure, peaceable, and impartial Christianity of Christ: I therefore hate the corrupt, slaveholding, women-whipping, cradle-plundering, partial and hypocritical Christianity of this land. Indeed, I can see no reason, but the most deceitful one, for calling the religion of this land Christianity. I look upon it as the climax of all misnomers, the boldest of all frauds, and the grossest of all libels. Never was there a clearer case of "stealing the livery of the court of heaven to serve the devil in." I am filled with unutterable loathing when I contemplate the religious pomp and show, together with the horrible inconsistencies, which every where surround me. We have men-stealers for ministers, women-whippers for missionaries, and cradle-plunderers for church members. The man who wields the blood-clotted cowskin during the week fills the pulpit on Sunday, and claims to be a minister of the meek and lowly Jesus. The man who robs me of my earnings at the end of each week meets me as a class-leader on Sunday morning, to show me the way of life, and the path of salvation. He who sells my sister, for purposes of prostitution, stands forth as the pious advocate of purity. He who proclaims it a religious duty to read the Bible denies me the right of learning to read the name of the God who made me. He who is the religious advocate of marriage robs whole millions of its sacred influence, and leaves them to the ravages of wholesale pollution. The warm defender of the sacredness of the family relation is the same that scatters whole families,—sundering husbands and wives, parents and children, sisters and brothers,—leaving the hut vacant, and the hearth desolate. We see the thief preaching against theft, and the adulterer against adultery. We have men sold to build churches, women sold to support the gospel, and babes sold to purchase Bibles for the *Poor Heathen! All For The Glory Of God And The Good Of Souls!* The slave auctioneer's bell and the church-going bell chime in with each other, and the bitter cries of the heart-broken slave are drowned in the religious shouts of his pious master. Revivals of religion and revivals in the slave-trade go hand in hand together. The slave prison and the church stand near each other. The clanking of fetters and the rattling of chains in the prison, and the pious psalm and solemn prayer in the church, may be heard at the same time. The dealers in the bodies and souls of men erect their stand in the presence of the pulpit, and they mutually help each other. The dealer gives his blood-stained gold to support the pulpit, and the pulpit, in return, covers his infernal business with the garb of Christianity. Here we have religion and robbery the allies of each other—devils dressed in angels' robes, and hell presenting the semblance of paradise.

> "Just God! and these are they,v Who minister at thine altar, God of right!
> Men who their hands, with prayer and blessing, lay
> On Israel's ark of light.
>
> "What! preach, and kidnap men?
> Give thanks, and rob thy own afflicted poor?
> Talk of thy glorious liberty, and then
> Bolt hard the captive's door?
>
> "What! servants of thy own
> Merciful Son, who came to seek and save
> The homeless and the outcast, fettering down
> The tasked and plundered slave!
>
> "Pilate and Herod friends!
> Chief priests and rulers, as of old, combine!
> Just God and holy! is that church which lends
> Strength to the spoiler thine?"

The Christianity of America is a Christianity, of whose votaries it may be as truly said, as it was of the ancient scribes and Pharisees, "They bind heavy burdens, and grievous to be borne, and lay them on men's shoulders, but they themselves will not move them with one of their fingers. All their works they do for to be seen of men.—They love the uppermost rooms at feasts, and the chief seats in the synagogues, ... and to be called of men, Rabbi, Rabbi.—But woe unto you, scribes and Pharisees, hypocrites! for ye shut up the kingdom of heaven against men; for ye neither go in yourselves, neither suffer ye them that are entering to go in. Ye devour widows' houses, and for a pretence make long prayers; therefore ye shall receive the greater damnation. Ye compass sea and land to make one proselyte, and when he is made, ye make him twofold more the child of hell than yourselves.—Woe unto you, scribes and Pharisees, hypocrites! for ye pay tithe of mint, and anise, and cumin, and have omitted the weightier matters of the law, judgment, mercy, and faith; these ought ye to have done, and not to leave the other undone. Ye blind guides! which strain at a gnat, and swallow a camel. Woe unto you, scribes and Pharisees, hypocrites! for ye make clean the outside of the cup and of the platter; but within, they are full of extortion and excess.—Woe unto you, scribes and Pharisees, hypocrites! for ye are like unto whited sepulchres, which indeed appear beautiful outward, but are within full of dead men's bones, and of all uncleanness. Even so ye also outwardly appear righteous unto men, but within ye are full of hypocrisy and iniquity."

Dark and terrible as is this picture, I hold it to be strictly true of the overwhelming mass of professed Christians in America. They strain at a gnat, and swallow a camel. Could any thing be more true of our churches? They would be shocked at the proposition of fellowshipping a *sheep*-stealer; and at the same time they hug to their communion a *man*-stealer, and brand me with being an infidel, if I find fault with them for it. They attend with Pharisaical strictness to the outward forms of religion, and at the same time neglect the weightier matters of the law, judgment, mercy, and faith. They are always ready to sacrifice, but seldom to show mercy. They are they who are represented as professing to love God whom they have not seen, whilst they hate their brother whom they have seen. They love the heathen on the other side of the globe. They can pray for him, pay money to have the Bible put into his hand, and missionaries to instruct him; while they despise and totally neglect the heathen at their own doors.

Such is, very briefly, my view of the religion of this land; and to avoid any misunderstanding, growing out of the use of general terms, I mean by the religion of this land, that which is revealed in the words, deeds, and actions, of those bodies, north and south, calling themselves Christian churches, and yet in union with slaveholders. It is against religion, as presented by these bodies, that I have felt it my duty to testify.

I conclude these remarks by copying the following portrait of the religion of the south, (which is, by communion and fellowship, the religion of the north,) which I soberly affirm is "true to the life," and without caricature or the slightest exaggeration. It is said to have been drawn, several years before the present anti-slavery agitation began, by a northern Methodist preacher, who, while residing at the south, had an opportunity to see slaveholding morals, manners, and piety, with his own eyes. "Shall I not visit for these things? saith the Lord. Shall not my soul be avenged on such a nation as this?"

A PARODY

"Come, saints and sinners, hear me tell
How pious priests whip Jack and Nell,
And women buy and children sell,
And preach all sinners down to hell,
And sing of heavenly union.

"They'll bleat and baa, dona like goats,
Gorge down black sheep, and strain at motes,
Array their backs in fine black coats,
Then seize their negroes by their throats,
And choke, for heavenly union.

"They'll church you if you sip a dram,
And damn you if you steal a lamb;
Yet rob old Tony, Doll, and Sam,
Of human rights, and bread and ham;
Kidnapper's heavenly union.

"They'll loudly talk of Christ's reward,
And bind his image with a cord,
And scold, and swing the lash abhorred,
And sell their brother in the Lord
To handcuffed heavenly union.

"They'll read and sing a sacred song,
And make a prayer both loud and long,
And teach the right and do the wrong,
Hailing the brother, sister throng,
With words of heavenly union.

"We wonder how such saints can sing,
Or praise the Lord upon the wing,
Who roar, and scold, and whip, and sting,
And to their slaves and mammon cling,
In guilty conscience union.

"They'll raise tobacco, corn, and rye,
And drive, and thieve, and cheat, and lie,
And lay up treasures in the sky,
By making switch and cowskin fly,
In hope of heavenly union.

"They'll crack old Tony on the skull,
And preach and roar like Bashan bull,
Or braying ass, of mischief full,
Then seize old Jacob by the wool,
And pull for heavenly union.

"A roaring, ranting, sleek man-thief,
Who lived on mutton, veal, and beef,
Yet never would afford relief
To needy, sable sons of grief,
Was big with heavenly union.

"'Love not the world,' the preacher said,
And winked his eye, and shook his head;
He seized on Tom, and Dick, and Ned,
Cut short their meat, and clothes, and bread,
Yet still loved heavenly union.

"Another preacher whining spoke
Of One whose heart for sinners broke:
He tied old Nanny to an oak,
And drew the blood at every stroke,
And prayed for heavenly union.

"Two others oped their iron jaws,
And waved their children-stealing paws;
There sat their children in gewgaws;
By stinting negroes' backs and maws,
They kept up heavenly union.

"All good from Jack another takes,
And entertains their flirts and rakes,
Who dress as sleek as glossy snakes,
And cram their mouths with sweetened cakes;
And this goes down for union."

Sincerely and earnestly hoping that this little book may do something toward throwing light on the American slave system, and hastening the glad day of deliverance to the millions of my brethren in bonds—faithfully relying upon the power of truth, love, and justice, for success in my humble efforts—and solemnly pledging my self anew to the sacred cause,—I subscribe myself,

FREDERICK DOUGLASS.
LYNN, *Mass., April* 28, 1845.

MY BONDAGE AND MY FREEDOM

By a principle essential to Christianity, a PERSON is eternally differenced from a THING; so that the idea of a HUMAN BEING, necessarily excludes the idea of PROPERTY IN THAT BEING. —COLERIDGE

Entered according to Act of Congress in 1855
by Frederick Douglass in the Clerk's Office of the District Court
of the Northern District of New York

TO
HONORABLE GERRIT SMITH,
AS A SLIGHT TOKEN OF
ESTEEM FOR HIS CHARACTER,
ADMIRATION FOR HIS GENIUS AND BENEVOLENCE,
AFFECTION FOR HIS PERSON, AND
GRATITUDE FOR HIS FRIENDSHIP,
AND AS
A Small but most Sincere Acknowledgement of
HIS PRE-EMINENT SERVICES IN BEHALF OF THE RIGHTS AND
LIBERTIES
OF AN
AFFLICTED, DESPISED AND DEEPLY OUTRAGED PEOPLE,
BY RANKING SLAVERY WITH PIRACY AND MURDER,
AND BY
DENYING IT EITHER A LEGAL OR CONSTITUTIONAL EXISTENCE,
This Volume is Respectfully Dedicated,
BY HIS FAITHFUL AND FIRMLY ATTACHED FRIEND,

FREDERICK DOUGLAS.
ROCHESTER, N.Y.

EDITOR'S PREFACE

If the volume now presented to the public were a mere work of ART, the history of its misfortune might be written in two very simple words—TOO LATE. The nature and character of slavery have been subjects of an almost endless variety of artistic representation; and after the brilliant achievements in that field, and while those achievements are yet fresh in the memory of the million, he who would add another to the legion, must possess the charm of transcendent excellence, or apologize for something worse than rashness. The reader is, therefore, assured, with all due promptitude, that his attention is not invited to a work of ART, but to a work of FACTS—Facts, terrible and almost incredible, it may be yet FACTS, nevertheless.

I am authorized to say that there is not a fictitious name nor place in the whole volume; but that names and places are literally given, and that every transaction therein described actually transpired.

Perhaps the best Preface to this volume is furnished in the following letter of Mr. Douglass, written in answer to my urgent solicitation for such a work:

ROCHESTER, N. Y. *July* 2, 1855.

DEAR FRIEND: I have long entertained, as you very well know, a somewhat positive repugnance to writing or speaking anything for the public, which could, with any degree of plausibilty, make me liable to the imputation of seeking personal notoriety, for its own sake. Entertaining that feeling very sincerely, and permitting its control, perhaps, quite unreasonably, I have often refused to narrate my personal experience in public anti-slavery meetings, and in sympathizing circles, when urged to do so by friends, with whose views and wishes, ordinarily, it were a pleasure to comply. In my letters and speeches, I have generally aimed to discuss the question of Slavery in the light of fundamental principles, and upon facts, notorious and open to all; making, I trust, no more of the fact of my own former enslavement, than circumstances seemed absolutely to require. I have never placed my opposition to slavery on a basis so narrow as my own enslavement, but rather upon the indestructible and unchangeable laws of human nature, every one of which is perpetually and flagrantly violated by the slave system. I have also felt that it was best for those having histories worth the writing—or supposed to be so—to commit such work to hands other than their own. To write of one's self, in such a manner as not to incur the imputation of weakness, vanity, and egotism, is a work within the ability of but few; and I have little reason to believe that I belong to that fortunate few.

These considerations caused me to hesitate, when first you kindly urged me to prepare for publication a full account of my life as a slave, and my life as a freeman.

Nevertheless, I see, with you, many reasons for regarding my autobiography as exceptional in its character, and as being, in some sense, naturally beyond the reach of those reproaches which honorable and sensitive minds dislike to incur. It is not to illustrate any heroic achievements of a man, but to vindicate a just and beneficent principle, in its application to the whole human family, by letting in the light of truth upon a system, esteemed by some as a blessing, and by others as a curse and a crime. I agree with you, that this system is now at the bar of public opinion—not only of this country, but of the whole civilized world—for judgment. Its friends have made for it the usual plea—"not guilty;" the case must, therefore, proceed. Any facts, either from slaves, slaveholders, or by-standers, calculated to enlighten the public mind, by revealing the true nature, character, and tendency of the slave system, are in order, and can scarcely be innocently withheld.

I see, too, that there are special reasons why I should write my own biography, in preference to employing another to do it. Not only is slavery on trial, but unfortunately, the enslaved people are also on trial. It is alleged, that they are, naturally, inferior; that they are *so low* in the scale of humanity, and so utterly stupid, that they are unconscious of their wrongs, and do not apprehend their rights. Looking, then, at your request, from this stand-point, and wishing everything of which you think me capable to go to the benefit of my afflicted people, I part with my doubts and hesitation, and proceed to furnish you the desired manuscript; hoping that you may be able to make such arrangements for its publication as shall be best adapted to accomplish that good which you so enthusiastically anticipate.

FREDERICK DOUGLASS

There was little necessity for doubt and hesitation on the part of Mr. Douglass, as to the propriety of his giving to the world a full account of himself. A man who was born and brought up in slavery, a living witness of its horrors; who often himself experienced its cruelties; and who, despite the depressing influences surrounding his birth, youth and manhood, has risen, from a dark and almost absolute obscurity, to the distinguished position which he now occupies, might very well assume the existence of a commendable curiosity, on the part of the public, to know the facts of his remarkable history.

EDITOR

INTRODUCTION

When a man raises himself from the lowest condition in society to the highest, mankind pay him the tribute of their admiration; when he accomplishes this elevation by native energy, guided by prudence and wisdom, their admiration is increased; but when his course, onward and upward, excellent in itself, furthermore proves a possible, what had hitherto been regarded as an impossible, reform, then he becomes a burning and a shining light, on which the aged may look with gladness, the young with hope, and the down-trodden, as a representative of what they may themselves become. To such a man, dear reader, it is my privilege to introduce you.

The life of Frederick Douglass, recorded in the pages which follow, is not merely an example of self-elevation under the most adverse circumstances; it is, moreover, a noble vindication of the highest aims of the American anti-slavery movement. The real object of that movement is not only to disenthrall, it is, also, to bestow upon the Negro the exercise of all those rights, from the possession of which he has been so long debarred.

But this full recognition of the colored man to the right, and the entire admission of the same to the full privileges, political, religious and social, of manhood, requires powerful effort on the part of the enthralled, as well as on the part of those who would disenthrall them. The people at large must feel the conviction, as well as admit the abstract logic, of human equality; the Negro, for the first time in the world's history, brought in full contact with high civilization, must prove his title first to all that is demanded for him; in the teeth of unequal chances, he must prove himself equal to the mass of those who oppress him—therefore, absolutely superior to his apparent fate, and to their relative ability. And it is most cheering to the friends of freedom, today, that evidence of this equality is rapidly accumulating, not from the ranks of the half-freed colored people of the free states, but from the very depths of slavery itself; the indestructible equality of man to man is demonstrated by the ease with which black men, scarce one remove from barbarism—if slavery can be honored with such a distinction—vault into the high places of the most advanced and painfully acquired civilization. Ward and Garnett, Wells Brown and Pennington, Loguen and Douglass, are banners on the outer wall, under which abolition is fighting its most successful battles, because they are living exemplars of the practicability of the most radical abolitionism; for, they were all of them born to the doom of slavery, some of them remained slaves until adult age, yet they all have not only won equality to their white fellow citizens, in civil, religious, political and social rank, but they have also illustrated and adorned our common country by their genius, learning and eloquence.

The characteristics whereby Mr. Douglass has won first rank among these remarkable men, and is still rising toward highest rank among living Americans, are abundantly laid bare in the book before us. Like the autobiography of Hugh Miller, it carries us so far back into early childhood, as to throw light upon the question, "when positive and persistent memory begins in the human being." And, like Hugh Miller, he must have been a shy old-fashioned child, occasionally oppressed by what he could not well account for, peering and poking about among the layers of right and wrong, of tyrant and thrall, and the wonderfulness of that hopeless tide of things which brought power to one race, and unrequited toil to another, until, finally, he stumbled upon his "first-found Ammonite," hidden away down in the depths of his own nature, and which revealed to him the fact that liberty and right, for all men, were anterior to slavery and wrong. When his knowledge of the world was bounded by the visible horizon on Col. Lloyd's plantation, and while every thing around him bore a fixed, iron stamp, as if it had always been so, this was, for one so young, a notable discovery.

To his uncommon memory, then, we must add a keen and accurate insight into men and things; an original breadth of common sense which enabled him to see, and weigh, and compare whatever passed before him, and which kindled a desire to search out and define their relations to other things not so patent, but which never succumbed to the marvelous nor the supernatural; a sacred thirst for liberty and for learning, first as a means of attaining liberty, then as an end in itself most desirable; a will; an unfaltering energy and determination to obtain what his soul pronounced desirable; a majestic self-hood; determined courage; a deep and agonizing sympathy with his embruted, crushed and bleeding fellow slaves, and an extraordinary depth of passion, together with that rare alliance between passion and intellect, which enables the former, when deeply roused, to excite, develop and sustain the latter.

With these original gifts in view, let us look at his schooling; the fearful discipline through which it pleased God to prepare him for the high calling on which he has since entered—the advocacy of emancipation by the people who are not slaves. And for this special mission, his plantation education was better than any he could have acquired in any lettered school. What he needed, was facts and experiences, welded to acutely wrought up sympathies, and these he could not elsewhere have obtained, in a manner so peculiarly adapted to his nature. His physical being was well trained, also, running wild until advanced into boyhood; hard work and light diet, thereafter, and a skill in handicraft in youth.

For his special mission, then, this was, considered in connection with his natural gifts, a good schooling; and, for his special mission, he doubtless "left school" just at the proper moment. Had he remained longer in slavery—had he fretted under bonds until the ripening of manhood and its passions, until the drear agony of slave-wife and slave-children had been piled upon his already bitter experiences—then, not only would his own history have had another termination, but the drama of American slavery would have been essentially varied; for I cannot resist the belief, that the boy who learned to read and write as he did, who taught his fellow slaves these precious acquirements as he did, who plotted for their mutual escape as he did, would, when a man at bay, strike a blow which would make slavery reel and stagger. Furthermore, blows and insults he bore, at the moment, without resentment; deep but suppressed emotion rendered him insensible to their sting; but it was afterward, when the memory of them went seething through his brain, breeding a fiery indignation at his injured self-hood, that the resolve came to resist, and the time fixed when to resist, and the plot laid, how to resist; and he always kept his self-pledged word. In what he undertook, in this line, he looked fate in the face, and had a cool, keen look at the relation of means to ends. Henry Bibb, to avoid chastisement, strewed his master's bed with charmed leaves and *was whipped*. Frederick Douglass quietly pocketed a like *fetiche*, compared his muscles with those of Covey—and *whipped him*.

In the history of his life in bondage, we find, well developed, that inherent and continuous energy of character which will ever render him distinguished. What his hand found to do, he did with his might; even while conscious that he was wronged out of his daily earnings, he worked, and worked hard. At his daily labor he went with a will; with keen, well set eye, brawny chest, lithe figure, and fair sweep of arm, he would have been king among calkers, had that been his mission.

It must not be overlooked, in this glance at his education, that Mr. Douglass lacked one aid to which so many men of mark have been deeply indebted— he had neither a mother's care, nor a mother's culture, save that which slavery grudgingly meted out to him. Bitter nurse! may not even her features relax with human feeling, when she gazes at such offspring! How susceptible he was to the kindly influences of mother-culture, may be gathered from his own words, on page 57: "It has been a life-long standing grief to me, that I know so little of my mother, and that I was so early separated from her. The counsels of her love must have been beneficial to me. The side view of her face is imaged on my memory, and I take few steps in life, without feeling her presence; but the image is mute, and I have no striking words of hers treasured up."

From the depths of chattel slavery in Maryland, our author escaped into the caste-slavery of the north, in New Bedford, Massachusetts. Here he found oppression assuming another, and hardly less bitter, form; of that very handicraft which the greed of slavery had taught him, his half-freedom denied him the exercise for an honest living; he found himself one of a class—free colored men—whose position he has described in the following words:

"Aliens are we in our native land. The fundamental principles of the republic, to which the humblest white man, whether born here or elsewhere, may appeal with confidence, in the hope of awakening a favorable response, are held to be inapplicable to us. The glorious doctrines of your revolutionary fathers, and the more glorious teachings of the Son of God, are construed and applied against us. We are literally scourged beyond the beneficent range of both authorities, human and divine. * * * * American humanity hates us, scorns us, disowns and denies, in a thousand ways, our very personality. The outspread wing of American christianity, apparently broad enough to give shelter to a perishing world, refuses to cover us. To us, its bones are brass, and its features iron. In running thither for shelter and succor, we have only fled from the hungry blood-hound to the devouring wolf—from a corrupt and selfish world, to a hollow and hypocritical church."—*Speech before American and Foreign Anti-Slavery Society, May,* 1854.

Four years or more, from 1837 to 1841, he struggled on, in New Bedford, sawing wood, rolling casks, or doing what labor he might, to support himself and young family; four years he brooded over the scars which slavery and semi-slavery had inflicted upon his body and soul; and then, with his wounds yet unhealed, he fell among the Garrisonians—a glorious waif to those most ardent reformers. It happened one day, at Nantucket, that he, diffidently and reluctantly, was led to address an anti-slavery meeting. He was about the age when the younger Pitt entered the House of Commons; like Pitt, too, he stood up a born orator.

William Lloyd Garrison, who was happily present, writes thus of Mr. Douglass' maiden effort; "I shall never forget his first speech at the convention—the extraordinary emotion it excited in my own mind—the powerful impression it created upon a crowded auditory, completely taken by surprise. * * * I think I never hated slavery so intensely as at that moment; certainly, my perception of the enormous outrage which is inflicted by it on the godlike nature of its victims, was rendered far more clear than ever. There stood one in physical proportions and stature commanding and exact—in intellect richly endowed—in natural eloquence a prodigy."*

It is of interest to compare Mr. Douglass's account of this meeting with Mr. Garrison's. Of the two, I think the latter the most correct. It must have been

---

* Letter, Introduction to *Life of Frederick Douglass,* Boston, 1841.

a grand burst of eloquence! The pent up agony, indignation and pathos of an abused and harrowed boyhood and youth, bursting out in all their freshness and overwhelming earnestness!

This unique introduction to its great leader, led immediately to the employment of Mr. Douglass as an agent by the American Anti-Slavery Society. So far as his self-relying and independent character would permit, he became, after the strictest sect, a Garrisonian. It is not too much to say, that he formed a complement which they needed, and they were a complement equally necessary to his "make-up." With his deep and keen sensitiveness to wrong, and his wonderful memory, he came from the land of bondage full of its woes and its evils, and painting them in characters of living light; and, on his part, he found, told out in sound Saxon phrase, all those principles of justice and right and liberty, which had dimly brooded over the dreams of his youth, seeking definite forms and verbal expression. It must have been an electric flashing of thought, and a knitting of soul, granted to but few in this life, and will be a life-long memory to those who participated in it. In the society, moreover, of Wendell Phillips, Edmund Quincy, William Lloyd Garrison, and other men of earnest faith and refined culture, Mr. Douglass enjoyed the high advantage of their assistance and counsel in the labor of self-culture, to which he now addressed himself with wonted energy. Yet, these gentlemen, although proud of Frederick Douglass, failed to fathom, and bring out to the light of day, the highest qualities of his mind; the force of their own education stood in their own way: they did not delve into the mind of a colored man for capacities which the pride of race led them to believe to be restricted to their own Saxon blood. Bitter and vindictive sarcasm, irresistible mimicry, and a pathetic narrative of his own experiences of slavery, were the intellectual manifestations which they encouraged him to exhibit on the platform or in the lecture desk.

A visit to England, in 1845, threw Mr. Douglass among men and women of earnest souls and high culture, and who, moreover, had never drank of the bitter waters of American caste. For the first time in his life, he breathed an atmosphere congenial to the longings of his spirit, and felt his manhood free and unrestricted. The cordial and manly greetings of the British and Irish audiences in public, and the refinement and elegance of the social circles in which he mingled, not only as an equal, but as a recognized man of genius, were, doubtless, genial and pleasant resting places in his hitherto thorny and troubled journey through life. There are joys on the earth, and, to the wayfaring fugitive from American slavery or American caste, this is one of them.

But his sojourn in England was more than a joy to Mr. Douglass. Like the platform at Nantucket, it awakened him to the consciousness of new powers that lay in him. From the pupilage of Garrisonism he rose to the dignity of a teacher and a thinker; his opinions on the broader aspects of the great American question were earnestly and incessantly sought, from various points of view, and he must, perforce, bestir himself to give suitable answer. With that prompt and truthful perception which has led their sisters in all ages of the world to gather at the feet and support the hands of reformers, the gentlewomen of England* were foremost to encourage and strengthen him to carve out for himself a path fitted to his powers and energies, in the life-battle against slavery and caste to which he was pledged. And one stirring thought, inseparable from the British idea of the evangel of freedom, must have smote his ear from every side—

> Hereditary bondmen! know ye not
> Who would be free, themselves mast strike the blow?

The result of this visit was, that on his return to the United States, he established a newspaper. This proceeding was sorely against the wishes and the advice of the leaders of the American Anti-Slavery Society, but our author had fully grown up to the conviction of a truth which they had once promulged, but now forgotten, to wit: that in their own elevation—self-elevation—colored men have a blow to strike "on their own hook," against slavery and caste. Differing from his Boston friends in this matter, diffident in his own abilities, reluctant at their dissuadings, how beautiful is the loyalty with which he still clung to their principles in all things else, and even in this.

Now came the trial hour. Without cordial support from any large body of men or party on this side the Atlantic, and too far distant in space and immediate interest to expect much more, after the much already done, on the other side, he stood up, almost alone, to the arduous labor and heavy expenditure of editor and lecturer. The Garrison party, to which he still adhered, did not want a *colored* newspaper—there was an odor of *caste* about it; the Liberty party could hardly be expected to give warm support to a man who smote their principles as with a hammer; and the wide gulf which separated the free colored people from the Garrisonians, also separated them from their brother, Frederick Douglass.

The arduous nature of his labors, from the date of the establishment of his paper, may be estimated by the fact, that anti-slavery papers in the United States, even while organs of, and when supported by, anti-slavery parties, have, with a single exception, failed to pay expenses. Mr. Douglass has maintained, and does maintain, his paper without the support of any party, and even in the teeth of the opposition of those from whom he had reason to expect counsel and encouragement. He has been compelled, at one and the same time, and almost constantly, during the past seven years, to contribute matter to its columns as

---

* One of these ladies, impelled by the same noble spirit which carried Miss Nightingale to Scutari, has devoted her time, her untiring energies, to a great extent her means, and her high literary abilities, to the advancement and support of Frederick Douglass' Paper, the only organ of the downtrodden, edited and published by one of themselves, in the United States.

editor, and to raise funds for its support as lecturer. It is within bounds to say, that he has expended twelve thousand dollars of his own hard earned money, in publishing this paper, a larger sum than has been contributed by any one individual for the general advancement of the colored people. There had been many other papers published and edited by colored men, beginning as far back as 1827, when the Rev. Samuel E. Cornish and John B. Russworm (a graduate of Bowdoin college, and afterward Governor of Cape Palmas) published the *Freedom's Journal*, in New York City; probably not less than one hundred newspaper enterprises have been started in the United States, by free colored men, born free, and some of them of liberal education and fair talents for this work; but, one after another, they have fallen through, although, in several instances, anti-slavery friends contributed to their support.* It had almost been given up, as an impracticable thing, to maintain a colored newspaper, when Mr. Douglass, with fewest early advantages of all his competitors, essayed, and has proved the thing perfectly practicable, and, moreover, of great public benefit. This paper, in addition to its power in holding up the hands of those to whom it is especially devoted, also affords irrefutable evidence of the justice, safety and practicability of Immediate Emancipation; it further proves the immense loss which slavery inflicts on the land while it dooms such energies as his to the hereditary degradation of slavery.

It has been said in this Introduction, that Mr. Douglass had raised himself by his own efforts to the highest position in society. As a successful editor, in our land, he occupies this position. Our editors rule the land, and he is one of them. As an orator and thinker, his position is equally high, in the opinion of his countrymen. If a stranger in the United States would seek its most distinguished men—the movers of public opinion—he will find their names mentioned, and their movements chronicled, under the head of "BY MAGNETIC TELEGRAPH," in the daily papers. The keen caterers for the public attention, set down, in this column, such men only as have won high mark in the public esteem. During the past winter—1854-5—very frequent mention of Frederick Douglass was made under this head in the daily papers; his name glided as often—this week from Chicago, next week from Boston—over the lightning wires, as the name of any other man, of whatever note. To no man did the people more widely nor more earnestly say, *"Tell me thy thought!"* And, somehow or other, revolution seemed to follow in his wake. His were not the mere words of eloquence which Kossuth speaks of, that delight the ear and then pass away. No! They were *work*-able, *do*-able words, that brought forth fruits in the revolution in Illinois, and in the passage of the franchise resolutions by the Assembly of New York.

---

* Mr. Stephen Myers, of Albany, deserves mention as one of the most persevering among the colored editorial fraternity.

And the secret of his power, what is it? He is a Representative American man—a type of his countrymen. Naturalists tell us that a full grown man is a resultant or representative of all animated nature on this globe; beginning with the early embryo state, then representing the lowest forms of organic life,[*] and passing through every subordinate grade or type, until he reaches the last and highest—manhood. In like manner, and to the fullest extent, has Frederick Douglass passed through every gradation of rank comprised in our national make-up, and bears upon his person and upon his soul every thing that is American. And he has not only full sympathy with every thing American; his proclivity or bent, to active toil and visible progress, are in the strictly national direction, delighting to outstrip "all creation."

Nor have the natural gifts, already named as his, lost anything by his severe training. When unexcited, his mental processes are probably slow, but singularly clear in perception, and wide in vision, the unfailing memory bringing up all the facts in their every aspect; incongruities he lays hold of incontinently, and holds up on the edge of his keen and telling wit. But this wit never descends to frivolity; it is rigidly in the keeping of his truthful common sense, and always used in illustration or proof of some point which could not so readily be reached any other way. "Beware of a Yankee when he is feeding," is a shaft that strikes home in a matter never so laid bare by satire before. "The Garrisonian views of disunion, if carried to a successful issue, would only place the people of the north in the same relation to American slavery which they now bear to the slavery of Cuba or the Brazils," is a statement, in a few words, which contains the result and the evidence of an argument which might cover pages, but could not carry stronger conviction, nor be stated in less pregnable form. In proof of this, I may say, that having been submitted to the attention of the Garrisonians in print, in March, it was repeated before them at their business meeting in May—the platform, *par excellence*, on which they invite free fight, *a l'outrance*, to all comers. It was given out in the clear, ringing tones, wherewith the hall of shields was wont to resound of old, yet neither Garrison, nor Phillips, nor May, nor Remond, nor Foster, nor Burleigh, with his subtle steel of "the ice brook's temper," ventured to break a lance upon it! The doctrine of the dissolution of the Union, as a means for the abolition of American slavery, was silenced upon the lips that gave it birth, and in the presence of an array of defenders who compose the keenest intellects in the land.

"The man who is right is a majority" is an aphorism struck out by Mr. Douglass in that great gathering of the friends of freedom, at Pittsburgh, in 1852, where he towered among the highest, because, with abilities inferior to

---

[*] The German physiologists have even discovered vegetable matter—starch—in the human body. See *Med. Chirurgical Rev.*, Oct., 1854, p. 339.

none, and moved more deeply than any, there was neither policy nor party to trammel the outpourings of his soul. Thus we find, opposed to all disadvantages which a black man in the United States labors and struggles under, is this one vantage ground—when the chance comes, and the audience where he may have a say, he stands forth the freest, most deeply moved and most earnest of all men.

It has been said of Mr. Douglass, that his descriptive and declamatory powers, admitted to be of the very highest order, take precedence of his logical force. Whilst the schools might have trained him to the exhibition of the formulas of deductive logic, nature and circumstances forced him into the exercise of the higher faculties required by induction. The first ninety pages of this "Life in Bondage," afford specimens of observing, comparing, and careful classifying, of such superior character, that it is difficult to believe them the results of a child's thinking; he questions the earth, and the children and the slaves around him again and again, and finally looks to *"God in the sky"* for the why and the wherefore of the unnatural thing, slavery. *"Yes, if indeed thou art, wherefore dost thou suffer us to be slain?"* is the only prayer and worship of the God-forsaken Dodos in the heart of Africa. Almost the same was his prayer. One of his earliest observations was that white children should know their ages, while the colored children were ignorant of theirs; and the songs of the slaves grated on his inmost soul, because a something told him that harmony in sound, and music of the spirit, could not consociate with miserable degradation.

To such a mind, the ordinary processes of logical deduction are like proving that two and two make four. Mastering the intermediate steps by an intuitive glance, or recurring to them as Ferguson resorted to geometry, it goes down to the deeper relation of things, and brings out what may seem, to some, mere statements, but which are new and brilliant generalizations, each resting on a broad and stable basis. Thus, Chief Justice Marshall gave his decisions, and then told Brother Story to look up the authorities—and they never differed from him. Thus, also, in his "Lecture on the Anti-Slavery Movement," delivered before the Rochester Ladies' Anti-Slavery Society, Mr. Douglass presents a mass of thought, which, without any showy display of logic on his part, requires an exercise of the reasoning faculties of the reader to keep pace with him. And his "Claims of the Negro Ethnologically Considered," is full of new and fresh thoughts on the dawning science of race-history.

If, as has been stated, his intellection is slow, when unexcited, it is most prompt and rapid when he is thoroughly aroused. Memory, logic, wit, sarcasm, invective pathos and bold imagery of rare structural beauty, well up as from a copious fountain, yet each in its proper place, and contributing to form a whole, grand in itself, yet complete in the minutest proportions. It is most difficult to hedge him in a corner, for his positions are taken so deliberately, that it is rare to find a point in them undefended aforethought. Professor Reason tells me the following: "On a recent visit of a public nature, to Philadelphia, and in a meeting composed mostly of his colored brethren, Mr. Douglass proposed a comparison of views in the matters of the relations and duties of 'our people;' he holding that prejudice was the result of condition, and could be conquered by the efforts of the degraded themselves. A gentleman present, distinguished for logical acumen and subtlety, and who had devoted no small portion of the last twenty-five years to the study and elucidation of this very question, held the opposite view, that prejudice is innate and unconquerable. He terminated a series of well dove-tailed, Socratic questions to Mr. Douglass, with the following: 'If the legislature at Harrisburgh should awaken, to-morrow morning, and find each man's skin turned black and his hair woolly, what could they do to remove prejudice?' 'Immediately pass laws entitling black men to all civil, political and social privileges,' was the instant reply—and the questioning ceased."

The most remarkable mental phenomenon in Mr. Douglass, is his style in writing and speaking. In March, 1855, he delivered an address in the assembly chamber before the members of the legislature of the state of New York. An eye witness* describes the crowded and most intelligent audience, and their rapt attention to the speaker, as the grandest scene he ever witnessed in the capitol. Among those whose eyes were riveted on the speaker full two hours and a half, were Thurlow Weed and Lieutenant Governor Raymond; the latter, at the conclusion of the address, exclaimed to a friend, "I would give twenty thousand dollars, if I could deliver that address in that manner." Mr. Raymond is a first class graduate of Dartmouth, a rising politician, ranking foremost in the legislature; of course, his ideal of oratory must be of the most polished and finished description.

The style of Mr. Douglass in writing, is to me an intellectual puzzle. The strength, affluence and terseness may easily be accounted for, because the style of a man is the man; but how are we to account for that rare polish in his style of writing, which, most critically examined, seems the result of careful early culture among the best classics of our language; it equals if it does not surpass the style of Hugh Miller, which was the wonder of the British literary public, until he unraveled the mystery in the most interesting of autobiographies. But Frederick Douglass was still calking the seams of Baltimore clippers, and had only written a "pass," at the age when Miller's style was already formed.

I asked William Whipper, of Pennsylvania, the gentleman alluded to above, whether he thought Mr. Douglass's power inherited from the Negroid, or from what is called the Caucasian side of his make up? After some reflection, he frankly answered, "I must admit, although sorry to do so, that the Caucasian

---

* Mr. Wm. H. Topp, of Albany.

predominates." At that time, I almost agreed with him; but, facts narrated in the first part of this work, throw a different light on this interesting question.

We are left in the dark as to who was the paternal ancestor of our author; a fact which generally holds good of the Romuluses and Remuses who are to inaugurate the new birth of our republic. In the absence of testimony from the Caucasian side, we must see what evidence is given on the other side of the house.

"My grandmother, though advanced in years, * * * was yet a woman of power and spirit. She was marvelously straight in figure, elastic and muscular." (p. 46.)

After describing her skill in constructing nets, her perseverance in using them, and her wide-spread fame in the agricultural way he adds, "It happened to her—as it will happen to any careful and thrifty person residing in an ignorant and improvident neighborhood—to enjoy the reputation of being born to good luck." And his grandmother was a black woman.

"My mother was tall, and finely proportioned; of deep black, glossy complexion; had regular features; and among other slaves was remarkably sedate in her manners." "Being a field hand, she was obliged to walk twelve miles and return, between nightfall and daybreak, to see her children" (p. 54.) "I shall never forget the indescribable expression of her countenance when I told her that I had had no food since morning. * * * There was pity in her glance at me, and a fiery indignation at Aunt Katy at the same time; * * * * she read Aunt Katy a lecture which she never forgot." (p. 56.) "I learned after my mother's death, that she could read, and that she was the *only* one of all the slaves and colored people in Tuckahoe who enjoyed that advantage. How she acquired this knowledge, I know not, for Tuckahoe is the last place in the world where she would be apt to find facilities for learning." (p. 57.) "There is, in *Prichard's Natural History of Man*, the head of a figure—on page 157—the features of which so resemble those of my mother, that I often recur to it with something of the feeling which I suppose others experience when looking upon the pictures of dear departed ones." (p. 52.)

The head alluded to is copied from the statue of Ramses the Great, an Egyptian king of the nineteenth dynasty. The authors of the *Types of Mankind* give a side view of the same on page 148, remarking that the profile, "like Napoleon's, is superbly European!" The nearness of its resemblance to Mr. Douglass' mother rests upon the evidence of his memory, and judging from his almost marvelous feats of recollection of forms and outlines recorded in this book, this testimony may be admitted.

These facts show that for his energy, perseverance, eloquence, invective, sagacity, and wide sympathy, he is indebted to his Negro blood. The very marvel of his style would seem to be a development of that other marvel—how his mother learned to read. The versatility of talent which he wields, in common with Dumas, Ira Aldridge, and Miss Greenfield, would seem to be the result of the grafting of the Anglo-Saxon on good, original, Negro stock. If the friends of "Caucasus" choose to claim, for that region, what remains after this analysis—to wit: combination—they are welcome to it. They will forgive me for reminding them that the term "Caucasian" is dropped by recent writers on Ethnology; for the people about Mount Caucasus, are, and have ever been, Mongols. The great "white race" now seek paternity, according to Dr. Pickering, in Arabia—"Arida Nutrix" of the best breed of horses &c. Keep on, gentlemen; you will find yourselves in Africa, by-and-by. The Egyptians, like the Americans, were a *mixed race*, with some Negro blood circling around the throne, as well as in the mud hovels.

This is the proper place to remark of our author, that the same strong self-hood, which led him to measure strength with Mr. Covey, and to wrench himself from the embrace of the Garrisonians, and which has borne him through many resistances to the personal indignities offered him as a colored man, sometimes becomes a hyper-sensitiveness to such assaults as men of his mark will meet with, on paper. Keen and unscrupulous opponents have sought, and not unsuccessfully, to pierce him in this direction; for well they know, that if assailed, he will smite back.

It is not without a feeling of pride, dear reader, that I present you with this book. The son of a self-emancipated bond-woman, I feel joy in introducing to you my brother, who has rent his own bonds, and who, in his every relation—as a public man, as a husband and as a father—is such as does honor to the land which gave him birth. I shall place this book in the hands of the only child spared me, bidding him to strive and emulate its noble example. You may do likewise. It is an American book, for Americans, in the fullest sense of the idea. It shows that the worst of our institutions, in its worst aspect, cannot keep down energy, truthfulness, and earnest struggle for the right. It proves the justice and practicability of Immediate Emancipation. It shows that any man in our land, "no matter in what battle his liberty may have been cloven down, * * * * no matter what complexion an Indian or an African sun may have burned upon him," not only may "stand forth redeemed and disenthralled," but may also stand up a candidate for the highest suffrage of a great people—the tribute of their honest, hearty admiration. Reader, *Vale! New York*

JAMES M'CUNE SMITH

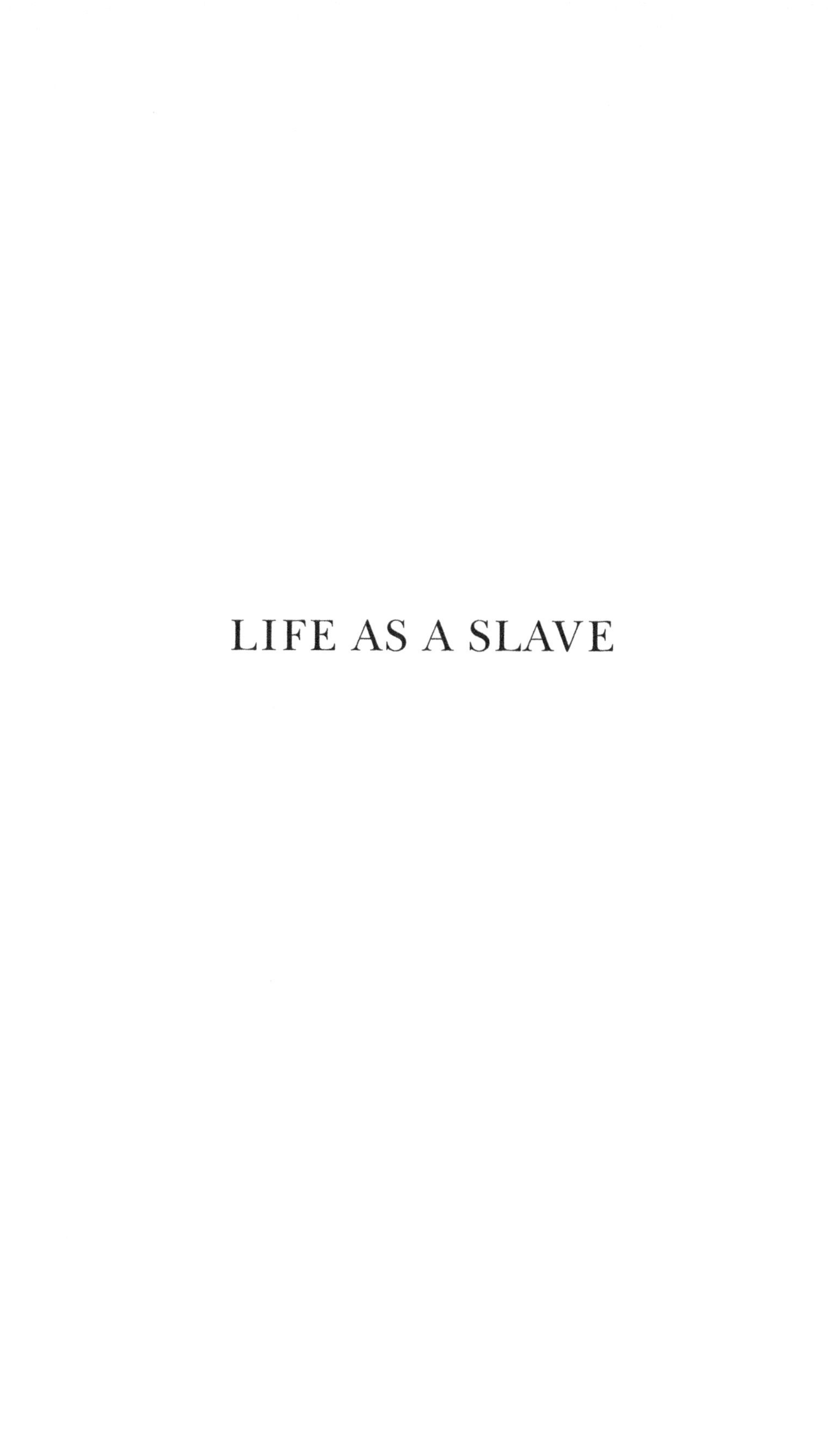

LIFE AS A SLAVE

CHAPTER I

Childhood

PLACE OF BIRTH—CHARACTER OF THE DISTRICT—TUCKAHOE—ORIGIN OF THE NAME—CHOPTANK RIVER—TIME OF BIRTH—GENEALOGICAL TREES—MODE OF COUNTING TIME—NAMES OF GRANDPARENTS—THEIR POSITION—GRANDMOTHER ESPECIALLY ESTEEMED—"BORN TO GOOD LUCK"—SWEET POTATOES—SUPERSTITION—THE LOG CABIN—ITS CHARMS—SEPARATING CHILDREN—MY AUNTS—THEIR NAMES—FIRST KNOWLEDGE OF BEING A SLAVE—OLD MASTER—GRIEFS AND JOYS OF CHILDHOOD—COMPARATIVE HAPPINESS OF THE SLAVE-BOY AND THE SON OF A SLAVEHOLDER.

In Talbot county, Eastern Shore, Maryland, near Easton, the county town of that county, there is a small district of country, thinly populated, and remarkable for nothing that I know of more than for the worn-out, sandy, desert-like appearance of its soil, the general dilapidation of its farms and fences, the indigent and spiritless character of its inhabitants, and the prevalence of ague and fever.

The name of this singularly unpromising and truly famine stricken district is Tuckahoe, a name well known to all Marylanders, black and white. It was given to this section of country probably, at the first, merely in derision; or it may possibly have been applied to it, as I have heard, because some one of its earlier inhabitants had been guilty of the petty meanness of stealing a hoe—or taking a hoe that did not belong to him. Eastern Shore men usually pronounce the word *took*, as *tuck*; *Took-a-hoe*, therefore, is, in Maryland parlance, *Tuckahoe*. But, whatever may have been its origin—and about this I will not be positive— that name has stuck to the district in question; and it is seldom mentioned but with contempt and derision, on account of the barrenness of its soil, and the ignorance, indolence, and poverty of its people. Decay and ruin are everywhere visible, and the thin population of the place would have quitted it long ago, but for the Choptank river, which runs through it, from which they take abundance of shad and herring, and plenty of ague and fever.

It was in this dull, flat, and unthrifty district, or neighborhood, surrounded by a white population of the lowest order, indolent and drunken to a proverb, and among slaves, who seemed to ask, *"Oh! what's the use?"* every time they lifted a hoe, that I—without any fault of mine was born, and spent the first years of my childhood.

The reader will pardon so much about the place of my birth, on the score that it is always a fact of some importance to know where a man is born, if, indeed, it be important to know anything about him. In regard to the *time* of my birth, I cannot be as definite as I have been respecting the *place*. Nor, indeed, can I impart much knowledge concerning my parents. Genealogical trees do not flourish among slaves. A person of some consequence here in the north, sometimes designated *father*, is literally abolished in slave law and slave practice. It is only once in a while that an exception is found to this statement. I never met with a slave who could tell me how old he was. Few slave-mothers know anything of the months of the year, nor of the days of the month. They keep no family records, with marriages, births, and deaths. They measure the ages of their children by spring time, winter time, harvest time, planting time, and the like; but these soon become undistinguishable and forgotten. Like other slaves, I cannot tell how old I am. This destitution was among my earliest troubles. I learned when I grew up, that my master—and this is the case with masters generally—allowed no questions to be put to him, by which a slave might learn his age. Such questions deemed evidence of impatience, and even of impudent curiosity. From certain events, however, the dates of which I have since learned, I suppose myself to have been born about the year 1817.

The first experience of life with me that I now remember—and I remember it but hazily—began in the family of my grandmother and grandfather. Betsey and Isaac Baily. They were quite advanced in life, and had long lived on the spot where they then resided. They were considered old settlers in the neighborhood, and, from certain circumstances, I infer that my grandmother, especially, was held in high esteem, far higher than is the lot of most colored persons in the slave states. She was a good nurse, and a capital hand at making nets for catching shad and herring; and these nets were in great demand, not only in Tuckahoe, but at Denton and Hillsboro, neighboring villages. She was not only good at making the nets, but was also somewhat famous for her good fortune in taking the fishes referred to. I have known her to be in the water half the day. Grandmother was likewise more provident than most of her neighbors in the preservation of seedling sweet potatoes, and it happened to her—as it will happen to any careful and thrifty person residing in an ignorant and improvident community—to enjoy the reputation of having been born to "good luck." Her "good luck" was owing to the exceeding care which she took in preventing the succulent root from getting bruised in the digging, and in placing it beyond the reach of frost, by actually burying it under the hearth of her cabin during the winter months. In the time of planting sweet potatoes, "Grandmother Betty," as she was familiarly called, was sent for in all directions, simply to place the seedling potatoes in the hills; for superstition had it, that if "Grandmamma Betty but touches them at planting, they will be sure to grow and flourish." This high reputation was full of advantage to her, and to the children around her. Though Tuckahoe had but few of the good things of life, yet of such as it did possess grandmother got a full share, in the way of presents. If good potato crops came after her planting, she was not forgotten by those for whom she planted; and as she was remembered by others, so she remembered the hungry little ones around her.

The dwelling of my grandmother and grandfather had few pretensions. It was a log hut, or cabin, built of clay, wood, and straw. At a distance it resembled— though it was smaller, less commodious and less substantial—the cabins erected in the western states by the first settlers. To my child's eye, however, it was a noble structure, admirably adapted to promote the comforts and conveniences of its inmates. A few rough, Virginia fence-rails, flung loosely over the rafters above, answered the triple purpose of floors, ceilings, and bedsteads. To be sure, this upper apartment was reached only by a ladder—but what in the world for climbing could be better than a ladder? To me, this ladder was really a high invention, and possessed a sort of charm as I played with delight upon the rounds of it. In this little hut there was a large family of children: I dare not say how many. My grandmother—whether because too old for field service, or because she had so faithfully discharged the duties of her station in early life, I know not—enjoyed the high privilege of living in a cabin, separate from the quarter, with no other burden than her own support, and the necessary care of the little children, imposed. She evidently esteemed it a great fortune to live so. The children were not her own, but her grandchildren—the children of her daughters. She took delight in having them around her, and in attending to their few wants. The practice of separating children from their mother, and hiring the latter out at distances too great to admit of their meeting, except at long intervals, is a marked feature of the cruelty and barbarity of the slave system. But it is in harmony with the grand aim of slavery, which, always and everywhere, is to reduce man to a level with the brute. It is a successful method of obliterating from the mind and heart of the slave, all just ideas of the sacredness of *the family*, as an institution.

Most of the children, however, in this instance, being the children of my grandmother's daughters, the notions of family, and the reciprocal duties and benefits of the relation, had a better chance of being understood than where children are placed—as they often are in the hands of strangers, who have no care for them, apart from the wishes of their masters. The daughters of my grandmother were five in number. Their names were JENNY, ESTHER, MILLY, PRISCILLA, and HARRIET. The daughter last named was my mother, of whom the reader shall learn more by-and-by.

Living here, with my dear old grandmother and grandfather, it was a long time before I knew myself to be *a slave*. I knew many other things before I knew that. Grandmother and grandfather were the greatest people in the world to me; and being with them so snugly in their own little cabin—I supposed it be their own—knowing no higher authority over me or the other children than the authority of grandmamma, for a time there was nothing to disturb me; but, as I grew larger and older, I learned by degrees the sad fact, that the "little hut," and the lot on which it stood, belonged not to my dear old grandparents, but to some person who lived a great distance off, and who was called, by grandmother, "OLD MASTER." I further learned the sadder fact, that not only the house and lot, but that grandmother herself, (grandfather was free,) and all the little children around her, belonged to this mysterious personage, called by grandmother, with every mark of reverence, "Old Master." Thus early did clouds and shadows begin to fall upon my path. Once on the track—troubles never come singly—I was not long in finding out another fact, still more grievous to my childish heart. I was told that this "old master," whose name seemed ever to be mentioned with fear and shuddering, only allowed the children to live with grandmother for a limited time, and that in fact as soon as they were big enough, they were promptly taken away, to live with the said "old master." These were distressing revelations indeed; and though I was quite too young to comprehend the full import of the intelligence, and mostly spent my childhood days in gleesome sports with the other children, a shade of disquiet rested upon me.

The absolute power of this distant "old master" had touched my young spirit with but the point of its cold, cruel iron, and left me something to brood over after the play and in moments of repose. Grandmammy was, indeed, at that time, all the world to me; and the thought of being separated from her, in any considerable time, was more than an unwelcome intruder. It was intolerable.

Children have their sorrows as well as men and women; and it would be well to remember this in our dealings with them. SLAVE-children *are* children, and prove no exceptions to the general rule. The liability to be separated from my grandmother, seldom or never to see her again, haunted me. I dreaded the thought of going to live with that mysterious "old master," whose name I never heard mentioned with affection, but always with fear. I look back to this as among the heaviest of my childhood's sorrows. My grandmother! my grandmother! and the little hut, and the joyous circle under her care, but especially *she*, who made us sorry when she left us but for an hour, and glad on her return,—how could I leave her and the good old home?

But the sorrows of childhood, like the pleasures of after life, are transient. It is not even within the power of slavery to write *indelible* sorrow, at a single dash, over the heart of a child.

> The tear down childhood's cheek that flows,
> Is like the dew-drop on the rose—
> When next the summer breeze comes by,
> And waves the bush—the flower is dry.

There is, after all, but little difference in the measure of contentment felt by the slave-child neglected and the slaveholder's child cared for and petted. The spirit of the All Just mercifully holds the balance for the young.

The slaveholder, having nothing to fear from impotent childhood, easily affords to refrain from cruel inflictions; and if cold and hunger do not pierce the tender frame, the first seven or eight years of the slave-boy's life are about as full of sweet content as those of the most favored and petted *white* children of the slaveholder. The slave-boy escapes many troubles which befall and vex his white brother. He seldom has to listen to lectures on propriety of behavior, or on anything else. He is never chided for handling his little knife and fork improperly or awkwardly, for he uses none. He is never reprimanded for soiling the table-cloth, for he takes his meals on the clay floor. He never has the misfortune, in his games or sports, of soiling or tearing his clothes, for he has almost none to soil or tear. He is never expected to act like a nice little gentleman, for he is only a rude little slave. Thus, freed from all restraint, the slave-boy can be, in his life and conduct, a genuine boy, doing whatever his boyish nature suggests; enacting, by turns, all the strange antics and freaks of horses, dogs, pigs, and barn-door fowls, without in any manner compromising his dignity, or incurring reproach of any sort. He literally runs wild; has no pretty little verses to learn in the nursery; no nice little speeches to make for aunts, uncles, or cousins, to show how smart he is; and, if he can only manage to keep out of the way of the heavy feet and fists of the older slave boys, he may trot on, in his joyous and roguish tricks, as happy as any little heathen under the palm trees of Africa. To be sure, he is occasionally reminded, when he stumbles in the path of his master—and this he early learns to avoid—that he is eating his *"white bread,"* and that he will be made to *"see sights"* by-and-by. The threat is soon forgotten; the shadow soon passes, and our sable boy continues to roll in the dust, or play in the mud, as bests suits him, and in the veriest freedom. If he feels uncomfortable, from mud or from dust, the coast is clear; he can plunge into the river or the pond, without the ceremony of undressing, or the fear of wetting his clothes; his little tow-linen shirt—for that is all he has on—is easily dried; and it needed ablution as much as did his skin. His food is of the coarsest kind, consisting for the most part of cornmeal mush, which often finds it way from the wooden tray to his mouth in an oyster shell. His days, when the weather is warm, are spent in the pure, open air, and in the bright sunshine. He always sleeps in airy apartments; he seldom has to take powders, or to be paid to swallow pretty little sugar-coated pills, to cleanse his blood, or to quicken his appetite. He eats no candies; gets no lumps of loaf sugar; always relishes his food; cries but little, for nobody cares for his crying; learns to esteem his bruises but slight, because others so esteem them. In a word, he is, for the most part of the first eight years of his life, a spirited, joyous, uproarious, and happy boy, upon whom troubles fall only like water on a duck's back. And such a boy, so far as I can now remember, was the boy whose life in slavery I am now narrating.

CHAPTER II

Removed from My First Home

THE NAME "OLD MASTER" A TERROR—COLONEL LLOYD'S PLANTATION—
WYE RIVER—WHENCE ITS NAME—POSITION OF THE LLOYDS—HOME
ATTRACTION—MEET OFFERING—JOURNEY FROM TUCKAHOE TO
WYE RIVER—SCENE ON REACHING OLD MASTER'S—DEPARTURE OF
GRANDMOTHER—STRANGE MEETING OF SISTERS AND BROTHERS—
REFUSAL TO BE COMFORTED—SWEET SLEEP.

That mysterious individual referred to in the first chapter as an object of terror among the inhabitants of our little cabin, under the ominous title of "old master," was really a man of some consequence. He owned several farms in Tuckahoe; was the chief clerk and butler on the home plantation of Col. Edward Lloyd; had overseers on his own farms; and gave directions to overseers on the farms belonging to Col. Lloyd. This plantation is situated on Wye river—the river receiving its name, doubtless, from Wales, where the Lloyds originated. They (the Lloyds) are an old and honored family in Maryland, exceedingly wealthy. The home plantation, where they have resided, perhaps for a century or more, is one of the largest, most fertile, and best appointed, in the state.

About this plantation, and about that queer old master—who must be something more than a man, and something worse than an angel—the reader will easily imagine that I was not only curious, but eager, to know all that could be known. Unhappily for me, however, all the information I could get concerning him increased my great dread of being carried thither—of being separated from and deprived of the protection of my grandmother and grandfather. It was, evidently, a great thing to go to Col. Lloyd's; and I was not without a little curiosity to see the place; but no amount of coaxing could induce in me the wish to remain there. The fact is, such was my dread of leaving the little cabin, that I wished to remain little forever, for I knew the taller I grew the shorter my stay. The old cabin, with its rail floor and rail bedsteads upstairs, and its clay floor downstairs, and its dirt chimney, and windowless sides, and that most curious piece of workmanship dug in front of the fireplace, beneath which grandmammy placed the sweet potatoes to keep them from the frost, was MY HOME—the only home I ever had; and I loved it, and all connected with it. The old fences around it, and the stumps in the edge of the woods near it, and the squirrels that ran, skipped, and played upon them, were objects of interest and affection. There, too, right at the side of the hut, stood the old well, with its stately and skyward-pointing beam, so aptly placed between the limbs of what had once been a tree, and so nicely balanced that I could move it up and down with only one hand, and could get a drink myself without calling for help. Where else in the world could such a well be found, and where could such another home be met with? Nor were these all the attractions of the place. Down in a little valley, not far from grandmammy's cabin, stood Mr. Lee's mill, where the people came often in large numbers to get their corn ground. It was a watermill; and I never shall be able to tell the many things thought and felt, while I sat on the bank and watched that mill, and the turning of that ponderous wheel. The mill-pond, too, had its charms; and with my pinhook, and thread line, I could get *nibbles*, if I could catch no fish. But, in all my sports and plays, and in spite of them, there would, occasionally, come the painful foreboding that I was not long to remain there, and that I must soon be called away to the home of old master.

I was A SLAVE—born a slave and though the fact was incomprehensible to me, it conveyed to my mind a sense of my entire dependence on the will of *somebody* I had never seen; and, from some cause or other, I had been made to fear this somebody above all else on earth. Born for another's benefit, as the *firstling* of the cabin flock I was soon to be selected as a meet offering to the fearful and inexorable *demigod*, whose huge image on so many occasions haunted my childhood's imagination. When the time of my departure was decided upon, my grandmother, knowing my fears, and in pity for them, kindly kept me ignorant of the dreaded event about to transpire. Up to the morning (a beautiful summer morning) when we were to start, and, indeed, during the whole journey—a journey which, child as I was, I remember as well as if it were yesterday—she kept the sad fact hidden from me. This reserve was necessary; for, could I have known all, I should have given grandmother some trouble in getting me started. As it was, I was helpless, and she—dear woman!—led me along by the hand, resisting, with the reserve and solemnity of a priestess, all my inquiring looks to the last.

The distance from Tuckahoe to Wye river—where my old master lived— was full twelve miles, and the walk was quite a severe test of the endurance of my young legs. The journey would have proved too severe for me, but that my dear old grandmother—blessings on her memory!—afforded occasional relief by "toting" me (as Marylanders have it) on her shoulder. My grandmother, though advanced in years—as was evident from more than one gray hair, which peeped from between the ample and graceful folds of her newly-ironed bandana turban—was yet a woman of power and spirit. She was marvelously straight in figure, elastic, and muscular. I seemed hardly to be a burden to her. She would have "toted" me farther, but that I felt myself too much of a man to allow it, and insisted on walking. Releasing dear grandmamma from carrying me, did not make me altogether independent of her, when we happened to pass through portions of the somber woods which lay between Tuckahoe and Wye river. She often found me increasing the energy of my grip, and holding her clothing, lest something should come out of the woods and eat me up. Several old logs and stumps imposed upon me, and got themselves taken for wild beasts. I could see their legs, eyes, and ears, or I could see something like eyes, legs, and ears, till I got close enough to them to see that the eyes were knots, washed white with rain, and the legs were broken limbs, and the ears, only ears owing to the point from which they were seen. Thus early I learned that the point from which a thing is viewed is of some importance.

As the day advanced the heat increased; and it was not until the afternoon that we reached the much dreaded end of the journey. I found myself in the midst of a group of children of many colors; black, brown, copper colored, and nearly white. I had not seen so many children before. Great houses loomed up in different directions, and a great many men and women were at work in the fields. All this hurry, noise, and singing was very different from the stillness of Tuckahoe. As a new comer, I was an object of special interest; and, after laughing and yelling around me, and playing all sorts of wild tricks, they (the children) asked me to go out and play with them. This I refused to do, preferring to stay with grandmamma. I could not help feeling that our being there boded no good to me. Grandmamma looked sad. She was soon to lose another object of affection, as she had lost many before. I knew she was unhappy, and the shadow fell from her brow on me, though I knew not the cause.

All suspense, however, must have an end; and the end of mine, in this instance, was at hand. Affectionately patting me on the head, and exhorting me to be a good boy, grandmamma told me to go and play with the little children. "They are kin to you," said she; "go and play with them." Among a number of cousins were Phil, Tom, Steve, and Jerry, Nance and Betty.

Grandmother pointed out my brother PERRY, my sister SARAH, and my sister ELIZA, who stood in the group. I had never seen my brother nor my sisters before; and, though I had sometimes heard of them, and felt a curious interest in them, I really did not understand what they were to me, or I to them. We were brothers and sisters, but what of that? Why should they be attached to me, or I to them? Brothers and sisters we were by blood; but *slavery* had made us strangers. I heard the words brother and sisters, and knew they must mean something; but slavery had robbed these terms of their true meaning. The experience through which I was passing, they had passed through before. They had already been initiated into the mysteries of old master's domicile, and they seemed to look upon me with a certain degree of compassion; but my heart clave to my grandmother. Think it not strange, dear reader, that so little sympathy of feeling existed between us. The conditions of brotherly and sisterly feeling were wanting—we had never nestled and played together. My poor mother, like many other slave-women, had many *children*, but NO FAMILY! The domestic hearth, with its holy lessons and precious endearments, is abolished in the case of a slave-mother and her children. "Little children, love one another," are words seldom heard in a slave cabin.

I really wanted to play with my brother and sisters, but they were strangers to me, and I was full of fear that grandmother might leave without taking me with her. Entreated to do so, however, and that, too, by my dear grandmother, I went to the back part of the house, to play with them and the other children. *Play*, however, I did not, but stood with my back against the wall, witnessing the playing of the others. At last, while standing there, one of the children, who had been in the kitchen, ran up to me, in a sort of roguish glee, exclaiming, "Fed, Fed! grandmammy gone! grandmammy gone!" I could not believe it; yet, fearing the worst, I ran into the kitchen, to see for myself, and found it even so. Grandmammy had indeed gone, and was now far away, "clean" out of sight. I need not tell all that happened now. Almost heart-broken at the discovery, I fell upon the ground, and wept a boy's bitter tears, refusing to be comforted. My brother and sisters came around me, and said, "Don't cry," and gave me peaches and pears, but I flung them away, and refused all their kindly advances. I had never been deceived before; and I felt not only grieved at parting—as I supposed forever—with my grandmother, but indignant that a trick had been played upon me in a matter so serious.

It was now late in the afternoon. The day had been an exciting and wearisome one, and I knew not how or where, but I suppose I sobbed myself to sleep. There is a healing in the angel wing of sleep, even for the slave-boy; and its balm was never more welcome to any wounded soul than it was to mine, the first night I spent at the domicile of old master. The reader may be surprised that I narrate so minutely an incident apparently so trivial, and which must have occurred when I was not more than seven years old; but as I wish to give a faithful history of my experience in slavery, I cannot withhold a circumstance which, at the time, affected me so deeply. Besides, this was, in fact, my first introduction to the realities of slavery.

CHAPTER III

Parentage

MY FATHER SHROUDED IN MYSTERY—MY MOTHER—HER PERSONAL APPEARANCE—INTERFERENCE OF SLAVERY WITH THE NATURAL AFFECTIONS OF MOTHER AND CHILDREN—SITUATION OF MY MOTHER— HER NIGHTLY VISITS TO HER BOY—STRIKING INCIDENT—HER DEATH— HER PLACE OF BURIAL.

If the reader will now be kind enough to allow me time to grow bigger, and afford me an opportunity for my experience to become greater, I will tell him something, by-and-by, of slave life, as I saw, felt, and heard it, on Col. Edward Lloyd's plantation, and at the house of old master, where I had now, despite of myself, most suddenly, but not unexpectedly, been dropped. Meanwhile, I will redeem my promise to say something more of my dear mother.

I say nothing of *father*, for he is shrouded in a mystery I have never been able to penetrate. Slavery does away with fathers, as it does away with families. Slavery has no use for either fathers or families, and its laws do not recognize their existence in the social arrangements of the plantation. When they *do* exist, they are not the outgrowths of slavery, but are antagonistic to that system. The order of civilization is reversed here. The name of the child is not expected to be that of its father, and his condition does not necessarily affect that of the child. He may be the slave of Mr. Tilgman; and his child, when born, may be the slave of Mr. Gross. He may be a *freeman*; and yet his child may be a *chattel*. He may be white, glorying in the purity of his Anglo-Saxon blood; and his child may be ranked with the blackest slaves. Indeed, he *may* be, and often *is*, master and father to the same child. He can be father without being a husband, and may sell his child without incurring reproach, if the child be by a woman in whose veins courses one thirty-second part of African blood. My father was a white man, or nearly white. It was sometimes whispered that my master was my father.

But to return, or rather, to begin. My knowledge of my mother is very scanty, but very distinct. Her personal appearance and bearing are ineffaceably stamped upon my memory. She was tall, and finely proportioned; of deep black, glossy complexion; had regular features, and, among the other slaves, was remarkably sedate in her manners. There is in *Prichard's Natural History of Man*, the head of a figure—on page 157—the features of which so resemble those of my mother, that I often recur to it with something of the feeling which I suppose others experience when looking upon the pictures of dear departed ones.

Yet I cannot say that I was very deeply attached to my mother; certainly not so deeply as I should have been had our relations in childhood been different. We were separated, according to the common custom, when I was but an infant, and, of course, before I knew my mother from any one else.

The germs of affection with which the Almighty, in his wisdom and mercy, arms the hopeless infant against the ills and vicissitudes of his lot, had been directed in their growth toward that loving old grandmother, whose gentle hand and kind deportment it was in the first effort of my infantile understanding to comprehend and appreciate. Accordingly, the tenderest affection which a beneficent Father allows, as a partial compensation to the mother for the pains and lacerations of her heart, incident to the maternal relation, was, in my case, diverted from its true and natural object, by the envious, greedy, and treacherous hand of slavery. The slave-mother can be spared long enough from the field to endure all the bitterness of a mother's anguish, when it adds another name to a master's ledger, but *not* long enough to receive the joyous reward afforded by the intelligent smiles of her child. I never think of this terrible interference of slavery with my infantile affections, and its diverting them from their natural course, without feelings to which I can give no adequate expression.

I do not remember to have seen my mother at my grandmother's at any time. I remember her only in her visits to me at Col. Lloyd's plantation, and in the kitchen of my old master. Her visits to me there were few in number, brief in duration, and mostly made in the night. The pains she took, and the toil she endured, to see me, tells me that a true mother's heart was hers, and that slavery had difficulty in paralyzing it with unmotherly indifference.

My mother was hired out to a Mr. Stewart, who lived about twelve miles from old master's, and, being a field hand, she seldom had leisure, by day, for the performance of the journey. The nights and the distance were both obstacles to her visits. She was obliged to walk, unless chance flung into her way an opportunity to ride; and the latter was sometimes her good luck. But she always had to walk one way or the other. It was a greater luxury than slavery could afford, to allow a black slave-mother a horse or a mule, upon which to travel twenty-four miles, when she could walk the distance. Besides, it is deemed a foolish whim for a slave-mother to manifest concern to see her children, and, in one point of view, the case is made out—she can do nothing for them. She has no control over them; the master is even more than the mother, in all matters touching the fate of her child. Why, then, should she give herself any concern? She has no responsibility. Such is the reasoning, and such the practice. The iron rule of the plantation, always passionately and violently enforced in that neighborhood, makes flogging the penalty of failing to be in the field before sunrise in the morning, unless special permission be given to the absenting slave. "I went to see my child," is no excuse to the ear or heart of the overseer.

One of the visits of my mother to me, while at Col. Lloyd's, I remember very vividly, as affording a bright gleam of a mother's love, and the earnestness of a mother's care.

"I had on that day offended "Aunt Katy," (called "Aunt" by way of respect,) the cook of old master's establishment. I do not now remember the nature of my offense in this instance, for my offenses were numerous in that quarter, greatly depending, however, upon the mood of Aunt Katy, as to their heinousness; but she had adopted, that day, her favorite mode of punishing me, namely, making me go without food all day—that is, from after breakfast. The first hour or two after dinner, I succeeded pretty well in keeping up my spirits; but though I made an excellent stand against the foe, and fought bravely during the afternoon, I knew I must be conquered at last, unless I got the accustomed reenforcement of a slice of corn bread, at sundown. Sundown came, but *no bread*, and, in its stead, their came the threat, with a scowl well suited to its terrible import, that she "meant to *starve the life out of me!*" Brandishing her knife, she chopped off the heavy slices for the other children, and put the loaf away, muttering, all the while, her savage designs upon myself. Against this disappointment, for I was expecting that her heart would relent at last, I made an extra effort to maintain my dignity; but when I saw all the other children around me with merry and satisfied faces, I could stand it no longer. I went out behind the house, and cried like a fine fellow! When tired of this, I returned to the kitchen, sat by the fire, and brooded over my hard lot. I was too hungry to sleep. While I sat in the corner, I caught sight of an ear of Indian corn on an upper shelf of the kitchen. I watched my chance, and got it, and, shelling off a few grains, I put it back again. The grains in my hand, I quickly put in some ashes, and covered them with embers, to roast them. All this I did at the risk of getting a brutal thumping, for Aunt Katy could beat, as well as starve me. My corn was not long in roasting, and, with my keen appetite, it did not matter even if the grains were not exactly done. I eagerly pulled them out, and placed them on my stool, in a clever little pile. Just as I began to help myself to my very dry meal, in came my dear mother. And now, dear reader, a scene occurred which was altogether worth beholding, and to me it was instructive as well as interesting. The friendless and hungry boy, in his extremest need—and when he did not dare to look for succor—found himself in the strong, protecting arms of a mother; a mother who was, at the moment (being endowed with high powers of manner as well as matter) more than a match for all his enemies. I shall never forget the indescribable expression of her countenance, when I told her that I had had no food since morning; and that Aunt Katy said she "meant to starve the life out of me." There was pity in her glance at me, and a fiery indignation at Aunt Katy at the same time; and, while she took the corn from me, and gave me a large ginger cake, in its stead, she read Aunt Katy a lecture which she never forgot. My mother threatened her with complaining to old master in my behalf; for the latter, though harsh and cruel himself, at times, did not sanction the meanness, injustice, partiality and oppressions enacted by Aunt Katy in the kitchen. That night I learned the fact, that I was, not only a child, but *somebody's* child. The "sweet cake" my mother gave me was in the shape of a heart, with a rich, dark ring glazed upon the edge of it. I was victorious, and well off for the moment; prouder, on my mother's knee, than a king upon his throne. But my triumph was short. I dropped off to sleep, and waked in the morning only to find my mother gone, and myself left at the mercy of the sable virago, dominant in my old master's kitchen, whose fiery wrath was my constant dread.

I do not remember to have seen my mother after this occurrence. Death soon ended the little communication that had existed between us; and with it, I believe, a life judging from her weary, sad, down-cast countenance and mute demeanor—full of heartfelt sorrow. I was not allowed to visit her during any part of her long illness; nor did I see her for a long time before she was taken ill and died. The heartless and ghastly form of *slavery* rises between mother and child, even at the bed of death. The mother, at the verge of the grave, may not gather her children, to impart to them her holy admonitions, and invoke for them her dying benediction. The bond-woman lives as a slave, and is left to die as a beast; often with fewer attentions than are paid to a favorite horse. Scenes of sacred tenderness, around the death-bed, never forgotten, and which often arrest the vicious and confirm the virtuous during life, must be looked for among the free, though they sometimes occur among the slaves. It has been a life-long, standing grief to me, that I knew so little of my mother; and that I was so early separated from her. The counsels of her love must have been beneficial to me. The side view of her face is imaged on my memory, and I take few steps in life, without feeling her presence; but the image is mute, and I have no striking words of her's treasured up.

I learned, after my mother's death, that she could read, and that she was the *only* one of all the slaves and colored people in Tuckahoe who enjoyed that advantage. How she acquired this knowledge, I know not, for Tuckahoe is the last place in the world where she would be apt to find facilities for learning. I can, therefore, fondly and proudly ascribe to her an earnest love of knowledge. That a "field hand" should learn to read, in any slave state, is remarkable; but the achievement of my mother, considering the place, was very extraordinary;

and, in view of that fact, I am quite willing, and even happy, to attribute any love of letters I possess, and for which I have got—despite of prejudices only too much credit, *not* to my admitted Anglo-Saxon paternity, but to the native genius of my sable, unprotected, and uncultivated *mother*—a woman, who belonged to a race whose mental endowments it is, at present, fashionable to hold in disparagement and contempt.

Summoned away to her account, with the impassable gulf of slavery between us during her entire illness, my mother died without leaving me a single intimation of *who* my father was. There was a whisper, that my master was my father; yet it was only a whisper, and I cannot say that I ever gave it credence. Indeed, I now have reason to think he was not; nevertheless, the fact remains, in all its glaring odiousness, that, by the laws of slavery, children, in all cases, are reduced to the condition of their mothers. This arrangement admits of the greatest license to brutal slaveholders, and their profligate sons, brothers, relations and friends, and gives to the pleasure of sin, the additional attraction of profit. A whole volume might be written on this single feature of slavery, as I have observed it.

One might imagine, that the children of such connections, would fare better, in the hands of their masters, than other slaves. The rule is quite the other way; and a very little reflection will satisfy the reader that such is the case. A man who will enslave his own blood, may not be safely relied on for magnanimity. Men do not love those who remind them of their sins unless they have a mind to repent—and the mulatto child's face is a standing accusation against him who is master and father to the child. What is still worse, perhaps, such a child is a constant offense to the wife. She hates its very presence, and when a slaveholding woman hates, she wants not means to give that hate telling effect. Women—white women, I mean—are IDOLS at the south, not WIVES, for the slave women are preferred in many instances; and if these *idols* but nod, or lift a finger, woe to the poor victim: kicks, cuffs and stripes are sure to follow. Masters are frequently compelled to sell this class of their slaves, out of deference to the feelings of their white wives; and shocking and scandalous as it may seem for a man to sell his own blood to the traffickers in human flesh, it is often an act of humanity toward the slave-child to be thus removed from his merciless tormentors.

It is not within the scope of the design of my simple story, to comment upon every phase of slavery not within my experience as a slave.

But, I may remark, that, if the lineal descendants of Ham are only to be enslaved, according to the scriptures, slavery in this country will soon become an unscriptural institution; for thousands are ushered into the world, annually, who—like myself—owe their existence to white fathers, and, most frequently, to their masters, and master's sons. The slave-woman is at the mercy of the fathers, sons or brothers of her master. The thoughtful know the rest.

After what I have now said of the circumstances of my mother, and my relations to her, the reader will not be surprised, nor be disposed to censure me, when I tell but the simple truth, viz: that I received the tidings of her death with no strong emotions of sorrow for her, and with very little regret for myself on account of her loss. I had to learn the value of my mother long after her death, and by witnessing the devotion of other mothers to their children.

There is not, beneath the sky, an enemy to filial affection so destructive as slavery. It had made my brothers and sisters strangers to me; it converted the mother that bore me, into a myth; it shrouded my father in mystery, and left me without an intelligible beginning in the world.

My mother died when I could not have been more than eight or nine years old, on one of old master's farms in Tuckahoe, in the neighborhood of Hillsborough. Her grave is, as the grave of the dead at sea, unmarked, and without stone or stake.

CHAPTER IV

A General Survey of the Slave Plantation

ISOLATION OF LLOYD S PLANTATION—PUBLIC OPINION THERE NO
PROTECTION TO THE SLAVE—ABSOLUTE POWER OF THE OVERSEER—
NATURAL AND ARTIFICIAL CHARMS OF THE PLACE—ITS BUSINESS-LIKE
APPEARANCE—SUPERSTITION ABOUT THE BURIAL GROUND—GREAT
IDEAS OF COL. LLOYD—ETIQUETTE AMONG SLAVES—THE COMIC SLAVE
DOCTOR—PRAYING AND FLOGGING—OLD MASTER LOSING ITS TERRORS—
HIS BUSINESS—CHARACTER OF AUNT KATY—SUFFERINGS FROM HUNGER—
OLD MASTER'S HOME—JARGON OF THE PLANTATION—GUINEA SLAVES—
MASTER DANIEL—FAMILY OF COL. LLOYD—FAMILY OF CAPT. ANTHONY—
HIS SOCIAL POSITION—NOTIONS OF RANK AND STATION.

It is generally supposed that slavery, in the state of Maryland, exists in its mildest
form, and that it is totally divested of those harsh and terrible peculiarities,
which mark and characterize the slave system, in the southern and south-
western states of the American union. The argument in favor of this opinion,
is the contiguity of the free states, and the exposed condition of slavery in
Maryland to the moral, religious and humane sentiment of the free states.

I am not about to refute this argument, so far as it relates to slavery
in that state, generally; on the contrary, I am willing to admit that, to this
general point, the arguments is well grounded. Public opinion is, indeed, an
unfailing restraint upon the cruelty and barbarity of masters, overseers, and
slave-drivers, whenever and wherever it can reach them; but there are certain
secluded and out-of-the-way places, even in the state of Maryland, seldom
visited by a single ray of healthy public sentiment—where slavery, wrapt in its
own congenial, midnight darkness, *can*, and *does*, develop all its malign and
shocking characteristics; where it can be indecent without shame, cruel without
shuddering, and murderous without apprehension or fear of exposure.

Just such a secluded, dark, and out-of-the-way place, is the "home
plantation" of Col. Edward Lloyd, on the Eastern Shore, Maryland. It is far away

from all the great thoroughfares, and is proximate to no town or village. There is neither school-house, nor town-house in its neighborhood. The school-house is unnecessary, for there are no children to go to school. The children and grand-children of Col. Lloyd were taught in the house, by a private tutor—a Mr. Page a tall, gaunt sapling of a man, who did not speak a dozen words to a slave in a whole year. The overseers' children go off somewhere to school; and they, therefore, bring no foreign or dangerous influence from abroad, to embarrass the natural operation of the slave system of the place. Not even the mechanics—through whom there is an occasional out-burst of honest and telling indignation, at cruelty and wrong on other plantations—are white men, on this plantation. Its whole public is made up of, and divided into, three classes—SLAVEHOLDERS, SLAVES and OVERSEERS. Its blacksmiths, wheelwrights, shoemakers, weavers, and coopers, are slaves. Not even commerce, selfish and iron-hearted at it is, and ready, as it ever is, to side with the strong against the weak—the rich against the poor—is trusted or permitted within its secluded precincts. Whether with a view of guarding against the escape of its secrets, I know not, but it is a fact, the every leaf and grain of the produce of this plantation, and those of the neighboring farms belonging to Col. Lloyd, are transported to Baltimore in Col. Lloyd's own vessels; every man and boy on board of which—except the captain—are owned by him. In return, everything brought to the plantation, comes through the same channel. Thus, even the glimmering and unsteady light of trade, which sometimes exerts a civilizing influence, is excluded from this "tabooed" spot.

Nearly all the plantations or farms in the vicinity of the "home plantation" of Col. Lloyd, belong to him; and those which do not, are owned by personal friends of his, as deeply interested in maintaining the slave system, in all its rigor, as Col. Lloyd himself. Some of his neighbors are said to be even more stringent than he. The Skinners, the Peakers, the Tilgmans, the Lockermans, and the Gipsons, are in the same boat; being slaveholding neighbors, they may have strengthened each other in their iron rule. They are on intimate terms, and their interests and tastes are identical.

Public opinion in such a quarter, the reader will see, is not likely to very efficient in protecting the slave from cruelty. On the contrary, it must increase and intensify his wrongs. Public opinion seldom differs very widely from public practice. To be a restraint upon cruelty and vice, public opinion must emanate from a humane and virtuous community. To no such humane and virtuous community, is Col. Lloyd's plantation exposed. That plantation is a little nation of its own, having its own language, its own rules, regulations and customs. The laws and institutions of the state, apparently touch it nowhere. The troubles arising here, are not settled by the civil power of the state. The overseer is generally accuser, judge, jury, advocate and executioner. The criminal is always dumb. The overseer attends to all sides of a case.

There are no conflicting rights of property, for all the people are owned by one man; and they can themselves own no property. Religion and politics are alike excluded. One class of the population is too high to be reached by the preacher; and the other class is too low to be cared for by the preacher. The poor have the gospel preached to them, in this neighborhood, only when they are able to pay for it. The slaves, having no money, get no gospel. The politician keeps away, because the people have no votes, and the preacher keeps away, because the people have no money. The rich planter can afford to learn politics in the parlor, and to dispense with religion altogether.

In its isolation, seclusion, and self-reliant independence, Col. Lloyd's plantation resembles what the baronial domains were during the middle ages in Europe. Grim, cold, and unapproachable by all genial influences from communities without, *there it stands;* full three hundred years behind the age, in all that relates to humanity and morals.

This, however, is not the only view that the place presents. Civilization is shut out, but nature cannot be. Though separated from the rest of the world; though public opinion, as I have said, seldom gets a chance to penetrate its dark domain; though the whole place is stamped with its own peculiar, ironlike individuality; and though crimes, high-handed and atrocious, may there be committed, with almost as much impunity as upon the deck of a pirate ship—it is, nevertheless, altogether, to outward seeming, a most strikingly interesting place, full of life, activity, and spirit; and presents a very favorable contrast to the indolent monotony and languor of Tuckahoe. Keen as was my regret and great as was my sorrow at leaving the latter, I was not long in adapting myself to this, my new home. A man's troubles are always half disposed of, when he finds endurance his only remedy. I found myself here; there was no getting away; and what remained for me, but to make the best of it? Here were plenty of children to play with, and plenty of places of pleasant resort for boys of my age, and boys older. The little tendrils of affection, so rudely and treacherously broken from around the darling objects of my grandmother's hut, gradually began to extend, and to entwine about the new objects by which I now found myself surrounded.

There was a windmill (always a commanding object to a child's eye) on Long Point—a tract of land dividing Miles river from the Wye a mile or more from my old master's house. There was a creek to swim in, at the bottom of an open flat space, of twenty acres or more, called "the Long Green"—a very beautiful play-ground for the children.

In the river, a short distance from the shore, lying quietly at anchor, with her small boat dancing at her stern, was a large sloop—the Sally Lloyd; called by that name in honor of a favorite daughter of the colonel. The sloop and the mill were wondrous things, full of thoughts and ideas. A child cannot well look at such objects without *thinking*.

Then here were a great many houses; human habitations, full of the mysteries of life at every stage of it. There was the little red house, up the road, occupied by Mr. Sevier, the overseer. A little nearer to my old master's, stood a very long, rough, low building, literally alive with slaves, of all ages, conditions and sizes. This was called "the Longe Quarter." Perched upon a hill, across the Long Green, was a very tall, dilapidated, old brick building—the architectural dimensions of which proclaimed its erection for a different purpose—now occupied by slaves, in a similar manner to the Long Quarter. Besides these, there were numerous other slave houses and huts, scattered around in the neighborhood, every nook and corner of which was completely occupied. Old master's house, a long, brick building, plain, but substantial, stood in the center of the plantation life, and constituted one independent establishment on the premises of Col. Lloyd.

Besides these dwellings, there were barns, stables, store-houses, and tobacco-houses; blacksmiths' shops, wheelwrights' shops, coopers' shops—all objects of interest; but, above all, there stood the grandest building my eyes had then ever beheld, called, by every one on the plantation, the "Great House." This was occupied by Col. Lloyd and his family. They occupied it; *I* enjoyed it. The great house was surrounded by numerous and variously shaped out-buildings. There were kitchens, wash-houses, dairies, summer-house, green-houses, hen-houses, turkey-houses, pigeon-houses, and arbors, of many sizes and devices, all neatly painted, and altogether interspersed with grand old trees, ornamental and primitive, which afforded delightful shade in summer, and imparted to the scene a high degree of stately beauty. The great house itself was a large, white, wooden building, with wings on three sides of it. In front, a large portico, extending the entire length of the building, and supported by a long range of columns, gave to the whole establishment an air of solemn grandeur. It was a treat to my young and gradually opening mind, to behold this elaborate exhibition of wealth, power, and vanity. The carriage entrance to the house was a large gate, more than a quarter of a mile distant from it; the intermediate space was a beautiful lawn, very neatly trimmed, and watched with the greatest care. It was dotted thickly over with delightful trees, shrubbery, and flowers. The road, or lane, from the gate to the great house, was richly paved with white pebbles from the beach, and, in its course, formed a complete circle around the beautiful lawn. Carriages going in and retiring from the great house, made the circuit of the lawn, and their passengers were permitted to behold a scene of almost Eden-like beauty. Outside this select inclosure, were parks, where as about the residences of the English nobility—rabbits, deer, and other wild game, might be seen, peering and playing about, with none to molest them or make them afraid. The tops of the stately poplars were often covered with the red-winged black-birds, making all nature vocal with the joyous life and beauty of their wild, warbling notes. These all belonged to me, as well as to Col. Edward Lloyd, and for a time I greatly enjoyed them.

A short distance from the great house, were the stately mansions of the dead, a place of somber aspect. Vast tombs, embowered beneath the weeping willow and the fir tree, told of the antiquities of the Lloyd family, as well as of their wealth. Superstition was rife among the slaves about this family burying ground. Strange sights had been seen there by some of the older slaves. Shrouded ghosts, riding on great black horses, had been seen to enter; balls of fire had been seen to fly there at midnight, and horrid sounds had been repeatedly heard. Slaves know enough of the rudiments of theology to believe that those go to hell who die slaveholders; and they often fancy such persons wishing themselves back again, to wield the lash. Tales of sights and sounds, strange and terrible, connected with the huge black tombs, were a very great security to the grounds about them, for few of the slaves felt like approaching them even in the day time. It was a dark, gloomy and forbidding place, and it was difficult to feel that the spirits of the sleeping dust there deposited, reigned with the blest in the realms of eternal peace.

The business of twenty or thirty farms was transacted at this, called, by way of eminence, "great house farm." These farms all belonged to Col. Lloyd, as did, also, the slaves upon them. Each farm was under the management of an overseer. As I have said of the overseer of the home plantation, so I may say of the overseers on the smaller ones; they stand between the slave and all civil constitutions—their word is law, and is implicitly obeyed.

The colonel, at this time, was reputed to be, and he apparently was, very rich. His slaves, alone, were an immense fortune. These, small and great, could not have been fewer than one thousand in number, and though scarcely a month passed without the sale of one or more lots to the Georgia traders, there was no apparent diminution in the number of his human stock: the home plantation merely groaned at a removal of the young increase, or human crop, then proceeded as lively as ever. Horse-shoeing, cart-mending, plow-repairing, coopering, grinding, and weaving, for all the neighboring farms, were performed here, and slaves were employed in all these branches. "Uncle Tony" was the blacksmith; "Uncle Harry" was the cartwright; "Uncle Abel" was the shoemaker; and all these had hands to assist them in their several departments.

These mechanics were called "uncles" by all the younger slaves, not because they really sustained that relationship to any, but according to plantation *etiquette*, as a mark of respect, due from the younger to the older slaves. Strange, and even ridiculous as it may seem, among a people so uncultivated, and with so many stern trials to look in the face, there is not to be found, among any people, a more rigid enforcement of the law of respect to elders, than they maintain. I set this down as partly constitutional with my race, and partly conventional. There is no better material in the world for making a gentleman, than is furnished in the African. He shows to others, and exacts for himself, all the tokens of respect which he is compelled to manifest toward his master. A young slave must approach the company of the older with hat in hand, and woe betide him, if he fails to acknowledge a favor, of any sort, with the accustomed *"tank'ee,"* &c. So uniformly are good manners enforced among slaves, I can easily detect a "bogus" fugitive by his manners.

Among other slave notabilities of the plantation, was one called by everybody Uncle Isaac Copper. It is seldom that a slave gets a surname from anybody in Maryland; and so completely has the south shaped the manners of the north, in this respect, that even abolitionists make very little of the surname of a Negro. The only improvement on the "Bills," "Jacks," "Jims," and "Neds" of the south, observable here is, that "William," "John," "James," "Edward," are substituted. It goes against the grain to treat and address a Negro precisely as they would treat and address a white man. But, once in a while, in slavery as in the free states, by some extraordinary circumstance, the Negro has a surname fastened to him, and holds it against all conventionalities. This was the case with Uncle Isaac Copper. When the "uncle" was dropped, he generally had the prefix "doctor," in its stead. He was our doctor of medicine, and doctor of divinity as well. Where he took his degree I am unable to say, for he was not very communicative to inferiors, and I was emphatically such, being but a boy seven or eight years old. He was too well established in his profession to permit questions as to his native skill, or his attainments. One qualification he undoubtedly had—he was a confirmed *cripple;* and he could neither work, nor would he bring anything if offered for sale in the market. The old man, though lame, was no sluggard. He was a man that made his crutches do him good service. He was always on the alert, looking up the sick, and all such as were supposed to need his counsel. His remedial prescriptions embraced four articles. For diseases of the body, *Epsom salts and castor oil;* for those of the soul, *the Lord's Prayer,* and *hickory switches*!

I was not long at Col. Lloyd's before I was placed under the care of Doctor Issac Copper. I was sent to him with twenty or thirty other children, to learn the "Lord's Prayer." I found the old gentleman seated on a huge three-legged oaken stool, armed with several large hickory switches; and, from his position, he could reach—lame as he was—any boy in the room. After standing awhile to learn what was expected of us, the old gentleman, in any other than a devotional tone, commanded us to kneel down. This done, he commenced telling us to say everything he said. "Our Father"—this was repeated after him with promptness and uniformity; "Who art in heaven"—was less promptly and uniformly repeated; and the old gentleman paused in the prayer, to give us a short lecture upon the consequences of inattention, both immediate and future, and especially those more immediate. About these he was absolutely certain, for he held in his right hand the means of bringing all his predictions and warnings to pass. On he proceeded with the prayer; and we with our thick tongues and unskilled ears, followed him to the best of our ability. This, however, was not sufficient to please the old gentleman. Everybody, in the south, wants the privilege of whipping somebody else. Uncle Isaac shared the common passion of his country, and, therefore, seldom found any means of keeping his disciples in order short of flogging. "Say everything I say;" and bang would come the switch on some poor boy's undevotional head. *"What you looking at there"*—*"Stop that pushing"*—and down again would come the lash.

The whip is all in all. It is supposed to secure obedience to the slaveholder, and is held as a sovereign remedy among the slaves themselves, for every form of disobedience, temporal or spiritual. Slaves, as well as slaveholders, use it with an unsparing hand. Our devotions at Uncle Isaac's combined too much of the tragic and comic, to make them very salutary in a spiritual point of view; and it is due to truth to say, I was often a truant when the time for attending the praying and flogging of Doctor Isaac Copper came on.

The windmill under the care of Mr. Kinney, a kind hearted old Englishman, was to me a source of infinite interest and pleasure. The old man always seemed pleased when he saw a troop of darkey little urchins, with their tow-linen shirts fluttering in the breeze, approaching to view and admire the whirling wings of his wondrous machine. From the mill we could see other objects of deep interest. These were, the vessels from St. Michael's, on their way to Baltimore. It was a source of much amusement to view the flowing sails and complicated rigging, as the little crafts dashed by, and to speculate upon Baltimore, as to the kind and quality of the place. With so many sources of interest around me, the reader may be prepared to learn that I began to think very highly of Col. L.'s plantation. It was just a place to my boyish taste. There were fish to be caught in the creek, if one only had a hook and line; and crabs, clams and oysters were to be caught by wading, digging and raking for them. Here was a field for industry and enterprise, strongly inviting; and the reader may be assured that I entered upon it with spirit.

Even the much dreaded old master, whose merciless fiat had brought me from Tuckahoe, gradually, to my mind, parted with his terrors. Strange enough, his reverence seemed to take no particular notice of me, nor of my coming. Instead of leaping out and devouring me, he scarcely seemed conscious of my presence. The fact is, he was occupied with matters more weighty and important than either looking after or vexing me. He probably thought as little of my advent, as he would have thought of the addition of a single pig to his stock!

As the chief butler on Col. Lloyd's plantation, his duties were numerous and perplexing. In almost all important matters he answered in Col. Lloyd's stead. The overseers of all the farms were in some sort under him, and received the law from his mouth. The colonel himself seldom addressed an overseer, or allowed an overseer to address him. Old master carried the keys of all store houses; measured out the allowance for each slave at the end of every month; superintended the storing of all goods brought to the plantation; dealt out the raw material to all the handicraftsmen; shipped the grain, tobacco, and all saleable produce of the plantation to market, and had the general oversight of the coopers' shop, wheelwrights' shop, blacksmiths' shop, and shoemakers' shop. Besides the care of these, he often had business for the plantation which required him to be absent two and three days.

Thus largely employed, he had little time, and perhaps as little disposition, to interfere with the children individually. What he was to Col. Lloyd, he made Aunt Katy to him. When he had anything to say or do about us, it was said or done in a wholesale manner; disposing of us in classes or sizes, leaving all minor details to Aunt Katy, a person of whom the reader has already received no very favorable impression. Aunt Katy was a woman who never allowed herself to act greatly within the margin of power granted to her, no matter how broad that authority might be. Ambitious, ill-tempered and cruel, she found in her present position an ample field for the exercise of her ill-omened qualities. She had a strong hold on old master she was considered a first rate cook, and she really was very industrious. She was, therefore, greatly favored by old master, and as one mark of his favor, she was the only mother who was permitted to retain her children around her. Even to these children she was often fiendish in her brutality. She pursued her son Phil, one day, in my presence, with a huge butcher knife, and dealt a blow with its edge which left a shocking gash on his arm, near the wrist. For this, old master did sharply rebuke her, and threatened that if she ever should do the like again, he would take the skin off her back. Cruel, however, as Aunt Katy was to her own children, at times she was not destitute of maternal feeling, as I often had occasion to know, in the bitter pinches of hunger I had to endure. Differing from the practice of Col. Lloyd, old master, instead of allowing so much for each slave, committed the allowance for all to the care of Aunt Katy, to be divided after cooking it, amongst us. The allowance, consisting of coarse corn-meal, was not very abundant—indeed, it was very slender; and in passing through Aunt Katy's hands, it was made more slender still, for some of us. William, Phil and Jerry were her children, and it is not to accuse her too severely, to allege that she was often guilty of starving myself and the other children, while she was literally cramming her own. Want of food was my chief trouble the first summer at my old master's. Oysters and clams would do very well, with an occasional supply of bread, but they soon failed in the absence of bread. I speak but the simple truth, when I say, I have often been so pinched with hunger, that I have fought with the dog—"Old Nep"—for the smallest crumbs that fell from the kitchen table, and have been glad when I won a single crumb in the combat. Many times have I followed, with eager step, the waiting-girl when she went out to shake the table cloth, to get the crumbs and small bones flung out for the cats. The water, in which meat had been boiled, was as eagerly sought for by me. It was a great thing to get the privilege of dipping a piece of bread in such water; and the skin taken from rusty bacon, was a positive luxury. Nevertheless, I sometimes got full meals and kind words from sympathizing old slaves, who knew my sufferings, and received the comforting assurance that I should be a man some day. "Never mind, honey—better day comin'," was even then a solace, a cheering consolation to me in my troubles. Nor were all the kind words I received from slaves. I had a friend in the parlor, as well, and one to whom I shall be glad to do justice, before I have finished this part of my story.

I was not long at old master's, before I learned that his surname was Anthony, and that he was generally called "Captain Anthony"—a title which he probably acquired by sailing a craft in the Chesapeake Bay. Col. Lloyd's slaves never called Capt. Anthony "old master," but always Capt. Anthony; and *me* they called "Captain Anthony Fred." There is not, probably, in the whole south, a plantation where the English language is more imperfectly spoken than on Col. Lloyd's. It is a mixture of Guinea and everything else you please. At the time of which I am now writing, there were slaves there who had been brought from the coast of Africa. They never used the "s" in indication of the possessive case. "Cap'n Ant'ney Tom," "Lloyd Bill," "Aunt Rose Harry," means "Captain Anthony's Tom," "Lloyd's Bill," &c. *"Oo you dem long to?"* means, "Whom do you belong to?" *"Oo dem got any peachy?"* means, "Have you got any peaches?" I could scarcely understand them when I first went among them, so broken was their speech; and I am persuaded that I could not have been dropped anywhere on the globe, where I could reap less, in the way of knowledge, from my immediate associates, than on this plantation. Even "MAS' DANIEL," by his association with his father's slaves, had measurably adopted their dialect and their ideas, so far as they had ideas to be adopted. The equality of nature is strongly asserted in childhood, and childhood requires children for associates. *Color* makes no difference with a child. Are you a child with wants, tastes and pursuits common to children, not put on, but natural? then, were you black as ebony you would be welcome to the child of alabaster whiteness. The law of compensation holds here, as well as elsewhere. Mas' Daniel could not associate with ignorance without sharing its shade; and he could not give his black playmates his company, without giving them his intelligence, as well. Without knowing this, or caring about it, at the time, I, for some cause or other, spent much of my time with Mas' Daniel, in preference to spending it with most of the other boys.

Mas' Daniel was the youngest son of Col. Lloyd; his older brothers were Edward and Murray—both grown up, and fine looking men. Edward was especially esteemed by the children, and by me among the rest; not that he ever said anything to us or for us, which could be called especially kind; it was enough for us, that he never looked nor acted scornfully toward us. There were also three sisters, all married; one to Edward Winder; a second to Edward Nicholson; a third to Mr. Lownes.

The family of old master consisted of two sons, Andrew and Richard; his daughter, Lucretia, and her newly married husband, Capt. Auld. This was the house family. The kitchen family consisted of Aunt Katy, Aunt Esther, and ten or a dozen children, most of them older than myself. Capt. Anthony was not considered a rich slaveholder, but was pretty well off in the world. He owned about thirty *"head"* of slaves, and three farms in Tuckahoe. The most valuable part of his property was his slaves, of whom he could afford to sell one every year. This crop, therefore, brought him seven or eight hundred dollars a year, besides his yearly salary, and other revenue from his farms.

The idea of rank and station was rigidly maintained on Col. Lloyd's plantation. Our family never visited the great house, and the Lloyds never came to our home. Equal non-intercourse was observed between Capt. Anthony's family and that of Mr. Sevier, the overseer.

Such, kind reader, was the community, and such the place, in which my earliest and most lasting impressions of slavery, and of slave-life, were received; of which impressions you will learn more in the coming chapters of this book.

CHAPTER V

Gradual Initiation to the Mysteries of Slavery

GROWING ACQUAINTANCE WITH OLD MASTER—HIS CHARACTER—EVILS OF UNRESTRAINED PASSION—APPARENT TENDERNESS—OLD MASTER A MAN OF TROUBLE—CUSTOM OF MUTTERING TO HIMSELF—NECESSITY OF BEING AWARE OF HIS WORDS—THE SUPPOSED OBTUSENESS OF SLAVE-CHILDREN—BRUTAL OUTRAGE—DRUNKEN OVERSEER—SLAVEHOLDER'S IMPATIENCE—WISDOM OF APPEALING TO SUPERIORS—THE SLAVEHOLDER S WRATH BAD AS THAT OF THE OVERSEER—A BASE AND SELFISH ATTEMPT TO BREAK UP A COURTSHIP—A HARROWING SCENE.

Although my old master—Capt. Anthony—gave me at first, (as the reader will have already seen) very little attention, and although that little was of a remarkably mild and gentle description, a few months only were sufficient to convince me that mildness and gentleness were not the prevailing or governing traits of his character. These excellent qualities were displayed only occasionally. He could, when it suited him, appear to be literally insensible to the claims of humanity, when appealed to by the helpless against an aggressor, and he could himself commit outrages, deep, dark and nameless. Yet he was not by nature worse than other men. Had he been brought up in a free state, surrounded by the just restraints of free society—restraints which are necessary to the freedom of all its members, alike and equally—Capt. Anthony might have been as humane a man, and every way as respectable, as many who now oppose the slave system; certainly as humane and respectable as are members of society generally. The slaveholder, as well as the slave, is the victim of the slave system. A man's character greatly takes its hue and shape from the form and color of things about him. Under the whole heavens there is no relation more unfavorable to the development of honorable character, than that sustained by the slaveholder to the slave. Reason is imprisoned here, and passions run wild. Like the fires of the prairie, once lighted, they are at the mercy of every wind, and must burn, till they have consumed all that is combustible within their remorseless grasp.

Capt. Anthony could be kind, and, at times, he even showed an affectionate disposition. Could the reader have seen him gently leading me by the hand—as he sometimes did—patting me on the head, speaking to me in soft, caressing tones and calling me his "little Indian boy," he would have deemed him a kind old man, and really, almost fatherly. But the pleasant moods of a slaveholder are remarkably brittle; they are easily snapped; they neither come often, nor remain long. His temper is subjected to perpetual trials; but, since these trials are never borne patiently, they add nothing to his natural stock of patience.

Old master very early impressed me with the idea that he was an unhappy man. Even to my child's eye, he wore a troubled, and at times, a haggard aspect. His strange movements excited my curiosity, and awakened my compassion. He seldom walked alone without muttering to himself; and he occasionally stormed about, as if defying an army of invisible foes. "He would do this, that, and the other; he'd be d—d if he did not,"—was the usual form of his threats. Most of his leisure was spent in walking, cursing and gesticulating, like one possessed by a demon. Most evidently, he was a wretched man, at war with his own soul, and with all the world around him. To be overheard by the children, disturbed him very little. He made no more of our presence, than of that of the ducks and geese which he met on the green. He little thought that the little black urchins around him, could see, through those vocal crevices, the very secrets of his heart. Slaveholders ever underrate the intelligence with which they have to grapple. I really understood the old man's mutterings, attitudes and gestures, about as well as he did himself. But slaveholders never encourage that kind of communication, with the slaves, by which they might learn to measure the depths of his knowledge. Ignorance is a high virtue in a human chattel; and as the master studies to keep the slave ignorant, the slave is cunning enough to make the master think he succeeds. The slave fully appreciates the saying, "where ignorance is bliss, 'tis folly to be wise." When old master's gestures were violent, ending with a threatening shake of the head, and a sharp snap of his middle finger and thumb, I deemed it wise to keep at a respectable distance from him; for, at such times, trifling faults stood, in his eyes, as momentous offenses; and, having both the power and the disposition, the victim had only to be near him to catch the punishment, deserved or undeserved.

One of the first circumstances that opened my eyes to the cruelty and wickedness of slavery, and the heartlessness of my old master, was the refusal of the latter to interpose his authority, to protect and shield a young woman, who had been most cruelly abused and beaten by his overseer in Tuckahoe. This overseer—a Mr. Plummer—was a man like most of his class, little better than a human brute; and, in addition to his general profligacy and repulsive coarseness, the creature was a miserable drunkard. He was, probably, employed by my old master, less on account of the excellence of his services, than for the cheap rate at which they could be obtained. He was not fit to have the management of a drove of mules. In a fit of drunken madness, he committed the outrage which brought the young woman in question down to my old master's for protection. This young woman was the daughter of Milly, an own aunt of mine. The poor girl, on arriving at our house, presented a pitiable appearance. She had left in haste, and without preparation; and, probably, without the knowledge of Mr. Plummer. She had traveled twelve miles, bare-footed, bare-necked and bare-headed. Her neck and shoulders were covered with scars, newly made; and not content with marring her neck and shoulders, with the cowhide, the cowardly brute had dealt her a blow on the head with a hickory club, which cut a horrible gash, and left her face literally covered with blood. In this condition, the poor young woman came down, to implore protection at the hands of my old master. I expected to see him boil over with rage at the revolting deed, and to hear him fill the air with curses upon the brutal Plummer; but I was disappointed. He sternly told her, in an angry tone, he "believed she deserved every bit of it," and, if she did not go home instantly, he would himself take the remaining skin from her neck and back. Thus was the poor girl compelled to return, without redress, and perhaps to receive an additional flogging for daring to appeal to old master against the overseer.

Old master seemed furious at the thought of being troubled by such complaints. I did not, at that time, understand the philosophy of his treatment of my cousin. It was stern, unnatural, violent. Had the man no bowels of compassion? Was he dead to all sense of humanity? No. I think I now understand it. This treatment is a part of the system, rather than a part of the man. Were slaveholders to listen to complaints of this sort against the overseers, the luxury of owning large numbers of slaves, would be impossible. It would do away with the office of overseer, entirely; or, in other words, it would convert the master himself into an overseer. It would occasion great loss of time and labor, leaving the overseer in fetters, and without the necessary power to secure obedience to his orders. A privilege so dangerous as that of appeal, is, therefore, strictly prohibited; and any one exercising it, runs a fearful hazard. Nevertheless, when a slave has nerve enough to exercise it, and boldly approaches his master, with a well-founded complaint against an overseer, though he may be repulsed, and may even have that of which he complains repeated at the time, and, though he may be beaten by his master, as well as by the overseer, for his temerity, in the end the policy of complaining is, generally, vindicated by the relaxed rigor of the overseer's treatment. The latter becomes more careful, and less disposed to use the lash upon such slaves thereafter. It is with this final result in view, rather than with any expectation of immediate good, that the outraged slave is induced to meet his master with a complaint. The overseer very naturally dislikes to have the ear of the master disturbed by complaints; and, either upon this consideration, or upon advice and warning privately given him by his employers, he generally modifies the rigor of his rule, after an outbreak of the kind to which I have been referring.

Howsoever the slaveholder may allow himself to act toward his slave, and, whatever cruelty he may deem it wise, for example's sake, or for the gratification of his humor, to inflict, he cannot, in the absence of all provocation, look with pleasure upon the bleeding wounds of a defenseless slave-woman. When he drives her from his presence without redress, or the hope of redress, he acts, generally, from motives of policy, rather than from a hardened nature, or from innate brutality. Yet, let but his own temper be stirred, his own passions get loose, and the slave-owner will go *far beyond* the overseer in cruelty. He will convince the slave that his wrath is far more terrible and boundless, and vastly more to be dreaded, than that of the underling overseer. What may have been mechanically and heartlessly done by the overseer, is now done with a will. The man who now wields the lash is irresponsible. He may, if he pleases, cripple or kill, without fear of consequences; except in so far as it may concern profit or loss. To a man of violent temper—as my old master was—this was but a very slender and inefficient restraint. I have seen him in a tempest of passion, such as I have just described—a passion into which entered all the bitter ingredients of pride, hatred, envy, jealousy, and the thrist(sic) for revenge.

The circumstances which I am about to narrate, and which gave rise to this fearful tempest of passion, are not singular nor isolated in slave life, but are common in every slaveholding community in which I have lived. They are incidental to the relation of master and slave, and exist in all sections of slave-holding countries.

The reader will have noticed that, in enumerating the names of the slaves who lived with my old master, *Esther* is mentioned. This was a young woman who possessed that which is ever a curse to the slave-girl; namely—personal beauty. She was tall, well formed, and made a fine appearance. The daughters of Col. Lloyd could scarcely surpass her in personal charms. Esther was courted by Ned Roberts, and he was as fine looking a young man, as she was a woman. He was the son of a favorite slave of Col. Lloyd. Some slaveholders would have been glad to promote the marriage of two such persons; but, for some reason or other, my old master took it upon him to break up the growing intimacy between Esther and Edward. He strictly ordered her to quit the company of said Roberts, telling her that he would punish her severely if he ever found her again in Edward's company. This unnatural and heartless order was, of course, broken. A woman's love is not to be annihilated by the peremptory command of any one, whose breath is in his nostrils. It was impossible to keep Edward and Esther apart. Meet they would, and meet they did. Had old master been a man of honor and purity, his motives, in this matter, might have been viewed more favorably. As it was, his motives were as abhorrent, as his methods were foolish and contemptible. It was too evident that he was not concerned for the girl's welfare. It is one of the damning characteristics of the slave system, that it robs its victims of every earthly incentive to a holy life. The fear of God, and the hope of heaven, are found sufficient to sustain many slave-women, amidst the snares and dangers of their strange lot; but, this side of God and heaven, a slave-woman is at the mercy of the power, caprice and passion of her owner. Slavery provides no means for the honorable continuance of the race. Marriage as imposing obligations on the parties to it—has no existence here, except in such hearts as are purer and higher than the standard morality around them. It is one of the consolations of my life, that I know of many honorable instances of persons who maintained their honor, where all around was corrupt.

Esther was evidently much attached to Edward, and abhorred—as she had reason to do—the tyrannical and base behavior of old master. Edward was young, and fine looking, and he loved and courted her. He might have been her husband, in the high sense just alluded to; but WHO and *what* was this old master? His attentions were plainly brutal and selfish, and it was as natural that Esther should loathe him, as that she should love Edward. Abhorred and circumvented as he was, old master, having the power, very easily took revenge. I happened to see this exhibition of his rage and cruelty toward Esther. The time selected was singular. It was early in the morning, when all besides was still, and before any of the family, in the house or kitchen, had left their beds. I saw but few of the shocking preliminaries, for the cruel work had begun before I awoke. I was probably awakened by the shrieks and piteous cries of poor Esther. My sleeping place was on the floor of a little, rough closet, which opened into the kitchen; and through the cracks of its unplaned boards, I could distinctly see and hear what was going on, without being seen by old master. Esther's wrists were firmly tied, and the twisted rope was fastened to a strong staple in a heavy wooden joist above, near the fireplace. Here she stood, on a bench, her arms tightly drawn over her breast. Her back and shoulders were bare to the waist. Behind her stood old master, with cowskin in hand, preparing his barbarous work with all manner of harsh, coarse, and tantalizing epithets. The screams of his victim were most piercing. He was cruelly deliberate, and protracted the torture, as one who was delighted with the scene. Again and again he drew the hateful whip through his hand, adjusting it with a view of dealing the most pain-giving blow. Poor Esther had never yet been severely whipped, and her shoulders were plump and tender. Each blow, vigorously laid on, brought screams as well as blood. *"Have mercy; Oh! have mercy"* she cried; *"I won't do so no more;"* but her piercing cries seemed only to increase his fury. His answers to them are too coarse and blasphemous to be produced here. The whole scene, with all its attendants, was revolting and shocking, to the last degree; and when the motives of this brutal castigation are considered,—language has no power to convey a just sense of its awful criminality. After laying on some thirty or forty stripes, old master untied his suffering victim, and let her get down. She could scarcely stand, when untied. From my heart I pitied her, and—child though I was—the outrage kindled in me a feeling far from peaceful; but I was hushed, terrified, stunned, and could do nothing, and the fate of Esther might be mine next. The scene here described was often repeated in the case of poor Esther, and her life, as I knew it, was one of wretchedness.

CHAPTER VI

Treatment of Slaves on Lloyd's Plantation

EARLY REFLECTIONS ON SLAVERY—PRESENTIMENT OF ONE DAY BEING A FREEMAN—COMBAT BETWEEN AN OVERSEER AND A SLAVEWOMAN—THE ADVANTAGES OF RESISTANCE—ALLOWANCE DAY ON THE HOME PLANTATION—THE SINGING OF SLAVES—AN EXPLANATION—THE SLAVES FOOD AND CLOTHING—NAKED CHILDREN—LIFE IN THE QUARTER—DEPRIVATION OF SLEEP—NURSING CHILDREN CARRIED TO THE FIELD—DESCRIPTION OF THE COWSKIN—THE ASH-CAKE—MANNER OF MAKING IT—THE DINNER HOUR—THE CONTRAST.

The heart-rending incidents, related in the foregoing chapter, led me, thus early, to inquire into the nature and history of slavery. *Why am I a slave? Why are some people slaves, and others masters? Was there ever a time this was not so? How did the relation commence?* These were the perplexing questions which began now to claim my thoughts, and to exercise the weak powers of my mind, for I was still but a child, and knew less than children of the same age in the free states. As my questions concerning these things were only put to children a little older, and little better informed than myself, I was not rapid in reaching a solid footing. By some means I learned from these inquiries that *"God, up in the sky,"* made every body; and that he made *white* people to be masters and mistresses, and *black* people to be slaves. This did not satisfy me, nor lessen my interest in the subject. I was told, too, that God was good, and that He knew what was best for me, and best for everybody. This was less satisfactory than the first statement; because it came, point blank, against all my notions of goodness. It was not good to let old master cut the flesh off Esther, and make her cry so. Besides, how did people know that God made black people to be slaves? Did they go up in the sky and learn it? or, did He come down and tell them so? All was dark here. It was some relief to my hard notions of the goodness of God, that, although he made white men to be slaveholders, he did not make them to be *bad* slaveholders, and that, in due time, he would punish the bad slaveholders; that he would, when they died, send them to the bad place, where they would be "burnt up." Nevertheless, I could not reconcile the relation of slavery with my crude notions of goodness.

Then, too, I found that there were puzzling exceptions to this theory of slavery on both sides, and in the middle. I knew of blacks who were *not* slaves; I knew of whites who were *not* slaveholders; and I knew of persons who were *nearly* white, who were slaves. *Color*, therefore, was a very unsatisfactory basis for slavery.

Once, however, engaged in the inquiry, I was not very long in finding out the true solution of the matter. It was not *color*, but *crime*, not *God*, but *man*, that afforded the true explanation of the existence of slavery; nor was I long in finding out another important truth, viz: what man can make, man can unmake. The appalling darkness faded away, and I was master of the subject. There were slaves here, direct from Guinea; and there were many who could say that their fathers and mothers were stolen from Africa—forced from their homes, and compelled to serve as slaves. This, to me, was knowledge; but it was a kind of knowledge which filled me with a burning hatred of slavery, increased my suffering, and left me without the means of breaking away from my bondage. Yet it was knowledge quite worth possessing. I could not have been more than seven or eight years old, when I began to make this subject my study. It was with me in the woods and fields; along the shore of the river, and wherever my boyish wanderings led me; and though I was, at that time, quite ignorant of the existence of the free states, I distinctly remember being, *even then*, most strongly impressed with the idea of being a freeman some day. This cheering assurance was an inborn dream of my human nature a constant menace to slavery—and one which all the powers of slavery were unable to silence or extinguish.

Up to the time of the brutal flogging of my Aunt Esther—for she was my own aunt—and the horrid plight in which I had seen my cousin from Tuckahoe, who had been so badly beaten by the cruel Mr. Plummer, my attention had not been called, especially, to the gross features of slavery. I had, of course, heard of whippings and of savage *rencontres* between overseers and slaves, but I had always been out of the way at the times and places of their occurrence. My plays and sports, most of the time, took me from the corn and tobacco fields, where the great body of the hands were at work, and where scenes of cruelty were enacted and witnessed. But, after the whipping of Aunt Esther, I saw many cases of the same shocking nature, not only in my master's house, but on Col. Lloyd's plantation. One of the first which I saw, and which greatly agitated me, was the whipping of a woman belonging to Col. Lloyd, named Nelly. The offense alleged against Nelly, was one of the commonest and most indefinite in the whole catalogue of offenses usually laid to the charge of slaves, viz: "impudence." This may mean almost anything, or nothing at all, just according to the caprice of the master or overseer, at the moment. But, whatever it is, or is not, if it gets the name of "impudence," the party charged with it is sure of a flogging. This offense may be committed in various ways; in the tone of an answer; in answering at all; in not answering; in the expression of countenance; in the motion of the head; in the gait, manner and bearing of the slave. In the case under consideration, I can easily believe that, according to all slaveholding standards, here was a genuine instance of impudence. In Nelly there were all the necessary conditions for committing the offense. She was a bright mulatto, the recognized wife of a favorite "hand" on board Col. Lloyd's sloop, and the mother of five sprightly children. She was a vigorous and spirited woman, and one of the most likely, on the plantation, to be guilty of impudence. My attention was called to the scene, by the noise, curses and screams that proceeded from it; and, on going a little in that direction, I came upon the parties engaged in the skirmish. Mr. Siever, the overseer, had hold of Nelly, when I caught sight of them; he was endeavoring to drag her toward a tree, which endeavor Nelly was sternly resisting; but to no purpose, except to retard the progress of the overseer's plans. Nelly—as I have said—was the mother of five children; three of them were present, and though quite small (from seven to ten years old, I should think) they gallantly came to their mother's defense, and gave the overseer an excellent pelting with stones. One of the little fellows ran up, seized the overseer by the leg and bit him; but the monster was too busily engaged with Nelly, to pay any attention to the assaults of the children. There were numerous bloody marks on Mr. Sevier's face, when I first saw him, and they increased as the struggle went on. The imprints of Nelly's fingers were visible, and I was glad to see them. Amidst the wild screams of the children—*"Let my mammy go"*—*"let my mammy go"*—there escaped, from between the teeth of the bullet-headed overseer, a few bitter curses, mingled with threats, that "he would teach the d—d b—h how to give a white man impudence." There is no doubt that Nelly felt herself superior, in some respects, to the slaves around her. She was a wife and a mother; her husband was a valued and favorite slave. Besides, he was one of the first hands on board of the sloop, and the sloop hands—since they had to represent the plantation abroad—were generally treated tenderly. The overseer never was allowed to whip Harry; why then should he be allowed to whip Harry's wife? Thoughts of this kind, no doubt, influenced her; but, for whatever reason, she nobly resisted, and, unlike most of the slaves, seemed determined to make her whipping cost Mr. Sevier as much as possible. The blood on his (and her) face, attested her skill, as well as her courage and dexterity in using her nails. Maddened by her resistance, I expected to see Mr. Sevier level her to the ground by a stunning blow; but no; like a savage bull-dog—which he resembled both in temper and appearance—he maintained his grip, and steadily dragged his victim toward the tree, disregarding alike her blows, and the cries of the children for their mother's release. He would, doubtless, have knocked her down with his hickory stick, but that such act might have cost him his place. It is often deemed advisable to knock a *man* slave down, in order to tie him, but it is considered cowardly and inexcusable, in an overseer, thus to deal with a *woman*. He is expected to tie her up, and to give her what is called, in southern parlance, a "genteel flogging," without any very great outlay of strength or skill. I watched, with palpitating interest, the course of the preliminary struggle, and was saddened by every new advantage gained over her by the ruffian. There were times when she seemed likely to get the better of the brute, but he finally overpowered her, and succeeded in getting his rope around her arms, and in firmly tying her to the tree, at which he had been aiming. This done, and Nelly was at the mercy of his merciless lash; and now, what followed, I have no heart to describe. The cowardly creature made good his every threat; and wielded the lash with all the hot zest of furious revenge. The cries of the woman, while undergoing the terrible infliction, were mingled with those of the children, sounds which I hope the reader may never be called upon to hear. When Nelly was untied, her back was covered with blood. The red stripes were all over her shoulders. She was whipped—severely whipped; but she was not subdued, for she continued to denounce the overseer, and to call him every vile name. He had bruised her flesh, but had left her invincible spirit undaunted. Such floggings are seldom repeated by the same overseer. They prefer to whip those who are most easily whipped. The old doctrine that submission is the very best cure for outrage and wrong, does not hold good on the slave plantation. He is whipped oftenest, who is whipped easiest; and that slave who has the courage to stand up for himself against the overseer, although he may have many hard stripes at the first, becomes, in the end, a freeman, even though he sustain the formal relation of a slave. "You can shoot me but you can't whip me," said a slave to Rigby Hopkins; and the result was that he was neither whipped nor shot. If the latter had been his fate, it would have been less deplorable than the living and lingering death to which cowardly and slavish souls are subjected. I do not know that Mr. Sevier ever undertook to whip Nelly again. He probably never did, for it was not long after his attempt to subdue her, that he was taken sick, and died. The wretched man died as he had lived, unrepentant; and it was said—with how much truth I know not—that in the very last hours of his life, his ruling passion showed itself, and that when wrestling with death, he was uttering horrid oaths, and flourishing the cowskin, as though he was tearing the flesh off some helpless slave. One thing is certain, that when he was in health, it was enough to chill the blood, and to stiffen the hair of an ordinary man, to hear Mr. Sevier talk. Nature, or his cruel habits, had given to his face an expression of unusual savageness, even for a slave-driver. Tobacco and rage had worn his teeth short, and nearly every sentence that escaped their compressed grating, was commenced or concluded with some outburst of profanity. His presence made the field alike the field of blood, and of blasphemy. Hated for his cruelty, despised for his cowardice, his death was deplored by no one outside his own house—if indeed it was deplored there; it was regarded by the slaves as a merciful interposition of Providence. Never went there a man to the grave loaded with heavier curses. Mr. Sevier's place was promptly taken by a Mr. Hopkins, and the change was quite a relief, he being a very different man. He was, in all respects, a better man than his predecessor; as good as any man can be, and yet be an overseer. His course was characterized by no extraordinary cruelty; and when he whipped a slave, as he sometimes did, he seemed to take no especial pleasure in it, but, on the contrary, acted as though he felt it to be a mean business. Mr. Hopkins stayed but a short time; his place much to the regret of the slaves generally—was taken by a Mr. Gore, of whom more will be said hereafter. It is enough, for the present, to say, that he was no improvement on Mr. Sevier, except that he was less noisy and less profane.

I have already referred to the business-like aspect of Col. Lloyd's plantation. This business-like appearance was much increased on the two days at the end of each month, when the slaves from the different farms came to get their monthly allowance of meal and meat. These were gala days for the slaves, and there was much rivalry among them as to *who* should be elected to go up to the great house farm for the allowance, and, indeed, to attend to any business at this (for them) the capital. The beauty and grandeur of the place, its numerous slave population, and the fact that Harry, Peter and Jake the sailors of the sloop— almost always kept, privately, little trinkets which they bought at Baltimore, to sell, made it a privilege to come to the great house farm. Being selected, too, for this office, was deemed a high honor. It was taken as a proof of confidence and favor; but, probably, the chief motive of the competitors for the place, was, a desire to break the dull monotony of the field, and to get beyond the overseer's eye and lash. Once on the road with an ox team, and seated on the tongue of his cart, with no overseer to look after him, the slave was comparatively free; and, if thoughtful, he had time to think. Slaves are generally expected to sing as well as to work. A silent slave is not liked by masters or overseers. *"Make a noise," "make a noise,"* and *"bear a hand,"* are the words usually addressed to the slaves when there is silence amongst them. This may account for the almost constant singing heard in the southern states. There was, generally, more or less singing among the teamsters, as it was one means of letting the overseer know where they were, and that they were moving on with the work. But, on allowance day, those who visited the great house farm were peculiarly excited and noisy. While on their way, they would make the dense old woods, for miles around, reverberate with their wild notes. These were not always merry because they were wild. On the contrary, they were mostly of a plaintive cast, and told a tale of grief and sorrow. In the most boisterous outbursts of rapturous sentiment, there was ever a tinge of deep melancholy. I have never heard any songs like those anywhere since I left slavery, except when in Ireland. There I heard the same *wailing notes*, and was much affected by them. It was during the famine of 1845-6. In all the songs of the slaves, there was ever some expression in praise of the great house farm; something which would flatter the pride of the owner, and, possibly, draw a favorable glance from him.

> I am going away to the great house farm,
> O yea! O yea! O yea!
> My old master is a good old master,
> O yea! O yea! O yea!

This they would sing, with other words of their own improvising—jargon to others, but full of meaning to themselves. I have sometimes thought, that the mere hearing of those songs would do more to impress truly spiritual-minded men and women with the soul-crushing and death-dealing character of slavery, than the reading of whole volumes of its mere physical cruelties. They speak to the heart and to the soul of the thoughtful. I cannot better express my sense of them now, than ten years ago, when, in sketching my life, I thus spoke of this feature of my plantation experience:

I did not, when a slave, understand the deep meanings of those rude, and apparently incoherent songs. I was myself within the circle, so that I neither saw or heard as those without might see and hear. They told a tale which was then altogether beyond my feeble comprehension; they were tones, loud, long and deep, breathing the prayer and complaint of souls boiling over with the bitterest anguish. Every tone was a testimony against slavery, and a prayer to God for deliverance from chains. The hearing of those wild notes always depressed my spirits, and filled my heart with ineffable sadness. The mere recurrence, even now, afflicts my spirit, and while I am writing these lines, my tears are falling. To those songs I trace my first glimmering conceptions of the dehumanizing character of slavery. I can never get rid of that conception. Those songs still follow me, to deepen my hatred of slavery, and quicken my sympathies for my brethren in bonds. If any one wishes to be impressed with a sense of the soul-killing power of slavery, let him go to Col. Lloyd's plantation, and, on allowance day, place himself in the deep, pine woods, and there let him, in silence, thoughtfully analyze the sounds that shall pass through the chambers of his soul, and if he is not thus impressed, it will only be because "there is no flesh in his obdurate heart."

The remark is not unfrequently made, that slaves are the most contended and happy laborers in the world. They dance and sing, and make all manner of joyful noises—so they do; but it is a great mistake to suppose them happy because they sing. The songs of the slave represent the sorrows, rather than the joys, of his heart; and he is relieved by them, only as an aching heart is relieved by its tears. Such is the constitution of the human mind, that, when pressed to extremes, it often avails itself of the most opposite methods. Extremes meet in mind as in matter. When the slaves on board of the "Pearl" were overtaken, arrested, and carried to prison—their hopes for freedom blasted—as they marched in chains they sang, and found (as Emily Edmunson tells us) a melancholy relief in singing. The singing of a man cast away on a desolate island, might be as appropriately considered an evidence of his contentment and happiness, as the singing of a slave. Sorrow and desolation have their songs, as well as joy and peace. Slaves sing more to *make* themselves happy, than to express their happiness.

It is the boast of slaveholders, that their slaves enjoy more of the physical comforts of life than the peasantry of any country in the world. My experience contradicts this. The men and the women slaves on Col. Lloyd's farm, received, as their monthly allowance of food, eight pounds of pickled pork, or their equivalent in fish. The pork was often tainted, and the fish was of the poorest quality—herrings, which would bring very little if offered for sale in any northern market. With their pork or fish, they had one bushel of Indian meal—unbolted—of which quite fifteen per cent was fit only to feed pigs. With this, one pint of salt was given; and this was the entire monthly allowance of a full grown slave, working constantly in the open field, from morning until night, every day in the month except Sunday, and living on a fraction more than a quarter of a pound of meat per day, and less than a peck of corn-meal per week. There is no kind of work that a man can do which requires a better supply of food to prevent physical exhaustion, than the field-work of a slave. So much for the slave's allowance of food; now for his raiment. The yearly allowance of clothing for the slaves on this plantation, consisted of two tow-linen shirts—such linen as the coarsest crash towels are made of; one pair of trowsers of the same material, for summer, and a pair of trowsers and a jacket of woolen, most slazily put together, for winter; one pair of yarn stockings, and one pair of shoes of the coarsest description. The slave's entire apparel could not have cost more than eight dollars per year. The allowance of food and clothing for the little children, was committed to their mothers, or to the older slavewomen having the care of them. Children who were unable to work in the field, had neither shoes, stockings, jackets nor trowsers given them. Their clothing consisted of two coarse tow-linen shirts—already described—per year; and when these failed them, as they often did, they went naked until the next allowance day. Flocks of little children from five to ten years old, might be seen on Col. Lloyd's plantation, as destitute of clothing as any little heathen on the west coast of Africa; and this, not merely during the summer months, but during the frosty weather of March. The little girls were no better off than the boys; all were nearly in a state of nudity.

As to beds to sleep on, they were known to none of the field hands; nothing but a coarse blanket—not so good as those used in the north to cover horses—was given them, and this only to the men and women. The children stuck themselves in holes and corners, about the quarters; often in the corner of the huge chimneys, with their feet in the ashes to keep them warm. The want of beds, however, was not considered a very great privation. Time to sleep was of far greater importance, for, when the day's work is done, most of the slaves have their washing, mending and cooking to do; and, having few or none of the ordinary facilities for doing such things, very many of their sleeping hours are consumed in necessary preparations for the duties of the coming day.

The sleeping apartments—if they may be called such—have little regard to comfort or decency. Old and young, male and female, married and single, drop down upon the common clay floor, each covering up with his or her blanket,— the only protection they have from cold or exposure. The night, however, is shortened at both ends. The slaves work often as long as they can see, and are late in cooking and mending for the coming day; and, at the first gray streak of morning, they are summoned to the field by the driver's horn.

More slaves are whipped for oversleeping than for any other fault. Neither age nor sex finds any favor. The overseer stands at the quarter door, armed with stick and cowskin, ready to whip any who may be a few minutes behind time. When the horn is blown, there is a rush for the door, and the hindermost one is sure to get a blow from the overseer. Young mothers who worked in the field, were allowed an hour, about ten o'clock in the morning, to go home to nurse their children. Sometimes they were compelled to take their children with them, and to leave them in the corner of the fences, to prevent loss of time in nursing them. The overseer generally rides about the field on horseback. A cowskin and a hickory stick are his constant companions. The cowskin is a kind of whip seldom seen in the northern states. It is made entirely of untanned, but dried, ox hide, and is about as hard as a piece of well-seasoned live oak. It is made of various sizes, but the usual length is about three feet. The part held in the hand is nearly an inch in thickness; and, from the extreme end of the butt or handle, the cowskin tapers its whole length to a point. This makes it quite elastic and springy. A blow with it, on the hardest back, will gash the flesh, and make the blood start. Cowskins are painted red, blue and green, and are the favorite slave whip. I think this whip worse than the "cat-o'nine-tails." It condenses the whole strength of the arm to a single point, and comes with a spring that makes the air whistle. It is a terrible instrument, and is so handy, that the overseer can always have it on his person, and ready for use. The temptation to use it is ever strong; and an overseer can, if disposed, always have cause for using it. With him, it is literally a word and a blow, and, in most cases, the blow comes first.

As a general rule, slaves do not come to the quarters for either breakfast or dinner, but take their "ash cake" with them, and eat it in the field. This was so on the home plantation; probably, because the distance from the quarter to the field, was sometimes two, and even three miles.

The dinner of the slaves consisted of a huge piece of ash cake, and a small piece of pork, or two salt herrings. Not having ovens, nor any suitable cooking utensils, the slaves mixed their meal with a little water, to such thickness that a spoon would stand erect in it; and, after the wood had burned away to coals and ashes, they would place the dough between oak leaves and lay it carefully in the ashes, completely covering it; hence, the bread is called ash cake. The surface of this peculiar bread is covered with ashes, to the depth of a sixteenth part of an inch, and the ashes, certainly, do not make it very grateful to the teeth, nor render it very palatable. The bran, or coarse part of the meal, is baked with the fine, and bright scales run through the bread. This bread, with its ashes and bran, would disgust and choke a northern man, but it is quite liked by the slaves. They eat it with avidity, and are more concerned about the quantity than about the quality. They are far too scantily provided for, and are worked too steadily, to be much concerned for the quality of their food. The few minutes allowed them at dinner time, after partaking of their coarse repast, are variously spent. Some lie down on the "turning row," and go to sleep; others draw together, and talk; and others are at work with needle and thread, mending their tattered garments. Sometimes you may hear a wild, hoarse laugh arise from a circle, and often a song. Soon, however, the overseer comes dashing through the field. "*Tumble up! Tumble up*, and to *work, work*," is the cry; and, now, from twelve o'clock (mid-day) till dark, the human cattle are in motion, wielding their clumsy hoes; hurried on by no hope of reward, no sense of gratitude, no love of children, no prospect of bettering their condition; nothing, save the dread and terror of the slave-driver's lash. So goes one day, and so comes and goes another.

But, let us now leave the rough usage of the field, where vulgar coarseness and brutal cruelty spread themselves and flourish, rank as weeds in the tropics; where a vile wretch, in the shape of a man, rides, walks, or struts about, dealing blows, and leaving gashes on broken-spirited men and helpless women, for thirty dollars per month—a business so horrible, hardening and disgraceful, that, rather, than engage in it, a decent man would blow his own brains out— and let the reader view with me the equally wicked, but less repulsive aspects of slave life; where pride and pomp roll luxuriously at ease; where the toil of a thousand men supports a single family in easy idleness and sin. This is the great house; it is the home of the LLOYDS! Some idea of its splendor has already been given—and, it is here that we shall find that height of luxury which is the opposite of that depth of poverty and physical wretchedness that we have just now been contemplating. But, there is this difference in the two extremes; viz:

that in the case of the slave, the miseries and hardships of his lot are imposed by others, and, in the master's case, they are imposed by himself. The slave is a subject, subjected by others; the slaveholder is a subject, but he is the author of his own subjection. There is more truth in the saying, that slavery is a greater evil to the master than to the slave, than many, who utter it, suppose. The self-executing laws of eternal justice follow close on the heels of the evil-doer here, as well as elsewhere; making escape from all its penalties impossible. But, let others philosophize; it is my province here to relate and describe; only allowing myself a word or two, occasionally, to assist the reader in the proper understanding of the facts narrated.

CHAPTER VII

Life in the Great House

The close-fisted stinginess that fed the poor slave on coarse corn-meal and tainted meat; that clothed him in crashy tow-linen, and hurried him to toil through the field, in all weathers, with wind and rain beating through his tattered garments; that scarcely gave even the young slave-mother time to nurse her hungry infant in the fence corner; wholly vanishes on approaching the sacred precincts of the great house, the home of the Lloyds. There the scriptural phrase finds an exact illustration; the highly favored inmates of this mansion are literally arrayed "in purple and fine linen," and fare sumptuously every day! The table groans under the heavy and blood-bought luxuries gathered with painstaking care, at home and abroad. Fields, forests, rivers and seas, are made tributary here. Immense wealth, and its lavish expenditure, fill the great house with all that can please the eye, or tempt the taste. Here, appetite, not food, is the great *desideratum*. Fish, flesh and fowl, are here in profusion. Chickens, of all breeds; ducks, of all kinds, wild and tame, the common, and the huge Muscovite; Guinea fowls, turkeys, geese, and pea fowls, are in their several pens, fat and fatting for the destined vortex. The graceful swan, the mongrels, the black-necked wild goose; partridges, quails, pheasants and pigeons; choice water fowl, with all their strange varieties, are caught in this huge family net. Beef, veal, mutton and venison, of the most select kinds and quality, roll bounteously to this grand consumer. The teeming riches of the Chesapeake bay, its rock, perch, drums, crocus, trout, oysters, crabs, and terrapin, are drawn hither to adorn the glittering table of the great house. The dairy, too, probably the finest on the Eastern Shore of Maryland—supplied by cattle of the best English stock, imported for the purpose, pours its rich donations of fragant cheese, golden butter, and delicious cream, to heighten the attraction of the gorgeous, unending round of feasting. Nor are the fruits of the earth forgotten or neglected. The fertile garden, many acres in size, constituting a separate establishment, distinct from the common farm—with its scientific gardener, imported from Scotland (a Mr. McDermott) with four men under his direction, was not behind, either in the abundance or in the delicacy of its contributions to the same full board. The tender asparagus, the succulent celery, and the delicate cauliflower; egg plants, beets, lettuce, parsnips, peas, and French beans, early and late; radishes, cantelopes, melons of all kinds; the fruits and flowers of all climes and of all descriptions, from the hardy apple of the north, to the lemon and orange of the south, culminated at this point. Baltimore gathered figs, raisins, almonds and juicy grapes from Spain. Wines and brandies from France; teas of various flavor, from China; and rich, aromatic coffee from Java, all conspired to swell the tide of high life, where pride and indolence rolled and lounged in magnificence and satiety.

Behind the tall-backed and elaborately wrought chairs, stand the servants, men and maidens—fifteen in number—discriminately selected, not only with a view to their industry and faithfulness, but with special regard to their personal appearance, their graceful agility and captivating address. Some of these are armed with fans, and are fanning reviving breezes toward the over-heated brows of the alabaster ladies; others watch with eager eye, and with fawn-like step anticipate and supply wants before they are sufficiently formed to be announced by word or sign.

These servants constituted a sort of black aristocracy on Col. Lloyd's plantation. They resembled the field hands in nothing, except in color, and in this they held the advantage of a velvet-like glossiness, rich and beautiful. The hair, too, showed the same advantage. The delicate colored maid rustled in the scarcely worn silk of her young mistress, while the servant men were equally well attired from the over-flowing wardrobe of their young masters; so that, in dress, as well as in form and feature, in manner and speech, in tastes and habits, the distance between these favored few, and the sorrow and hunger-smitten multitudes of the quarter and the field, was immense; and this is seldom passed over.

Let us now glance at the stables and the carriage house, and we shall find the same evidences of pride and luxurious extravagance. Here are three splendid coaches, soft within and lustrous without. Here, too, are gigs, phaetons, barouches, sulkeys and sleighs. Here are saddles and harnesses—beautifully wrought and silver mounted—kept with every care. In the stable you will find, kept only for pleasure, full thirty-five horses, of the most approved blood for speed and beauty. There are two men here constantly employed in taking care of these horses. One of these men must be always in the stable, to answer every call from the great house. Over the way from the stable, is a house built expressly for the hounds—a pack of twenty-five or thirty—whose fare would have made glad the heart of a dozen slaves. Horses and hounds are not the only consumers of the slave's toil. There was practiced, at the Lloyd's, a hospitality which would have astonished and charmed any health-seeking northern divine or merchant, who might have chanced to share it. Viewed from his own table, and *not* from the field, the colonel was a model of generous hospitality. His house was, literally, a hotel, for weeks during the summer months. At these times, especially, the air was freighted with the rich fumes of baking, boiling, roasting and broiling. The odors I shared with the winds; but the meats were under a more stringent monopoly except that, occasionally, I got a cake from Mas' Daniel. In Mas' Daniel I had a friend at court, from whom I learned many things which my eager curiosity was excited to know. I always knew when company was expected, and who they were, although I was an outsider, being the property, not of Col. Lloyd, but of a servant of the wealthy colonel. On these occasions, all that pride, taste and money could do, to dazzle and charm, was done.

Who could say that the servants of Col. Lloyd were not well clad and cared for, after witnessing one of his magnificent entertainments? Who could say that they did not seem to glory in being the slaves of such a master? Who, but a fanatic, could get up any sympathy for persons whose every movement was agile, easy and graceful, and who evinced a consciousness of high superiority? And who would ever venture to suspect that Col. Lloyd was subject to the troubles of ordinary mortals? Master and slave seem alike in their glory here? Can it all be seeming? Alas! it may only be a sham at last! This immense wealth; this gilded splendor; this profusion of luxury; this exemption from toil; this life of ease; this sea of plenty; aye, what of it all? Are the pearly gates of happiness and sweet content flung open to such suitors? *far from it!* The poor slave, on his hard, pine plank, but scantily covered with his thin blanket, sleeps more soundly than the feverish voluptuary who reclines upon his feather bed and downy pillow. Food, to the indolent lounger, is poison, not sustenance. Lurking beneath all their dishes, are invisible spirits of evil, ready to feed the self-deluded gormandizers which aches, pains, fierce temper, uncontrolled passions, dyspepsia, rheumatism, lumbago and gout; and of these the Lloyds got their full share. To the pampered love of ease, there is no resting place. What is pleasant today, is repulsive tomorrow; what is soft now, is hard at another time; what is sweet in the morning, is bitter in the evening. Neither to the wicked, nor to the idler, is there any solid peace: *"Troubled, like the restless sea."*

I had excellent opportunities of witnessing the restless discontent and the capricious irritation of the Lloyds. My fondness for horses—not peculiar to me more than to other boys attracted me, much of the time, to the stables. This establishment was especially under the care of "old" and "young" Barney—father and son. Old Barney was a fine looking old man, of a brownish complexion, who was quite portly, and wore a dignified aspect for a slave. He was, evidently, much devoted to his profession, and held his office an honorable one. He was a farrier as well as an ostler; he could bleed, remove lampers from the mouths of the horses, and was well instructed in horse medicines. No one on the farm knew, so well as Old Barney, what to do with a sick horse. But his gifts and acquirements were of little advantage to him. His office was by no means an enviable one. He often got presents, but he got stripes as well; for in nothing was Col. Lloyd more unreasonable and exacting, than in respect to the management of his pleasure horses. Any supposed inattention to these animals were sure to be visited with degrading punishment. His horses and dogs fared better than his men. Their beds must be softer and cleaner than those of his human cattle. No excuse could shield Old Barney, if the colonel only suspected something wrong about his horses; and, consequently, he was often punished when faultless. It was absolutely painful to listen to the many unreasonable and fretful scoldings, poured out at the stable, by Col. Lloyd, his sons and sons-in-law. Of the latter, he had three—Messrs. Nicholson, Winder and Lownes. These all lived at the great house a portion of the year, and enjoyed the luxury of whipping the servants when they pleased, which was by no means unfrequently. A horse was seldom brought out of the stable to which no objection could be raised. "There was dust in his hair;" "there was a twist in his reins;" "his mane did not lie straight;" "he had not been properly grained;" "his head did not look well;" "his fore-top was not combed out;" "his fetlocks had not been properly trimmed;" something was always wrong. Listening to complaints, however groundless, Barney must stand, hat in hand, lips sealed, never answering a word. He must make no reply, no explanation; the judgment of the master must be deemed infallible, for his power is absolute and irresponsible. In a free state, a master, thus complaining without cause, of his ostler, might be told—"Sir, I am sorry I cannot please you, but, since I have done the best I can, your remedy is to dismiss me." Here, however, the ostler must stand, listen and tremble. One of the most heart-saddening and humiliating scenes I ever witnessed, was the whipping of Old Barney, by Col. Lloyd himself. Here were two men, both advanced in years; there were the silvery locks of Col. L., and there was the bald and toil-worn brow of Old Barney; master and slave; superior and inferior here, but *equals* at the bar of God; and, in the common course of events, they must both soon meet in another world, in a world where all distinctions, except those based on obedience and disobedience, are blotted out forever. "Uncover your head!" said the imperious master; he was obeyed. "Take off your jacket, you old rascal!" and off came Barney's jacket. "Down on your knees!" down knelt the old man, his shoulders bare, his bald head glistening in the sun, and his aged knees on the cold, damp ground. In his humble and debasing attitude, the master—that master to whom he had given the best years and the best strength of his life—came forward, and laid on thirty lashes, with his horse whip. The old man bore it patiently, to the last, answering each blow with a slight shrug of the shoulders, and a groan. I cannot think that Col. Lloyd succeeded in marring the flesh of Old Barney very seriously, for the whip was a light, riding whip; but the spectacle of an aged man—a husband and a father—humbly kneeling before a worm of the dust, surprised and shocked me at the time; and since I have grown old enough to think on the wickedness of slavery, few facts have been of more value to me than this, to which I was a witness. It reveals slavery in its true color, and in its maturity of repulsive hatefulness. I owe it to truth, however, to say, that this was the first and the last time I ever saw Old Barney, or any other slave, compelled to kneel to receive a whipping.

I saw, at the stable, another incident, which I will relate, as it is illustrative of a phase of slavery to which I have already referred in another connection. Besides two other coachmen, Col. Lloyd owned one named William, who, strangely enough, was often called by his surname, Wilks, by white and colored people on the home plantation. Wilks was a very fine looking man. He was about as white as anybody on the plantation; and in manliness of form, and comeliness of features, he bore a very striking resemblance to Mr. Murray Lloyd. It was whispered, and pretty generally admitted as a fact, that William Wilks was a son of Col. Lloyd, by a highly favored slave-woman, who was still on the plantation. There were many reasons for believing this whisper, not only in William's appearance, but in the undeniable freedom which he enjoyed over all others, and his apparent consciousness of being something more than a slave to his master. It was notorious, too, that William had a deadly enemy in Murray Lloyd, whom he so much resembled, and that the latter greatly worried his father with importunities to sell William. Indeed, he gave his father no rest until he did sell him, to Austin Woldfolk, the great slave-trader at that time. Before selling him, however, Mr. L. tried what giving William a whipping would do, toward making things smooth; but this was a failure. It was a compromise, and defeated itself; for, immediately after the infliction, the heart-sickened colonel atoned to William for the abuse, by giving him a gold watch and chain. Another fact, somewhat curious, is, that though sold to the remorseless *Woldfolk*, taken in irons to Baltimore and cast into prison, with a view to being driven to the south, William, by *some* means—always a mystery to me—outbid all his purchasers, paid for himself, *and now resides in Baltimore, a* FREEMAN. Is there not room to suspect, that, as the gold watch was presented to atone for the whipping, a purse of gold was given him by the same hand, with which to effect his purchase, as an atonement for the indignity involved in selling his own flesh and blood. All the circumstances of William, on the great house farm, show him to have occupied a different position from the other slaves, and, certainly, there is nothing in the supposed hostility of slaveholders to amalgamation, to forbid the supposition that William Wilks was the son of Edward Lloyd. *Practical* amalgamation is common in every neighborhood where I have been in slavery.

Col. Lloyd was not in the way of knowing much of the real opinions and feelings of his slaves respecting him. The distance between him and them was far too great to admit of such knowledge. His slaves were so numerous, that he did not know them when he saw them. Nor, indeed, did all his slaves know him. In this respect, he was inconveniently rich. It is reported of him, that, while riding along the road one day, he met a colored man, and addressed him in the usual way of speaking to colored people on the public highways of the south: "Well, boy, who do you belong to?" "To Col. Lloyd," replied the slave. "Well, does the colonel treat you well?" "No, sir," was the ready reply. "What? does he work you too hard?" "Yes, sir." "Well, don't he give enough to eat?" "Yes, sir, he gives me enough, such as it is." The colonel, after ascertaining where the slave belonged, rode on; the slave also went on about his business, not dreaming that he had been conversing with his master. He thought, said and heard nothing more of the matter, until two or three weeks afterwards. The poor man was then informed by his overseer, that, for having found fault with his master, he was now to be sold to a Georgia trader. He was immediately chained and handcuffed; and thus, without a moment's warning he was snatched away, and forever sundered from his family and friends, by a hand more unrelenting than that of death. *This* is the penalty of telling the simple truth, in answer to a series of plain questions. It is partly in consequence of such facts, that slaves, when inquired of as to their condition and the character of their masters, almost invariably say they are contented, and that their masters are kind. Slaveholders have been known to send spies among their slaves, to ascertain, if possible, their views and feelings in regard to their condition. The frequency of this had the effect to establish among the slaves the maxim, that a still tongue makes a wise head. They suppress the truth rather than take the consequence of telling it, and, in so doing, they prove themselves a part of the human family. If they have anything to say of their master, it is, generally, something in his favor, especially when speaking to strangers. I was frequently asked, while a slave, if I had a kind master, and I do not remember ever to have given a negative reply. Nor did I, when pursuing this course, consider myself as uttering what was utterly false; for I always measured the kindness of my master by the standard of kindness set up by slaveholders around us. However, slaves are like other people, and imbibe similar prejudices. They are apt to think *their condition* better than that of others. Many, under the influence of this prejudice, think their own masters are better than the masters of other slaves; and this, too, in some cases, when the very reverse is true. Indeed, it is not uncommon for slaves even to fall out and quarrel among themselves about the relative kindness of their masters, contending for the superior goodness of his own over that of others. At the very same time, they mutually execrate their masters, when viewed separately. It was so on our plantation. When Col. Lloyd's slaves met those of Jacob Jepson, they seldom parted without a quarrel about their masters; Col. Lloyd's slaves contending that he was the richest, and Mr. Jepson's slaves that he was the smartest, man of the two. Col. Lloyd's slaves would boost his ability to buy and sell Jacob Jepson; Mr. Jepson's slaves would boast his ability to whip Col. Lloyd. These quarrels would almost always end in a fight between the parties; those that beat were supposed to have gained the point at issue. They seemed to think that the greatness of their masters was transferable to themselves. To be a SLAVE, was thought to be bad enough; but to be a *poor man's* slave, was deemed a disgrace, indeed.

CHAPTER VIII

A Chapter of Horrors

AUSTIN GORE—A SKETCH OF HIS CHARACTER—OVERSEERS AS A CLASS—THEIR PECULIAR CHARACTERISTICS—THE MARKED INDIVIDUALITY OF AUSTIN GORE—HIS SENSE OF DUTY—HOW HE WHIPPED—MURDER OF POOR DENBY—HOW IT OCCURRED—SENSATION—HOW GORE MADE PEACE WITH COL. LLOYD—THE MURDER UNPUNISHED—ANOTHER DREADFUL MURDER NARRATED—NO LAWS FOR THE PROTECTION OF SLAVES CAN BE ENFORCED IN THE SOUTHERN STATES.

As I have already intimated elsewhere, the slaves on Col. Lloyd's plantation, whose hard lot, under Mr. Sevier, the reader has already noticed and deplored, were not permitted to enjoy the comparatively moderate rule of Mr. Hopkins. The latter was succeeded by a very different man. The name of the new overseer was Austin Gore. Upon this individual I would fix particular attention; for under his rule there was more suffering from violence and bloodshed than had—according to the older slaves ever been experienced before on this plantation. I confess, I hardly know how to bring this man fitly before the reader. He was, it is true, an overseer, and possessed, to a large extent, the peculiar characteristics of his class; yet, to call him merely an overseer, would not give the reader a fair notion of the man. I speak of overseers as a class. They are such. They are as distinct from the slaveholding gentry of the south, as are the fishwomen of Paris, and the coal-heavers of London, distinct from other members of society. They constitute a separate fraternity at the south, not less marked than is the fraternity of Park Lane bullies in New York. They have been arranged and classified by that great law of attraction, which determines the spheres and affinities of men; which ordains, that men, whose malign and brutal propensities predominate over their moral and intellectual endowments, shall, naturally, fall into those employments which promise the largest gratification to those predominating instincts or propensities. The office of overseer takes this raw material of vulgarity and brutality, and stamps it as a distinct class of

155

southern society. But, in this class, as in all other classes, there are characters of marked individuality, even while they bear a general resemblance to the mass. Mr. Gore was one of those, to whom a general characterization would do no manner of justice. He was an overseer; but he was something more. With the malign and tyrannical qualities of an overseer, he combined something of the lawful master. He had the artfulness and the mean ambition of his class; but he was wholly free from the disgusting swagger and noisy bravado of his fraternity. There was an easy air of independence about him; a calm self-possession, and a sternness of glance, which might well daunt hearts less timid than those of poor slaves, accustomed from childhood and through life to cower before a driver's lash. The home plantation of Col. Lloyd afforded an ample field for the exercise of the qualifications for overseership, which he possessed in such an eminent degree.

Mr. Gore was one of those overseers, who could torture the slightest word or look into impudence; he had the nerve, not only to resent, but to punish, promptly and severely. He never allowed himself to be answered back, by a slave. In this, he was as lordly and as imperious as Col. Edward Lloyd, himself; acting always up to the maxim, practically maintained by slaveholders, that it is better that a dozen slaves suffer under the lash, without fault, than that the master or the overseer should *seem* to have been wrong in the presence of the slave. *Everything must be absolute here.* Guilty or not guilty, it is enough to be accused, to be sure of a flogging. The very presence of this man Gore was painful, and I shunned him as I would have shunned a rattlesnake. His piercing, black eyes, and sharp, shrill voice, ever awakened sensations of terror among the slaves. For so young a man (I describe him as he was, twenty-five or thirty years ago) Mr. Gore was singularly reserved and grave in the presence of slaves. He indulged in no jokes, said no funny things, and kept his own counsels. Other overseers, how brutal soever they might be, were, at times, inclined to gain favor with the slaves, by indulging a little pleasantry; but Gore was never known to be guilty of any such weakness. He was always the cold, distant, unapproachable *overseer* of Col. Edward Lloyd's plantation, and needed no higher pleasure than was involved in a faithful discharge of the duties of his office. When he whipped, he seemed to do so from a sense of duty, and feared no consequences. What Hopkins did reluctantly, Gore did with alacrity. There was a stern will, an iron-like reality, about this Gore, which would have easily made him the chief of a band of pirates, had his environments been favorable to such a course of life. All the coolness, savage barbarity and freedom from moral restraint, which are necessary in the character of a pirate-chief, centered, I think, in this man Gore. Among many other deeds of shocking cruelty which he perpetrated, while I was at Mr. Lloyd's, was the murder of a young colored man, named Denby. He was sometimes called Bill Denby, or Demby; (I write from sound, and the sounds on Lloyd's plantation are not very certain.) I knew him well. He was a powerful young man, full of animal spirits, and, so far as I know, he was among the most valuable of Col. Lloyd's slaves. In something—I know not what—he offended this Mr. Austin Gore, and, in accordance with the custom of the latter, he under took to flog him. He gave Denby but few stripes; the latter broke away from him and plunged into the creek, and, standing there to the depth of his neck in water, he refused to come out at the order of the overseer; whereupon, for this refusal, *Gore shot him dead!* It is said that Gore gave Denby three calls, telling him that if he did not obey the last call, he would shoot him. When the third call was given, Denby stood his ground firmly; and this raised the question, in the minds of the by-standing slaves—"Will he dare to shoot?" Mr. Gore, without further parley, and without making any further effort to induce Denby to come out of the water, raised his gun deliberately to his face, took deadly aim at his standing victim, and, in an instant, poor Denby was numbered with the dead. His mangled body sank out of sight, and only his warm, red blood marked the place where he had stood.

This devilish outrage, this fiendish murder, produced, as it was well calculated to do, a tremendous sensation. A thrill of horror flashed through every soul on the plantation, if I may except the guilty wretch who had committed the hell-black deed. While the slaves generally were panic-struck, and howling with alarm, the murderer himself was calm and collected, and appeared as though nothing unusual had happened. The atrocity roused my old master, and he spoke out, in reprobation of it; but the whole thing proved to be less than a nine days' wonder. Both Col. Lloyd and my old master arraigned Gore for his cruelty in the matter, but this amounted to nothing. His reply, or explanation—as I remember to have heard it at the time was, that the extraordinary expedient was demanded by necessity; that Denby had become unmanageable; that he had set a dangerous example to the other slaves; and that, without some such prompt measure as that to which he had resorted, were adopted, there would be an end to all rule and order on the plantation. That very convenient covert for all manner of cruelty and outrage that cowardly alarm-cry, that the slaves would *"take the place,"* was pleaded, in extenuation of this revolting crime, just as it had been cited in defense of a thousand similar ones. He argued, that if one slave refused to be corrected, and was allowed to escape with his life, when he had been told that he should lose it if he persisted in his course, the other slaves would soon copy his example; the result of which would be, the freedom of the slaves, and the enslavement of the whites. I have every reason to believe that Mr. Gore's defense, or explanation, was deemed satisfactory—at least to Col. Lloyd. He was continued in his office on the plantation. His fame as an overseer went abroad, and his horrid crime was not even submitted to judicial investigation. The murder was committed in the presence of slaves, and they, of course, could neither institute a suit, nor testify against the murderer. His bare word would go further in a court of law, than the united testimony of ten thousand black witnesses.

All that Mr. Gore had to do, was to make his peace with Col. Lloyd. This done, and the guilty perpetrator of one of the most foul murders goes unwhipped of justice, and uncensured by the community in which he lives. Mr. Gore lived in St. Michael's, Talbot county, when I left Maryland; if he is still alive he probably yet resides there; and I have no reason to doubt that he is now as highly esteemed, and as greatly respected, as though his guilty soul had never been stained with innocent blood. I am well aware that what I have now written will by some be branded as false and malicious. It will be denied, not only that such a thing ever did transpire, as I have now narrated, but that such a thing could happen in *Maryland*. I can only say—believe it or not—that I have said nothing but the literal truth, gainsay it who may.

I speak advisedly when I say this,—that killing a slave, or any colored person, in Talbot county, Maryland, is not treated as a crime, either by the courts or the community. Mr. Thomas Lanman, ship carpenter, of St. Michael's, killed two slaves, one of whom he butchered with a hatchet, by knocking his brains out. He used to boast of the commission of the awful and bloody deed. I have heard him do so, laughingly, saying, among other things, that he was the only benefactor of his country in the company, and that when "others would do as much as he had done, we should be relieved of the d—d niggers."

As an evidence of the reckless disregard of human life where the life is that of a slave I may state the notorious fact, that the wife of Mr. Giles Hicks, who lived but a short distance from Col. Lloyd's, with her own hands murdered my wife's cousin, a young girl between fifteen and sixteen years of age—mutilating her person in a most shocking manner. The atrocious woman, in the paroxysm of her wrath, not content with murdering her victim, literally mangled her face, and broke her breast bone. Wild, however, and infuriated as she was, she took the precaution to cause the slave-girl to be buried; but the facts of the case coming abroad, very speedily led to the disinterment of the remains of the murdered slave-girl. A coroner's jury was assembled, who decided that the girl had come to her death by severe beating. It was ascertained that the offense for which this girl was thus hurried out of the world, was this: she had been set that night, and several preceding nights, to mind Mrs. Hicks's baby, and having fallen into a sound sleep, the baby cried, waking Mrs. Hicks, but not the slave-girl. Mrs. Hicks, becoming infuriated at the girl's tardiness, after calling several times, jumped from her bed and seized a piece of fire-wood from the fireplace; and then, as she lay fast asleep, she deliberately pounded in her skull and breast-bone, and thus ended her life. I will not say that this most horrid murder produced no sensation in the community. It *did* produce a sensation; but, incredible to tell, the moral sense of the community was blunted too entirely by the ordinary nature of slavery horrors, to bring the murderess to punishment. A warrant was issued for her arrest, but, for some reason or other, that warrant was never served. Thus did Mrs. Hicks not only escape condign punishment, but even the pain and mortification of being arraigned before a court of justice.

Whilst I am detailing the bloody deeds that took place during my stay on Col. Lloyd's plantation, I will briefly narrate another dark transaction, which occurred about the same time as the murder of Denby by Mr. Gore.

On the side of the river Wye, opposite from Col. Lloyd's, there lived a Mr. Beal Bondley, a wealthy slaveholder. In the direction of his land, and near the shore, there was an excellent oyster fishing ground, and to this, some of the slaves of Col. Lloyd occasionally resorted in their little canoes, at night, with a view to make up the deficiency of their scanty allowance of food, by the oysters that they could easily get there. This, Mr. Bondley took it into his head to regard as a trespass, and while an old man belonging to Col. Lloyd was engaged in catching a few of the many millions of oysters that lined the bottom of that creek, to satisfy his hunger, the villainous Mr. Bondley, lying in ambush, without the slightest ceremony, discharged the contents of his musket into the back and shoulders of the poor old man. As good fortune would have it, the shot did not prove mortal, and Mr. Bondley came over, the next day, to see Col. Lloyd—whether to pay him for his property, or to justify himself for what he had done, I know not; but this I *can* say, the cruel and dastardly transaction was speedily hushed up; there was very little said about it at all, and nothing was publicly done which looked like the application of the principle of justice to the man whom *chance*, only, saved from being an actual murderer. One of the commonest sayings to which my ears early became accustomed, on Col. Lloyd's plantation and elsewhere in Maryland, was, that it was *"worth but half a cent to kill a nigger, and a half a cent to bury him;"* and the facts of my experience go far to justify the practical truth of this strange proverb. Laws for the protection of the lives of the slaves, are, as they must needs be, utterly incapable of being enforced, where the very parties who are nominally protected, are not permitted to give evidence, in courts of law, against the only class of persons from whom abuse, outrage and murder might be reasonably apprehended. While I heard of numerous murders committed by slaveholders on the Eastern Shores of Maryland, I never knew a solitary instance in which a slaveholder was either hung or imprisoned for having murdered a slave. The usual pretext for killing a slave is, that the slave has offered resistance. Should a slave, when assaulted, but raise his hand in self defense, the white assaulting party is fully justified by southern, or Maryland, public opinion, in shooting the slave down. Sometimes this is done, simply because it is alleged that the slave has been saucy. But here I leave this phase of the society of my early childhood, and will relieve the kind reader of these heart-sickening details.

CHAPTER IX

Personal Treatment

MISS LUCRETIA—HER KINDNESS—HOW IT WAS MANIFESTED—"IKE"—A BATTLE WITH HIM—THE CONSEQUENCES THEREOF—MISS LUCRETIA'S BALSAM—BREAD—HOW I OBTAINED IT—BEAMS OF SUNLIGHT AMIDST THE GENERAL DARKNESS—SUFFERING FROM COLD—HOW WE TOOK OUR MEALS—ORDERS TO PREPARE FOR BALTIMORE—OVERJOYED AT THE THOUGHT OF QUITTING THE PLANTATION—EXTRAORDINARY CLEANSING—COUSIN TOM'S VERSION OF BALTIMORE—ARRIVAL THERE—KIND RECEPTION GIVEN ME BY MRS. SOPHIA AULD—LITTLE TOMMY—MY NEW POSITION—MY NEW DUTIES—A TURNING POINT IN MY HISTORY.

I have nothing cruel or shocking to relate of my own personal experience, while I remained on Col. Lloyd's plantation, at the home of my old master. An occasional cuff from Aunt Katy, and a regular whipping from old master, such as any heedless and mischievous boy might get from his father, is all that I can mention of this sort. I was not old enough to work in the field, and, there being little else than field work to perform, I had much leisure. The most I had to do, was, to drive up the cows in the evening, to keep the front yard clean, and to perform small errands for my young mistress, Lucretia Auld. I have reasons for thinking this lady was very kindly disposed toward me, and, although I was not often the object of her attention, I constantly regarded her as my friend, and was always glad when it was my privilege to do her a service. In a family where there was so much that was harsh, cold and indifferent, the slightest word or look of kindness passed, with me, for its full value. Miss Lucretia—as we all continued to call her long after her marriage—had bestowed upon me such words and looks as taught me that she pitied me, if she did not love me. In addition to words and looks, she sometimes gave me a piece of bread and butter; a thing not set down in the bill of fare, and which must have been an extra ration, planned aside from either Aunt Katy or old master, solely out of the tender regard and friendship she had for me. Then, too, I one day got into the wars with Uncle

Able's son, "Ike," and had got sadly worsted; in fact, the little rascal had struck me directly in the forehead with a sharp piece of cinder, fused with iron, from the old blacksmith's forge, which made a cross in my forehead very plainly to be seen now. The gash bled very freely, and I roared very loudly and betook myself home. The coldhearted Aunt Katy paid no attention either to my wound or my roaring, except to tell me it served me right; I had no business with Ike; it was good for me; I would now keep away *from dem Lloyd niggers.*" Miss Lucretia, in this state of the case, came forward; and, in quite a different spirit from that manifested by Aunt Katy, she called me into the parlor (an extra privilege of itself) and, without using toward me any of the hard-hearted and reproachful epithets of my kitchen tormentor, she quietly acted the good Samaritan. With her own soft hand she washed the blood from my head and face, fetched her own balsam bottle, and with the balsam wetted a nice piece of white linen, and bound up my head. The balsam was not more healing to the wound in my head, than her kindness was healing to the wounds in my spirit, made by the unfeeling words of Aunt Katy. After this, Miss Lucretia was my friend. I felt her to be such; and I have no doubt that the simple act of binding up my head, did much to awaken in her mind an interest in my welfare. It is quite true, that this interest was never very marked, and it seldom showed itself in anything more than in giving me a piece of bread when I was hungry; but this was a great favor on a slave plantation, and I was the only one of the children to whom such attention was paid. When very hungry, I would go into the back yard and play under Miss Lucretia's window. When pretty severely pinched by hunger, I had a habit of singing, which the good lady very soon came to understand as a petition for a piece of bread. When I sung under Miss Lucretia's window, I was very apt to get well paid for my music. The reader will see that I now had two friends, both at important points—Mas' Daniel at the great house, and Miss Lucretia at home. From Mas' Daniel I got protection from the bigger boys; and from Miss Lucretia I got bread, by singing when I was hungry, and sympathy when I was abused by that termagant, who had the reins of government in the kitchen. For such friendship I felt deeply grateful, and bitter as are my recollections of slavery, I love to recall any instances of kindness, any sunbeams of humane treatment, which found way to my soul through the iron grating of my house of bondage. Such beams seem all the brighter from the general darkness into which they penetrate, and the impression they make is vividly distinct and beautiful.

As I have before intimated, I was seldom whipped—and never severely— by my old master. I suffered little from the treatment I received, except from hunger and cold. These were my two great physical troubles. I could neither get a sufficiency of food nor of clothing; but I suffered less from hunger than from cold. In hottest summer and coldest winter, I was kept almost in a state of nudity; no shoes, no stockings, no jacket, no trowsers; nothing but coarse sackcloth or tow-linen, made into a sort of shirt, reaching down to my knees. This I wore night and day, changing it once a week. In the day time I could protect myself pretty well, by keeping on the sunny side of the house; and in bad weather, in the corner of the kitchen chimney. The great difficulty was, to keep warm during the night. I had no bed. The pigs in the pen had leaves, and the horses in the stable had straw, but the children had no beds. They lodged anywhere in the ample kitchen. I slept, generally, in a little closet, without even a blanket to cover me. In very cold weather. I sometimes got down the bag in which corn-meal was usually carried to the mill, and crawled into that. Sleeping there, with my head in and feet out, I was partly protected, though not comfortable. My feet have been so cracked with the frost, that the pen with which I am writing might be laid in the gashes. The manner of taking our meals at old master's, indicated but little refinement. Our corn-meal mush, when sufficiently cooled, was placed in a large wooden tray, or trough, like those used in making maple sugar here in the north. This tray was set down, either on the floor of the kitchen, or out of doors on the ground; and the children were called, like so many pigs; and like so many pigs they would come, and literally devour the mush—some with oyster shells, some with pieces of shingles, and none with spoons. He that eat fastest got most, and he that was strongest got the best place; and few left the trough really satisfied. I was the most unlucky of any, for Aunt Katy had no good feeling for me; and if I pushed any of the other children, or if they told her anything unfavorable of me, she always believed the worst, and was sure to whip me.

As I grew older and more thoughtful, I was more and more filled with a sense of my wretchedness. The cruelty of Aunt Katy, the hunger and cold I suffered, and the terrible reports of wrong and outrage which came to my ear, together with what I almost daily witnessed, led me, when yet but eight or nine years old, to wish I had never been born. I used to contrast my condition with the black-birds, in whose wild and sweet songs I fancied them so happy! Their apparent joy only deepened the shades of my sorrow. There are thoughtful days in the lives of children—at least there were in mine when they grapple with all the great, primary subjects of knowledge, and reach, in a moment, conclusions which no subsequent experience can shake. I was just as well aware of the unjust, unnatural and murderous character of slavery, when nine years old, as I am now. Without any appeal to books, to laws, or to authorities of any kind, it was enough to accept God as a father, to regard slavery as a crime.

I was not ten years old when I left Col. Lloyd's plantation for Balitmore(sic). I left that plantation with inexpressible joy. I never shall forget the ecstacy with which I received the intelligence from my friend, Miss Lucretia, that my old master had determined to let me go to Baltimore to live with Mr. Hugh Auld, a brother to Mr. Thomas Auld, my old master's son-in-law. I received this information about three days before my departure. They were three of the happiest days of my childhood. I spent the largest part of these three days in the creek, washing off the plantation scurf, and preparing for my new home. Mrs. Lucretia took a lively interest in getting me ready. She told me I must get all the dead skin off my feet and knees, before I could go to Baltimore, for the people there were very cleanly, and would laugh at me if I looked dirty; and, besides, she was intending to give me a pair of trowsers, which I should not put on unless I got all the dirt off. This was a warning to which I was bound to take heed; for the thought of owning a pair of trowsers, was great, indeed. It was almost a sufficient motive, not only to induce me to scrub off the *mange* (as pig drovers would call it) but the skin as well. So I went at it in good earnest, working for the first time in the hope of reward. I was greatly excited, and could hardly consent to sleep, lest I should be left. The ties that, ordinarily, bind children to their homes, were all severed, or they never had any existence in my case, at least so far as the home plantation of Col. L. was concerned. I therefore found no severe trail at the moment of my departure, such as I had experienced when separated from my home in Tuckahoe. My home at my old master's was charmless to me; it was not home, but a prison to me; on parting from it, I could not feel that I was leaving anything which I could have enjoyed by staying. My mother was now long dead; my grandmother was far away, so that I seldom saw her; Aunt Katy was my unrelenting tormentor; and my two sisters and brothers, owing to our early separation in life, and the family-destroying power of slavery, were, comparatively, strangers to me. The fact of our relationship was almost blotted out. I looked for *home* elsewhere, and was confident of finding none which I should relish less than the one I was leaving. If, however, I found in my new home to which I was going with such blissful anticipations—hardship, whipping and nakedness, I had the questionable consolation that I should not have escaped any one of these evils by remaining under the management of Aunt Katy. Then, too, I thought, since I had endured much in this line on Lloyd's plantation, I could endure as much elsewhere, and especially at Baltimore; for I had something of the feeling about that city which is expressed in the saying, that being "hanged in England, is better than dying a natural death in Ireland." I had the strongest desire to see Baltimore. My cousin Tom—a boy two or three years older than I— had been there, and though not fluent (he stuttered immoderately) in speech, he had inspired me with that desire, by his eloquent description of the place. Tom was, sometimes, Capt. Auld's cabin boy; and when he came from Baltimore, he was always a sort of hero amongst us, at least till his Baltimore trip was forgotten. I could never tell him of anything, or point out anything that struck me as beautiful or powerful, but that he had seen something in Baltimore far surpassing it. Even the great house itself, with all its pictures within, and pillars without, he had the hardihood to say "was nothing to Baltimore." He bought a trumpet (worth six pence) and brought it home; told what he had seen in the windows of stores; that he had heard shooting crackers, and seen soldiers; that he had seen a steamboat; that there were ships in Baltimore that could carry four such sloops as the "Sally Lloyd." He said a great deal about the market-house; he spoke of the bells ringing; and of many other things which roused my curiosity very much; and, indeed, which heightened my hopes of happiness in my new home.

We sailed out of Miles river for Baltimore early on a Saturday morning. I remember only the day of the week; for, at that time, I had no knowledge of the days of the month, nor, indeed, of the months of the year. On setting sail, I walked aft, and gave to Col. Lloyd's plantation what I hoped would be the last look I should ever give to it, or to any place like it. My strong aversion to the great farm, was not owing to my own personal suffering, but the daily suffering of others, and to the certainty that I must, sooner or later, be placed under the barbarous rule of an overseer, such as the accomplished Gore, or the brutal and drunken Plummer. After taking this last view, I quitted the quarter deck, made my way to the bow of the sloop, and spent the remainder of the day in looking ahead; interesting myself in what was in the distance, rather than what was near by or behind. The vessels, sweeping along the bay, were very interesting objects. The broad bay opened like a shoreless ocean on my boyish vision, filling me with wonder and admiration.

Late in the afternoon, we reached Annapolis, the capital of the state, stopping there not long enough to admit of my going ashore. It was the first large town I had ever seen; and though it was inferior to many a factory village in New England, my feelings, on seeing it, were excited to a pitch very little below that reached by travelers at the first view of Rome. The dome of the state house was especially imposing, and surpassed in grandeur the appearance of the great house. The great world was opening upon me very rapidly, and I was eagerly acquainting myself with its multifarious lessons.

We arrived in Baltimore on Sunday morning, and landed at Smith's wharf, not far from Bowly's wharf. We had on board the sloop a large flock of sheep, for the Baltimore market; and, after assisting in driving them to the slaughter house of Mr. Curtis, on Loudon Slater's Hill, I was speedily conducted by Rich—one of the hands belonging to the sloop—to my new home in Alliciana street, near Gardiner's ship-yard, on Fell's Point. Mr. and Mrs. Hugh Auld, my new mistress and master, were both at home, and met me at the door with their rosy cheeked little son, Thomas, to take care of whom was to constitute my future occupation. In fact, it was to "little Tommy," rather than to his parents, that old master made a present of me; and though there was no *legal* form or arrangement entered into, I have no doubt that Mr. and Mrs. Auld felt that, in due time, I should be the legal property of their bright-eyed and beloved boy, Tommy. I was struck with the appearance, especially, of my new mistress. Her face was lighted with the kindliest emotions; and the reflex influence of her countenance, as well as the tenderness with which she seemed to regard me, while asking me sundry little questions, greatly delighted me, and lit up, to my fancy, the pathway of my future. Miss Lucretia was kind; but my new mistress, "Miss Sophy," surpassed her in kindness of manner. Little Thomas was affectionately told by his mother, that *"there was his Freddy,"* and that "Freddy would take care of him;" and I was told to "be kind to little Tommy"—an injunction I scarcely needed, for I had already fallen in love with the dear boy; and with these little ceremonies I was initiated into my new home, and entered upon my peculiar duties, with not a cloud above the horizon.

I may say here, that I regard my removal from Col. Lloyd's plantation as one of the most interesting and fortunate events of my life. Viewing it in the light of human likelihoods, it is quite probable that, but for the mere circumstance of being thus removed before the rigors of slavery had fastened upon me; before my young spirit had been crushed under the iron control of the slave-driver, instead of being, today, a FREEMAN, I might have been wearing the galling chains of slavery. I have sometimes felt, however, that there was something more intelligent than *chance,* and something more certain than *luck,* to be seen in the circumstance. If I have made any progress in knowledge; if I have cherished any honorable aspirations, or have, in any manner, worthily discharged the duties of a member of an oppressed people; this little circumstance must be allowed its due weight in giving my life that direction. I have ever regarded it as the first plain manifestation of that

> Divinity that shapes our ends,
> Rough hew them as we will.

I was not the only boy on the plantation that might have been sent to live in Baltimore. There was a wide margin from which to select. There were boys younger, boys older, and boys of the same age, belonging to my old master some at his own house, and some at his farm—but the high privilege fell to my lot.

I may be deemed superstitious and egotistical, in regarding this event as a special interposition of Divine Providence in my favor; but the thought is a part of my history, and I should be false to the earliest and most cherished sentiments of my soul, if I suppressed, or hesitated to avow that opinion, although it may be characterized as irrational by the wise, and ridiculous by the scoffer. From my earliest recollections of serious matters, I date the entertainment of something like an ineffaceable conviction, that slavery would not always be able to hold me within its foul embrace; and this conviction, like a word of living faith, strengthened me through the darkest trials of my lot. This good spirit was from God; and to him I offer thanksgiving and praise.

CHAPTER X

Life in Baltimore

CITY ANNOYANCES—PLANTATION REGRETS—MY MISTRESS, MISS SOPHA—
HER HISTORY—HER KINDNESS TO ME—MY MASTER, HUGH AULD—
HIS SOURNESS—MY INCREASED SENSITIVENESS—MY COMFORTS—MY
OCCUPATION—THE BANEFUL EFFECTS OF SLAVEHOLDING ON MY DEAR
AND GOOD MISTRESS—HOW SHE COMMENCED TEACHING ME TO READ—
WHY SHE CEASED TEACHING ME—CLOUDS GATHERING OVER MY BRIGHT
PROSPECTS—MASTER AULD'S EXPOSITION OF THE TRUE PHILOSOPHY
OF SLAVERY—CITY SLAVES—PLANTATION SLAVES—THE CONTRAST—
EXCEPTIONS—MR. HAMILTON'S TWO SLAVES, HENRIETTA AND MARY—
MRS. HAMILTON'S CRUEL TREATMENT OF THEM—THE PITEOUS ASPECT
THEY PRESENTED—NO POWER MUST COME BETWEEN THE SLAVE AND THE
SLAVEHOLDER.

Once in Baltimore, with hard brick pavements under my feet, which almost
raised blisters, by their very heat, for it was in the height of summer; walled in
on all sides by towering brick buildings; with troops of hostile boys ready to
pounce upon me at every street corner; with new and strange objects glaring
upon me at every step, and with startling sounds reaching my ears from all
directions, I for a time thought that, after all, the home plantation was a more
desirable place of residence than my home on Alliciana street, in Baltimore. My
country eyes and ears were confused and bewildered here; but the boys were
my chief trouble. They chased me, and called me *"Eastern Shore man,"* till really
I almost wished myself back on the Eastern Shore. I had to undergo a sort of
moral acclimation, and when that was over, I did much better. My new mistress
happily proved to be all she *seemed* to be, when, with her husband, she met me
at the door, with a most beaming, benignant countenance. She was, naturally,
of an excellent disposition, kind, gentle and cheerful. The supercilious contempt
for the rights and feelings of the slave, and the petulance and bad humor which
generally characterize slaveholding ladies, were all quite absent from kind
"Miss" Sophia's manner and bearing toward me. She had, in truth, never been

a slaveholder, but had—a thing quite unusual in the south—depended almost entirely upon her own industry for a living. To this fact the dear lady, no doubt, owed the excellent preservation of her natural goodness of heart, for slavery can change a saint into a sinner, and an angel into a demon. I hardly knew how to behave toward "Miss Sopha," as I used to call Mrs. Hugh Auld. I had been treated as a *pig* on the plantation; I was treated as a *child* now. I could not even approach her as I had formerly approached Mrs. Thomas Auld. How could I hang down my head, and speak with bated breath, when there was no pride to scorn me, no coldness to repel me, and no hatred to inspire me with fear? I therefore soon learned to regard her as something more akin to a mother, than a slaveholding mistress. The crouching servility of a slave, usually so acceptable a quality to the haughty slaveholder, was not understood nor desired by this gentle woman. So far from deeming it impudent in a slave to look her straight in the face, as some slaveholding ladies do, she seemed ever to say, "look up, child; don't be afraid; see, I am full of kindness and good will toward you." The hands belonging to Col. Lloyd's sloop, esteemed it a great privilege to be the bearers of parcels or messages to my new mistress; for whenever they came, they were sure of a most kind and pleasant reception. If little Thomas was her son, and her most dearly beloved child, she, for a time, at least, made me something like his half-brother in her affections. If dear Tommy was exalted to a place on his mother's knee, "Feddy" was honored by a place at his mother's side. Nor did he lack the caressing strokes of her gentle hand, to convince him that, though *motherless*, he was not *friendless*. Mrs. Auld was not only a kind-hearted woman, but she was remarkably pious; frequent in her attendance of public worship, much given to reading the bible, and to chanting hymns of praise, when alone. Mr. Hugh Auld was altogether a different character. He cared very little about religion, knew more of the world, and was more of the world, than his wife. He set out, doubtless to be—as the world goes—a respectable man, and to get on by becoming a successful ship builder, in that city of ship building. This was his ambition, and it fully occupied him. I was, of course, of very little consequence to him, compared with what I was to good Mrs. Auld; and, when he smiled upon me, as he sometimes did, the smile was borrowed from his lovely wife, and, like all borrowed light, was transient, and vanished with the source whence it was derived. While I must characterize Master Hugh as being a very sour man, and of forbidding appearance, it is due to him to acknowledge, that he was never very cruel to me, according to the notion of cruelty in Maryland. The first year or two which I spent in his house, he left me almost exclusively to the management of his wife. She was my law-giver. In hands so tender as hers, and in the absence of the cruelties of the plantation, I became, both physically and mentally, much more sensitive to good and ill treatment; and, perhaps, suffered more from a frown from my mistress, than I formerly did from a cuff at the hands of Aunt Katy. Instead of the cold, damp floor of my old master's kitchen, I found myself on carpets; for the corn bag in winter, I now had a good straw bed, well furnished with covers; for the coarse corn-meal in the morning, I now had good bread, and mush occasionally; for my poor tow-lien shirt, reaching to my knees, I had good, clean clothes. I was really well off. My employment was to run errands, and to take care of Tommy; to prevent his getting in the way of carriages, and to keep him out of harm's way generally. Tommy, and I, and his mother, got on swimmingly together, for a time. I say *for a time,* because the fatal poison of irresponsible power, and the natural influence of slavery customs, were not long in making a suitable impression on the gentle and loving disposition of my excellent mistress. At first, Mrs. Auld evidently regarded me simply as a child, like any other child; she had not come to regard me as *property.* This latter thought was a thing of conventional growth. The first was natural and spontaneous. A noble nature, like hers, could not, instantly, be wholly perverted; and it took several years to change the natural sweetness of her temper into fretful bitterness. In her worst estate, however, there were, during the first seven years I lived with her, occasional returns of her former kindly disposition.

The frequent hearing of my mistress reading the bible for she often read aloud when her husband was absent soon awakened my curiosity in respect to this *mystery* of reading, and roused in me the desire to learn. Having no fear of my kind mistress before my eyes, (she had then given me no reason to fear,) I frankly asked her to teach me to read; and, without hesitation, the dear woman began the task, and very soon, by her assistance, I was master of the alphabet, and could spell words of three or four letters. My mistress seemed almost as proud of my progress, as if I had been her own child; and, supposing that her husband would be as well pleased, she made no secret of what she was doing for me. Indeed, she exultingly told him of the aptness of her pupil, of her intention to persevere in teaching me, and of the duty which she felt it to teach me, at least to read *the bible.* Here arose the first cloud over my Baltimore prospects, the precursor of drenching rains and chilling blasts.

Master Hugh was amazed at the simplicity of his spouse, and, probably for the first time, he unfolded to her the true philosophy of slavery, and the peculiar rules necessary to be observed by masters and mistresses, in the management of their human chattels. Mr. Auld promptly forbade continuance of her instruction; telling her, in the first place, that the thing itself was unlawful; that it was also unsafe, and could only lead to mischief. To use his own words, further, he said, "if you give a nigger an inch, he will take an ell;" "he should know nothing but the will of his master, and learn to obey it." "if you teach that nigger—speaking of myself—how to read the bible, there will be no keeping him;" "it would forever unfit him for the duties of a slave;" and "as to himself, learning would do him no good, but probably, a great deal of harm—making him disconsolate and unhappy." "If you learn him now to read, he'll want to know how to write; and, this accomplished, he'll be running away with himself." Such was the tenor of Master Hugh's oracular exposition of the true philosophy of training a human chattel; and it must be confessed that he very clearly comprehended the nature and the requirements of the relation of master and slave. His discourse was the first decidedly anti-slavery lecture to which it had been my lot to listen. Mrs. Auld evidently felt the force of his remarks; and, like an obedient wife, began to shape her course in the direction indicated by her husband. The effect of his words, *on me*, was neither slight nor transitory. His iron sentences—cold and harsh—sunk deep into my heart, and stirred up not only my feelings into a sort of rebellion, but awakened within me a slumbering train of vital thought. It was a new and special revelation, dispelling a painful mystery, against which my youthful understanding had struggled, and struggled in vain, to wit: the *white* man's power to perpetuate the enslavement of the *black* man. "Very well," thought I; "knowledge unfits a child to be a slave." I instinctively assented to the proposition; and from that moment I understood the direct pathway from slavery to freedom. This was just what I needed; and I got it at a time, and from a source, whence I least expected it. I was saddened at the thought of losing the assistance of my kind mistress; but the information, so instantly derived, to some extent compensated me for the loss I had sustained in this direction. Wise as Mr. Auld was, he evidently underrated my comprehension, and had little idea of the use to which I was capable of putting the impressive lesson he was giving to his wife. *He* wanted me to be *a slave;* I had already voted against that on the home plantation of Col. Lloyd. That which he most loved I most hated; and the very determination which he expressed to keep me in ignorance, only rendered me the more resolute in seeking intelligence. In learning to read, therefore, I am not sure that I do not owe quite as much to the opposition of my master, as to the kindly assistance of my amiable mistress. I acknowledge the benefit rendered me by the one, and by the other; believing, that but for my mistress, I might have grown up in ignorance.

I had resided but a short time in Baltimore, before I observed a marked difference in the manner of treating slaves, generally, from which I had witnessed in that isolated and out-of-the-way part of the country where I began life. A city slave is almost a free citizen, in Baltimore, compared with a slave on Col. Lloyd's plantation. He is much better fed and clothed, is less dejected in his appearance, and enjoys privileges altogether unknown to the whip-driven slave on the plantation. Slavery dislikes a dense population, in which there is a majority of non-slaveholders. The general sense of decency that must pervade such a population, does much to check and prevent those outbreaks of atrocious cruelty, and those dark crimes without a name, almost openly perpetrated on the plantation. He is a desperate slaveholder who will shock the humanity of his non-slaveholding neighbors, by the cries of the lacerated slaves; and very few in the city are willing to incur the odium of being cruel masters. I found, in Baltimore, that no man was more odious to the white, as well as to the colored people, than he, who had the reputation of starving his slaves. Work them, flog them, if need be, but don't starve them. These are, however, some painful exceptions to this rule. While it is quite true that most of the slaveholders in Baltimore feed and clothe their slaves well, there are others who keep up their country cruelties in the city.

An instance of this sort is furnished in the case of a family who lived directly opposite to our house, and were named Hamilton. Mrs. Hamilton owned two slaves. Their names were Henrietta and Mary. They had always been house slaves. One was aged about twenty-two, and the other about fourteen. They were a fragile couple by nature, and the treatment they received was enough to break down the constitution of a horse. Of all the dejected, emaciated, mangled and excoriated creatures I ever saw, those two girls—in the refined, church going and Christian city of Baltimore were the most deplorable. Of stone must that heart be made, that could look upon Henrietta and Mary, without being sickened to the core with sadness. Especially was Mary a heart-sickening object. Her head, neck and shoulders, were literally cut to pieces. I have frequently felt her head, and found it nearly covered over with festering sores, caused by the lash of her cruel mistress. I do not know that her master ever whipped her, but I have often been an eye witness of the revolting and brutal inflictions by Mrs. Hamilton; and what lends a deeper shade to this woman's conduct, is the fact, that, almost in the very moments of her shocking outrages of humanity and decency, she would charm you by the sweetness of her voice and her seeming piety. She used to sit in a large rocking chair, near the middle of the room, with a heavy cowskin, such as I have elsewhere described; and I speak within the truth when I say, that these girls seldom passed that chair, during the day, without a blow from that cowskin, either upon their bare arms, or upon their shoulders. As they passed her, she would draw her cowskin and give them a blow, saying, *"move faster, you black jip!"* and, again, *"take that, you black jip!"* continuing, *"if you don't move faster, I will give you more."* Then the lady would go on, singing her sweet hymns, as though her *righteous* soul were sighing for the holy realms of paradise.

Added to the cruel lashings to which these poor slave-girls were subjected— enough in themselves to crush the spirit of men—they were, really, kept nearly half starved; they seldom knew what it was to eat a full meal, except when they got it in the kitchens of neighbors, less mean and stingy than the psalm-singing Mrs. Hamilton. I have seen poor Mary contending for the offal, with the pigs in the street. So much was the poor girl pinched, kicked, cut and pecked to pieces, that the boys in the street knew her only by the name of *"pecked,"* a name derived from the scars and blotches on her neck, head and shoulders.

It is some relief to this picture of slavery in Baltimore, to say—what is but the simple truth—that Mrs. Hamilton's treatment of her slaves was generally condemned, as disgraceful and shocking; but while I say this, it must also be remembered, that the very parties who censured the cruelty of Mrs. Hamilton, would have condemned and promptly punished any attempt to interfere with Mrs. Hamilton's *right* to cut and slash her slaves to pieces. There must be no force between the slave and the slaveholder, to restrain the power of the one, and protect the weakness of the other; and the cruelty of Mrs. Hamilton is as justly chargeable to the upholders of the slave system, as drunkenness is chargeable on those who, by precept and example, or by indifference, uphold the drinking system.

CHAPTER XI

"A Change Came O'er the Spirit of My Dream"

HOW I LEARNED TO READ—MY MISTRESS—HER SLAVEHOLDING DUTIES—
THEIR DEPLORABLE EFFECTS UPON HER ORIGINALLY NOBLE NATURE—
THE CONFLICT IN HER MIND—HER FINAL OPPOSITION TO MY LEARNING
TO READ—TOO LATE—SHE HAD GIVEN ME THE INCH, I WAS RESOLVED
TO TAKE THE ELL—HOW I PURSUED MY EDUCATION—MY TUTORS—HOW
I COMPENSATED THEM—WHAT PROGRESS I MADE—SLAVERY—WHAT I
HEARD SAID ABOUT IT—THIRTEEN YEARS OLD—THE *Columbian Orator*—A
RICH SCENE—A DIALOGUE—SPEECHES OF CHATHAM, SHERIDAN, PITT
AND FOX—KNOWLEDGE EVER INCREASING—MY EYES OPENED—LIBERTY—
HOW I PINED FOR IT—MY SADNESS—THE DISSATISFACTION OF MY POOR
MISTRESS—MY HATRED OF SLAVERY—ONE UPAS TREE OVERSHADOWED US
BOTH.

I lived in the family of Master Hugh, at Baltimore, seven years, during which time—as the almanac makers say of the weather—my condition was variable. The most interesting feature of my history here, was my learning to read and write, under somewhat marked disadvantages. In attaining this knowledge, I was compelled to resort to indirections by no means congenial to my nature, and which were really humiliating to me. My mistress—who, as the reader has already seen, had begun to teach me was suddenly checked in her benevolent design, by the strong advice of her husband. In faithful compliance with this advice, the good lady had not only ceased to instruct me, herself, but had set her face as a flint against my learning to read by any means. It is due, however, to my mistress to say, that she did not adopt this course in all its stringency at the first. She either thought it unnecessary, or she lacked the depravity indispensable to shutting me up in mental darkness. It was, at least, necessary for her to have some training, and some hardening, in the exercise of the slaveholder's prerogative, to make her equal to forgetting my human nature and character, and to treating me as a thing destitute of a moral or an intellectual nature. Mrs. Auld—my mistress—was, as I have said, a most kind and tender-hearted woman; and, in the humanity of her heart, and the simplicity of her mind, she set out, when I first went to live with her, to treat me as she supposed one human being ought to treat another.

It is easy to see, that, in entering upon the duties of a slaveholder, some little experience is needed. Nature has done almost nothing to prepare men and women to be either slaves or slaveholders. Nothing but rigid training, long persisted in, can perfect the character of the one or the other. One cannot easily forget to love freedom; and it is as hard to cease to respect that natural love in our fellow creatures. On entering upon the career of a slaveholding mistress, Mrs. Auld was singularly deficient; nature, which fits nobody for such an office, had done less for her than any lady I had known. It was no easy matter to induce her to think and to feel that the curly-headed boy, who stood by her side, and even leaned on her lap; who was loved by little Tommy, and who loved little Tommy in turn; sustained to her only the relation of a chattel. I was *more* than that, and she felt me to be more than that. I could talk and sing; I could laugh and weep; I could reason and remember; I could love and hate. I was human, and she, dear lady, knew and felt me to be so. How could she, then, treat me as a brute, without a mighty struggle with all the noble powers of her own soul. That struggle came, and the will and power of the husband was victorious. Her noble soul was overthrown; but, he that overthrew it did not, himself, escape the consequences. He, not less than the other parties, was injured in his domestic peace by the fall.

When I went into their family, it was the abode of happiness and contentment. The mistress of the house was a model of affection and tenderness. Her fervent piety and watchful uprightness made it impossible to see her without thinking and feeling—*"that woman is a Christian."* There was no sorrow nor suffering for which she had not a tear, and there was no innocent joy for which she did not a smile. She had bread for the hungry, clothes for the naked, and comfort for every mourner that came within her reach. Slavery soon proved its ability to divest her of these excellent qualities, and her home of its early happiness. Conscience cannot stand much violence. Once thoroughly broken down, *who* is he that can repair the damage? It may be broken toward the slave, on Sunday, and toward the master on Monday. It cannot endure such shocks. It must stand entire, or it does not stand at all. If my condition waxed bad, that of the family waxed not better. The first step, in the wrong direction, was the violence done to nature and to conscience, in arresting the benevolence that would have enlightened my young mind. In ceasing to instruct me, she must begin to justify herself *to* herself; and, once consenting to take sides in such a debate, she was riveted to her position. One needs very little knowledge of moral philosophy, to see *where* my mistress now landed. She finally became even more violent in her opposition to my learning to read, than was her husband himself. She was not satisfied with simply doing as *well* as her husband had commanded her, but seemed resolved to better his instruction. Nothing appeared to make my poor mistress—after her turning toward the downward path—more angry, than seeing me, seated in some nook or corner, quietly reading a book or a newspaper. I have had her rush at me, with the utmost fury, and snatch from my hand such newspaper or book, with something of the wrath and consternation which a traitor might be supposed to feel on being discovered in a plot by some dangerous spy.

Mrs. Auld was an apt woman, and the advice of her husband, and her own experience, soon demonstrated, to her entire satisfaction, that education and slavery are incompatible with each other. When this conviction was thoroughly established, I was most narrowly watched in all my movements. If I remained in a separate room from the family for any considerable length of time, I was sure to be suspected of having a book, and was at once called upon to give an account of myself. All this, however, was entirely *too late*. The first, and never to be retraced, step had been taken. In teaching me the alphabet, in the days of her simplicity and kindness, my mistress had given me the *"inch,"* and now, no ordinary precaution could prevent me from taking the *"ell."*

Seized with a determination to learn to read, at any cost, I hit upon many expedients to accomplish the desired end. The plea which I mainly adopted, and the one by which I was most successful, was that of using my young white playmates, with whom I met in the streets as teachers. I used to carry, almost constantly, a copy of Webster's spelling book in my pocket; and, when sent of errands, or when play time was allowed me, I would step, with my young friends, aside, and take a lesson in spelling. I generally paid my *tuition fee* to the boys, with bread, which I also carried in my pocket. For a single biscuit, any of my hungry little comrades would give me a lesson more valuable to me than bread. Not every one, however, demanded this consideration, for there were those who took pleasure in teaching me, whenever I had a chance to be taught by them. I am strongly tempted to give the names of two or three of those little boys, as a slight testimonial of the gratitude and affection I bear them, but prudence forbids; not that it would injure me, but it might, possibly, embarrass them; for it is almost an unpardonable offense to do any thing, directly or indirectly, to promote a slave's freedom, in a slave state. It is enough to say, of my warm-hearted little play fellows, that they lived on Philpot street, very near Durgin & Bailey's shipyard.

Although slavery was a delicate subject, and very cautiously talked about among grown up people in Maryland, I frequently talked about it—and that very freely—with the white boys. I would, sometimes, say to them, while seated on a curb stone or a cellar door, "I wish I could be free, as you will be when you get to be men." "You will be free, you know, as soon as you are twenty-one, and can go where you like, but I am a slave for life. Have I not as good a right to be free as you have?" Words like these, I observed, always troubled them; and I had no small satisfaction in wringing from the boys, occasionally, that fresh and bitter condemnation of slavery, that springs from nature, unseared and unperverted. Of all consciences let me have those to deal with which have not been bewildered by the cares of life. I do not remember ever to have met with a *boy*, while I was in slavery, who defended the slave system; but I have often had boys to console me, with the hope that something would yet occur, by which I might be made free. Over and over again, they have told me, that "they believed I had as good a right to be free as *they* had;" and that "they did not believe God ever made any one to be a slave." The reader will easily see, that such little conversations with my play fellows, had no tendency to weaken my love of liberty, nor to render me contented with my condition as a slave.

When I was about thirteen years old, and had succeeded in learning to read, every increase of knowledge, especially respecting the FREE STATES, added something to the almost intolerable burden of the thought—I AM A SLAVE FOR LIFE. To my bondage I saw no end. It was a terrible reality, and I shall never be able to tell how sadly that thought chafed my young spirit. Fortunately, or unfortunately, about this time in my life, I had made enough money to buy what was then a very popular school book, viz: the *Columbian Orator*. I bought this addition to my library, of Mr. Knight, on Thames street, Fell's Point, Baltimore, and paid him fifty cents for it. I was first led to buy this book, by hearing some little boys say they were going to learn some little pieces out of it for the Exhibition. This volume was, indeed, a rich treasure, and every opportunity afforded me, for a time, was spent in diligently perusing it. Among much other interesting matter, that which I had perused and reperused with unflagging satisfaction, was a short dialogue between a master and his slave. The slave is represented as having been recaptured, in a second attempt to run away; and the master opens the dialogue with an upbraiding speech, charging the slave with ingratitude, and demanding to know what he has to say in his own defense. Thus upbraided, and thus called upon to reply, the slave rejoins, that he knows how little anything that he can say will avail, seeing that he is completely in the hands of his owner; and with noble resolution, calmly says, "I submit to my fate." Touched by the slave's answer, the master insists upon his further speaking, and recapitulates the many acts of kindness which he has performed toward the slave, and tells him he is permitted to speak for himself. Thus invited to the debate, the quondam slave made a spirited defense of himself, and thereafter the whole argument, for and against slavery, was brought out. The master was vanquished at every turn in the argument; and seeing himself to be thus vanquished, he generously and meekly emancipates the slave, with his best wishes for his prosperity. It is scarcely neccessary(sic) to say, that a dialogue, with such an origin, and such an ending—read when the fact of my being a slave was a constant burden of grief—powerfully affected me; and I could not help feeling that the day might come, when the well-directed answers made by the slave to the master, in this instance, would find their counterpart in myself.

This, however, was not all the fanaticism which I found in this *Columbian Orator*. I met there one of Sheridan's mighty speeches, on the subject of Catholic Emancipation, Lord Chatham's speech on the American war, and speeches by the great William Pitt and by Fox. These were all choice documents to me, and I read them, over and over again, with an interest that was ever increasing, because it was ever gaining in intelligence; for the more I read them, the better I understood them. The reading of these speeches added much to my limited stock of language, and enabled me to give tongue to many interesting thoughts, which had frequently flashed through my soul, and died away for want of utterance. The mighty power and heart-searching directness of truth, penetrating even the heart of a slaveholder, compelling him to yield up his earthly interests to the claims of eternal justice, were finely illustrated in the dialogue, just referred to; and from the speeches of Sheridan, I got a bold and powerful denunciation of oppression, and a most brilliant vindication of the rights of man. Here was, indeed, a noble acquisition. If I ever wavered under the consideration, that the Almighty, in some way, ordained slavery, and willed my enslavement for his own glory, I wavered no longer. I had now penetrated the secret of all slavery and oppression, and had ascertained their true foundation to be in the pride, the power and the avarice of man. The dialogue and the speeches were all redolent of the principles of liberty, and poured floods of light on the nature and character of slavery. With a book of this kind in my hand, my own human nature, and the facts of my experience, to help me, I was equal to a contest with the religious advocates of slavery, whether among the whites or among the colored people, for blindness, in this matter, is not confined to the former. I have met many religious colored people, at the south, who are under the delusion that God requires them to submit to slavery, and to wear their chains with meekness and humility. I could entertain no such nonsense as this; and I almost lost my patience when I found any colored man weak enough to believe such stuff. Nevertheless, the increase of knowledge was attended with bitter, as well as sweet results. The more I read, the more I was led to abhor and detest slavery, and my enslavers. "Slaveholders," thought I, "are only a band of successful robbers, who left their homes and went into Africa for the purpose of stealing and reducing my people to slavery." I loathed them as the meanest and the most wicked of men. As I read, behold! the very discontent so graphically predicted by Master

Hugh, had already come upon me. I was no longer the light-hearted, gleesome boy, full of mirth and play, as when I landed first at Baltimore. Knowledge had come; light had penetrated the moral dungeon where I dwelt; and, behold! there lay the bloody whip, for my back, and here was the iron chain; and my good, *kind master*, he was the author of my situation. The revelation haunted me, stung me, and made me gloomy and miserable. As I writhed under the sting and torment of this knowledge, I almost envied my fellow slaves their stupid contentment. This knowledge opened my eyes to the horrible pit, and revealed the teeth of the frightful dragon that was ready to pounce upon me, but it opened no way for my escape. I have often wished myself a beast, or a bird—anything, rather than a slave. I was wretched and gloomy, beyond my ability to describe. I was too thoughtful to be happy. It was this everlasting thinking which distressed and tormented me; and yet there was no getting rid of the subject of my thoughts. All nature was redolent of it. Once awakened by the silver trump of knowledge, my spirit was roused to eternal wakefulness. Liberty! the inestimable birthright of every man, had, for me, converted every object into an asserter of this great right. It was heard in every sound, and beheld in every object. It was ever present, to torment me with a sense of my wretched condition. The more beautiful and charming were the smiles of nature, the more horrible and desolate was my condition. I saw nothing without seeing it, and I heard nothing without hearing it. I do not exaggerate, when I say, that it looked from every star, smiled in every calm, breathed in every wind, and moved in every storm.

I have no doubt that my state of mind had something to do with the change in the treatment adopted, by my once kind mistress toward me. I can easily believe, that my leaden, downcast, and discontented look, was very offensive to her. Poor lady! She did not know my trouble, and I dared not tell her. Could I have freely made her acquainted with the real state of my mind, and given her the reasons therefor, it might have been well for both of us. Her abuse of me fell upon me like the blows of the false prophet upon his ass; she did not know that an *angel* stood in the way; and—such is the relation of master and slave I could not tell her. Nature had made us *friends;* slavery made us *enemies.* My interests were in a direction opposite to hers, and we both had our private thoughts and plans. She aimed to keep me ignorant; and I resolved to know, although knowledge only increased my discontent. My feelings were not the result of any marked cruelty in the treatment I received; they sprung from the consideration of my being a slave at all. It was *slavery*—not its mere *incidents*—that I hated. I had been cheated. I saw through the attempt to keep me in ignorance; I saw that slaveholders would have gladly made me believe that they were merely acting under the authority of God, in making a slave of me, and in making slaves of others; and I treated them as robbers and deceivers. The feeding and clothing me well, could not atone for taking my liberty from me. The smiles of my mistress could not remove the deep sorrow that dwelt in my young bosom. Indeed, these, in time, came only to deepen my sorrow. She had changed; and the reader will see that I had changed, too. We were both victims to the same overshadowing evil—*she*, as mistress, I, as slave. I will not censure her harshly; she cannot censure me, for she knows I speak but the truth, and have acted in my opposition to slavery, just as she herself would have acted, in a reverse of circumstances.

CHAPTER XII

Religious Nature Awakened

ABOLITIONISTS SPOKEN OF—MY EAGERNESS TO KNOW WHAT THIS WORD MEANT—MY CONSULTATION OF THE DICTIONARY—INCENDIARY INFORMATION—HOW AND WHERE DERIVED—THE ENIGMA SOLVED— NATHANIEL TURNER'S INSURRECTION—THE CHOLERA—RELIGION—FIRST AWAKENED BY A METHODIST MINISTER NAMED HANSON—MY DEAR AND GOOD OLD COLORED FRIEND, LAWSON—HIS CHARACTER AND OCCUPATION—HIS INFLUENCE OVER ME—OUR MUTUAL ATTACHMENT— THE COMFORT I DERIVED FROM HIS TEACHING—NEW HOPES AND ASPIRATIONS—HEAVENLY LIGHT AMIDST EARTHLY DARKNESS—THE TWO IRISHMEN ON THE WHARF—THEIR CONVERSATION—HOW I LEARNED TO WRITE—WHAT WERE MY AIMS.

Whilst in the painful state of mind described in the foregoing chapter, almost regretting my very existence, because doomed to a life of bondage, so goaded and so wretched, at times, that I was even tempted to destroy my own life, I was keenly sensitive and eager to know any, and every thing that transpired, having any relation to the subject of slavery. I was all ears, all eyes, whenever the words *slave, slavery,* dropped from the lips of any white person, and the occasions were not unfrequent when these words became leading ones, in high, social debate, at our house. Every little while, I could hear Master Hugh, or some of his company, speaking with much warmth and excitement about *"abolitionists."* Of *who* or *what* these were, I was totally ignorant. I found, however, that whatever they might be, they were most cordially hated and soundly abused by slaveholders, of every grade. I very soon discovered, too, that slavery was, in some sort, under consideration, whenever the abolitionists were alluded to. This made the term a very interesting one to me. If a slave, for instance, had made good his escape from slavery, it was generally alleged, that he had been persuaded and assisted by the abolitionists. If, also, a slave killed his master—as was sometimes the case—or struck down his overseer, or set fire to his master's dwelling, or committed any violence or crime, out of the common way, it was certain to be said, that such a crime was the legitimate fruits of the abolition movement. Hearing such charges often repeated, I, naturally enough, received the impression that abolition—whatever else it might be—could not be unfriendly to the slave, nor very friendly to the slaveholder. I therefore set about finding out, if possible, *who* and *what* the abolitionists were, and *why* they were so obnoxious to the slaveholders. The dictionary afforded me very little help. It taught me that abolition was the "act of abolishing;" but it left me in ignorance at the very point where I most wanted information—and that was, as to the *thing* to be abolished. A city newspaper, the *Baltimore American*, gave me the incendiary information denied me by the dictionary. In its columns I found, that, on a certain day, a vast number of petitions and memorials had been presented to congress, praying for the abolition of slavery in the District of Columbia, and for the abolition of the slave trade between the states of the Union. This was enough. The vindictive bitterness, the marked caution, the studied reverse, and the cumbrous ambiguity, practiced by our white folks, when alluding to this subject, was now fully explained. Ever, after that, when I heard the words "abolition," or "abolition movement," mentioned, I felt the matter one of a personal concern; and I drew near to listen, when I could do so, without seeming too solicitous and prying. There was HOPE in those words. Ever and anon, too, I could see some terrible denunciation of slavery, in our papers—copied from abolition papers at the north—and the injustice of such denunciation commented on. These I read with avidity. I had a deep satisfaction in the thought, that the rascality of slaveholders was not concealed from the eyes of the world, and that I was not alone in abhorring the cruelty and brutality of slavery. A still deeper train of thought was stirred. I saw that there was *fear*, as well as *rage*, in the manner of speaking of the abolitionists. The latter, therefore, I was compelled to regard as having some power in the country; and I felt that they might, possibly, succeed in their designs. When I met with a slave to whom I deemed it safe to talk on the subject, I would impart to him so much of the mystery as I had been able to penetrate. Thus, the light of this grand movement broke in upon my mind, by degrees; and I must say, that, ignorant as I then was of the philosophy of that movement, I believe in it from the first—and I believed in it, partly, because I saw that it alarmed the consciences of slaveholders. The insurrection of Nathaniel Turner had been quelled, but the alarm and terror had not subsided. The cholera was on its way, and the thought was present, that God was angry with the white people because of their slaveholding wickedness, and, therefore, his judgments were abroad in the land. It was impossible for me not to hope much from the abolition movement, when I saw it supported by the Almighty, and armed with DEATH!

Previous to my contemplation of the anti-slavery movement, and its probable results, my mind had been seriously awakened to the subject of religion. I was not more than thirteen years old, when I felt the need of God, as a father and protector. My religious nature was awakened by the preaching of a white Methodist minister, named Hanson. He thought that all men, great and small, bond and free, were sinners in the sight of God; that they were, by nature, rebels against His government; and that they must repent of their sins, and be reconciled to God, through Christ. I cannot say that I had a very distinct notion of what was required of me; but one thing I knew very well—I was wretched, and had no means of making myself otherwise. Moreover, I knew that I could pray for light. I consulted a good colored man, named Charles Johnson; and, in tones of holy affection, he told me to pray, and what to pray for. I was, for weeks, a poor, brokenhearted mourner, traveling through the darkness and misery of doubts and fears. I finally found that change of heart which comes by "casting all one's care" upon God, and by having faith in Jesus Christ, as the Redeemer, Friend, and Savior of those who diligently seek Him.

After this, I saw the world in a new light. I seemed to live in a new world, surrounded by new objects, and to be animated by new hopes and desires. I loved all mankind—slaveholders not excepted; though I abhorred slavery more than ever. My great concern was, now, to have the world converted. The desire for knowledge increased, and especially did I want a thorough acquaintance with the contents of the bible. I have gathered scattered pages from this holy book, from the filthy street gutters of Baltimore, and washed and dried them, that in the moments of my leisure, I might get a word or two of wisdom from them. While thus religiously seeking knowledge, I became acquainted with a good old colored man, named Lawson. A more devout man than he, I never saw. He drove a dray for Mr. James Ramsey, the owner of a rope-walk on Fell's Point, Baltimore. This man not only prayed three time a day, but he prayed as he walked through the streets, at his work—on his dray everywhere. His life was a life of prayer, and his words (when he spoke to his friends,) were about a better world. Uncle Lawson lived near Master Hugh's house; and, becoming deeply attached to the old man, I went often with him to prayer-meeting, and spent much of my leisure time with him on Sunday. The old man could read a little, and I was a great help to him, in making out the hard words, for I was a better reader than he. I could teach him *"the letter,"* but he could teach me *"the spirit;"* and high, refreshing times we had together, in singing, praying and glorifying God. These meetings with Uncle Lawson went on for a long time, without the knowledge of Master Hugh or my mistress. Both knew, however, that I had become religious, and they seemed to respect my conscientious piety. My mistress was still a professor of religion, and belonged to class. Her leader was no less a person than the Rev. Beverly Waugh, the presiding elder, and now one of the bishops of the Methodist Episcopal church. Mr. Waugh was then stationed over Wilk street church. I am careful to state these facts, that the reader may be able to form an idea of the precise influences which had to do with shaping and directing my mind.

In view of the cares and anxieties incident to the life she was then leading, and, especially, in view of the separation from religious associations to which she was subjected, my mistress had, as I have before stated, become lukewarm, and needed to be looked up by her leader. This brought Mr. Waugh to our house, and gave me an opportunity to hear him exhort and pray. But my chief instructor, in matters of religion, was Uncle Lawson. He was my spiritual father; and I loved him intensely, and was at his house every chance I got.

This pleasure was not long allowed me. Master Hugh became averse to my going to Father Lawson's, and threatened to whip me if I ever went there again. I now felt myself persecuted by a wicked man; and I *would* go to Father Lawson's, notwithstanding the threat. The good old man had told me, that the "Lord had a great work for me to do;" and I must prepare to do it; and that he had been shown that I must preach the gospel. His words made a deep impression on my mind, and I verily felt that some such work was before me, though I could not see *how* I should ever engage in its performance. "The good Lord," he said, "would bring it to pass in his own good time," and that I must go on reading and studying the scriptures. The advice and the suggestions of Uncle Lawson, were not without their influence upon my character and destiny. He threw my thoughts into a channel from which they have never entirely diverged. He fanned my already intense love of knowledge into a flame, by assuring me that I was to be a useful man in the world. When I would say to him, "How can these things be and what can *I* do?" his simple reply was, *"Trust in the Lord."* When I told him that "I was a slave, and a slave FOR LIFE," he said, "the Lord can make you free, my dear. All things are possible with him, only *have faith in God."* "Ask, and it shall be given." "If you want liberty," said the good old man, "ask the Lord for it, *in faith*, AND HE WILL GIVE IT TO YOU."

Thus assured, and cheered on, under the inspiration of hope, I worked and prayed with a light heart, believing that my life was under the guidance of a wisdom higher than my own. With all other blessings sought at the mercy seat, I always prayed that God would, of His great mercy, and in His own good time, deliver me from my bondage.

I went, one day, on the wharf of Mr. Waters; and seeing two Irishmen unloading a large scow of stone, or ballast I went on board, unasked, and helped them. When we had finished the work, one of the men came to me, aside, and asked me a number of questions, and among them, if I were a slave. I told him "I was a slave, and a slave for life." The good Irishman gave his shoulders a shrug, and seemed deeply affected by the statement. He said, "it was a pity so fine a little fellow as myself should be a slave for life." They both had much to say about the matter, and expressed the deepest sympathy with me, and the most decided hatred of slavery. They went so far as to tell me that I ought to run away, and go to the north; that I should find friends there, and that I would be as free as anybody. I, however, pretended not to be interested in what they said, for I feared they might be treacherous. White men have been known to encourage slaves to escape, and then—to get the reward—they have kidnapped them, and returned them to their masters. And while I mainly inclined to the notion that these men were honest and meant me no ill, I feared it might be otherwise. I nevertheless remembered their words and their advice, and looked forward to an escape to the north, as a possible means of gaining the liberty for which my heart panted. It was not my enslavement, at the then present time, that most affected me; the being a slave *for life*, was the saddest thought. I was too young to think of running away immediately; besides, I wished to learn how to write, before going, as I might have occasion to write my own pass. I now not only had the hope of freedom, but a foreshadowing of the means by which I might, some day, gain that inestimable boon. Meanwhile, I resolved to add to my educational attainments the art of writing.

After this manner I began to learn to write: I was much in the ship yard—Master Hugh's, and that of Durgan & Bailey—and I observed that the carpenters, after hewing and getting a piece of timber ready for use, wrote on it the initials of the name of that part of the ship for which it was intended. When, for instance, a piece of timber was ready for the starboard side, it was marked with a capital "S." A piece for the larboard side was marked "L;" larboard forward, "L. F.;" larboard aft, was marked "L. A.;" starboard aft, "S. A.;" and starboard forward "S. F." I soon learned these letters, and for what they were placed on the timbers.

My work was now, to keep fire under the steam box, and to watch the ship yard while the carpenters had gone to dinner. This interval gave me a fine opportunity for copying the letters named. I soon astonished myself with the ease with which I made the letters; and the thought was soon present, "if I can make four, I can make more." But having made these easily, when I met boys about Bethel church, or any of our play-grounds, I entered the lists with them in the art of writing, and would make the letters which I had been so fortunate as to learn, and ask them to "beat that if they could." With playmates for my teachers, fences and pavements for my copy books, and chalk for my pen and ink, I learned the art of writing. I, however, afterward adopted various methods of improving my hand. The most successful, was copying the *italics* in Webster's spelling book, until I could make them all without looking on the book. By this time, my little "Master Tommy" had grown to be a big boy, and had written over a number of copy books, and brought them home. They had been shown to the neighbors, had elicited due praise, and were now laid carefully away. Spending my time between the ship yard and house, I was as often the lone keeper of the latter as of the former. When my mistress left me in charge of the house,

I had a grand time; I got Master Tommy's copy books and a pen and ink, and, in the ample spaces between the lines, I wrote other lines, as nearly like his as possible. The process was a tedious one, and I ran the risk of getting a flogging for marring the highly prized copy books of the oldest son. In addition to those opportunities, sleeping, as I did, in the kitchen loft—a room seldom visited by any of the family—I got a flour barrel up there, and a chair; and upon the head of that barrel I have written (or endeavored to write) copying from the bible and the Methodist hymn book, and other books which had accumulated on my hands, till late at night, and when all the family were in bed and asleep. I was supported in my endeavors by renewed advice, and by holy promises from the good Father Lawson, with whom I continued to meet, and pray, and read the scriptures. Although Master Hugh was aware of my going there, I must say, for his credit, that he never executed his threat to whip me, for having thus, innocently, employed-my leisure time.

CHAPTER XIII

The Vicissitudes of Slave Life

DEATH OF OLD MASTER'S SON RICHARD, SPEEDILY FOLLOWED BY THAT OF OLD MASTER—VALUATION AND DIVISION OF ALL THE PROPERTY, INCLUDING THE SLAVES—MY PRESENCE REQUIRED AT HILLSBOROUGH TO BE APPRAISED AND ALLOTTED TO A NEW OWNER—MY SAD PROSPECTS AND GRIEF—PARTING—THE UTTER POWERLESSNESS OF THE SLAVES TO DECIDE THEIR OWN DESTINY—A GENERAL DREAD OF MASTER ANDREW—HIS WICKEDNESS AND CRUELTY—MISS LUCRETIA MY NEW OWNER—MY RETURN TO BALTIMORE—JOY UNDER THE ROOF OF MASTER HUGH—DEATH OF MRS. LUCRETIA—MY POOR OLD GRANDMOTHER—HER SAD FATE—THE LONE COT IN THE WOODS—MASTER THOMAS AULD'S SECOND MARRIAGE—AGAIN REMOVED FROM MASTER HUGH'S—REASONS FOR REGRETTING THE CHANGE—A PLAN OF ESCAPE ENTERTAINED.

I must now ask the reader to go with me a little back in point of time, in my humble story, and to notice another circumstance that entered into my slavery experience, and which, doubtless, has had a share in deepening my horror of slavery, and increasing my hostility toward those men and measures that practically uphold the slave system.

It has already been observed, that though I was, after my removal from Col. Lloyd's plantation, in *form* the slave of Master Hugh, I was, in *fact*, and in *law*, the slave of my old master, Capt. Anthony. Very well.

In a very short time after I went to Baltimore, my old master's youngest son, Richard, died; and, in three years and six months after his death, my old master himself died, leaving only his son, Andrew, and his daughter, Lucretia, to share his estate. The old man died while on a visit to his daughter, in Hillsborough, where Capt. Auld and Mrs. Lucretia now lived. The former, having given up the command of Col. Lloyd's sloop, was now keeping a store in that town.

Cut off, thus unexpectedly, Capt. Anthony died intestate; and his property must now be equally divided between his two children, Andrew and Lucretia.

The valuation and the division of slaves, among contending heirs, is an important incident in slave life. The character and tendencies of the heirs, are generally well understood among the slaves who are to be divided, and all have their aversions and preferences. But, neither their aversions nor their preferences avail them anything.

On the death of old master, I was immediately sent for, to be valued and divided with the other property. Personally, my concern was, mainly, about my possible removal from the home of Master Hugh, which, after that of my grandmother, was the most endeared to me. But, the whole thing, as a feature of slavery, shocked me. It furnished me anew insight into the unnatural power to which I was subjected. My detestation of slavery, already great, rose with this new conception of its enormity.

That was a sad day for me, a sad day for little Tommy, and a sad day for my dear Baltimore mistress and teacher, when I left for the Eastern Shore, to be valued and divided. We, all three, wept bitterly that day; for we might be parting, and we feared we were parting, forever. No one could tell among which pile of chattels I should be flung. Thus early, I got a foretaste of that painful uncertainty which slavery brings to the ordinary lot of mortals. Sickness, adversity and death may interfere with the plans and purposes of all; but the slave has the added danger of changing homes, changing hands, and of having separations unknown to other men. Then, too, there was the intensified degradation of the spectacle. What an assemblage! Men and women, young and old, married and single; moral and intellectual beings, in open contempt of their humanity, level at a blow with horses, sheep, horned cattle and swine! Horses and men—cattle and women—pigs and children—all holding the same rank in the scale of social existence; and all subjected to the same narrow inspection, to ascertain their value in gold and silver—the only standard of worth applied by slaveholders to slaves! How vividly, at that moment, did the brutalizing power of slavery flash before me! Personality swallowed up in the sordid idea of property! Manhood lost in chattelhood!

After the valuation, then came the division. This was an hour of high excitement and distressing anxiety. Our destiny was now to be *fixed for life*, and we had no more voice in the decision of the question, than the oxen and cows that stood chewing at the haymow. One word from the appraisers, against all preferences or prayers, was enough to sunder all the ties of friendship and affection, and even to separate husbands and wives, parents and children. We were all appalled before that power, which, to human seeming, could bless or blast us in a moment. Added to the dread of separation, most painful to the majority of the slaves, we all had a decided horror of the thought of falling into the hands of Master Andrew. He was distinguished for cruelty and intemperance.

Slaves generally dread to fall into the hands of drunken owners. Master Andrew was almost a confirmed sot, and had already, by his reckless mismanagement and profligate dissipation, wasted a large portion of old master's property. To fall into his hands, was, therefore, considered merely as the first step toward being sold away to the far south. He would spend his fortune in a few years, and his farms and slaves would be sold, we thought, at public outcry; and we should be hurried away to the cotton fields, and rice swamps, of the sunny south. This was the cause of deep consternation.

The people of the north, and free people generally, I think, have less attachment to the places where they are born and brought up, than have the slaves. Their freedom to go and come, to be here and there, as they list, prevents any extravagant attachment to any one particular place, in their case. On the other hand, the slave is a fixture; he has no choice, no goal, no destination; but is pegged down to a single spot, and must take root here, or nowhere. The idea of removal elsewhere, comes, generally, in the shape of a threat, and in punishment of crime. It is, therefore, attended with fear and dread. A slave seldom thinks of bettering his condition by being sold, and hence he looks upon separation from his native place, with none of the enthusiasm which animates the bosoms of young freemen, when they contemplate a life in the far west, or in some distant country where they intend to rise to wealth and distinction. Nor can those from whom they separate, give them up with that cheerfulness with which friends and relations yield each other up, when they feel that it is for the good of the departing one that he is removed from his native place. Then, too, there is correspondence, and there is, at least, the hope of reunion, because reunion is *possible*. But, with the slave, all these mitigating circumstances are wanting. There is no improvement in his condition *probable*,—no correspondence *possible*,—no reunion attainable. His going out into the world, is like a living man going into the tomb, who, with open eyes, sees himself buried out of sight and hearing of wife, children and friends of kindred tie.

In contemplating the likelihoods and possibilities of our circumstances, I probably suffered more than most of my fellow servants. I had known what it was to experience kind, and even tender treatment; they had known nothing of the sort. Life, to them, had been rough and thorny, as well as dark. They had—most of them—lived on my old master's farm in Tuckahoe, and had felt the reign of Mr. Plummer's rule. The overseer had written his character on the living parchment of most of their backs, and left them callous; my back (thanks to my early removal from the plantation to Baltimore) was yet tender. I had left a kind mistress at Baltimore, who was almost a mother to me. She was in tears when we parted, and the probabilities of ever seeing her again, trembling in the balance as they did, could not be viewed without alarm and agony. The thought of leaving that kind mistress forever, and, worse still, of being the slave of Andrew

Anthony—a man who, but a few days before the division of the property, had, in my presence, seized my brother Perry by the throat, dashed him on the ground, and with the heel of his boot stamped him on the head, until the blood gushed from his nose and ears—was terrible! This fiendish proceeding had no better apology than the fact, that Perry had gone to play, when Master Andrew wanted him for some trifling service. This cruelty, too, was of a piece with his general character. After inflicting his heavy blows on my brother, on observing me looking at him with intense astonishment, he said, "*That* is the way I will serve you, one of these days;" meaning, no doubt, when I should come into his possession. This threat, the reader may well suppose, was not very tranquilizing to my feelings. I could see that he really thirsted to get hold of me. But I was there only for a few days. I had not received any orders, and had violated none, and there was, therefore, no excuse for flogging me.

At last, the anxiety and suspense were ended; and they ended, thanks to a kind Providence, in accordance with my wishes. I fell to the portion of Mrs. Lucretia—the dear lady who bound up my head, when the savage Aunt Katy was adding to my sufferings her bitterest maledictions.

Capt. Thomas Auld and Mrs. Lucretia at once decided on my return to Baltimore. They knew how sincerely and warmly Mrs. Hugh Auld was attached to me, and how delighted Mr. Hugh's son would be to have me back; and, withal, having no immediate use for one so young, they willingly let me off to Baltimore.

I need not stop here to narrate my joy on returning to Baltimore, nor that of little Tommy; nor the tearful joy of his mother; nor the evident saticfaction(sic) of Master Hugh. I was just one month absent from Baltimore, before the matter was decided; and the time really seemed full six months.

One trouble over, and on comes another. The slave's life is full of uncertainty. I had returned to Baltimore but a short time, when the tidings reached me, that my friend, Mrs. Lucretia, who was only second in my regard to Mrs. Hugh Auld, was dead, leaving her husband and only one child—a daughter, named Amanda.

Shortly after the death of Mrs. Lucretia, strange to say, Master Andrew died, leaving his wife and one child. Thus, the whole family of Anthonys was swept away; only two children remained. All this happened within five years of my leaving Col. Lloyd's.

No alteration took place in the condition of the slaves, in consequence of these deaths, yet I could not help feeling less secure, after the death of my friend, Mrs. Lucretia, than I had done during her life. While she lived, I felt that I had a strong friend to plead for me in any emergency. Ten years ago, while speaking of the state of things in our family, after the events just named, I used this language:

Now all the property of my old master, slaves included, was in the hands of strangers—strangers who had nothing to do in accumulating it. Not a slave was left free. All remained slaves, from youngest to oldest. If any one thing in my experience, more than another, served to deepen my conviction of the infernal character of slavery, and to fill me with unutterable loathing of slaveholders, it was their base ingratitude to my poor old grandmother. She had served my old master faithfully from youth to old age. She had been the source of all his wealth; she had peopled his plantation with slaves; she had become a great-grandmother in his service. She had rocked him in infancy, attended him in childhood, served him through life, and at his death wiped from his icy brow the cold death-sweat, and closed his eyes forever. She was nevertheless left a slave—a slave for life—a slave in the hands of strangers; and in their hands she saw her children, her grandchildren, and her great-grandchildren, divided, like so many sheep, without being gratified with the small privilege of a single word, as to their or her own destiny. And, to cap the climax of their base ingratitude and fiendish barbarity, my grandmother, who was now very old, having outlived my old master and all his children, having seen the beginning and end of all of them, and her present owners finding she was of but little value, her frame already racked with the pains of old age, and complete helplessness fast stealing over her once active limbs, they took her to the woods, built her a little hut, put up a little mud-chimney, and then made her welcome to the privilege of supporting herself there in perfect loneliness; thus virtually turning her out to die! If my poor old grandmother now lives, she lives to suffer in utter loneliness; she lives to remember and mourn over the loss of children, the loss of grandchildren, and the loss of great-grandchildren. They are, in the language of the slave's poet, Whittier—

> Gone, gone, sold and gone,
> To the rice swamp dank and lone,
> Where the slave-whip ceaseless swings,
> Where the noisome insect stings,
> Where the fever-demon strews
> Poison with the falling dews,
> Where the sickly sunbeams glare
> Through the hot and misty air:—
>> Gone, gone, sold and gone
>> To the rice swamp dank and lone,
>> From Virginia hills and waters—
>> Woe is me, my stolen daughters!

The hearth is desolate. The children, the unconscious children, who once sang and danced in her presence, are gone. She gropes her way, in the darkness of age, for a drink of water. Instead of the voices of her children, she hears by day the moans of the dove, and by night the screams of the hideous owl. All is gloom. The grave is at the door. And now, when weighed down by the pains and aches of old age, when the head inclines to the feet, when the beginning and ending of human existence meet, and helpless infancy and painful old age combine together—at this time, this most needful time, the time for the exercise of that tenderness and affection which children only can exercise toward a declining parent—my poor old grandmother, the devoted mother of twelve children, is left all alone, in yonder little hut, before a few dim embers.

Two years after the death of Mrs. Lucretia, Master Thomas married his second wife. Her name was Rowena Hamilton, the eldest daughter of Mr. William Hamilton, a rich slaveholder on the Eastern Shore of Maryland, who lived about five miles from St. Michael's, the then place of my master's residence.

Not long after his marriage, Master Thomas had a misunderstanding with Master Hugh, and, as a means of punishing his brother, he ordered him to send me home.

As the ground of misunderstanding will serve to illustrate the character of southern chivalry, and humanity, I will relate it.

Among the children of my Aunt Milly, was a daughter, named Henny. When quite a child, Henny had fallen into the fire, and burnt her hands so bad that they were of very little use to her. Her fingers were drawn almost into the palms of her hands. She could make out to do something, but she was considered hardly worth the having—of little more value than a horse with a broken leg. This unprofitable piece of human property, ill shapen, and disfigured, Capt. Auld sent off to Baltimore, making his brother Hugh welcome to her services.

After giving poor Henny a fair trial, Master Hugh and his wife came to the conclusion, that they had no use for the crippled servant, and they sent her back to Master Thomas. Thus, the latter took as an act of ingratitude, on the part of his brother; and, as a mark of his displeasure, he required him to send me immediately to St. Michael's, saying, if he cannot keep *"Hen,"* he shall not have *"Fred."*

Here was another shock to my nerves, another breaking up of my plans, and another severance of my religious and social alliances. I was now a big boy. I had become quite useful to several young colored men, who had made me their teacher. I had taught some of them to read, and was accustomed to spend many of my leisure hours with them. Our attachment was strong, and I greatly dreaded the separation. But regrets, especially in a slave, are unavailing. I was only a slave; my wishes were nothing, and my happiness was the sport of my masters.

My regrets at now leaving Baltimore, were not for the same reasons as when I before left that city, to be valued and handed over to my proper owner. My home was not now the pleasant place it had formerly been. A change had taken place, both in Master Hugh, and in his once pious and affectionate wife. The influence of brandy and bad company on him, and the influence of slavery and social isolation upon her, had wrought disastrously upon the characters of both.

Thomas was no longer "little Tommy," but was a big boy, and had learned to assume the airs of his class toward me. My condition, therefore, in the house of Master Hugh, was not, by any means, so comfortable as in former years. My attachments were now outside of our family. They were felt to those to whom I *imparted* instruction, and to those little white boys from whom I *received* instruction. There, too, was my dear old father, the pious Lawson, who was, in christian graces, the very counterpart of "Uncle" Tom. The resemblance is so perfect, that he might have been the original of Mrs. Stowe's christian hero. The thought of leaving these dear friends, greatly troubled me, for I was going without the hope of ever returning to Baltimore again; the feud between Master Hugh and his brother being bitter and irreconcilable, or, at least, supposed to be so.

In addition to thoughts of friends from whom I was parting, as I supposed, *forever*, I had the grief of neglected chances of escape to brood over. I had put off running away, until now I was to be placed where the opportunities for escaping were much fewer than in a large city like Baltimore.

On my way from Baltimore to St. Michael's, down the Chesapeake bay, our sloop—the "Amanda"—was passed by the steamers plying between that city and Philadelphia, and I watched the course of those steamers, and, while going to St. Michael's, I formed a plan to escape from slavery; of which plan, and matters connected therewith the kind reader shall learn more hereafter.

CHAPTER XIV

Experience in St. Michael's

THE VILLAGE—ITS INHABITANTS—THEIR OCCUPATION AND LOW PROPENSITIES CAPTAN(sic) THOMAS AULD—HIS CHARACTER—HIS SECOND WIFE, ROWENA—WELL MATCHED—SUFFERINGS FROM HUNGER—OBLIGED TO TAKE FOOD—MODE OF ARGUMENT IN VINDICATION THEREOF—NO MORAL CODE OF FREE SOCIETY CAN APPLY TO SLAVE SOCIETY—SOUTHERN CAMP MEETING—WHAT MASTER THOMAS DID THERE—HOPES—SUSPICIONS ABOUT HIS CONVERSION—THE RESULT—FAITH AND WORKS ENTIRELY AT VARIANCE—HIS RISE AND PROGRESS IN THE CHURCH—POOR COUSIN "HENNY"—HIS TREATMENT OF HER—THE METHODIST PREACHERS—THEIR UTTER DISREGARD OF US—ONE EXCELLENT EXCEPTION—REV. GEORGE COOKMAN—SABBATH SCHOOL—HOW BROKEN UP AND BY WHOM—A FUNERAL PALL CAST OVER ALL MY PROSPECTS—COVEY THE NEGRO-BREAKER.

St. Michael's, the village in which was now my new home, compared favorably with villages in slave states, generally. There were a few comfortable dwellings in it, but the place, as a whole, wore a dull, slovenly, enterprise-forsaken aspect. The mass of the buildings were wood; they had never enjoyed the artificial adornment of paint, and time and storms had worn off the bright color of the wood, leaving them almost as black as buildings charred by a conflagration.

St. Michael's had, in former years, (previous to 1833, for that was the year I went to reside there,) enjoyed some reputation as a ship building community, but that business had almost entirely given place to oyster fishing, for the Baltimore and Philadelphia markets—a course of life highly unfavorable to morals, industry, and manners. Miles river was broad, and its oyster fishing grounds were extensive; and the fishermen were out, often, all day, and a part of the night, during autumn, winter and spring. This exposure was an excuse for carrying with them, in considerable quanties(sic), spirituous liquors, the then supposed best antidote for cold. Each canoe was supplied with its jug of rum; and tippling, among this class of the citizens of St. Michael's, became general.

This drinking habit, in an ignorant population, fostered coarseness, vulgarity and an indolent disregard for the social improvement of the place, so that it was admitted, by the few sober, thinking people who remained there, that St. Michael's had become a very *unsaintly*, as well as unsightly place, before I went there to reside.

I left Baltimore for St. Michael's in the month of March, 1833. I know the year, because it was the one succeeding the first cholera in Baltimore, and was the year, also, of that strange phenomenon, when the heavens seemed about to part with its starry train. I witnessed this gorgeous spectacle, and was awe-struck. The air seemed filled with bright, descending messengers from the sky. It was about daybreak when I saw this sublime scene. I was not without the suggestion, at the moment, that it might be the harbinger of the coming of the Son of Man; and, in my then state of mind, I was prepared to hail Him as my friend and deliverer. I had read, that the "stars shall fall from heaven"; and they were now falling. I was suffering much in my mind. It did seem that every time the young tendrils of my affection became attached, they were rudely broken by some unnatural outside power; and I was beginning to look away to heaven for the rest denied me on earth.

But, to my story. It was now more than seven years since I had lived with Master Thomas Auld, in the family of my old master, on Col. Lloyd's plantation. We were almost entire strangers to each other; for, when I knew him at the house of my old master, it was not as a *master*, but simply as "Captain Auld," who had married old master's daughter. All my lessons concerning his temper and disposition, and the best methods of pleasing him, were yet to be learnt. Slaveholders, however, are not very ceremonious in approaching a slave; and my ignorance of the new material in shape of a master was but transient. Nor was my mistress long in making known her animus. She was not a "Miss Lucretia," traces of whom I yet remembered, and the more especially, as I saw them shining in the face of little Amanda, her daughter, now living under a step-mother's government. I had not forgotten the soft hand, guided by a tender heart, that bound up with healing balsam the gash made in my head by Ike, the son of Abel. Thomas and Rowena, I found to be a well-matched pair. *He* was stingy, and *she* was cruel; and—what was quite natural in such cases—she possessed the ability to make him as cruel as herself, while she could easily descend to the level of his meanness. In the house of Master Thomas, I was made—for the first time in seven years to feel the pinchings of hunger, and this was not very easy to bear.

For, in all the changes of Master Hugh's family, there was no change in the bountifulness with which they supplied me with food. Not to give a slave enough to eat, is meanness intensified, and it is so recognized among slaveholders generally, in Maryland. The rule is, no matter how coarse the food, only let there be enough of it. This is the theory, and—in the part of Maryland I came from—the general practice accords with this theory. Lloyd's plantation was an exception, as was, also, the house of Master Thomas Auld.

All know the lightness of Indian corn-meal, as an article of food, and can easily judge from the following facts whether the statements I have made of the stinginess of Master Thomas, are borne out. There were four slaves of us in the kitchen, and four whites in the great house Thomas Auld, Mrs. Auld, Hadaway Auld (brother of Thomas Auld) and little Amanda. The names of the slaves in the kitchen, were Eliza, my sister; Priscilla, my aunt; Henny, my cousin; and myself. There were eight persons in the family. There was, each week, one half bushel of corn-meal brought from the mill; and in the kitchen, corn-meal was almost our exclusive food, for very little else was allowed us. Out of this bushel of corn-meal, the family in the great house had a small loaf every morning; thus leaving us, in the kitchen, with not quite a half a peck per week, apiece. This allowance was less than half the allowance of food on Lloyd's plantation. It was not enough to subsist upon; and we were, therefore, reduced to the wretched necessity of living at the expense of our neighbors. We were compelled either to beg, or to steal, and we did both. I frankly confess, that while I hated everything like stealing, *as such*, I nevertheless did not hesitate to take food, when I was hungry, wherever I could find it. Nor was this practice the mere result of an unreasoning instinct; it was, in my case, the result of a clear apprehension of the claims of morality. I weighed and considered the matter closely, before I ventured to satisfy my hunger by such means. Considering that my labor and person were the property of Master Thomas, and that I was by him deprived of the necessaries of life necessaries obtained by my own labor—it was easy to deduce the right to supply myself with what was my own. It was simply appropriating what was my own to the use of my master, since the health and strength derived from such food were exerted in *his* service. To be sure, this was stealing, according to the law and gospel I heard from St. Michael's pulpit; but I had already begun to attach less importance to what dropped from that quarter, on that point, while, as yet, I retained my reverence for religion. It was not always convenient to steal from master, and the same reason why I might, innocently, steal from him, did not seem to justify me in stealing from others. In the case of my master, it was only a question of *removal*—the taking his meat out of one tub, and putting it into another; the ownership of the meat was not affected by the transaction. At first, he owned it in the *tub*, and last, he owned it in *me*. His meat house was not always open. There was a strict watch kept on that point, and the key was on a large bunch in Rowena's pocket. A great many times have we, poor creatures, been severely pinched with hunger, when meat and bread have been moulding under the lock, while the key was in the pocket of our mistress. This had been so when she *knew* we were nearly half starved; and yet, that mistress, with saintly air, would kneel with her husband, and pray each morning that a merciful God would bless them in basket and in store, and save them, at last, in his kingdom. But I proceed with the argument.

It was necessary that right to steal from *others* should be established; and this could only rest upon a wider range of generalization than that which supposed the right to steal from my master.

It was sometime before I arrived at this clear right. The reader will get some idea of my train of reasoning, by a brief statement of the case. "I am," thought I, "not only the slave of Thomas, but I am the slave of society at large. Society at large has bound itself, in form and in fact, to assist Master Thomas in robbing me of my rightful liberty, and of the just reward of my labor; therefore, whatever rights I have against Master Thomas, I have, equally, against those confederated with him in robbing me of liberty. As society has marked me out as privileged plunder, on the principle of self-preservation I am justified in plundering in turn. Since each slave belongs to all; all must, therefore, belong to each."

I shall here make a profession of faith which may shock some, offend others, and be dissented from by all. It is this: Within the bounds of his just earnings, I hold that the slave is fully justified in helping himself to the *gold and silver, and the best apparel of his master, or that of any other slaveholder; and that such taking is not stealing in any just sense of that word.*

The morality of *free* society can have no application to *slave* society. Slaveholders have made it almost impossible for the slave to commit any crime, known either to the laws of God or to the laws of man. If he steals, he takes his own; if he kills his master, he imitates only the heroes of the revolution. Slaveholders I hold to be individually and collectively responsible for all the evils which grow out of the horrid relation, and I believe they will be so held at the judgment, in the sight of a just God. Make a man a slave, and you rob him of moral responsibility. Freedom of choice is the essence of all accountability. But my kind readers are, probably, less concerned about my opinions, than about that which more nearly touches my personal experience; albeit, my opinions have, in some sort, been formed by that experience.

Bad as slaveholders are, I have seldom met with one so entirely destitute of every element of character capable of inspiring respect, as was my present master, Capt. Thomas Auld.

When I lived with him, I thought him incapable of a noble action. The leading trait in his character was intense selfishness. I think he was fully aware of this fact himself, and often tried to conceal it. Capt. Auld was not a *born* slaveholder—not a birthright member of the slaveholding oligarchy. He was only a slaveholder by *marriage-right*; and, of all slaveholders, these latter are, *by far*, the most exacting. There was in him all the love of domination, the pride of mastery, and the swagger of authority, but his rule lacked the vital element of consistency. He could be cruel; but his methods of showing it were cowardly, and evinced his meanness rather than his spirit. His commands were strong, his enforcement weak.

Slaves are not insensible to the whole-souled characteristics of a generous, dashing slaveholder, who is fearless of consequences; and they prefer a master of this bold and daring kind—even with the risk of being shot down for impudence to the fretful, little soul, who never uses the lash but at the suggestion of a love of gain.

Slaves, too, readily distinguish between the birthright bearing of the original slaveholder and the assumed attitudes of the accidental slaveholder; and while they cannot respect either, they certainly despise the latter more than the former.

The luxury of having slaves wait upon him was something new to Master Thomas; and for it he was wholly unprepared. He was a slaveholder, without the ability to hold or manage his slaves. We seldom called him "master," but generally addressed him by his "bay craft" title—"*Capt. Auld.*" It is easy to see that such conduct might do much to make him appear awkward, and, consequently, fretful. His wife was especially solicitous to have us call her husband "master." Is your *master* at the store?"—"Where is your *master*?"—"Go and tell your *master*"—"I will make your *master* acquainted with your conduct"—she would say; but we were inapt scholars. Especially were I and my sister Eliza inapt in this particular. Aunt Priscilla was less stubborn and defiant in her spirit than Eliza and myself; and, I think, her road was less rough than ours.

In the month of August, 1833, when I had almost become desperate under the treatment of Master Thomas, and when I entertained more strongly than ever the oft-repeated determination to run away, a circumstance occurred which seemed to promise brighter and better days for us all. At a Methodist camp-meeting, held in the Bay Side (a famous place for campmeetings) about eight miles from St. Michael's, Master Thomas came out with a profession of religion. He had long been an object of interest to the church, and to the ministers, as I had seen by the repeated visits and lengthy exhortations of the latter. He was a fish quite worth catching, for he had money and standing. In the community of St. Michael's he was equal to the best citizen. He was strictly temperate; *perhaps*, from principle, but most likely, from interest. There was very little to do for him, to give him the appearance of piety, and to make him a pillar in the church. Well, the camp-meeting continued a week; people gathered from all parts of the county, and two steamboat loads came from Baltimore. The ground was happily chosen; seats were arranged; a stand erected; a rude altar fenced in, fronting the preachers' stand, with straw in it for the accommodation of mourners. This latter would hold at least one hundred persons. In front, and on the sides of the preachers' stand, and outside the long rows of seats, rose the first class of stately tents, each vieing with the other in strength, neatness, and capacity for accommodating its inmates. Behind this first circle of tents was another, less imposing, which reached round the camp-ground to the speakers' stand. Outside this second class of tents were covered wagons, ox carts, and vehicles of every shape and size. These served as tents to their owners. Outside of these, huge fires were burning, in all directions, where roasting, and boiling, and frying, were going on, for the benefit of those who were attending to their own spiritual welfare within the circle. *Behind* the preachers' stand, a narrow space was marked out for the use of the colored people. There were no seats provided for this class of persons; the preachers addressed them, *"over the left,"* if they addressed them at all. After the preaching was over, at every service, an invitation was given to mourners to come into the pen; and, in some cases, ministers went out to persuade men and women to come in. By one of these ministers, Master Thomas Auld was persuaded to go inside the pen. I was deeply interested in that matter, and followed; and, though colored people were not allowed either in the pen or in front of the preachers' stand, I ventured to take my stand at a sort of half-way place between the blacks and whites, where I could distinctly see the movements of mourners, and especially the progress of Master Thomas.

"If he has got religion," thought I, "he will emancipate his slaves; and if he should not do so much as this, he will, at any rate, behave toward us more kindly, and feed us more generously than he has heretofore done." Appealing to my own religious experience, and judging my master by what was true in my own case, I could not regard him as soundly converted, unless some such good results followed his profession of religion.

But in my expectations I was doubly disappointed; Master Thomas was *Master Thomas* still. The fruits of his righteousness were to show themselves in no such way as I had anticipated. His conversion was not to change his relation toward men—at any rate not toward BLACK men—but toward God. My faith, I confess, was not great. There was something in his appearance that, in my mind, cast a doubt over his conversion. Standing where I did, I could see his every movement. I watched narrowly while he remained in the little pen; and although I saw that his face was extremely red, and his hair disheveled, and though I heard him groan, and saw a stray tear halting on his cheek, as if inquiring "which way shall I go?"—I could not wholly confide in the genuineness of his conversion. The hesitating behavior of that tear-drop and its loneliness, distressed me, and cast a doubt upon the whole transaction, of which it was a part. But people said, *"Capt. Auld had come through,"* and it was for me to hope for the best. I was bound to do this, in charity, for I, too, was religious, and had been in the church full three years, although now I was not more than sixteen years old. Slaveholders may, sometimes, have confidence in the piety of some of their slaves; but the slaves seldom have confidence in the piety of their masters. *"He cant go to heaven with our blood in his skirts,"* is a settled point in the creed of every slave; rising superior to all teaching to the contrary, and standing forever as a fixed fact. The highest evidence the slaveholder can give the slave of his acceptance with God, is the emancipation of his slaves. This is proof that he is willing to give up all to God, and for the sake of God. Not to do this, was, in my estimation, and in the opinion of all the slaves, an evidence of half-heartedness, and wholly inconsistent with the idea of genuine conversion. I had read, also, somewhere in the Methodist Discipline, the following question and answer:

"*Question.* What shall be done for the extirpation of slavery?

"*Answer.* We declare that we are much as ever convinced of the great evil of slavery; therefore, no slaveholder shall be eligible to any official station in our church."

These words sounded in my ears for a long time, and encouraged me to hope. But, as I have before said, I was doomed to disappointment. Master Thomas seemed to be aware of my hopes and expectations concerning him. I have thought, before now, that he looked at me in answer to my glances, as much as to say, "I will teach you, young man, that, though I have parted with my sins, I have not parted with my sense. I shall hold my slaves, and go to heaven too."

Possibly, to convince us that we must not presume *too much* upon his recent conversion, he became rather more rigid and stringent in his exactions. There always was a scarcity of good nature about the man; but now his whole countenance was *soured* over with the seemings of piety. His religion, therefore, neither made him emancipate his slaves, nor caused him to treat them with greater humanity. If religion had any effect on his character at all, it made him more cruel and hateful in all his ways. The natural wickedness of his heart had not been removed, but only reinforced, by the profession of religion. Do I judge him harshly? God forbid. Facts *are* facts. Capt. Auld made the greatest profession of piety. His house was, literally, a house of prayer. In the morning, and in the evening, loud prayers and hymns were heard there, in which both himself and his wife joined; yet, *no more meal* was brought from the mill, *no more attention* was paid to the moral welfare of the kitchen; and nothing was done to make us feel that the heart of Master Thomas was one whit better than it was before he went into the little pen, opposite to the preachers' stand, on the camp ground.

Our hopes (founded on the discipline) soon vanished; for the authorities let him into the church *at once,* and before he was out of his term of *probation,* I heard of his leading class! He distinguished himself greatly among the brethren, and was soon an exhorter. His progress was almost as rapid as the growth of the fabled vine of Jack's bean. No man was more active than he, in revivals. He would go many miles to assist in carrying them on, and in getting outsiders interested in religion. His house being one of the holiest, if not the happiest in St. Michael's, became the "preachers' home." These preachers evidently liked to share Master Thomas's hospitality; for while he *starved us,* he *stuffed* them. Three or four of these ambassadors of the gospel—according to slavery—have been there at a time; all living on the fat of the land, while we, in the kitchen, were nearly starving. Not often did we get a smile of recognition from these holy men. They seemed almost as unconcerned about our getting to heaven, as they were about our getting out of slavery. To this general charge there was one exception—the Rev. GEORGE COOKMAN. Unlike Rev. Messrs. Storks, Ewry, Hickey, Humphrey and Cooper (all whom were on the St. Michael's circuit) he kindly took an interest in our temporal and spiritual welfare. Our souls and our bodies were all alike sacred in his sight; and he really had a good deal of genuine anti-slavery feeling mingled with his colonization ideas. There was not a slave in our neighborhood that did not love, and almost venerate, Mr. Cookman. It was pretty generally believed that he had been chiefly instrumental in bringing one of the largest slaveholders—Mr. Samuel Harrison—in that neighborhood, to emancipate all his slaves, and, indeed, the general impression was, that Mr. Cookman had labored faithfully with slaveholders, whenever he met them, to induce them to emancipate their bondmen, and that he did this as a religious duty. When this good man was at our house, we were all sure to be called in to prayers in the morning; and he was not slow in making inquiries as to the state of our minds, nor in giving us a word of exhortation and of encouragement. Great was the sorrow of all the slaves, when this faithful preacher of the gospel was removed from the Talbot county circuit. He was an eloquent preacher, and possessed what few ministers, south of Mason Dixon's line, possess, or *dare* to show, viz: a warm and philanthropic heart. The Mr. Cookman, of whom I speak, was an Englishman by birth, and perished while on his way to England, on board the ill-fated "President". Could the thousands of slaves in Maryland know the fate of the good man, to whose words of comfort they were so largely indebted, they would thank me for dropping a tear on this page, in memory of their favorite preacher, friend and benefactor.

But, let me return to Master Thomas, and to my experience, after his conversion. In Baltimore, I could, occasionally, get into a Sabbath school, among the free children, and receive lessons, with the rest; but, having already learned both to read and to write, I was more of a teacher than a pupil, even there. When, however, I went back to the Eastern Shore, and was at the house of Master Thomas, I was neither allowed to teach, nor to be taught. The whole community—with but a single exception, among the whites—frowned upon everything like imparting instruction either to slaves or to free colored persons. That single exception, a pious young man, named Wilson, asked me, one day, if I would like to assist him in teaching a little Sabbath school, at the house of a free colored man in St. Michael's, named James Mitchell. The idea was to me a delightful one, and I told him I would gladly devote as much of my Sabbath as I could command, to that most laudable work. Mr. Wilson soon mustered up a dozen old spelling books, and a few testaments; and we commenced operations, with some twenty scholars, in our Sunday school. Here, thought I, is something worth living for; here is an excellent chance for usefulness; and I shall soon have a company of young friends, lovers of knowledge, like some of my Baltimore friends, from whom I now felt parted forever.

Our first Sabbath passed delightfully, and I spent the week after very joyously. I could not go to Baltimore, but I could make a little Baltimore here. At our second meeting, I learned that there was some objection to the existence of the Sabbath school; and, sure enough, we had scarcely got at work—*good work*, simply teaching a few colored children how to read the gospel of the Son of God—when in rushed a mob, headed by Mr. Wright Fairbanks and Mr. Garrison West—two class-leaders—and Master Thomas; who, armed with sticks and other missiles, drove us off, and commanded us never to meet for such a purpose again. One of this pious crew told me, that as for my part, I wanted to be another Nat Turner; and if I did not look out, I should get as many balls into me, as Nat did into him. Thus ended the infant Sabbath school, in the town of St. Michael's. The reader will not be surprised when I say, that the breaking up of my Sabbath school, by these class-leaders, and professedly holy men, did not serve to strengthen my religious convictions. The cloud over my St. Michael's home grew heavier and blacker than ever.

It was not merely the agency of Master Thomas, in breaking up and destroying my Sabbath school, that shook my confidence in the power of southern religion to make men wiser or better; but I saw in him all the cruelty and meanness, *after* his conversion, which he had exhibited before he made a profession of religion. His cruelty and meanness were especially displayed in his treatment of my unfortunate cousin, Henny, whose lameness made her a burden to him. I have no extraordinary personal hard usage toward myself to complain of, against him, but I have seen him tie up the lame and maimed woman, and whip her in a manner most brutal, and shocking; and then, with blood-chilling blasphemy, he would quote the passage of scripture, "That servant which knew his lord's will, and prepared not himself, neither did according to his will, shall be beaten with many stripes." Master would keep this lacerated woman tied up by her wrists, to a bolt in the joist, three, four and five hours at a time. He would tie her up early in the morning, whip her with a cowskin before breakfast; leave her tied up; go to his store, and, returning to his dinner, repeat the castigation; laying on the rugged lash, on flesh already made raw by repeated blows. He seemed desirous to get the poor girl out of existence, or, at any rate, off his hands. In proof of this, he afterwards gave her away to his sister Sarah (Mrs. Cline) but, as in the case of Master Hugh, Henny was soon returned on his hands. Finally, upon a pretense that he could do nothing with her (I use his own words) he "set her adrift, to take care of herself." Here was a recently converted man, holding, with tight grasp, the well-framed, and able bodied slaves left him by old master—the persons, who, in freedom, could have taken care of themselves; yet, turning loose the only cripple among them, virtually to starve and die.

No doubt, had Master Thomas been asked, by some pious northern brother, *why* he continued to sustain the relation of a slaveholder, to those whom he retained, his answer would have been precisely the same as many other religious slaveholders have returned to that inquiry, viz: "I hold my slaves for their own good."

Bad as my condition was when I lived with Master Thomas, I was soon to experience a life far more goading and bitter. The many differences springing up between myself and Master Thomas, owing to the clear perception I had of his character, and the boldness with which I defended myself against his capricious complaints, led him to declare that I was unsuited to his wants; that my city life had affected me perniciously; that, in fact, it had almost ruined me for every good purpose, and had fitted me for everything that was bad. One of my greatest faults, or offenses, was that of letting his horse get away, and go down to the farm belonging to his father-in-law. The animal had a liking for that farm, with which I fully sympathized. Whenever I let it out, it would go dashing down the road to Mr. Hamilton's, as if going on a grand frolic. My horse gone, of course I must go after it. The explanation of our mutual attachment to the place is the same; the horse found there good pasturage, and I found there plenty of bread. Mr. Hamilton had his faults, but starving his slaves was not among them. He gave food, in abundance, and that, too, of an excellent quality. In Mr. Hamilton's cook—Aunt Mary—I found a most generous and considerate friend. She never allowed me to go there without giving me bread enough to make good the deficiencies of a day or two. Master Thomas at last resolved to endure my behavior no longer; he could neither keep me, nor his horse, we liked so well to be at his father-in-law's farm. I had now lived with him nearly nine months, and he had given me a number of severe whippings, without any visible improvement in my character, or my conduct; and now he was resolved to put me out—as he said—"*to be broken.*"

There was, in the Bay Side, very near the camp ground, where my master got his religious impressions, a man named Edward Covey, who enjoyed the execrated reputation, of being a first rate hand at breaking young Negroes. This Covey was a poor man, a farm renter; and this reputation (hateful as it was to the slaves and to all good men) was, at the same time, of immense advantage to him. It enabled him to get his farm tilled with very little expense, compared with what it would have cost him without this most extraordinary reputation. Some slaveholders thought it an advantage to let Mr. Covey have the government of their slaves a year or two, almost free of charge, for the sake of the excellent training such slaves got under his happy management! Like some horse breakers, noted for their skill, who ride the best horses in the country without expense, Mr. Covey could have under him, the most fiery bloods of the neighborhood, for the simple reward of returning them to their owners, *well broken*. Added to the natural fitness of Mr. Covey for the duties of his profession, he was said to "enjoy religion," and was as strict in the cultivation of piety, as he was in the cultivation of his farm. I was made aware of his character by some who had been under his hand; and while I could not look forward to going to him with any pleasure, I was glad to get away from St. Michael's. I was sure of getting enough to eat at Covey's, even if I suffered in other respects. *This*, to a hungry man, is not a prospect to be regarded with indifference.

CHAPTER XV

Covey, the Negro Breaker

The morning of the first of January, 1834, with its chilling wind and pinching frost, quite in harmony with the winter in my own mind, found me, with my little bundle of clothing on the end of a stick, swung across my shoulder, on the main road, bending my way toward Covey's, whither I had been imperiously ordered by Master Thomas. The latter had been as good as his word, and had committed me, without reserve, to the mastery of Mr. Edward Covey. Eight or ten years had now passed since I had been taken from my grandmother's cabin, in Tuckahoe; and these years, for the most part, I had spent in Baltimore, where—as the reader has already seen—I was treated with comparative tenderness. I was now about to sound profounder depths in slave life. The rigors of a field, less tolerable than the field of battle, awaited me. My new master was notorious for his fierce and savage disposition, and my only consolation in going to live with him was, the certainty of finding him precisely as represented by common fame. There was neither joy in my heart, nor elasticity in my step, as I started in search of the tyrant's home. Starvation made me glad to leave Thomas Auld's, and the cruel lash made me dread to go to Covey's. Escape was impossible; so, heavy and sad, I paced the seven miles, which separated Covey's house from St. Michael's— thinking much by the solitary way—averse to my condition; but *thinking* was all I could do. Like a fish in a net, allowed to play for a time, I was now drawn rapidly to the shore, secured at all points. "I am," thought I, "but the sport of a power which makes no account, either of my welfare or of my happiness. By a law which I can clearly comprehend, but cannot evade nor resist, I am ruthlessly snatched from the hearth of a fond grandmother, and hurried away to the home of a mysterious 'old master;' again I am removed from there, to a master in Baltimore; thence am I snatched away to the Eastern Shore, to be valued with the beasts of the field, and, with them, divided and set apart for a possessor; then I am sent back to Baltimore; and by the time I have formed new attachments, and have begun to hope that no more rude shocks shall touch me, a difference arises between brothers, and I am again broken up, and sent to St. Michael's; and now, from the latter place, I am footing my way to the home of a new master, where, I am given to understand, that, like a wild young working animal, I am to be broken to the yoke of a bitter and life-long bondage."

With thoughts and reflections like these, I came in sight of a small wood-colored building, about a mile from the main road, which, from the description I had received, at starting, I easily recognized as my new home. The Chesapeake bay—upon the jutting banks of which the little wood-colored house was standing—white with foam, raised by the heavy north-west wind; Poplar Island, covered with a thick, black pine forest, standing out amid this half ocean; and Kent Point, stretching its sandy, desert-like shores out into the foam-cested bay—were all in sight, and deepened the wild and desolate aspect of my new home.

The good clothes I had brought with me from Baltimore were now worn thin, and had not been replaced; for Master Thomas was as little careful to provide us against cold, as against hunger. Met here by a north wind, sweeping through an open space of forty miles, I was glad to make any port; and, therefore, I speedily pressed on to the little wood-colored house. The family consisted of Mr. and Mrs. Covey; Miss Kemp (a broken-backed woman) a sister of Mrs. Covey; William Hughes, cousin to Edward Covey; Caroline, the cook; Bill Smith, a hired man; and myself. Bill Smith, Bill Hughes, and myself, were the working force of the farm, which consisted of three or four hundred acres. I was now, for the first time in my life, to be a field hand; and in my new employment I found myself even more awkward than a green country boy may be supposed to be, upon his first entrance into the bewildering scenes of city life; and my awkwardness gave me much trouble. Strange and unnatural as it may seem, I had been at my new home but three days, before Mr. Covey (my brother in the Methodist church) gave me a bitter foretaste of what was in reserve for me. I presume he thought, that since he had but a single year in which to complete his work, the sooner he began, the better. Perhaps he thought that by coming to blows at once, we should mutually better understand our relations. But to whatever motive, direct or indirect, the cause may be referred, I had not been in his possession three whole days, before he subjected me to a most brutal chastisement. Under his heavy blows, blood flowed freely, and wales were left on my back as large as my little finger. The sores on my back, from this flogging, continued for weeks, for they were kept open by the rough and coarse cloth which I wore for shirting. The occasion and details of this first chapter of my experience as a field hand, must be told, that the reader may see how unreasonable, as well as how cruel, my new master, Covey, was. The whole thing I found to be characteristic of the man; and I was probably treated no worse by him than scores of lads who had previously been committed to him, for reasons similar to those which induced my master to place me with him. But, here are the facts connected with the affair, precisely as they occurred.

On one of the coldest days of the whole month of January, 1834, I was ordered, at day break, to get a load of wood, from a forest about two miles from the house. In order to perform this work, Mr. Covey gave me a pair of unbroken oxen, for, it seems, his breaking abilities had not been turned in this direction; and I may remark, in passing, that working animals in the south, are seldom so well trained as in the north. In due form, and with all proper ceremony, I was introduced to this huge yoke of unbroken oxen, and was carefully told which was "Buck," and which was "Darby"—which was the "in hand," and which was the "off hand" ox. The master of this important ceremony was no less a person than Mr. Covey, himself; and the introduction was the first of the kind I had ever had. My life, hitherto, had led me away from horned cattle, and I had no knowledge of the art of managing them. What was meant by the "in ox," as against the "off ox," when both were equally fastened to one cart, and under one yoke, I could not very easily divine; and the difference, implied by the names, and the peculiar duties of each, were alike *Greek* to me. Why was not the "off ox" called the "in ox?" Where and what is the reason for this distinction in names, when there is none in the things themselves? After initiating me into the *"woa," "back" "gee," "hither"*—the entire spoken language between oxen and driver—Mr. Covey took a rope, about ten feet long and one inch thick, and placed one end of it around the horns of the "in hand ox," and gave the other end to me, telling me that if the oxen started to run away, as the scamp knew they would, I must hold on to the rope and stop them. I need not tell any one who is acquainted with either the strength of the disposition of an untamed ox, that this order was about as unreasonable as a command to shoulder a mad bull! I had never driven oxen before, and I was as awkward, as a driver, as it is possible to conceive. It did not answer for me to plead ignorance, to Mr. Covey; there was something in his manner that quite forbade that. He was a man to whom a slave seldom felt any disposition to speak. Cold, distant, morose, with a face wearing all the marks of captious pride and malicious sternness, he repelled all advances.

Covey was not a large man; he was only about five feet ten inches in height, I should think; short necked, round shoulders; of quick and wiry motion, of thin and wolfish visage; with a pair of small, greenish-gray eyes, set well back under a forehead without dignity, and constantly in motion, and floating his passions, rather than his thoughts, in sight, but denying them utterance in words. The creature presented an appearance altogether ferocious and sinister, disagreeable and forbidding, in the extreme. When he spoke, it was from the corner of his mouth, and in a sort of light growl, like a dog, when an attempt is made to take a bone from him. The fellow had already made me believe him even *worse* than he had been presented. With his directions, and without stopping to question, I started for the woods, quite anxious to perform my first exploit in driving, in a creditable manner. The distance from the house to the woods gate a full mile, I should think—was passed over with very little difficulty; for although the animals ran, I was fleet enough, in the open field, to keep pace with them; especially as they pulled me along at the end of the rope; but, on reaching the woods, I was speedily thrown into a distressing plight. The animals took fright, and started off ferociously into the woods, carrying the cart, full tilt, against trees, over stumps, and dashing from side to side, in a manner altogether frightful. As I held the rope, I expected every moment to be crushed between the cart and the huge trees, among which they were so furiously dashing. After running thus for several minutes, my oxen were, finally, brought to a stand, by a tree, against which they dashed themselves with great violence, upsetting the cart, and entangling themselves among sundry young saplings. By the shock, the body of the cart was flung in one direction, and the wheels and tongue in another, and all in the greatest confusion. There I was, all alone, in a thick wood, to which I was a stranger; my cart upset and shattered; my oxen entangled, wild, and enraged; and I, poor soul! but a green hand, to set all this disorder right. I knew no more of oxen than the ox driver is supposed to know of wisdom. After standing a few moments surveying the damage and disorder, and not without a presentiment that this trouble would draw after it others, even more distressing, I took one end of the cart body, and, by an extra outlay of strength, I lifted it toward the axle-tree, from which it had been violently flung; and after much pulling and straining, I succeeded in getting the body of the cart in its place. This was an important step out of the difficulty, and its performance increased my courage for the work which remained to be done. The cart was provided with an ax, a tool with which I had become pretty well acquainted in the ship yard at Baltimore. With this, I cut down the saplings by which my oxen were entangled, and again pursued my journey, with my heart in my mouth, lest the oxen should again take it into their senseless heads to cut up a caper. My fears were groundless. Their spree was over for the present, and the rascals now moved off as soberly as though their behavior had been natural and exemplary.

On reaching the part of the forest where I had been, the day before, chopping wood, I filled the cart with a heavy load, as a security against another running away. But, the neck of an ox is equal in strength to iron. It defies all ordinary burdens, when excited. Tame and docile to a proverb, when *well* trained, the ox is the most sullen and intractable of animals when but half broken to the yoke.

I now saw, in my situation, several points of similarity with that of the oxen. They were property, so was I; they were to be broken, so was I. Covey was to break me, I was to break them; break and be broken—such is life.

Half the day already gone, and my face not yet homeward! It required only two day's experience and observation to teach me, that such apparent waste of time would not be lightly overlooked by Covey. I therefore hurried toward home; but, on reaching the lane gate, I met with the crowning disaster for the day. This gate was a fair specimen of southern handicraft. There were two huge posts, eighteen inches in diameter, rough hewed and square, and the heavy gate was so hung on one of these, that it opened only about half the proper distance. On arriving here, it was necessary for me to let go the end of the rope on the horns of the "in hand ox;" and now as soon as the gate was open, and I let go of it to get the rope, again, off went my oxen—making nothing of their load—full tilt; and in doing so they caught the huge gate between the wheel and the cart body, literally crushing it to splinters, and coming only within a few inches of subjecting me to a similar crushing, for I was just in advance of the wheel when it struck the left gate post. With these two hair-breadth escape, I thought I could sucessfully(sic) explain to Mr. Covey the delay, and avert apprehended punishment. I was not without a faint hope of being commended for the stern resolution which I had displayed in accomplishing the difficult task—a task which, I afterwards learned, even Covey himself would not have undertaken, without first driving the oxen for some time in the open field, preparatory to their going into the woods. But, in this I was disappointed. On coming to him, his countenance assumed an aspect of rigid displeasure, and, as I gave him a history of the casualties of my trip, his wolfish face, with his greenish eyes, became intensely ferocious. "Go back to the woods again," he said, muttering something else about wasting time. I hastily obeyed; but I had not gone far on my way, when I saw him coming after me. My oxen now behaved themselves with singular propriety, opposing their present conduct to my representation of their former antics. I almost wished, now that Covey was coming, they would do something in keeping with the character I had given them; but no, they had already had their spree, and they could afford now to be extra good, readily obeying my orders, and seeming to understand them quite as well as I did myself. On reaching the woods, my tormentor—who seemed all the way to be remarking upon the good behavior of his oxen—came up to me, and ordered me to stop the cart, accompanying the same with the threat that he would now teach me how to break gates, and idle away my time, when he sent me to the woods. Suiting the action to the word, Covey paced off, in his own wiry fashion, to a large, black gum tree, the young shoots of which are generally used for ox *goads*, they being exceedingly tough. Three of these *goads*, from four to six feet long, he cut off, and trimmed up, with his large jack-knife. This done, he ordered me to take off my clothes. To this unreasonable order I made no reply, but sternly refused to take off my clothing. "If you will beat me," thought I, "you shall do so over my clothes." After many threats, which made no impression on me, he rushed at me with something of the savage fierceness of a wolf, tore off the few and thinly worn clothes I had on, and proceeded to wear out, on my back, the heavy goads which he had cut from the gum tree. This flogging was the first of a series of floggings; and though very severe, it was less so than many which came after it, and these, for offenses far lighter than the gate breaking.

I remained with Mr. Covey one year (I cannot say I *lived* with him) and during the first six months that I was there, I was whipped, either with sticks or cowskins, every week. Aching bones and a sore back were my constant companions. Frequent as the lash was used, Mr. Covey thought less of it, as a means of breaking down my spirit, than that of hard and long continued labor. He worked me steadily, up to the point of my powers of endurance. From the dawn of day in the morning, till the darkness was complete in the evening, I was kept at hard work, in the field or the woods. At certain seasons of the year, we were all kept in the field till eleven and twelve o'clock at night. At these times, Covey would attend us in the field, and urge us on with words or blows, as it seemed best to him. He had, in his life, been an overseer, and he well understood the business of slave driving. There was no deceiving him. He knew just what a man or boy could do, and he held both to strict account. When he pleased, he would work himself, like a very Turk, making everything fly before him. It was, however, scarcely necessary for Mr. Covey to be really present in the field, to have his work go on industriously. He had the faculty of making us feel that he was always present. By a series of adroitly managed surprises, which he practiced, I was prepared to expect him at any moment. His plan was, never to approach the spot where his hands were at work, in an open, manly and direct manner. No thief was ever more artful in his devices than this man Covey. He would creep and crawl, in ditches and gullies; hide behind stumps and bushes, and practice so much of the cunning of the serpent, that Bill Smith and I— between ourselves—never called him by any other name than *"the snake."* We fancied that in his eyes and his gait we could see a snakish resemblance. One half of his proficiency in the art of Negro breaking, consisted, I should think, in this species of cunning. We were never secure. He could see or hear us nearly all the time. He was, to us, behind every stump, tree, bush and fence on the plantation. He carried this kind of trickery so far, that he would sometimes mount his horse, and make believe he was going to St. Michael's; and, in thirty minutes afterward, you might find his horse tied in the woods, and the snake-like Covey lying flat in the ditch, with his head lifted above its edge, or in a fence corner, watching every movement of the slaves! I have known him walk up to us and give us special orders, as to our work, in advance, as if he were leaving home with a view to being absent several days; and before he got half way to the house, he would avail himself of our inattention to his movements, to turn short on his heels, conceal himself behind a fence corner or a tree, and watch us until the going down of the sun. Mean and contemptible as is all this, it is in keeping with the character which the life of a slaveholder is calculated to produce. There is no earthly inducement, in the slave's condition, to incite him to labor faithfully. The fear of punishment is the sole motive for any sort of industry, with him. Knowing this fact, as the slaveholder does, and judging the slave by himself, he naturally concludes the slave will be idle whenever the cause for this fear is absent. Hence, all sorts of petty deceptions are practiced, to inspire this fear.

But, with Mr. Covey, trickery was natural. Everything in the shape of learning or religion, which he possessed, was made to conform to this semi-lying propensity. He did not seem conscious that the practice had anything unmanly, base or contemptible about it. It was a part of an important system, with him, essential to the relation of master and slave. I thought I saw, in his very religious devotions, this controlling element of his character. A long prayer at night made up for the short prayer in the morning; and few men could seem more devotional than he, when he had nothing else to do.

Mr. Covey was not content with the cold style of family worship, adopted in these cold latitudes, which begin and end with a simple prayer. No! the voice of praise, as well as of prayer, must be heard in his house, night and morning. At first, I was called upon to bear some part in these exercises; but the repeated flogging given me by Covey, turned the whole thing into mockery. He was a poor singer, and mainly relied on me for raising the hymn for the family, and when I failed to do so, he was thrown into much confusion. I do not think that he ever abused me on account of these vexations. His religion was a thing altogether apart from his worldly concerns. He knew nothing of it as a holy principle, directing and controlling his daily life, making the latter conform to the requirements of the gospel. One or two facts will illustrate his character better than a volume of generalties(sic).

I have already said, or implied, that Mr. Edward Covey was a poor man. He was, in fact, just commencing to lay the foundation of his fortune, as fortune is regarded in a slave state. The first condition of wealth and respectability there, being the ownership of human property, every nerve is strained, by the poor man, to obtain it, and very little regard is had to the manner of obtaining it. In pursuit of this object, pious as Mr. Covey was, he proved himself to be as unscrupulous and base as the worst of his neighbors. In the beginning, he was only able—as he said—"to buy one slave;" and, scandalous and shocking as is the fact, he boasted that he bought her simply "*as a breeder.*" But the worst is not told in this naked statement. This young woman (Caroline was her name) was virtually compelled by Mr. Covey to abandon herself to the object for which he had purchased her; and the result was, the birth of twins at the end of the year. At this addition to his human stock, both Edward Covey and his wife, Susan, were ecstatic with joy. No one dreamed of reproaching the woman, or of finding fault with the hired man—Bill Smith—the father of the children, for Mr. Covey himself had locked the two up together every night, thus inviting the result.

But I will pursue this revolting subject no further. No better illustration of the unchaste and demoralizing character of slavery can be found, than is furnished in the fact that this professedly Christian slaveholder, amidst all his prayers and hymns, was shamelessly and boastfully encouraging, and actually compelling, in his own house, undisguised and unmitigated fornication, as a means of increasing his human stock. I may remark here, that, while this fact will be read with disgust and shame at the north, it will be *laughed at,* as smart and praiseworthy in Mr. Covey, at the south; for a man is no more condemned there for buying a woman and devoting her to this life of dishonor, than for buying a cow, and raising stock from her. The same rules are observed, with a view to increasing the number and quality of the former, as of the latter.

I will here reproduce what I said of my own experience in this wretched place, more than ten years ago:

If at any one time of my life, more than another, I was made to drink the bitterest dregs of slavery, that time was during the first six months of my stay with Mr. Covey. We were worked all weathers. It was never too hot or too cold; it could never rain, blow, snow, or hail too hard for us to work in the field. Work, work, work, was scarcely more the order of the day than the night. The longest days were too short for him, and the shortest nights were too long for him. I was somewhat unmanageable when I first went there; but a few months of his discipline tamed me. Mr. Covey succeeded in breaking me. I was broken in body, soul and spirit. My natural elasticity was crushed; my intellect languished; the disposition to read departed; the cheerful spark that lingered about my eye died; the dark night of slavery closed in upon me; and behold a man transformed into a brute!

Sunday was my only leisure time. I spent this in a sort of beast-like stupor, between sleep and wake, under some large tree. At times, I would rise up, a flash of energetic freedom would dart through my soul, accompanied with a faint beam of hope, flickered for a moment, and then vanished. I sank down again, mourning over my wretched condition. I was sometimes prompted to take my life, and that of Covey, but was prevented by a combination of hope and fear. My sufferings on this plantation seem now like a dream rather than a stern reality.

Our house stood within a few rods of the Chesapeake bay, whose broad bosom was ever white with sails from every quarter of the habitable globe. Those beautiful vessels, robed in purest white, so delightful to the eye of freemen, were to me so many shrouded ghosts, to terrify and torment me with thoughts of my wretched condition. I have often, in the deep stillness of a summer's Sabbath, stood all alone upon the banks of that noble bay, and traced, with saddened heart and tearful eye, the countless number of sails moving off to the mighty ocean. The sight of these always affected me powerfully. My thoughts would compel utterance; and there, with no audience but the Almighty, I would pour out my soul's complaint in my rude way, with an apostrophe to the moving multitude of ships:

"You are loosed from your moorings, and free; I am fast in my chains, and am a slave! You move merrily before the gentle gale, and I sadly before the bloody whip! You are freedom's swift-winged angels, that fly around the world; I am confined in bands of iron! O, that I were free! O, that I were on one of your gallant decks, and under your protecting wing! Alas! betwixt me and you the turbid waters roll. Go on, go on. O that I could also go! Could I but swim! If I could fly! O, why was I born a man, of whom to make a brute! The glad ship is gone; she hides in the dim distance. I am left in the hottest hell of unending slavery. O God, save me! God, deliver me! Let me be free! Is there any God? Why am I a slave? I will run away. I will not stand it. Get caught, or get clear, I'll try it. I had as well die with ague as with fever. I have only one life to lose. I had as well be killed running as die standing. Only think of it; one hundred miles straight north, and I am free! Try it? Yes! God helping me, I will. It cannot be that I shall live and die a slave. I will take to the water. This very bay shall yet bear me into freedom. The steamboats steered in a north-east coast from North Point. I will do the same; and when I get to the head of the bay, I will turn my canoe adrift, and walk straight through Delaware into Pennsylvania. When I get there, I shall not be required to have a pass; I will travel without being disturbed. Let but the first opportunity offer, and come what will, I am off. Meanwhile, I will try to bear up under the yoke. I am not the only slave in the world. Why should I fret? I can bear as much as any of them. Besides, I am but a boy, and all boys are bound to some one. It may be that my misery in slavery will only increase my happiness when I get free. There is a better day coming."

I shall never be able to narrate the mental experience through which it was my lot to pass during my stay at Covey's. I was completely wrecked, changed and bewildered; goaded almost to madness at one time, and at another reconciling myself to my wretched condition. Everything in the way of kindness, which I had experienced at Baltimore; all my former hopes and aspirations for usefulness in the world, and the happy moments spent in the exercises of religion, contrasted with my then present lot, but increased my anguish.

I suffered bodily as well as mentally. I had neither sufficient time in which to eat or to sleep, except on Sundays. The overwork, and the brutal chastisements of which I was the victim, combined with that ever-gnawing and soul-devouring thought—"*I am a slave—a slave for life—a slave with no rational ground to hope for freedom*"—rendered me a living embodiment of mental and physical wretchedness.

CHAPTER XVI

Another Pressure of the Tyrant's Vice

EXPERIENCE AT COVEY'S SUMMED UP—FIRST SIX MONTHS SEVERER THAN THE SECOND—PRELIMINARIES TO THE CHANCE—REASONS FOR NARRATING THE CIRCUMSTANCES—SCENE IN TREADING YARD—TAKEN ILL—UNUSUAL BRUTALITY OF COVEY—ESCAPE TO ST. MICHAEL'S—THE PURSUIT—SUFFERING IN THE WOODS—DRIVEN BACK AGAIN TO COVEY'S—BEARING OF MASTER THOMAS—THE SLAVE IS NEVER SICK—NATURAL TO EXPECT SLAVES TO FEIGN SICKNESS—LAZINESS OF SLAVEHOLDERS.

The foregoing chapter, with all its horrid incidents and shocking features, may be taken as a fair representation of the first six months of my life at Covey's. The reader has but to repeat, in his own mind, once a week, the scene in the woods, where Covey subjected me to his merciless lash, to have a true idea of my bitter experience there, during the first period of the breaking process through which Mr. Covey carried me. I have no heart to repeat each separate transaction, in which I was victim of his violence and brutality. Such a narration would fill a volume much larger than the present one. I aim only to give the reader a truthful impression of my slave life, without unnecessarily affecting him with harrowing details.

As I have elsewhere intimated that my hardships were much greater during the first six months of my stay at Covey's, than during the remainder of the year, and as the change in my condition was owing to causes which may help the reader to a better understanding of human nature, when subjected to the terrible extremities of slavery, I will narrate the circumstances of this change, although I may seem thereby to applaud my own courage. You have, dear reader, seen me humbled, degraded, broken down, enslaved, and brutalized, and you understand how it was done; now let us see the converse of all this, and how it was brought about; and this will take us through the year 1834.

On one of the hottest days of the month of August, of the year just mentioned, had the reader been passing through Covey's farm, he might have seen me at work, in what is there called the "treading yard"—a yard upon which wheat is trodden out from the straw, by the horses' feet. I was there, at work, feeding the "fan," or rather bringing wheat to the fan, while Bill Smith was feeding. Our force consisted of Bill Hughes, Bill Smith, and a slave by the name of Eli; the latter having been hired for this occasion. The work was simple, and required strength and activity, rather than any skill or intelligence, and yet, to one entirely unused to such work, it came very hard. The heat was intense and overpowering, and there was much hurry to get the wheat, trodden out that day, through the fan; since, if that work was done an hour before sundown, the hands would have, according to a promise of Covey, that hour added to their night's rest. I was not behind any of them in the wish to complete the day's work before sundown, and, hence, I struggled with all my might to get the work forward. The promise of one hour's repose on a week day, was sufficient to quicken my pace, and to spur me on to extra endeavor. Besides, we had all planned to go fishing, and I certainly wished to have a hand in that. But I was disappointed, and the day turned out to be one of the bitterest I ever experienced. About three o'clock, while the sun was pouring down his burning rays, and not a breeze was stirring, I broke down; my strength failed me; I was seized with a violent aching of the head, attended with extreme dizziness, and trembling in every limb. Finding what was coming, and feeling it would never do to stop work, I nerved myself up, and staggered on until I fell by the side of the wheat fan, feeling that the earth had fallen upon me. This brought the entire work to a dead stand. There was work for four; each one had his part to perform, and each part depended on the other, so that when one stopped, all were compelled to stop. Covey, who had now become my dread, as well as my tormentor, was at the house, about a hundred yards from where I was fanning, and instantly, upon hearing the fan stop, he came down to the treading yard, to inquire into the cause of our stopping. Bill Smith told him I was sick, and that I was unable longer to bring wheat to the fan.

I had, by this time, crawled away, under the side of a post-and-rail fence, in the shade, and was exceeding ill. The intense heat of the sun, the heavy dust rising from the fan, the stooping, to take up the wheat from the yard, together with the hurrying, to get through, had caused a rush of blood to my head. In this condition, Covey finding out where I was, came to me; and, after standing over me a while, he asked me what the matter was. I told him as well as I could, for it was with difficulty that I could speak. He then gave me a savage kick in the side, which jarred my whole frame, and commanded me to get up. The man had obtained complete control over me; and if he had commanded me to do any possible thing, I should, in my then state of mind, have endeavored to comply. I made an effort to rise, but fell back in the attempt, before gaining my feet. The brute now gave me another heavy kick, and again told me to rise. I again tried to rise, and succeeded in gaining my feet; but upon stooping to get the tub with which I was feeding the fan, I again staggered and fell to the ground; and I must have so fallen, had I been sure that a hundred bullets would have pierced me, as the consequence. While down, in this sad condition, and perfectly helpless, the merciless Negro breaker took up the hickory slab, with which Hughes had been striking off the wheat to a level with the sides of the half bushel measure (a very hard weapon) and with the sharp edge of it, he dealt me a heavy blow on my head which made a large gash, and caused the blood to run freely, saying, at the same time, "If *you have got the headache, I'll cure you.*" This done, he ordered me again to rise, but I made no effort to do so; for I had made up my mind that it was useless, and that the heartless monster might now do his worst; he could but kill me, and that might put me out of my misery. Finding me unable to rise, or rather despairing of my doing so, Covey left me, with a view to getting on with the work without me. I was bleeding very freely, and my face was soon covered with my warm blood. Cruel and merciless as was the motive that dealt that blow, dear reader, the wound was fortunate for me. Bleeding was never more efficacious. The pain in my head speedily abated, and I was soon able to rise. Covey had, as I have said, now left me to my fate; and the question was, shall I return to my work, or shall I find my way to St. Michael's, and make Capt. Auld acquainted with the atrocious cruelty of his brother Covey, and beseech him to get me another master? Remembering the object he had in view, in placing me under the management of Covey, and further, his cruel treatment of my poor crippled cousin, Henny, and his meanness in the matter of feeding and clothing his slaves, there was little ground to hope for a favorable reception at the hands of Capt. Thomas Auld. Nevertheless, I resolved to go straight to Capt. Auld, thinking that, if not animated by motives of humanity, he might be induced to interfere on my behalf from selfish considerations. "He cannot," thought I, "allow his property to be thus bruised and battered, marred and defaced; and I will go to him, and tell him the simple truth about the matter." In order to get to St. Michael's, by the most favorable and direct road, I must walk seven miles; and this, in my sad condition, was no easy performance. I had already lost much blood; I was exhausted by over exertion; my sides were sore from the heavy blows planted there by the stout boots of Mr. Covey; and I was, in every way, in an unfavorable plight for the journey. I however watched my chance, while the cruel and cunning Covey was looking in an opposite direction, and started off, across the field, for St. Michael's. This was a daring step; if it failed, it would only exasperate Covey, and increase the rigors of my bondage, during the remainder of my term of service under him; but the step was taken, and I must go forward. I succeeded in getting nearly half way across the broad field, toward the woods, before Mr. Covey observed me. I was still bleeding, and the exertion of running had started the blood afresh. *Come back! Come back!* vociferated Covey, with threats of what he would do if I did not return instantly. But, disregarding his calls and his threats, I pressed on toward the woods as fast as my feeble state would allow. Seeing no signs of my stopping, Covey caused his horse to be brought out and saddled, as if he intended to pursue me. The race was now to be an unequal one; and, thinking I might be overhauled by him, if I kept the main road, I walked nearly the whole distance in the woods, keeping far enough from the road to avoid detection and pursuit. But, I had not gone far, before my little strength again failed me, and I laid down. The blood was still oozing from the wound in my head; and, for a time, I suffered more than I can describe. There I was, in the deep woods, sick and emaciated, pursued by a wretch whose character for revolting cruelty beggars all opprobrious speech—bleeding, and almost bloodless. I was not without the fear of bleeding to death. The thought of dying in the woods, all alone, and of being torn to pieces by the buzzards, had not yet been rendered tolerable by my many troubles and hardships, and I was glad when the shade of the trees, and the cool evening breeze, combined with my matted hair to stop the flow of blood. After lying there about three quarters of an hour, brooding over the singular and mournful lot to which I was doomed, my mind passing over the whole scale or circle of belief and unbelief, from faith in the overruling providence of God, to the blackest atheism, I again took up my journey toward St. Michael's, more weary and sad than in the morning when I left Thomas Auld's for the home of Mr. Covey. I was bare-footed and bare-headed, and in my shirt sleeves. The way was through bogs and briers, and I tore my feet often during the journey. I was full five hours in going the seven or eight miles; partly, because of the difficulties of the way, and partly, because of the feebleness induced by my illness, bruises and loss of blood. On gaining my master's store, I presented an appearance of wretchedness and woe, fitted to move any but a heart of stone. From the crown of my head to the sole of my feet, there were marks of blood. My hair was all clotted with dust and blood, and the back of my shirt was literally stiff with the same. Briers and thorns had scarred and torn my feet and legs, leaving blood marks there. Had I escaped from a den of tigers, I could not have looked worse than I did on reaching St. Michael's. In this unhappy plight, I appeared before my professedly *Christian* master, humbly to invoke the interposition of his power and authority, to protect me from further abuse and violence. I had begun to hope, during the latter part of my tedious journey toward St. Michael's, that Capt. Auld would now show himself in a nobler light than I had ever before seen him. I was disappointed. I had jumped from a sinking ship into the sea; I had fled from the tiger to something worse. I told him all the circumstances, as well as I could; how I was endeavoring to please Covey; how hard I was at work in the present instance; how unwilling I sunk down under the heat, toil and pain; the brutal manner in which Covey had kicked me in the side; the gash cut in my head; my hesitation about troubling him (Capt. Auld) with complaints; but, that now I felt it would not be best longer to conceal from him the outrages committed on me from time to time by Covey. At first, master Thomas seemed somewhat affected by the story of my wrongs, but he soon repressed his feelings and became cold as iron. It was impossible—as I stood before him at the first—for him to seem indifferent. I distinctly saw his human nature asserting its conviction against the slave system, which made cases like mine *possible*; but, as I have said, humanity fell before the systematic tyranny of slavery. He first walked the floor, apparently much agitated by my story, and the sad spectacle I presented; but, presently, it was *his* turn to talk. He began moderately, by finding excuses for Covey, and ending with a full justification of him, and a passionate condemnation of me. "He had no doubt I deserved the flogging. He did not believe I was sick; I was only endeavoring to get rid of work. My dizziness was laziness, and Covey did right to flog me, as he had done." After thus fairly annihilating me, and rousing himself by his own eloquence, he fiercely demanded what I wished *him* to do in the case!

With such a complete knock-down to all my hopes, as he had given me, and feeling, as I did, my entire subjection to his power, I had very little heart to reply. I must not affirm my innocence of the allegations which he had piled up against me; for that would be impudence, and would probably call down fresh violence as well as wrath upon me. The guilt of a slave is always, and everywhere, presumed; and the innocence of the slaveholder or the slave employer, is always asserted. The word of the slave, against this presumption, is generally treated as impudence, worthy of punishment. "Do you contradict me, you rascal?" is a final silencer of counter statements from the lips of a slave.

Calming down a little in view of my silence and hesitation, and, perhaps, from a rapid glance at the picture of misery I presented, he inquired again, "what I would have him do?" Thus invited a second time, I told Master Thomas I wished him to allow me to get a new home and to find a new master; that, as sure as I went back to live with Mr. Covey again, I should be killed by him; that he would never forgive my coming to him (Capt. Auld) with a complaint against him (Covey); that, since I had lived with him, he almost crushed my spirit, and I believed that he would ruin me for future service; that my life was not safe in his hands. This, Master Thomas *(my brother in the church)* regarded as "nonsence(sic)." "There was no danger of Mr. Covey's killing me; he was a good man, industrious and religious, and he would not think of removing me from that home; besides," said he and this I found was the most distressing thought of all to him—"if you should leave Covey now, that your year has but half expired, I should lose your wages for the entire year. You belong to Mr. Covey for one year, and you *must go back* to him, come what will. You must not trouble me with any more stories about Mr. Covey; and if you do not go immediately home, I will get hold of you myself." This was just what I expected, when I found he had *prejudged* the case against me. "But, Sir," I said, "I am sick and tired, and I cannot get home to-night." At this, he again relented, and finally he allowed me to remain all night at St. Michael's; but said I must be off early in the morning, and concluded his directions by making me swallow a huge dose of *epsom salts*—about the only medicine ever administered to slaves.

It was quite natural for Master Thomas to presume I was feigning sickness to escape work, for he probably thought that were *he* in the place of a slave with no wages for his work, no praise for well doing, no motive for toil but the lash—he would try every possible scheme by which to escape labor. I say I have no doubt of this; the reason is, that there are not, under the whole heavens, a set of men who cultivate such an intense dread of labor as do the slaveholders. The charge of laziness against the slave is ever on their lips, and is the standing apology for every species of cruelty and brutality. These men literally "bind heavy burdens, grievous to be borne, and lay them on men's shoulders; but they, themselves, will not move them with one of their fingers."

My kind readers shall have, in the next chapter—what they were led, perhaps, to expect to find in this—namely: an account of my partial disenthrallment from the tyranny of Covey, and the marked change which it brought about.

CHAPTER XVII

The Last Flogging

Sleep itself does not always come to the relief of the weary in body, and the broken in spirit; especially when past troubles only foreshadow coming disasters. The last hope had been extinguished. My master, who I did not venture to hope would protect me as *a man*, had even now refused to protect me as *his property;* and had cast me back, covered with reproaches and bruises, into the hands of a stranger to that mercy which was the soul of the religion he professed. May the reader never spend such a night as that allotted to me, previous to the morning which was to herald my return to the den of horrors from which I had made a temporary escape.

I remained all night—sleep I did not—at St. Michael's; and in the morning (Saturday) I started off, according to the order of Master Thomas, feeling that I had no friend on earth, and doubting if I had one in heaven. I reached Covey's about nine o'clock; and just as I stepped into the field, before I had reached the house, Covey, true to his snakish habits, darted out at me from a fence corner, in which he had secreted himself, for the purpose of securing me. He was amply provided with a cowskin and a rope; and he evidently intended to *tie me up*, and to wreak his vengeance on me to the fullest extent. I should have been an easy prey, had he succeeded in getting his hands upon me, for I had taken no refreshment since noon on Friday; and this, together with the pelting, excitement, and the loss of blood, had reduced my strength. I, however, darted back into the woods, before the ferocious hound could get hold of me, and buried myself in a thicket, where he lost sight of me. The corn-field afforded me cover, in getting to the woods. But for the tall corn, Covey would have overtaken me, and made me his captive. He seemed very much chagrined that he did not catch me, and gave up the chase, very reluctantly; for I could see his angry movements, toward the house from which he had sallied, on his foray.

Well, now I am clear of Covey, and of his wrathful lash, for present. I am in the wood, buried in its somber gloom, and hushed in its solemn silence; hid from all human eyes; shut in with nature and nature's God, and absent from all human contrivances. Here was a good place to pray; to pray for help for deliverance—a prayer I had often made before. But how could I pray? Covey could pray—Capt. Auld could pray—I would fain pray; but doubts (arising partly from my own neglect of the means of grace, and partly from the sham religion which everywhere prevailed, cast in my mind a doubt upon all religion, and led me to the conviction that prayers were unavailing and delusive) prevented my embracing the opportunity, as a religious one. Life, in itself, had almost become burdensome to me. All my outward relations were against me; I must stay here and starve (I was already hungry) or go home to Covey's, and have my flesh torn to pieces, and my spirit humbled under the cruel lash of Covey. This was the painful alternative presented to me. The day was long and irksome. My physical condition was deplorable. I was weak, from the toils of the previous day, and from the want of food and rest; and had been so little concerned about my appearance, that I had not yet washed the blood from my garments. I was an object of horror, even to myself. Life, in Baltimore, when most oppressive, was a paradise to this. What had I done, what had my parents done, that such a life as this should be mine? That day, in the woods, I would have exchanged my manhood for the brutehood of an ox.

Night came. I was still in the woods, unresolved what to do. Hunger had not yet pinched me to the point of going home, and I laid myself down in the leaves to rest; for I had been watching for hunters all day, but not being molested during the day, I expected no disturbance during the night. I had come to the conclusion that Covey relied upon hunger to drive me home; and in this I was quite correct—the facts showed that he had made no effort to catch me, since morning.

During the night, I heard the step of a man in the woods. He was coming toward the place where I lay. A person lying still has the advantage over one walking in the woods, in the day time, and this advantage is much greater at night. I was not able to engage in a physical struggle, and I had recourse to the common resort of the weak. I hid myself in the leaves to prevent discovery. But, as the night rambler in the woods drew nearer, I found him to be a *friend*, not an enemy; it was a slave of Mr. William Groomes, of Easton, a kind hearted fellow, named "Sandy." Sandy lived with Mr. Kemp that year, about four miles from St. Michael's. He, like myself had been hired out by the year; but, unlike myself, had not been hired out to be broken. Sandy was the husband of a free woman, who lived in the lower part of *"Potpie Neck,"* and he was now on his way through the woods, to see her, and to spend the Sabbath with her.

As soon as I had ascertained that the disturber of my solitude was not an enemy, but the good-hearted Sandy—a man as famous among the slaves of the neighborhood for his good nature, as for his good sense I came out from my hiding place, and made myself known to him. I explained the circumstances of the past two days, which had driven me to the woods, and he deeply compassionated my distress. It was a bold thing for him to shelter me, and I could not ask him to do so; for, had I been found in his hut, he would have suffered the penalty of thirty-nine lashes on his bare back, if not something worse. But Sandy was too generous to permit the fear of punishment to prevent his relieving a brother bondman from hunger and exposure; and, therefore, on his own motion, I accompanied him to his home, or rather to the home of his wife—for the house and lot were hers. His wife was called up—for it was now about midnight—a fire was made, some Indian meal was soon mixed with salt and water, and an ash cake was baked in a hurry to relieve my hunger. Sandy's wife was not behind him in kindness—both seemed to esteem it a privilege to succor me; for, although I was hated by Covey and by my master, I was loved by the colored people, because *they* thought I was hated for my knowledge, and persecuted because I was feared. I was the *only* slave *now* in that region who could read and write. There had been one other man, belonging to Mr. Hugh Hamilton, who could read (his name was "Jim"), but he, poor fellow, had, shortly after my coming into the neighborhood, been sold off to the far south. I saw Jim ironed, in the cart, to be carried to Easton for sale—pinioned like a yearling for the slaughter. My knowledge was now the pride of my brother slaves; and, no doubt, Sandy felt something of the general interest in me on that account. The supper was soon ready, and though I have feasted since, with honorables, lord mayors and aldermen, over the sea, my supper on ash cake and cold water, with Sandy, was the meal, of all my life, most sweet to my taste, and now most vivid in my memory.

Supper over, Sandy and I went into a discussion of what was *possible* for me, under the perils and hardships which now overshadowed my path. The question was, must I go back to Covey, or must I now tempt to run away? Upon a careful survey, the latter was found to be impossible; for I was on a narrow neck of land, every avenue from which would bring me in sight of pursuers. There was the Chesapeake bay to the right, and "Pot-pie" river to the left, and St. Michael's and its neighborhood occupying the only space through which there was any retreat.

I found Sandy an old advisor. He was not only a religious man, but he professed to believe in a system for which I have no name. He was a genuine African, and had inherited some of the so-called magical powers, said to be possessed by African and eastern nations. He told me that he could help me; that, in those very woods, there was an herb, which in the morning might be found, possessing all the powers required for my protection (I put his thoughts in my own language); and that, if I would take his advice, he would procure me the root of the herb of which he spoke. He told me further, that if I would take that root and wear it on my right side, it would be impossible for Covey to strike me a blow; that with this root about my person, no white man could whip me. He said he had carried it for years, and that he had fully tested its virtues. He had never received a blow from a slaveholder since he carried it; and he never expected to receive one, for he always meant to carry that root as a protection. He knew Covey well, for Mrs. Covey was the daughter of Mr. Kemp; and he (Sandy) had heard of the barbarous treatment to which I was subjected, and he wanted to do something for me.

Now all this talk about the root, was to me, very absurd and ridiculous, if not positively sinful. I at first rejected the idea that the simple carrying a root on my right side (a root, by the way, over which I walked every time I went into the woods) could possess any such magic power as he ascribed to it, and I was, therefore, not disposed to cumber my pocket with it. I had a positive aversion to all pretenders to *"divination."* It was beneath one of my intelligence to countenance such dealings with the devil, as this power implied. But, with all my learning—it was really precious little—Sandy was more than a match for me. "My book learning," he said, "had not kept Covey off me" (a powerful argument just then) and he entreated me, with flashing eyes, to try this. If it did me no good, it could do me no harm, and it would cost me nothing, any way. Sandy was so earnest, and so confident of the good qualities of this weed, that, to please him, rather than from any conviction of its excellence, I was induced to take it. He had been to me the good Samaritan, and had, almost providentially, found me, and helped me when I could not help myself; how did I know but that the hand of the Lord was in it? With thoughts of this sort, I took the roots from Sandy, and put them in my right hand pocket.

This was, of course, Sunday morning. Sandy now urged me to go home, with all speed, and to walk up bravely to the house, as though nothing had happened. I saw in Sandy too deep an insight into human nature, with all his superstition, not to have some respect for his advice; and perhaps, too, a slight gleam or shadow of his superstition had fallen upon me. At any rate, I started off toward Covey's, as directed by Sandy. Having, the previous night, poured my griefs into Sandy's ears, and got him enlisted in my behalf, having made his wife a sharer in my sorrows, and having, also, become well refreshed by sleep and food, I moved off, quite courageously, toward the much dreaded Covey's. Singularly enough, just as I entered his yard gate, I met him and his wife, dressed in their Sunday best—looking as smiling as angels—on their way to church. The manner of Covey astonished me. There was something really benignant in his countenance. He spoke to me as never before; told me that the pigs had got into the lot, and he wished me to drive them out; inquired how I was, and seemed an altered man. This extraordinary conduct of Covey, really made me begin to think that Sandy's herb had more virtue in it than I, in my pride, had been willing to allow; and, had the day been other than Sunday, I should have attributed Covey's altered manner solely to the magic power of the root. I suspected, however, that the *Sabbath*, and not the *root*, was the real explanation of Covey's manner. His religion hindered him from breaking the Sabbath, but not from breaking my skin. He had more respect for the *day* than for the *man*, for whom the day was mercifully given; for while he would cut and slash my body during the week, he would not hesitate, on Sunday, to teach me the value of my soul, or the way of life and salvation by Jesus Christ.

All went well with me till Monday morning; and then, whether the root had lost its virtue, or whether my tormentor had gone deeper into the black art than myself (as was sometimes said of him), or whether he had obtained a special indulgence, for his faithful Sabbath day's worship, it is not necessary for me to know, or to inform the reader; but, this I *may* say—the pious and benignant smile which graced Covey's face on *Sunday*, wholly disappeared on *Monday*. Long before daylight, I was called up to go and feed, rub, and curry the horses. I obeyed the call, and would have so obeyed it, had it been made at an earilier(sic) hour, for I had brought my mind to a firm resolve, during that Sunday's reflection, viz: to obey every order, however unreasonable, if it were possible, and, if Mr. Covey should then undertake to beat me, to defend and protect myself to the best of my ability. My religious views on the subject of resisting my master, had suffered a serious shock, by the savage persecution to which I had been subjected, and my hands were no longer tied by my religion. Master Thomas's indifference had served the last link. I had now to this extent "backslidden" from this point in the slave's religious creed; and I soon had occasion to make my fallen state known to my Sunday-pious brother, Covey.

Whilst I was obeying his order to feed and get the horses ready for the field, and when in the act of going up the stable loft for the purpose of throwing down some blades, Covey sneaked into the stable, in his peculiar snake-like way, and seizing me suddenly by the leg, he brought me to the stable floor, giving my newly mended body a fearful jar. I now forgot my roots, and remembered my pledge to *stand up in my own defense*. The brute was endeavoring skillfully to get a slip-knot on my legs, before I could draw up my feet. As soon as I found what he was up to, I gave a sudden spring (my two day's rest had been of much service to me,) and by that means, no doubt, he was able to bring me to the floor so heavily. He was defeated in his plan of tying me. While down, he seemed to think he had me very securely in his power. He little thought he was—as the rowdies say—"in" for a "rough and tumble" fight; but such was the fact. Whence came the daring spirit necessary to grapple with a man who, eight-and-forty hours before, could, with his slightest word have made me tremble like a leaf in a storm, I do not know; at any rate, *I was resolved to fight*, and, what was better still, I was actually hard at it. The fighting madness had come upon me, and I found my strong fingers firmly attached to the throat of my cowardly tormentor; as heedless of consequences, at the moment, as though we stood as equals before the law. The very color of the man was forgotten. I felt as supple as a cat, and was ready for the snakish creature at every turn. Every blow of his was parried, though I dealt no blows in turn. I was strictly on the *defensive*, preventing him from injuring me, rather than trying to injure him. I flung him on the ground several times, when he meant to have hurled me there. I held him so firmly by the throat, that his blood followed my nails. He held me, and I held him.

All was fair, thus far, and the contest was about equal. My resistance was entirely unexpected, and Covey was taken all aback by it, for he trembled in every limb. *"Are you going to resist*, you scoundrel?" said he. To which, I returned a polite *"Yes sir;"* steadily gazing my interrogator in the eye, to meet the first approach or dawning of the blow, which I expected my answer would call forth. But, the conflict did not long remain thus equal. Covey soon cried out lustily for help; not that I was obtaining any marked advantage over him, or was injuring him, but because he was gaining none over me, and was not able, single handed, to conquer me. He called for his cousin Hughs, to come to his assistance, and now the scene was changed. I was compelled to give blows, as well as to parry them; and, since I was, in any case, to suffer for resistance, I felt (as the musty proverb goes) that "I might as well be hanged for an old sheep as a lamb." I was still *defensive* toward Covey, but *aggressive* toward Hughs; and, at the first approach of the latter, I dealt a blow, in my desperation, which fairly sickened my youthful assailant. He went off, bending over with pain, and manifesting no disposition to come within my reach again. The poor fellow was in the act of trying to catch and tie my right hand, and while flattering himself with success, I gave him the kick which sent him staggering away in pain, at the same time that I held Covey with a firm hand.

Taken completely by surprise, Covey seemed to have lost his usual strength and coolness. He was frightened, and stood puffing and blowing, seemingly unable to command words or blows. When he saw that poor Hughes was standing half bent with pain—his courage quite gone the cowardly tyrant asked if I "meant to persist in my resistance." I told him "*I did mean to resist, come what might;*" that I had been by him treated like a *brute*, during the last six months; and that I should stand it *no longer*. With that, he gave me a shake, and attempted to drag me toward a stick of wood, that was lying just outside the stable door. He meant to knock me down with it; but, just as he leaned over to get the stick, I seized him with both hands by the collar, and, with a vigorous and sudden snatch, I brought my assailant harmlessly, his full length, on the *not* overclean ground—for we were now in the cow yard. He had selected the place for the fight, and it was but right that he should have all the advantges(sic) of his own selection.

By this time, Bill, the hiredman, came home. He had been to Mr. Hemsley's, to spend the Sunday with his nominal wife, and was coming home on Monday morning, to go to work. Covey and I had been skirmishing from before daybreak, till now, that the sun was almost shooting his beams over the eastern woods, and we were still at it. I could not see where the matter was to terminate. He evidently was afraid to let me go, lest I should again make off to the woods; otherwise, he would probably have obtained arms from the house, to frighten me. Holding me, Covey called upon Bill for assistance. The scene here, had something comic about it. "Bill," who knew *precisely* what Covey wished him to do, affected ignorance, and pretended he did not know what to do. "What shall I do, Mr. Covey," said Bill. "Take hold of him—take hold of him!" said Covey. With a toss of his head, peculiar to Bill, he said, "indeed, Mr. Covey I want to go to work." "*This is* your work," said Covey; "take hold of him." Bill replied, with spirit, "My master hired me here, to work, and *not* to help you whip Frederick." It was now my turn to speak. "Bill," said I, "don't put your hands on me." To which he replied, "My GOD! Frederick, I ain't goin' to tech ye," and Bill walked off, leaving Covey and myself to settle our matters as best we might.

But, my present advantage was threatened when I saw Caroline (the slave-woman of Covey) coming to the cow yard to milk, for she was a powerful woman, and could have mastered me very easily, exhausted as I now was. As soon as she came into the yard, Covey attempted to rally her to his aid. Strangely—and, I may add, fortunately—Caroline was in no humor to take a hand in any such sport. We were all in open rebellion, that morning. Caroline answered the command of her master to *"take hold of me,"* precisely as Bill had answered, but in *her*, it was at greater peril so to answer; she was the slave of Covey, and he could do what he pleased with her. It was *not* so with Bill, and Bill knew it. Samuel Harris, to whom Bill belonged, did not allow his slaves to be beaten, unless they were guilty of some crime which the law would punish. But, poor Caroline, like myself, was at the mercy of the merciless Covey; nor did she escape the dire effects of her refusal. He gave her several sharp blows.

Covey at length (two hours had elapsed) gave up the contest. Letting me go, he said—puffing and blowing at a great rate—"Now, you scoundrel, go to your work; I would not have whipped you half so much as I have had you not resisted." The fact was, *he had not whipped me at all*. He had not, in all the scuffle, drawn a single drop of blood from me. I had drawn blood from him; and, even without this satisfaction, I should have been victorious, because my aim had not been to injure him, but to prevent his injuring me.

During the whole six months that I lived with Covey, after this transaction, he never laid on me the weight of his finger in anger. He would, occasionally, say he did not want to have to get hold of me again—a declaration which I had no difficulty in believing; and I had a secret feeling, which answered, "You need not wish to get hold of me again, for you will be likely to come off worse in a second fight than you did in the first."

Well, my dear reader, this battle with Mr. Covey—undignified as it was, and as I fear my narration of it is—was the turning point in my *"life as a slave."* It rekindled in my breast the smouldering embers of liberty; it brought up my Baltimore dreams, and revived a sense of my own manhood. I was a changed being after that fight. I was *nothing* before; I WAS A MAN NOW. It recalled to life my crushed self-respect and my self-confidence, and inspired me with a renewed determination to be A FREEMAN. A man, without force, is without the essential dignity of humanity. Human nature is so constituted, that it cannot *honor* a helpless man, although it can *pity* him; and even this it cannot do long, if the signs of power do not arise.

He can only understand the effect of this combat on my spirit, who has himself incurred something, hazarded something, in repelling the unjust and cruel aggressions of a tyrant. Covey was a tyrant, and a cowardly one, withal. After resisting him, I felt as I had never felt before. It was a resurrection from the dark and pestiferous tomb of slavery, to the heaven of comparative freedom. I was no longer a servile coward, trembling under the frown of a brother worm of the dust, but, my long-cowed spirit was roused to an attitude of manly independence. I had reached the point, at which I was *not afraid to die*. This spirit made me a freeman in *fact*, while I remained a slave in *form*. When a slave cannot be flogged he is more than half free. He has a domain as broad as his own manly heart to defend, and he is really *"a power on earth."* While slaves prefer their lives, with flogging, to instant death, they will always find Christians enough, like unto Covey, to accommodate that preference. From this time, until that of my escape from slavery, I was never fairly whipped. Several attempts were made to whip me, but they were always unsuccessful. Bruises I did get, as I shall hereafter inform the reader; but the case I have been describing, was the end of the brutification to which slavery had subjected me.

The reader will be glad to know why, after I had so grievously offended Mr. Covey, he did not have me taken in hand by the authorities; indeed, why the law of Maryland, which assigns hanging to the slave who resists his master, was not put in force against me; at any rate, why I was not taken up, as is usual in such cases, and publicly whipped, for an example to other slaves, and as a means of deterring me from committing the same offense again. I confess, that the easy manner in which I got off, for a long time, a surprise to me, and I cannot, even now, fully explain the cause.

The only explanation I can venture to suggest, is the fact, that Covey was, probably, ashamed to have it known and confessed that he had been mastered by a boy of sixteen. Mr. Covey enjoyed the unbounded and very valuable reputation, of being a first rate overseer and *Negro breaker*. By means of this reputation, he was able to procure his hands for *very trifling* compensation, and with very great ease. His interest and his pride mutually suggested the wisdom of passing the matter by, in silence. The story that he had undertaken to whip a lad, and had been resisted, was, of itself, sufficient to damage him; for his bearing should, in the estimation of slaveholders, be of that imperial order that should make such an occurrence *impossible*. I judge from these circumstances, that Covey deemed it best to give me the go-by. It is, perhaps, not altogether creditable to my natural temper, that, after this conflict with Mr. Covey, I did, at times, purposely aim to provoke him to an attack, by refusing to keep with the other hands in the field, but I could never bully him to another battle. I had made up my mind to do him serious damage, if he ever again attempted to lay violent hands on me.

> Hereditary bondmen, know ye not
> Who would be free, themselves must strike the blow?

CHAPTER XVIII

New Relations and Duties

My term of actual service to Mr. Edward Covey ended on Christmas day, 1834. I gladly left the snakish Covey, although he was now as gentle as a lamb. My home for the year 1835 was already secured—my next master was already selected. There is always more or less excitement about the matter of changing hands, but I had become somewhat reckless. I cared very little into whose hands I fell—I meant to fight my way. Despite of Covey, too, the report got abroad, that I was hard to whip; that I was guilty of kicking back; that though generally a good tempered Negro, I sometimes *"got the devil in me."* These sayings were rife in Talbot county, and they distinguished me among my servile brethren. Slaves, generally, will fight each other, and die at each other's hands; but there are few who are not held in awe by a white man. Trained from the cradle up, to think and feel that their masters are superior, and invested with a sort of sacredness, there are few who can outgrow or rise above the control which that sentiment exercises. I had now got free from it, and the thing was known. One bad sheep will spoil a whole flock. Among the slaves, I was a bad sheep. I hated slavery, slaveholders, and all pertaining to them; and I did not fail to inspire others with the same feeling, wherever and whenever opportunity was presented. This made me a marked lad among the slaves, and a suspected one among the slaveholders. A knowledge of my ability to read and write, got pretty widely spread, which was very much against me.

The days between Christmas day and New Year's, are allowed the slaves as holidays. During these days, all regular work was suspended, and there was nothing to do but to keep fires, and look after the stock. This time was regarded as our own, by the grace of our masters, and we, therefore used it, or abused it, as we pleased. Those who had families at a distance, were now expected to visit them, and to spend with them the entire week. The younger slaves, or the unmarried ones, were expected to see to the cattle, and attend to incidental duties at home. The holidays were variously spent. The sober, thinking and industrious ones of our number, would employ themselves in manufacturing corn brooms, mats, horse collars and baskets, and some of these were very well made. Another class spent their time in hunting opossums, coons, rabbits, and other game. But the majority spent the holidays in sports, ball playing, wrestling, boxing, running foot races, dancing, and drinking whisky; and this latter mode of spending the time was generally most agreeable to their masters. A slave who would work during the holidays, was thought, by his master, undeserving of holidays. Such an one had rejected the favor of his master. There was, in this simple act of continued work, an accusation against slaves; and a slave could not help thinking, that if he made three dollars during the holidays, he might make three hundred during the year. Not to be drunk during the holidays, was disgraceful; and he was esteemed a lazy and improvident man, who could not afford to drink whisky during Christmas.

The fiddling, dancing and "*jubilee beating,*" was going on in all directions. This latter performance is strictly southern. It supplies the place of a violin, or of other musical instruments, and is played so easily, that almost every farm has its "Juba" beater. The performer improvises as he beats, and sings his merry songs, so ordering the words as to have them fall pat with the movement of his hands. Among a mass of nonsense and wild frolic, once in a while a sharp hit is given to the meanness of slaveholders. Take the following, for an example:

> *We raise de wheat,*
> *Dey gib us de corn;*
> *We bake de bread,*
> *Dey gib us de cruss;*
> *We sif de meal,*
> *Dey gib us de huss;*
> *We peal de meat,*
> *Dey gib us de skin,*

And dat's de way
Dey takes us in.
We skim de pot,
Dey gib us the liquor,
And say dat's good enough for nigger.
  Walk over! walk over!
Tom butter and de fat;
  Poor nigger you can't get over dat;
   Walk over!

This is not a bad summary of the palpable injustice and fraud of slavery, giving—as it does—to the lazy and idle, the comforts which God designed should be given solely to the honest laborer. But to the holiday's.

Judging from my own observation and experience, I believe these holidays to be among the most effective means, in the hands of slaveholders, of keeping down the spirit of insurrection among the slaves.

To enslave men, successfully and safely, it is necessary to have their minds occupied with thoughts and aspirations short of the liberty of which they are deprived. A certain degree of attainable good must be kept before them. These holidays serve the purpose of keeping the minds of the slaves occupied with prospective pleasure, within the limits of slavery. The young man can go wooing; the married man can visit his wife; the father and mother can see their children; the industrious and money loving can make a few dollars; the great wrestler can win laurels; the young people can meet, and enjoy each other's society; the drunken man can get plenty of whisky; and the religious man can hold prayer meetings, preach, pray and exhort during the holidays. Before the holidays, these are pleasures in prospect; after the holidays, they become pleasures of memory, and they serve to keep out thoughts and wishes of a more dangerous character. Were slaveholders at once to abandon the practice of allowing their slaves these liberties, periodically, and to keep them, the year round, closely confined to the narrow circle of their homes, I doubt not that the south would blaze with insurrections. These holidays are conductors or safety valves to carry off the explosive elements inseparable from the human mind, when reduced to the condition of slavery. But for these, the rigors of bondage would become too severe for endurance, and the slave would be forced up to dangerous desperation. Woe to the slaveholder when he undertakes to hinder or to prevent the operation of these electric conductors. A succession of earthquakes would be less destructive, than the insurrectionary fires which would be sure to burst forth in different parts of the south, from such interference.

Thus, the holidays, became part and parcel of the gross fraud, wrongs and inhumanity of slavery. Ostensibly, they are institutions of benevolence, designed to mitigate the rigors of slave life, but, practically, they are a fraud, instituted by human selfishness, the better to secure the ends of injustice and oppression. The slave's happiness is not the end sought, but, rather, the master's safety. It is not from a generous unconcern for the slave's labor that this cessation from labor is allowed, but from a prudent regard to the safety of the slave system. I am strengthened in this opinion, by the fact, that most slaveholders like to have their slaves spend the holidays in such a manner as to be of no real benefit to the slaves. It is plain, that everything like rational enjoyment among the slaves, is frowned upon; and only those wild and low sports, peculiar to semi-civilized people, are encouraged. All the license allowed, appears to have no other object than to disgust the slaves with their temporary freedom, and to make them as glad to return to their work, as they were to leave it. By plunging them into exhausting depths of drunkenness and dissipation, this effect is almost certain to follow. I have known slaveholders resort to cunning tricks, with a view of getting their slaves deplorably drunk. A usual plan is, to make bets on a slave, that he can drink more whisky than any other; and so to induce a rivalry among them, for the mastery in this degradation. The scenes, brought about in this way, were often scandalous and loathsome in the extreme. Whole multitudes might be found stretched out in brutal drunkenness, at once helpless and disgusting. Thus, when the slave asks for a few hours of virtuous freedom, his cunning master takes advantage of his ignorance, and cheers him with a dose of vicious and revolting dissipation, artfully labeled with the name of LIBERTY. We were induced to drink, I among the rest, and when the holidays were over, we all staggered up from our filth and wallowing, took a long breath, and went away to our various fields of work; feeling, upon the whole, rather glad to go from that which our masters artfully deceived us into the belief was freedom, back again to the arms of slavery. It was not what we had taken it to be, nor what it might have been, had it not been abused by us. It was about as well to be a slave to *master*, as to be a slave to *rum* and *whisky*.

I am the more induced to take this view of the holiday system, adopted by slaveholders, from what I know of their treatment of slaves, in regard to other things. It is the commonest thing for them to try to disgust their slaves with what they do not want them to have, or to enjoy. A slave, for instance, likes molasses; he steals some; to cure him of the taste for it, his master, in many cases, will go away to town, and buy a large quantity of the *poorest* quality, and set it before his slave, and, with whip in hand, compel him to eat it, until the poor fellow is made to sicken at the very thought of molasses. The same course is often adopted to cure slaves of the disagreeable and inconvenient practice of asking for more food, when their allowance has failed them. The same disgusting process works well, too, in other things, but I need not cite them. When a slave is drunk, the slaveholder has no fear that he will plan an insurrection; no fear that he will escape to the north. It is the sober, thinking slave who is dangerous, and needs the vigilance of his master, to keep him a slave. But, to proceed with my narrative.

On the first of January, 1835, I proceeded from St. Michael's to Mr. William Freeland's, my new home. Mr. Freeland lived only three miles from St. Michael's, on an old worn out farm, which required much labor to restore it to anything like a self-supporting establishment.

I was not long in finding Mr. Freeland to be a very different man from Mr. Covey. Though not rich, Mr. Freeland was what may be called a well-bred southern gentleman, as different from Covey, as a well-trained and hardened Negro breaker is from the best specimen of the first families of the south. Though Freeland was a slaveholder, and shared many of the vices of his class, he seemed alive to the sentiment of honor. He had some sense of justice, and some feelings of humanity. He was fretful, impulsive and passionate, but I must do him the justice to say, he was free from the mean and selfish characteristics which distinguished the creature from which I had now, happily, escaped. He was open, frank, imperative, and practiced no concealments, disdaining to play the spy. In all this, he was the opposite of the crafty Covey.

Among the many advantages gained in my change from Covey's to Freeland's—startling as the statement may be—was the fact that the latter gentleman made no profession of religion. I assert *most unhesitatingly*, that the religion of the south—as I have observed it and proved it—is a mere covering for the most horrid crimes; the justifier of the most appalling barbarity; a sanctifier of the most hateful frauds; and a secure shelter, under which the darkest, foulest, grossest, and most infernal abominations fester and flourish. Were I again to be reduced to the condition of a slave, *next* to that calamity, I should regard the fact of being the slave of a religious slaveholder, the greatest that could befall me. For all slaveholders with whom I have ever met, religious slaveholders are the worst. I have found them, almost invariably, the vilest, meanest and basest of their class. Exceptions there may be, but this is true of religious slaveholders, *as a class*. It is not for me to explain the fact. Others may do that; I simply state it as a fact, and leave the theological, and psychological inquiry, which it raises, to be decided by others more competent than myself. Religious slaveholders, like religious persecutors, are ever extreme in their malice and violence. Very near my new home, on an adjoining farm, there lived the Rev. Daniel Weeden, who was both pious and cruel after the real Covey pattern. Mr. Weeden was a local preacher of the Protestant Methodist persuasion, and a most zealous supporter of the ordinances of religion, generally. This Weeden owned a woman called "Ceal," who was a standing proof of his mercilessness. Poor Ceal's back, always scantily clothed, was kept literally raw, by the lash of this religious man and gospel minister. The most notoriously wicked man—so called in distinction from church members—could hire hands more easily than this brute. When sent out to find a home, a slave would never enter the gates of the preacher Weeden, while a sinful sinner needed a hand. Be have ill, or behave well, it was the known maxim of Weeden, that it is the duty of a master to use the lash. If, for no other reason, he contended that this was essential to remind a slave of his condition, and of his master's authority. The good slave must be whipped, to be *kept* good, and the bad slave must be whipped, to be *made* good. Such was Weeden's theory, and such was his practice. The back of his slave-woman will, in the judgment, be the swiftest witness against him.

While I am stating particular cases, I might as well immortalize another of my neighbors, by calling him by name, and putting him in print. He did not think that a "chiel" was near, "taking notes," and will, doubtless, feel quite angry at having his character touched off in the ragged style of a slave's pen. I beg to introduce the reader to REV. RIGBY HOPKINS. Mr. Hopkins resides between Easton and St. Michael's, in Talbot county, Maryland. The severity of this man made him a perfect terror to the slaves of his neighborhood. The peculiar feature of his government, was, his system of whipping slaves, as he said, *in advance* of deserving it. He always managed to have one or two slaves to whip on Monday morning, so as to start his hands to their work, under the inspiration of a new assurance on Monday, that his preaching about kindness, mercy, brotherly love, and the like, on Sunday, did not interfere with, or prevent him from establishing his authority, by the cowskin. He seemed to wish to assure them, that his tears over poor, lost and ruined sinners, and his pity for them, did not reach to the blacks who tilled his fields. This saintly Hopkins used to boast, that he was the best hand to manage a Negro in the county. He whipped for the smallest offenses, by way of preventing the commission of large ones.

The reader might imagine a difficulty in finding faults enough for such frequent whipping. But this is because you have no idea how easy a matter it is to offend a man who is on the look-out for offenses. The man, unaccustomed to slaveholding, would be astonished to observe how many *foggable* offenses there are in the slaveholder's catalogue of crimes; and how easy it is to commit any one of them, even when the slave least intends it. A slaveholder, bent on finding fault, will hatch up a dozen a day, if he chooses to do so, and each one of these shall be of a punishable description. A mere look, word, or motion, a mistake, accident, or want of power, are all matters for which a slave may be whipped at any time. Does a slave look dissatisfied with his condition? It is said, that he has the devil in him, and it must be whipped out. Does he answer *loudly*, when spoken to by his master, with an air of self-consciousness? Then, must he be taken down a button-hole lower, by the lash, well laid on. Does he forget, and omit to pull off his hat, when approaching a white person? Then, he must, or may be, whipped for his bad manners. Does he ever venture to vindicate his conduct, when harshly and unjustly accused? Then, he is guilty of impudence, one of the greatest crimes in the social catalogue of southern society. To allow a slave to escape punishment, who has impudently attempted to exculpate himself from unjust charges, preferred against him by some white person, is to be guilty of great dereliction of duty. Does a slave ever venture to suggest a better way of doing a thing, no matter what? He is, altogether, too officious—wise above what is written—and he deserves, even if he does not get, a flogging for his presumption. Does he, while plowing, break a plow, or while hoeing, break a hoe, or while chopping, break an ax? No matter what were the imperfections of the implement broken, or the natural liabilities for breaking, the slave can be whipped for carelessness. The *reverend* slaveholder could always find something of this sort, to justify him in using the lash several times during the week. Hopkins—like Covey and Weeden—were shunned by slaves who had the privilege (as many had) of finding their own masters at the end of each year; and yet, there was not a man in all that section of country, who made a louder profession of religion, than did MR. RIGBY HOPKINS.

But, to continue the thread of my story, through my experience when at Mr. William Freeland's.

My poor, weather-beaten bark now reached smoother water, and gentler breezes. My stormy life at Covey's had been of service to me. The things that would have seemed very hard, had I gone direct to Mr. Freeland's, from the home of Master Thomas, were now (after the hardships at Covey's) "trifles light as air." I was still a field hand, and had come to prefer the severe labor of the field, to the enervating duties of a house servant. I had become large and strong; and had begun to take pride in the fact, that I could do as much hard work as some of the older men. There is much rivalry among slaves, at times, as to which can do the most work, and masters generally seek to promote such rivalry. But some of us were too wise to race with each other very long. Such racing, we had the sagacity to see, was not likely to pay. We had our times for measuring each other's strength, but we knew too much to keep up the competition so long as to produce an extraordinary day's work. We knew that if, by extraordinary exertion, a large quantity of work was done in one day, the fact, becoming known to the master, might lead him to require the same amount every day. This thought was enough to bring us to a dead halt when over so much excited for the race.

At Mr. Freeland's, my condition was every way improved. I was no longer the poor scape-goat that I was when at Covey's, where every wrong thing done was saddled upon me, and where other slaves were whipped over my shoulders. Mr. Freeland was too just a man thus to impose upon me, or upon any one else.

It is quite usual to make one slave the object of especial abuse, and to beat him often, with a view to its effect upon others, rather than with any expectation that the slave whipped will be improved by it, but the man with whom I now was, could descend to no such meanness and wickedness. Every man here was held individually responsible for his own conduct.

This was a vast improvement on the rule at Covey's. There, I was the general pack horse. Bill Smith was protected, by a positive prohibition made by his rich master, and the command of the rich slaveholder is LAW to the poor one; Hughes was favored, because of his relationship to Covey; and the hands hired temporarily, escaped flogging, except as they got it over my poor shoulders. Of course, this comparison refers to the time when Covey *could* whip me.

Mr. Freeland, like Mr. Covey, gave his hands enough to eat, but, unlike Mr. Covey, he gave them time to take their meals; he worked us hard during the day, but gave us the night for rest—another advantage to be set to the credit of the sinner, as against that of the saint. We were seldom in the field after dark in the evening, or before sunrise in the morning. Our implements of husbandry were of the most improved pattern, and much superior to those used at Covey's.

Nothwithstanding the improved condition which was now mine, and the many advantages I had gained by my new home, and my new master, I was still restless and discontented. I was about as hard to please by a master, as a master is by slave. The freedom from bodily torture and unceasing labor, had given my mind an increased sensibility, and imparted to it greater activity. I was not yet exactly in right relations. "How be it, that was not first which is spiritual, but that which is natural, and afterward that which is spiritual." When entombed at Covey's, shrouded in darkness and physical wretchedness, temporal wellbeing was the grand *desideratum;* but, temporal wants supplied, the spirit puts in its claims. Beat and cuff your slave, keep him hungry and spiritless, and he will follow the chain of his master like a dog; but, feed and clothe him well—work him moderately—surround him with physical comfort—and dreams of freedom intrude. Give him a *bad* master, and he aspires to a *good* master; give him a good master, and he wishes to become his *own* master. Such is human nature. You may hurl a man so low, beneath the level of his kind, that he loses all just ideas of his natural position; but elevate him a little, and the clear conception of rights arises to life and power, and leads him onward. Thus elevated, a little, at Freeland's, the dreams called into being by that good man, Father Lawson, when in Baltimore, began to visit me; and shoots from the tree of liberty began to put forth tender buds, and dim hopes of the future began to dawn.

I found myself in congenial society, at Mr. Freeland's. There were Henry Harris, John Harris, Handy Caldwell, and Sandy Jenkins.*

---

* This is the same man who gave me the roots to prevent my being whipped by Mr. Covey. He was "a clever soul." We used frequently to talk about the fight with Covey, and as often as we did so, he would claim my success as the result of the roots which he gave me. This superstition is very common among the more ignorant slaves. A slave seldom dies, but that his death is attributed to trickery.

Henry and John were brothers, and belonged to Mr. Freeland. They were both remarkably bright and intelligent, though neither of them could read. Now for mischief! I had not been long at Freeland's before I was up to my old tricks. I early began to address my companions on the subject of education, and the advantages of intelligence over ignorance, and, as far as I dared, I tried to show the agency of ignorance in keeping men in slavery. Webster's spelling book and the *Columbian Orator* were looked into again. As summer came on, and the long Sabbath days stretched themselves over our idleness, I became uneasy, and wanted a Sabbath school, in which to exercise my gifts, and to impart the little knowledge of letters which I possessed, to my brother slaves. A house was hardly necessary in the summer time; I could hold my school under the shade of an old oak tree, as well as any where else. The thing was, to get the scholars, and to have them thoroughly imbued with the desire to learn. Two such boys were quickly secured, in Henry and John, and from them the contagion spread. I was not long bringing around me twenty or thirty young men, who enrolled themselves, gladly, in my Sabbath school, and were willing to meet me regularly, under the trees or elsewhere, for the purpose of learning to read. It was surprising with what ease they provided themselves with spelling books. These were mostly the cast off books of their young masters or mistresses. I taught, at first, on our own farm. All were impressed with the necessity of keeping the matter as private as possible, for the fate of the St. Michael's attempt was notorious, and fresh in the minds of all. Our pious masters, at St. Michael's, must not know that a few of their dusky brothers were learning to read the word of God, lest they should come down upon us with the lash and chain. We might have met to drink whisky, to wrestle, fight, and to do other unseemly things, with no fear of interruption from the saints or sinners of St. Michael's.

But, to meet for the purpose of improving the mind and heart, by learning to read the sacred scriptures, was esteemed a most dangerous nuisance, to be instantly stopped. The slaveholders of St. Michael's, like slaveholders elsewhere, would always prefer to see the slaves engaged in degrading sports, rather than to see them acting like moral and accountable beings.

Had any one asked a religious white man, in St. Michael's, twenty years ago, the names of three men in that town, whose lives were most after the pattern of our Lord and Master, Jesus Christ, the first three would have been as follows:

GARRISON WEST, *Class Leader*.
WRIGHT FAIRBANKS, *Class Leader*.
THOMAS AULD, *Class Leader*.

And yet, these were men who ferociously rushed in upon my Sabbath school, at St. Michael's, armed with mob-like missiles, and I must say, I thought him a Christian, until he took part in bloody by the lash. This same Garrison

West was my class leader, and I must say, I thought him a Christian, until he took part in breaking up my school. He led me no more after that. The plea for this outrage was then, as it is now and at all times—the danger to good order. If the slaves learnt to read, they would learn something else, and something worse. The peace of slavery would be disturbed; slave rule would be endangered. I leave the reader to characterize a system which is endangered by such causes. I do not dispute the soundness of the reasoning. It is perfectly sound; and, if slavery be *right*, Sabbath schools for teaching slaves to read the bible are *wrong*, and ought to be put down. These Christian class leaders were, to this extent, consistent. They had settled the question, that slavery is *right*, and, by that standard, they determined that Sabbath schools are wrong. To be sure, they were Protestant, and held to the great Protestant right of every man to *"search the scriptures"* for himself; but, then, to all general rules, there are *exceptions*. How convenient! What crimes may not be committed under the doctrine of the last remark. But, my dear, class leading Methodist brethren, did not condescend to give me a reason for breaking up the Sabbath school at St. Michael's; it was enough that they had determined upon its destruction. I am, however, digressing.

After getting the school cleverly into operation, the second time holding it in the woods, behind the barn, and in the shade of trees—I succeeded in inducing a free colored man, who lived several miles from our house, to permit me to hold my school in a room at his house. He, very kindly, gave me this liberty; but he incurred much peril in doing so, for the assemblage was an unlawful one. I shall not mention, here, the name of this man; for it might, even now, subject him to persecution, although the offenses were committed more than twenty years ago. I had, at one time, more than forty scholars, all of the right sort; and many of them succeeded in learning to read. I have met several slaves from Maryland, who were once my scholars; and who obtained their freedom, I doubt not, partly in consequence of the ideas imparted to them in that school. I have had various employments during my short life; but I look back to *none* with more satisfaction, than to that afforded by my Sunday school. An attachment, deep and lasting, sprung up between me and my persecuted pupils, which made parting from them intensely grievous; and, when I think that most of these dear souls are yet shut up in this abject thralldom, I am overwhelmed with grief.

Besides my Sunday school, I devoted three evenings a week to my fellow slaves, during the winter. Let the reader reflect upon the fact, that, in this christian country, men and women are hiding from professors of religion, in barns, in the woods and fields, in order to learn to read the *holy bible*. Those dear souls, who came to my Sabbath school, came *not* because it was popular or reputable to attend such a place, for they came under the liability of having forty stripes laid on their naked backs. Every moment they spend in my school, they were under this terrible liability; and, in this respect, I was sharer with them. Their minds had been cramped and starved by their cruel masters; the light of education had been completely excluded; and their hard earnings had been taken to educate their master's children. I felt a delight in circumventing the tyrants, and in blessing the victims of their curses.

The year at Mr. Freeland's passed off very smoothly, to outward seeming. Not a blow was given me during the whole year. To the credit of Mr. Freeland— irreligious though he was—it must be stated, that he was the best master I ever had, until I became my own master, and assumed for myself, as I had a right to do, the responsibility of my own existence and the exercise of my own powers. For much of the happiness—or absence of misery—with which I passed this year with Mr. Freeland, I am indebted to the genial temper and ardent friendship of my brother slaves. They were, every one of them, manly, generous and brave, yes; I say they were brave, and I will add, fine looking. It is seldom the lot of mortals to have truer and better friends than were the slaves on this farm. It is not uncommon to charge slaves with great treachery toward each other, and to believe them incapable of confiding in each other; but I must say, that I never loved, esteemed, or confided in men, more than I did in these. They were as true as steel, and no band of brothers could have been more loving. There were no mean advantages taken of each other, as is sometimes the case where slaves are situated as we were; no tattling; no giving each other bad names to Mr. Freeland; and no elevating one at the expense of the other. We never undertook to do any thing, of any importance, which was likely to affect each other, without mutual consultation. We were generally a unit, and moved together. Thoughts and sentiments were exchanged between us, which might well be called very incendiary, by oppressors and tyrants; and perhaps the time has not even now come, when it is safe to unfold all the flying suggestions which arise in the minds of intelligent slaves. Several of my friends and brothers, if yet alive, are still in some part of the house of bondage; and though twenty years have passed away, the suspicious malice of slavery might punish them for even listening to my thoughts.

The slaveholder, kind or cruel, is a slaveholder still—the every hour violator of the just and inalienable rights of man; and he is, therefore, every hour silently whetting the knife of vengeance for his own throat. He never lisps a syllable in commendation of the fathers of this republic, nor denounces any attempted oppression of himself, without inviting the knife to his own throat, and asserting the rights of rebellion for his own slaves.

The year is ended, and we are now in the midst of the Christmas holidays, which are kept this year as last, according to the general description previously given.

CHAPTER XIX

The Run-Away Plot

NEW YEAR'S THOUGHTS AND MEDITATIONS—AGAIN BOUGHT BY FREELAND—NO AMBITION TO BE A SLAVE—KINDNESS NO COMPENSATION FOR SLAVERY—INCIPIENT STEPS TOWARD ESCAPE—CONSIDERATIONS LEADING THERETO—IRRECONCILABLE HOSTILITY TO SLAVERY—SOLEMN VOW TAKEN—PLAN DIVULGED TO THE SLAVES—*Columbian Orator*— SCHEME GAINS FAVOR, DESPITE PRO-SLAVERY PREACHING—DANGER OF DISCOVERY—SKILL OF SLAVEHOLDERS IN READING THE MINDS OF THEIR SLAVES—SUSPICION AND COERCION—HYMNS WITH DOUBLE MEANING— VALUE, IN DOLLARS, OF OUR COMPANY—PRELIMINARY CONSULTATION— PASS-WORD—CONFLICTS OF HOPE AND FEAR—DIFFICULTIES TO BE OVERCOME—IGNORANCE OF GEOGRAPHY—SURVEY OF IMAGINARY DIFFICULTIES—EFFECT ON OUR MINDS—PATRICK HENRY—SANDY BECOMES A DREAMER—ROUTE TO THE NORTH LAID OUT—OBJECTIONS CONSIDERED—FRAUDS PRACTICED ON FREEMEN—PASSES WRITTEN— ANXIETIES AS THE TIME DREW NEAR—DREAD OF FAILURE—APPEALS TO COMRADES—STRANGE PRESENTIMENT—COINCIDENCE—THE BETRAYAL DISCOVERED—THE MANNER OF ARRESTING US—RESISTANCE MADE BY HENRY HARRIS—ITS EFFECT—THE UNIQUE SPEECH OF MRS. FREELAND— OUR SAD PROCESSION TO PRISON—BRUTAL JEERS BY THE MULTITUDE ALONG THE ROAD—PASSES EATEN—THE DENIAL—SANDY TOO WELL LOVED TO BE SUSPECTED—DRAGGED BEHIND HORSES—THE JAIL A RELIEF—A NEW SET OF TORMENTORS—SLAVE-TRADERS—JOHN, CHARLES AND HENRY RELEASED—ALONE IN PRISON—I AM TAKEN OUT, AND SENT TO BALTIMORE.

I am now at the beginning of the year 1836, a time favorable for serious thoughts. The mind naturally occupies itself with the mysteries of life in all its phases—the ideal, the real and the actual. Sober people look both ways at the beginning of the year, surveying the errors of the past, and providing against possible errors of the future. I, too, was thus exercised. I had little pleasure in retrospect, and the prospect was not very brilliant. "Notwithstanding," thought I, "the many resolutions and prayers I have made, in behalf of freedom, I am, this first day of the year 1836, still a slave, still wandering in the depths of spirit-devouring thralldom. My faculties and powers of body and soul are not my own, but are the property of a fellow mortal, in no sense superior to me, except that he has the physical power to compel me to be owned and controlled by him. By the combined physical force of the community, I am his slave—a slave for life." With thoughts like these, I was perplexed and chafed; they rendered me gloomy and disconsolate. The anguish of my mind may not be written.

At the close of the year 1835, Mr. Freeland, my temporary master, had bought me of Capt. Thomas Auld, for the year 1836. His promptness in securing my services, would have been flattering to my vanity, had I been ambitious to win the reputation of being a valuable slave. Even as it was, I felt a slight degree of complacency at the circumstance. It showed he was as well pleased with me as a slave, as I was with him as a master. I have already intimated my regard for Mr. Freeland, and I may say here, in addressing northern readers—where is no selfish motive for speaking in praise of a slaveholder—that Mr. Freeland was a man of many excellent qualities, and to me quite preferable to any master I ever had.

But the kindness of the slavemaster only gilds the chain of slavery, and detracts nothing from its weight or power. The thought that men are made for other and better uses than slavery, thrives best under the gentle treatment of a kind master. But the grim visage of slavery can assume no smiles which can fascinate the partially enlightened slave, into a forgetfulness of his bondage, nor of the desirableness of liberty.

I was not through the first month of this, my second year with the kind and gentlemanly Mr. Freeland, before I was earnestly considering and advising plans for gaining that freedom, which, when I was but a mere child, I had ascertained to be the natural and inborn right of every member of the human family. The desire for this freedom had been benumbed, while I was under the brutalizing dominion of Covey; and it had been postponed, and rendered inoperative, by my truly pleasant Sunday school engagements with my friends, during the year 1835, at Mr. Freeland's. It had, however, never entirely subsided. I hated slavery, always, and the desire for freedom only needed a favorable breeze, to fan it into a blaze, at any moment. The thought of only being a creature of the *present* and the *past*, troubled me, and I longed to have a *future*—a future with hope in it. To be shut up entirely to the past and present, is abhorrent to the human mind; it is to the soul—whose life and happiness is unceasing progress—what the prison is to the body; a blight and mildew, a hell of horrors. The dawning of this, another year, awakened me from my temporary slumber, and roused into life my latent, but long cherished aspirations for freedom. I was now not only ashamed to be contented in slavery, but ashamed to *seem* to be contented, and in my present favorable condition, under the mild rule of Mr. F., I am not sure that some kind reader will not condemn me for being over ambitious, and greatly wanting in proper humility, when I say the truth, that I now drove from me all thoughts of making the best of my lot, and welcomed only such thoughts as led me away from the house of bondage. The intense desires, now felt, *to be free*, quickened by my present favorable circumstances, brought me to the determination to act, as well as to think and speak. Accordingly, at the beginning of this year 1836, I took upon me a solemn vow, that the year which had now dawned upon me should not close, without witnessing an earnest attempt, on my part, to gain my liberty. This vow only bound me to make my escape individually; but the year spent with Mr. Freeland had attached me, as with "hooks of steel," to my brother slaves. The most affectionate and confiding friendship existed between us; and I felt it my duty to give them an opportunity to share in my virtuous determination by frankly disclosing to them my plans and purposes. Toward Henry and John Harris, I felt a friendship as strong as one man can feel for another; for I could have died with and for them. To them, therefore, with a suitable degree of caution, I began to disclose my sentiments and plans; sounding them, the while on the subject of running away, provided a good chance should offer. I scarcely need tell the reader, that I did my *very best* to imbue the minds of my dear friends with my own views and feelings. Thoroughly awakened, now, and with a definite vow upon me, all my little reading, which had any bearing on the subject of human rights, was rendered available in my communications with my friends. That (to me) gem of a book, the *Columbian Orator*, with its eloquent orations and spicy dialogues, denouncing oppression and slavery—telling of what had been dared, done and suffered by men, to obtain the inestimable boon of liberty—was still fresh in my memory, and whirled into the ranks of my speech with the aptitude of well trained soldiers, going through the drill. The fact is, I here began my public speaking. I canvassed, with Henry and John, the subject of slavery, and dashed against it the condemning brand of God's eternal justice, which it every hour violates. My fellow servants were neither indifferent, dull, nor inapt. Our feelings were more alike than our opinions. All, however, were ready to act, when a feasible plan should be proposed. "Show us *how* the thing is to be done," said they, "and all is clear."

We were all, except Sandy, quite free from slaveholding priestcraft. It was in vain that we had been taught from the pulpit at St. Michael's, the duty of obedience to our masters; to recognize God as the author of our enslavement; to regard running away an offense, alike against God and man; to deem our enslavement a merciful and beneficial arrangement; to esteem our condition, in this country, a paradise to that from which we had been snatched in Africa; to consider our hard hands and dark color as God's mark of displeasure, and as pointing us out as the proper subjects of slavery; that the relation of master and slave was one of reciprocal benefits; that our work was not more serviceable to our masters, than our master's thinking was serviceable to us. I say, it was in vain that the pulpit of St. Michael's had constantly inculcated these plausible doctrine. Nature laughed them to scorn. For my own part, I had now become altogether too big for my chains. Father Lawson's solemn words, of what I ought to be, and might be, in the providence of God, had not fallen dead on my soul. I was fast verging toward manhood, and the prophecies of my childhood were still unfulfilled. The thought, that year after year had passed away, and my resolutions to run away had failed and faded—that I was *still a slave*, and a slave, too, with chances for gaining my freedom diminished and still diminishing—was not a matter to be slept over easily; nor did I easily sleep over it.

But here came a new trouble. Thoughts and purposes so incendiary as those I now cherished, could not agitate the mind long, without danger of making themselves manifest to scrutinizing and unfriendly beholders. I had reason to fear that my sable face might prove altogether too transparent for the safe concealment of my hazardous enterprise. Plans of greater moment have leaked through stone walls, and revealed their projectors. But, here was no stone wall to hide my purpose. I would have given my poor, tell tale face for the immoveable countenance of an Indian, for it was far from being proof against the daily, searching glances of those with whom I met.

It is the interest and business of slaveholders to study human nature, with a view to practical results, and many of them attain astonishing proficiency in discerning the thoughts and emotions of slaves. They have to deal not with earth, wood, or stone, but with *men;* and, by every regard they have for their safety and prosperity, they must study to know the material on which they are at work. So much intellect as the slaveholder has around him, requires watching. Their safety depends upon their vigilance. Conscious of the injustice and wrong they are every hour perpetrating, and knowing what they themselves would do if made the victims of such wrongs, they are looking out for the first signs of the dread retribution of justice. They watch, therefore, with skilled and practiced eyes, and have learned to read, with great accuracy, the state of mind and heart of the slaves, through his sable face. These uneasy sinners are quick to inquire into the matter, where the slave is concerned. Unusual sobriety, apparent abstraction, sullenness and indifference—indeed, any mood out of the common way—afford ground for suspicion and inquiry. Often relying on their superior position and wisdom, they hector and torture the slave into a confession, by affecting to know the truth of their accusations. "You have got the devil in you," say they, "and we will whip him out of you." I have often been put thus to the torture, on bare suspicion. This system has its disadvantages as well as their opposite. The slave is sometimes whipped into the confession of offenses which he never committed. The reader will see that the good old rule—"a man is to be held innocent until proved to be guilty"—does not hold good on the slave plantation. Suspicion and torture are the approved methods of getting at the truth, here. It was necessary for me, therefore, to keep a watch over my deportment, lest the enemy should get the better of me.

But with all our caution and studied reserve, I am not sure that Mr. Freeland did not suspect that all was not right with us. It *did* seem that he watched us more narrowly, after the plan of escape had been conceived and discussed amongst us. Men seldom see themselves as others see them; and while, to ourselves, everything connected with our contemplated escape appeared concealed, Mr. Freeland may have, with the peculiar prescience of a slaveholder, mastered the huge thought which was disturbing our peace in slavery.

I am the more inclined to think that he suspected us, because, prudent as we were, as I now look back, I can see that we did many silly things, very well calculated to awaken suspicion. We were, at times, remarkably buoyant, singing hymns and making joyous exclamations, almost as triumphant in their tone as if we reached a land of freedom and safety. A keen observer might have detected in our repeated singing of

> *O Canaan, sweet Canaan,*
> *I am bound for the land of Canaan,*

something more than a hope of reaching heaven. We meant to reach the *north*—and the north was our Canaan.

> *I thought I heard them say,*
> *There were lions in the way,*
> *I don't expect to Star*
>   *Much longer here.*
>
> *Run to Jesus—shun the danger—*
> *I don't expect to stay*
>   *Much longer here.*

was a favorite air, and had a double meaning. In the lips of some, it meant the expectation of a speedy summons to a world of spirits; but, in the lips of *our* company, it simply meant, a speedy pilgrimage toward a free state, and deliverance from all the evils and dangers of slavery.

I had succeeded in winning to my (what slaveholders would call wicked) scheme, a company of five young men, the very flower of the neighborhood, each one of whom would have commanded one thousand dollars in the home market. At New Orleans, they would have brought fifteen hundred dollars a piece, and, perhaps, more. The names of our party were as follows: Henry Harris; John Harris, brother to Henry; Sandy Jenkins, of root memory; Charles Roberts, and Henry Bailey. I was the youngest, but one, of the party. I had, however, the advantage of them all, in experience, and in a knowledge of letters. This gave me great influence over them. Perhaps not one of them, left to himself, would have dreamed of escape as a possible thing. Not one of them was self-moved in the matter. They all wanted to be free; but the serious thought of running away, had not entered into their minds, until I won them to the undertaking. They all were tolerably well off—for slaves—and had dim hopes of being set free, some day, by their masters. If any one is to blame for disturbing the quiet of the slaves and slave-masters of the neighborhood of St. Michael's, *I am the man*. I claim to be the instigator of the high crime (as the slaveholders regard it) and I kept life in it, until life could be kept in it no longer.

Pending the time of our contemplated departure out of our Egypt, we met often by night, and on every Sunday. At these meetings we talked the matter over; told our hopes and fears, and the difficulties discovered or imagined; and, like men of sense, we counted the cost of the enterprise to which we were committing ourselves.

These meetings must have resembled, on a small scale, the meetings of revolutionary conspirators, in their primary condition. We were plotting against our (so called) lawful rulers; with this difference that we sought our own good, and not the harm of our enemies. We did not seek to overthrow them, but to escape from them. As for Mr. Freeland, we all liked him, and would have gladly remained with him, *as freeman*. LIBERTY was our aim; and we had now come to think that we had a right to liberty, against every obstacle even against the lives of our enslavers.

We had several words, expressive of things, important to us, which we understood, but which, even if distinctly heard by an outsider, would convey no certain meaning. I have reasons for suppressing these *pass-words*, which the reader will easily divine. I hated the secrecy; but where slavery is powerful, and liberty is weak, the latter is driven to concealment or to destruction.

The prospect was not always a bright one. At times, we were almost tempted to abandon the enterprise, and to get back to that comparative peace of mind, which even a man under the gallows might feel, when all hope of escape had vanished. Quiet bondage was felt to be better than the doubts, fears and uncertainties, which now so sadly perplexed and disturbed us.

The infirmities of humanity, generally, were represented in our little band. We were confident, bold and determined, at times; and, again, doubting, timid and wavering; whistling, like the boy in the graveyard, to keep away the spirits.

To look at the map, and observe the proximity of Eastern Shore, Maryland, to Delaware and Pennsylvania, it may seem to the reader quite absurd, to regard the proposed escape as a formidable undertaking. But to *understand*, some one has said a man must *stand under*. The real distance was great enough, but the imagined distance was, to our ignorance, even greater. Every slaveholder seeks to impress his slave with a belief in the boundlessness of slave territory, and of his own almost illimitable power. We all had vague and indistinct notions of the geography of the country.

The distance, however, is not the chief trouble. The nearer are the lines of a slave state and the borders of a free one, the greater the peril. Hired kidnappers infest these borders. Then, too, we knew that merely reaching a free state did not free us; that, wherever caught, we could be returned to slavery. We could see no spot on this side the ocean, where we could be free. We had heard of Canada, the real Canaan of the American bondmen, simply as a country to which the wild goose and the swan repaired at the end of winter, to escape the heat of summer, but not as the home of man. I knew something of theology, but nothing of geography. I really did not, at that time, know that there was a state of New York, or a state of Massachusetts. I had heard of Pennsylvania, Delaware and New Jersey, and all the southern states, but was ignorant of the free states, generally. New York city was our northern limit, and to go there, and be forever harassed with the liability of being hunted down and returned to slavery—with the certainty of being treated ten times worse than we had ever been treated before was a prospect far from delightful, and it might well cause some hesitation about engaging in the enterprise. The case, sometimes, to our excited visions, stood thus: At every gate through which we had to pass, we saw a watchman; at every ferry, a guard; on every bridge, a sentinel; and in every wood, a patrol or slave-hunter. We were hemmed in on every side. The good to be sought, and the evil to be shunned, were flung in the balance, and weighed against each other. On the one hand, there stood slavery; a stern reality, glaring frightfully upon us, with the blood of millions in his polluted skirts—terrible to behold—greedily devouring our hard earnings and feeding himself upon our flesh. Here was the evil from which to escape. On the other hand, far away, back in the hazy distance, where all forms seemed but shadows, under the flickering light of the north star—behind some craggy hill or snow-covered mountain—stood a doubtful freedom, half frozen, beckoning us to her icy domain. This was the good to be sought. The inequality was as great as that between certainty and uncertainty. This, in itself, was enough to stagger us; but when we came to survey the untrodden road, and conjecture the many possible difficulties, we were appalled, and at times, as I have said, were upon the point of giving over the struggle altogether.

The reader can have little idea of the phantoms of trouble which flit, in such circumstances, before the uneducated mind of the slave. Upon either side, we saw grim death assuming a variety of horrid shapes. Now, it was starvation, causing us, in a strange and friendless land, to eat our own flesh. Now, we were contending with the waves (for our journey was in part by water) and were drowned. Now, we were hunted by dogs, and overtaken and torn to pieces by their merciless fangs. We were stung by scorpions—chased by wild beasts—bitten by snakes; and, worst of all, after having succeeded in swimming rivers—encountering wild beasts—sleeping in the woods—suffering hunger, cold, heat and nakedness—we supposed ourselves to be overtaken by hired kidnappers, who, in the name of the law, and for their thrice accursed reward, would, perchance, fire upon us—kill some, wound others, and capture all. This dark picture, drawn by ignorance and fear, at times greatly shook our determination, and not unfrequently caused us to

> Rather bear those ills we had
> Than fly to others which we knew not of.

I am not disposed to magnify this circumstance in my experience, and yet I think I shall seem to be so disposed, to the reader. No man can tell the intense agony which is felt by the slave, when wavering on the point of making his escape. All that he has is at stake; and even that which he has not, is at stake, also. The life which he has, may be lost, and the liberty which he seeks, may not be gained.

Patrick Henry, to a listening senate, thrilled by his magic eloquence, and ready to stand by him in his boldest flights, could say, GIVE ME LIBERTY OR GIVE ME DEATH, and this saying was a sublime one, even for a freeman; but, incomparably more sublime, is the same sentiment, when *practically* asserted by men accustomed to the lash and chain—men whose sensibilities must have become more or less deadened by their bondage. With us it was a *doubtful* liberty, at best, that we sought; and a certain, lingering death in the rice swamps and sugar fields, if we failed. Life is not lightly regarded by men of sane minds. It is precious, alike to the pauper and to the prince—to the slave, and to his master; and yet, I believe there was not one among us, who would not rather have been shot down, than pass away life in hopeless bondage.

In the progress of our preparations, Sandy, the root man, became troubled. He began to have dreams, and some of them were very distressing. One of these, which happened on a Friday night, was, to him, of great significance; and I am quite ready to confess, that I felt somewhat damped by it myself. He said, "I dreamed, last night, that I was roused from sleep, by strange noises, like the voices of a swarm of angry birds, that caused a roar as they passed, which fell upon my ear like a coming gale over the tops of the trees. Looking up to see what it could mean," said Sandy, "I saw you, Frederick, in the claws of a huge bird, surrounded by a large number of birds, of all colors and sizes. These were all picking at you, while you, with your arms, seemed to be trying to protect your eyes. Passing over me, the birds flew in a south-westerly direction, and I watched them until they were clean out of sight. Now, I saw this as plainly as I now see you; and furder, honey, watch de Friday night dream; dare is sumpon in it, shose you born; dare is, indeed, honey."

I confess I did not like this dream; but I threw off concern about it, by attributing it to the general excitement and perturbation consequent upon our contemplated plan of escape. I could not, however, shake off its effect at once. I felt that it boded me no good. Sandy was unusually emphatic and oracular, and his manner had much to do with the impression made upon me.

The plan of escape which I recommended, and to which my comrades assented, was to take a large canoe, owned by Mr. Hamilton, and, on the Saturday night previous to the Easter holidays, launch out into the Chesapeake bay, and paddle for its head—a distance of seventy miles with all our might. Our course, on reaching this point, was, to turn the canoe adrift, and bend our steps toward the north star, till we reached a free state.

There were several objections to this plan. One was, the danger from gales on the bay. In rough weather, the waters of the Chesapeake are much agitated, and there is danger, in a canoe, of being swamped by the waves. Another objection was, that the canoe would soon be missed; the absent persons would, at once, be suspected of having taken it; and we should be pursued by some of the fast sailing bay craft out of St. Michael's. Then, again, if we reached the head of the bay, and turned the canoe adrift, she might prove a guide to our track, and bring the land hunters after us.

These and other objections were set aside, by the stronger ones which could be urged against every other plan that could then be suggested. On the water, we had a chance of being regarded as fishermen, in the service of a master. On the other hand, by taking the land route, through the counties adjoining Delaware, we should be subjected to all manner of interruptions, and many very disagreeable questions, which might give us serious trouble. Any white man is authorized to stop a man of color, on any road, and examine him, and arrest him, if he so desires.

By this arrangement, many abuses (considered such even by slaveholders) occur. Cases have been known, where freemen have been called upon to show their free papers, by a pack of ruffians—and, on the presentation of the papers, the ruffians have torn them up, and seized their victim, and sold him to a life of endless bondage.

The week before our intended start, I wrote a pass for each of our party, giving them permission to visit Baltimore, during the Easter holidays. The pass ran after this manner:

This is to certify, that I, the undersigned, have given the bearer, my servant, John, full liberty to go to Baltimore, to spend the Easter holidays.

W.H.

Near St. Michael's, Talbot county, Maryland

Although we were not going to Baltimore, and were intending to land east of North Point, in the direction where I had seen the Philadelphia steamers go, these passes might be made useful to us in the lower part of the bay, while steering toward Baltimore. These were not, however, to be shown by us, until all other answers failed to satisfy the inquirer. We were all fully alive to the importance of being calm and self-possessed, when accosted, if accosted we should be; and we more times than one rehearsed to each other how we should behave in the hour of trial.

These were long, tedious days and nights. The suspense was painful, in the extreme. To balance probabilities, where life and liberty hang on the result, requires steady nerves. I panted for action, and was glad when the day, at the close of which we were to start, dawned upon us. Sleeping, the night before, was out of the question. I probably felt more deeply than any of my companions, because I was the instigator of the movement. The responsibility of the whole enterprise rested on my shoulders. The glory of success, and the shame and confusion of failure, could not be matters of indifference to me. Our food was prepared; our clothes were packed up; we were all ready to go, and impatient for Saturday morning—considering that the last morning of our bondage.

I cannot describe the tempest and tumult of my brain, that morning. The reader will please to bear in mind, that, in a slave state, an unsuccessful runaway is not only subjected to cruel torture, and sold away to the far south, but he is frequently execrated by the other slaves. He is charged with making the condition of the other slaves intolerable, by laying them all under the suspicion of their masters—subjecting them to greater vigilance, and imposing greater limitations on their privileges. I dreaded murmurs from this quarter. It is difficult, too, for a slavemaster to believe that slaves escaping have not been aided in their flight by some one of their fellow slaves. When, therefore, a slave is missing, every slave on the place is closely examined as to his knowledge of the undertaking; and they are sometimes even tortured, to make them disclose what they are suspected of knowing of such escape.

Our anxiety grew more and more intense, as the time of our intended departure for the north drew nigh. It was truly felt to be a matter of life and death with us; and we fully intended to *fight* as well as *run*, if necessity should occur for that extremity. But the trial hour was not yet to come. It was easy to resolve, but not so easy to act. I expected there might be some drawing back, at the last. It was natural that there should be; therefore, during the intervening time, I lost no opportunity to explain away difficulties, to remove doubts, to dispel fears, and to inspire all with firmness. It was too late to look back; and *now* was the time to go forward. Like most other men, we had done the talking part of our work, long and well; and the time had come to *act* as if we were in earnest, and meant to be as true in action as in words. I did not forget to appeal to the pride of my comrades, by telling them that, if after having solemnly promised to go, as they had done, they now failed to make the attempt, they would, in effect, brand themselves with cowardice, and might as well sit down, fold their arms, and acknowledge themselves as fit only to be *slaves*. This detestable character, all were unwilling to assume. Every man except Sandy (he, much to our regret, withdrew) stood firm; and at our last meeting we pledged ourselves afresh, and in the most solemn manner, that, at the time appointed, we *would* certainly start on our long journey for a free country. This meeting was in the middle of the week, at the end of which we were to start.

Early that morning we went, as usual, to the field, but with hearts that beat quickly and anxiously. Any one intimately acquainted with us, might have seen that all was not well with us, and that some monster lingered in our thoughts. Our work that morning was the same as it had been for several days past—drawing out and spreading manure. While thus engaged, I had a sudden presentiment, which flashed upon me like lightning in a dark night, revealing to the lonely traveler the gulf before, and the enemy behind. I instantly turned to Sandy Jenkins, who was near me, and said to him, *"Sandy, we are betrayed; something has just told me so."* I felt as sure of it, as if the officers were there in sight. Sandy said, "Man, dat is strange; but I feel just as you do." If my mother—then long in her grave—had appeared before me, and told me that we were betrayed, I could not, at that moment, have felt more certain of the fact.

In a few minutes after this, the long, low and distant notes of the horn summoned us from the field to breakfast. I felt as one may be supposed to feel before being led forth to be executed for some great offense. I wanted no breakfast; but I went with the other slaves toward the house, for form's sake. My feelings were not disturbed as to the right of running away; on that point I had no trouble, whatever. My anxiety arose from a sense of the consequences of failure.

In thirty minutes after that vivid presentiment came the apprehended crash. On reaching the house, for breakfast, and glancing my eye toward the lane gate, the worst was at once made known. The lane gate off Mr. Freeland's house, is nearly a half mile from the door, and shaded by the heavy wood which bordered the main road. I was, however, able to descry four white men, and two colored men, approaching. The white men were on horseback, and the colored men were walking behind, and seemed to be tied. *"It is all over with us,"* thought I, *"we are surely betrayed."* I now became composed, or at least comparatively so, and calmly awaited the result. I watched the ill-omened company, till I saw them enter the gate. Successful flight was impossible, and I made up my mind to stand, and meet the evil, whatever it might be; for I was not without a slight hope that things might turn differently from what I at first expected. In a few moments, in came Mr. William Hamilton, riding very rapidly, and evidently much excited. He was in the habit of riding very slowly, and was seldom known to gallop his horse. This time, his horse was nearly at full speed, causing the dust to roll thick behind him. Mr. Hamilton, though one of the most resolute men in the whole neighborhood, was, nevertheless, a remarkably mild spoken man; and, even when greatly excited, his language was cool and circumspect. He came to the door, and inquired if Mr. Freeland was in. I told him that Mr. Freeland was at the barn. Off the old gentleman rode, toward the barn, with unwonted speed. Mary, the cook, was at a loss to know what was the matter, and I did not profess any skill in making her understand. I knew she would have united, as readily as any one, in cursing me for bringing trouble into the family; so I held my peace, leaving matters to develop themselves, without my assistance. In a few moments, Mr. Hamilton and Mr. Freeland came down from the barn to the house; and, just as they made their appearance in the front yard, three men (who proved to be constables) came dashing into the lane, on horseback, as if summoned by a sign requiring quick work. A few seconds brought them into the front yard, where they hastily dismounted, and tied their horses. This done, they joined Mr. Freeland and Mr. Hamilton, who were standing a short distance from the kitchen. A few moments were spent, as if in consulting how to proceed, and then the whole party walked up to the kitchen door. There was now no one in the kitchen but myself and John Harris. Henry and Sandy were yet at the barn. Mr. Freeland came inside the kitchen door, and with an agitated voice, called me by name, and told me to come forward; that there was some gentlemen who wished to see me. I stepped toward them, at the door, and asked what they wanted, when the constables grabbed me, and told me that I had better not resist; that I had been in a scrape, or was said to have been in one; that they were merely going to take me where I could be examined; that they were going to carry me to St. Michael's, to have me brought before my master. They further said, that, in case the evidence against me was not true, I should be acquitted. I was now firmly tied, and completely at the mercy of my captors. Resistance was idle. They were five in number, armed to the very teeth. When they had secured me, they next turned to John Harris, and, in a few moments, succeeded in tying him as firmly as they had already tied me. They next turned toward Henry Harris, who had now returned from the barn. "Cross your hands," said the constables, to Henry. "I won't" said Henry, in a voice so firm and clear, and in a manner so determined, as for a moment to arrest all proceedings. "Won't you cross your hands?" said Tom Graham, the constable. "*No I won't,*" said Henry, with increasing emphasis. Mr. Hamilton, Mr. Freeland, and the officers, now came near to Henry. Two of the constables drew out their shining pistols, and swore by the name of God, that he should cross his hands, or they would shoot him down. Each of these hired ruffians now cocked their pistols, and, with fingers apparently on the triggers, presented their deadly weapons to the breast of the unarmed slave, saying, at the same time, if he did not cross his hands, they would "blow his d—d heart out of him."

"*Shoot! shoot me!*" said Henry. "*You can't kill me but once.* Shoot!—shoot! and be d—d. *I won't be tied.*" This, the brave fellow said in a voice as defiant and heroic in its tone, as was the language itself; and, at the moment of saying this, with the pistols at his very breast, he quickly raised his arms, and dashed them from the puny hands of his assassins, the weapons flying in opposite directions. Now came the struggle. All hands was now rushed upon the brave fellow, and, after beating him for some time, they succeeded in overpowering and tying him. Henry put me to shame; he fought, and fought bravely. John and I had made no resistance. The fact is, I never see much use in fighting, unless there is a reasonable probability of whipping somebody. Yet there was something almost providential in the resistance made by the gallant Henry. But for that resistance, every soul of us would have been hurried off to the far south. Just a moment previous to the trouble with Henry, Mr. Hamilton *mildly* said—and this gave me the unmistakable clue to the cause of our arrest—"Perhaps we had now better make a search for those protections, which we understand Frederick has written for himself and the rest." Had these passes been found, they would have been point blank proof against us, and would have confirmed all the statements of our betrayer. Thanks to the resistance of Henry, the excitement produced by the scuffle drew all attention in that direction, and I succeeded in flinging my pass, unobserved, into the fire. The confusion attendant upon the scuffle, and the apprehension of further trouble, perhaps, led our captors to forego, for the present, any search for *"those protections" which Frederick was said to have written for his companions*; so we were not yet convicted of the purpose to run away; and it was evident that there was some doubt, on the part of all, whether we had been guilty of such a purpose.

Just as we were all completely tied, and about ready to start toward St. Michael's, and thence to jail, Mrs. Betsey Freeland (mother to William, who was very much attached—after the southern fashion—to Henry and John, they having been reared from childhood in her house) came to the kitchen door, with her hands full of biscuits—for we had not had time to take our breakfast that morning—and divided them between Henry and John. This done, the lady made the following parting address to me, looking and pointing her bony finger at me. "You devil! you yellow devil! It was you that put it into the heads of Henry and John to run away. But for *you*, you *long legged yellow devil*, Henry and John would never have thought of running away." I gave the lady a look, which called forth a scream of mingled wrath and terror, as she slammed the kitchen door, and went in, leaving me, with the rest, in hands as harsh as her own broken voice.

Could the kind reader have been quietly riding along the main road to or from Easton, that morning, his eye would have met a painful sight. He would have seen five young men, guilty of no crime, save that of preferring *liberty* to a life of *bondage,* drawn along the public highway—firmly bound together—tramping through dust and heat, bare-footed and bare-headed—fastened to three strong horses, whose riders were armed to the teeth, with pistols and daggers—on their way to prison, like felons, and suffering every possible insult from the crowds of idle, vulgar people, who clustered around, and heartlessly made their failure the occasion for all manner of ribaldry and sport. As I looked upon this crowd of vile persons, and saw myself and friends thus assailed and persecuted, I could not help seeing the fulfillment of Sandy's dream. I was in the hands of moral vultures, and firmly held in their sharp talons, and was hurried away toward Easton, in a south-easterly direction, amid the jeers of new birds of the same feather, through every neighborhood we passed. It seemed to me (and this shows the good understanding between the slaveholders and their allies) that every body we met knew the cause of our arrest, and were out, awaiting our passing by, to feast their vindictive eyes on our misery and to gloat over our ruin. Some said, *I ought to be hanged,* and others, *I ought to be burnt,* others, I ought to have the *"hide"* taken from my back; while no one gave us a kind word or sympathizing look, except the poor slaves, who were lifting their heavy hoes, and who cautiously glanced at us through the post-and-rail fences, behind which they were at work. Our sufferings, that morning, can be more easily imagined than described. Our hopes were all blasted, at a blow. The cruel injustice, the victorious crime, and the helplessness of innocence, led me to ask, in my ignorance and weakness "Where now is the God of justice and mercy? And why have these wicked men the power thus to trample upon our rights, and to insult our feelings?" And yet, in the next moment, came the consoling thought, *"The day of oppressor will come at last."* Of one thing I could be glad—not one of my dear friends, upon whom I had brought this great calamity, either by word or look, reproached me for having led them into it. We were a band of brothers, and never dearer to each other than now. The thought which gave us the most pain, was the probable separation which would now take place, in case we were sold off to the far south, as we were likely to be. While the constables were looking forward, Henry and I, being fastened together, could occasionally exchange a word, without being observed by the kidnappers who had us in charge. "What shall I do with my pass?" said Henry. "Eat it with your biscuit," said I; "it won't do to tear it up." We were now near St. Michael's. The direction concerning the passes was passed around, and executed. *"Own nothing!"* said I. *"Own nothing!"* was passed around and enjoined, and assented to. Our confidence in each other was unshaken; and we were quite resolved to succeed or fail together—as much after the calamity which had befallen us, as before.

On reaching St. Michael's, we underwent a sort of examination at my master's store, and it was evident to my mind, that Master Thomas suspected the truthfulness of the evidence upon which they had acted in arresting us; and that he only affected, to some extent, the positiveness with which he asserted our guilt. There was nothing said by any of our company, which could, in any manner, prejudice our cause; and there was hope, yet, that we should be able to return to our homes—if for nothing else, at least to find out the guilty man or woman who had betrayed us.

To this end, we all denied that we had been guilty of intended flight. Master Thomas said that the evidence he had of our intention to run away, was strong enough to hang us, in a case of murder. "But," said I, "the cases are not equal. If murder were committed, some one must have committed it—the thing is done! In our case, nothing has been done! We have not run away. Where is the evidence against us? We were quietly at our work." I talked thus, with unusual freedom, to bring out the evidence against us, for we all wanted, above all things, to know the guilty wretch who had betrayed us, that we might have something tangible upon which to pour the execrations. From something which dropped, in the course of the talk, it appeared that there was but one witness against us—and that that witness could not be produced. Master Thomas would not tell us *who* his informant was; but we suspected, and suspected *one* person *only*. Several circumstances seemed to point SANDY out, as our betrayer. His entire knowledge of our plans his participation in them—his withdrawal from us—his dream, and his simultaneous presentiment that we were betrayed—the taking us, and the leaving him—were calculated to turn suspicion toward him; and yet, we could not suspect him. We all loved him too well to think it *possible* that he could have betrayed us. So we rolled the guilt on other shoulders.

We were literally dragged, that morning, behind horses, a distance of fifteen miles, and placed in the Easton jail. We were glad to reach the end of our journey, for our pathway had been the scene of insult and mortification. Such is the power of public opinion, that it is hard, even for the innocent, to feel the happy consolations of innocence, when they fall under the maledictions of this power. How could we regard ourselves as in the right, when all about us denounced us as criminals, and had the power and the disposition to treat us as such.

In jail, we were placed under the care of Mr. Joseph Graham, the sheriff of the county. Henry, and John, and myself, were placed in one room, and Henry Baily and Charles Roberts, in another, by themselves. This separation was intended to deprive us of the advantage of concert, and to prevent trouble in jail.

Once shut up, a new set of tormentors came upon us. A swarm of imps, in human shape the slave-traders, deputy slave-traders, and agents of slave-traders—that gather in every country town of the state, watching for chances to buy human flesh (as buzzards to eat carrion) flocked in upon us, to ascertain if our masters had placed us in jail to be sold. Such a set of debased and villainous creatures, I never saw before, and hope never to see again. I felt myself surrounded as by a pack of *fiends*, fresh from *perdition*. They laughed, leered, and grinned at us; saying, "Ah! boys, we've got you, havn't we? So you were about to make your escape? Where were you going to?" After taunting us, and peering at us, as long as they liked, they one by one subjected us to an examination, with a view to ascertain our value; feeling our arms and legs, and shaking us by the shoulders to see if we were sound and healthy; impudently asking us, "how we would like to have them for masters?" To such questions, we were, very much to their annoyance, quite dumb, disdaining to answer them. For one, I detested the whisky-bloated gamblers in human flesh; and I believe I was as much detested by them in turn. One fellow told me, "if he had me, he would cut the devil out of me pretty quick."

These Negro buyers are very offensive to the genteel southern Christian public. They are looked upon, in respectable Maryland society, as necessary, but detestable characters. As a class, they are hardened ruffians, made such by nature and by occupation. Their ears are made quite familiar with the agonizing cry of outraged and woe-smitten humanity. Their eyes are forever open to human misery. They walk amid desecrated affections, insulted virtue, and blasted hopes. They have grown intimate with vice and blood; they gloat over the wildest illustrations of their soul-damning and earth-polluting business, and are moral pests. Yes; they are a legitimate fruit of slavery; and it is a puzzle to make out a case of greater villainy for them, than for the slaveholders, who make such a class *possible*. They are mere hucksters of the surplus slave produce of Maryland and Virginia coarse, cruel, and swaggering bullies, whose very breathing is of blasphemy and blood.

Aside from these slave-buyers, who infested the prison, from time to time, our quarters were much more comfortable than we had any right to expect they would be. Our allowance of food was small and coarse, but our room was the best in the jail—neat and spacious, and with nothing about it necessarily reminding us of being in prison, but its heavy locks and bolts and the black, iron lattice-work at the windows. We were prisoners of state, compared with most slaves who are put into that Easton jail. But the place was not one of contentment. Bolts, bars and grated windows are not acceptable to freedom-loving people of any color. The suspense, too, was painful. Every step on the stairway was listened to, in the hope that the comer would cast a ray of light on our fate. We would have given the hair off our heads for half a dozen words with one of the waiters in Sol. Lowe's hotel. Such waiters were in the way of hearing, at the table, the probable course of things. We could see them flitting about in their white jackets in front of this hotel, but could speak to none of them.

Soon after the holidays were over, contrary to all our expectations, Messrs. Hamilton and Freeland came up to Easton; not to make a bargain with the "Georgia traders," nor to send us up to Austin Woldfolk, as is usual in the case of run-away slaves, but to release Charles, Henry Harris, Henry Baily and John Harris, from prison, and this, too, without the infliction of a single blow. I was now left entirely alone in prison. The innocent had been taken, and the guilty left. My friends were separated from me, and apparently forever. This circumstance caused me more pain than any other incident connected with our capture and imprisonment. Thirty-nine lashes on my naked and bleeding back, would have been joyfully borne, in preference to this separation from these, the friends of my youth. And yet, I could not but feel that I was the victim of something like justice. Why should these young men, who were led into this scheme by me, suffer as much as the instigator? I felt glad that they were leased from prison, and from the dread prospect of a life (or death I should rather say) in the rice swamps. It is due to the noble Henry, to say, that he seemed almost as reluctant to leave the prison with me in it, as he was to be tied and dragged to prison. But he and the rest knew that we should, in all the likelihoods of the case, be separated, in the event of being sold; and since we were now completely in the hands of our owners, we all concluded it would be best to go peaceably home.

Not until this last separation, dear reader, had I touched those profounder depths of desolation, which it is the lot of slaves often to reach. I was solitary in the world, and alone within the walls of a stone prison, left to a fate of life-long misery. I had hoped and expected much, for months before, but my hopes and expectations were now withered and blasted. The ever dreaded slave life in Georgia, Louisiana and Alabama—from which escape is next to impossible now, in my loneliness, stared me in the face. The possibility of ever becoming anything but an abject slave, a mere machine in the hands of an owner, had now fled, and it seemed to me it had fled forever. A life of living death, beset with the innumerable horrors of the cotton field, and the sugar plantation, seemed to be my doom. The fiends, who rushed into the prison when we were first put there, continued to visit me, and to ply me with questions and with their tantalizing remarks. I was insulted, but helpless; keenly alive to the demands of justice and liberty, but with no means of asserting them. To talk to those imps about justice and mercy, would have been as absurd as to reason with bears and tigers. Lead and steel are the only arguments that they understand.

After remaining in this life of misery and despair about a week, which, by the way, seemed a month, Master Thomas, very much to my surprise, and greatly to my relief, came to the prison, and took me out, for the purpose, as he said, of sending me to Alabama, with a friend of his, who would emancipate me at the end of eight years. I was glad enough to get out of prison; but I had no faith in the story that this friend of Capt. Auld would emancipate me, at the end of the time indicated. Besides, I never had heard of his having a friend in Alabama, and I took the announcement, simply as an easy and comfortable method of shipping me off to the far south. There was a little scandal, too, connected with the idea of one Christian selling another to the Georgia traders, while it was deemed every way proper for them to sell to others. I thought this friend in Alabama was an invention, to meet this difficulty, for Master Thomas was quite jealous of his Christian reputation, however unconcerned he might be about his real Christian character. In these remarks, however, it is possible that I do Master Thomas Auld injustice. He certainly did not exhaust his power upon me, in the case, but acted, upon the whole, very generously, considering the nature of my offense. He had the power and the provocation to send me, without reserve, into the very everglades of Florida, beyond the remotest hope of emancipation; and his refusal to exercise that power, must be set down to his credit.

After lingering about St. Michael's a few days, and no friend from Alabama making his appearance, to take me there, Master Thomas decided to send me back again to Baltimore, to live with his brother Hugh, with whom he was now at peace; possibly he became so by his profession of religion, at the camp-meeting in the Bay Side. Master Thomas told me that he wished me to go to Baltimore, and learn a trade; and that, if I behaved myself properly, he would *emancipate me at twenty-five!* Thanks for this one beam of hope in the future. The promise had but one fault; it seemed too good to be true.

CHAPTER XX

Apprenticeship Life

NOTHING LOST BY THE ATTEMPT TO RUN AWAY—COMRADES IN THEIR OLD HOMES—REASONS FOR SENDING ME AWAY—RETURN TO BALTIMORE—CONTRAST BETWEEN TOMMY AND THAT OF HIS COLORED COMPANION—TRIALS IN GARDINER'S SHIP YARD—DESPERATE FIGHT—ITS CAUSES—CONFLICT BETWEEN WHITE AND BLACK LABOR—DESCRIPTION OF THE OUTRAGE—COLORED TESTIMONY NOTHING—CONDUCT OF MASTER HUGH—SPIRIT OF SLAVERY IN BALTIMORE—MY CONDITION IMPROVES—NEW ASSOCIATIONS—SLAVEHOLDER'S RIGHT TO TAKE HIS WAGES—HOW TO MAKE A CONTENTED SLAVE.

Well! dear reader, I am not, as you may have already inferred, a loser by the general upstir, described in the foregoing chapter. The little domestic revolution, notwithstanding the sudden snub it got by the treachery of somebody—I dare not say or think who—did not, after all, end so disastrously, as when in the iron cage at Easton, I conceived it would. The prospect, from that point, did look about as dark as any that ever cast its gloom over the vision of the anxious, out-looking, human spirit. "All is well that ends well." My affectionate comrades, Henry and John Harris, are still with Mr. William Freeland. Charles Roberts and Henry Baily are safe at their homes. I have not, therefore, any thing to regret on their account. Their masters have mercifully forgiven them, probably on the ground suggested in the spirited little speech of Mrs. Freeland, made to me just before leaving for the jail—namely: that they had been allured into the wicked scheme of making their escape, by me; and that, but for me, they would never have dreamed of a thing so shocking! My friends had nothing to regret, either; for while they were watched more closely on account of what had happened, they were, doubtless, treated more kindly than before, and got new assurances that they would be legally emancipated, some day, provided their behavior should make them deserving, from that time forward. Not a blow, as I learned, was struck any one of them. As for Master William Freeland, good, unsuspecting soul, he did not believe that we were intending to run away at all. Having given—as he thought—no occasion to his boys to leave him, he could not think it probable that they had entertained a design so grievous. This, however, was not the view taken of the matter by "Mas' Billy," as we used to call the soft spoken, but crafty and resolute Mr. William Hamilton. He had no doubt that the crime had been meditated; and regarding me as the instigator of it, he frankly told Master Thomas that he must remove me from that neighborhood, or he would shoot me down. He would not have one so dangerous as "Frederick" tampering with his slaves. William Hamilton was not a man whose threat might be safely disregarded. I have no doubt that he would have proved as good as his word, had the warning given not been promptly taken. He was furious at the thought of such a piece of high-handed *theft*, as we were about to perpetrate the stealing of our own bodies and souls! The feasibility of the plan, too, could the first steps have been taken, was marvelously plain. Besides, this was a *new* idea, this use of the bay. Slaves escaping, until now, had taken to the woods; they had never dreamed of profaning and abusing the waters of the noble Chesapeake, by making them the highway from slavery to freedom. Here was a broad road of destruction to slavery, which, before, had been looked upon as a wall of security by slaveholders. But Master Billy could not get Mr. Freeland to see matters precisely as he did; nor could he get Master Thomas so excited as he was himself. The latter—I must say it to his credit—showed much humane feeling in his part of the transaction, and atoned for much that had been harsh, cruel and unreasonable in his former treatment of me and others. His clemency was quite unusual and unlooked for. "Cousin Tom" told me that while I was in jail, Master Thomas was very unhappy; and that the night before his going up to release me, he had walked the floor nearly all night, evincing great distress; that very tempting offers had been made to him, by the Negro-traders, but he had rejected them all, saying that *money could not tempt him to sell me to the far south*. All this I can easily believe, for he seemed quite reluctant to send me away, at all. He told me that he only consented to do so, because of the very strong prejudice against me in the neighborhood, and that he feared for my safety if I remained there.

Thus, after three years spent in the country, roughing it in the field, and experiencing all sorts of hardships, I was again permitted to return to Baltimore, the very place, of all others, short of a free state, where I most desired to live. The three years spent in the country, had made some difference in me, and in the household of Master Hugh. "Little Tommy" was no longer *little* Tommy; and I was not the slender lad who had left for the Eastern Shore just three years before. The loving relations between me and Mas' Tommy were broken up. He was no longer dependent on me for protection, but felt himself a *man*, with other and more suitable associates. In childhood, he scarcely considered me inferior to himself certainly, as good as any other boy with whom he played; but the time had come when his *friend* must become his *slave*. So we were cold, and we parted. It was a sad thing to me, that, loving each other as we had done, we must now take different roads. To him, a thousand avenues were open. Education had made him acquainted with all the treasures of the world, and liberty had flung open the gates thereunto; but I, who had attended him seven years, and had watched over him with the care of a big brother, fighting his battles in the street, and shielding him from harm, to an extent which had induced his mother to say, "Oh! Tommy is always safe, when he is with Freddy," must be confined to a single condition. He could grow, and become a MAN; I could grow, though I could *not* become a man, but must remain, all my life, a minor—a mere boy. Thomas Auld, Junior, obtained a situation on board the brig "Tweed," and went to sea. I know not what has become of him; he certainly has my good wishes for his welfare and prosperity. There were few persons to whom I was more sincerely attached than to him, and there are few in the world I would be more pleased to meet.

Very soon after I went to Baltimore to live, Master Hugh succeeded in getting me hired to Mr. William Gardiner, an extensive ship builder on Fell's Point. I was placed here to learn to calk, a trade of which I already had some knowledge, gained while in Mr. Hugh Auld's ship-yard, when he was a master builder. Gardiner's, however, proved a very unfavorable place for the accomplishment of that object. Mr. Gardiner was, that season, engaged in building two large man-of-war vessels, professedly for the Mexican government. These vessels were to be launched in the month of July, of that year, and, in failure thereof, Mr. G. would forfeit a very considerable sum of money. So, when I entered the ship-yard, all was hurry and driving. There were in the yard about one hundred men; of these about seventy or eighty were regular carpenters—privileged men. Speaking of my condition here I wrote, years ago—and I have now no reason to vary the picture as follows:

There was no time to learn any thing. Every man had to do that which he knew how to do. In entering the ship-yard, my orders from Mr. Gardiner were, to do whatever the carpenters commanded me to do. This was placing me at the beck and call of about seventy-five men. I was to regard all these as masters. Their word was to be my law. My situation was a most trying one. At times I needed a dozen pair of hands. I was called a dozen ways in the space of a single minute. Three or four voices would strike my ear at the same moment. It was—"Fred., come help me to cant this timber here." "Fred., come carry this timber yonder."—"Fred., bring that roller here."—"Fred., go get a fresh can of water."—"Fred., come help saw off the end of this timber."—"Fred., go quick and get the crow bar."—"Fred., hold on the end of this fall."—"Fred., go to the blacksmith's shop, and get a new punch."—

"Hurra, Fred.! run and bring me a cold chisel."—"I say, Fred., bear a hand, and get up a fire as quick as lightning under that steam-box."—"Halloo, nigger! come, turn this grindstone."—"Come, come! move, move! and *bowse* this timber forward."—"I say, darkey, blast your eyes, why don't you heat up some pitch?"—"Halloo! halloo! halloo!" (Three voices at the same time.) "Come here!—Go there!—Hold on where you are! D—n you, if you move, I'll knock your brains out!"

Such, dear reader, is a glance at the school which was mine, during, the first eight months of my stay at Baltimore. At the end of the eight months, Master Hugh refused longer to allow me to remain with Mr. Gardiner. The circumstance which led to his taking me away, was a brutal outrage, committed upon me by the white apprentices of the ship-yard. The fight was a desperate one, and I came out of it most shockingly mangled. I was cut and bruised in sundry places, and my left eye was nearly knocked out of its socket. The facts, leading to this barbarous outrage upon me, illustrate a phase of slavery destined to become an important element in the overthrow of the slave system, and I may, therefore state them with some minuteness. That phase is this: *the conflict of slavery with the interests of the white mechanics and laborers of the south.* In the country, this conflict is not so apparent; but, in cities, such as Baltimore, Richmond, New Orleans, Mobile, &c., it is seen pretty clearly. The slaveholders, with a craftiness peculiar to themselves, by encouraging the enmity of the poor, laboring white man against the blacks, succeeds in making the said white man almost as much a slave as the black slave himself. The difference between the white slave, and the black slave, is this: the latter belongs to *one* slaveholder, and the former belongs to *all* the slaveholders, collectively. The white slave has taken from him, by indirection, what the black slave has taken from him, directly, and without ceremony. Both are plundered, and by the same plunderers. The slave is robbed, by his master, of all his earnings, above what is required for his bare physical necessities; and the white man is robbed by the slave system, of the just results of his labor, because he is flung into competition with a class of laborers who work without wages. The competition, and its injurious consequences, will, one day, array the nonslaveholding white people of the slave states, against the slave system, and make them the most effective workers against the great evil. At present, the slaveholders blind them to this competition, by keeping alive their prejudice against the slaves, *as men*—not against them *as slaves.* They appeal to their pride, often denouncing emancipation, as tending to place the white man, on an equality with Negroes, and, by this means, they succeed in drawing off the minds of the poor whites from the real fact, that, by the rich slave-master, they are already regarded as but a single remove from equality with the slave. The impression is cunningly made, that slavery is the only power that can prevent the laboring white man from falling to the level of the slave's poverty and degradation. To make this enmity deep and broad, between the slave and the poor white man, the latter is allowed to abuse and whip the former, without hinderance. But—as I have suggested—this state of facts prevails *mostly* in the country. In the city of Baltimore, there are not unfrequent murmurs, that educating the slaves to be mechanics may, in the end, give slavemasters power to dispense with the services of the poor white man altogether. But, with characteristic dread of offending the slaveholders, these poor, white mechanics in Mr. Gardiner's ship-yard—instead of applying the natural, honest remedy for the apprehended evil, and objecting at once to work there by the side of slaves—made a cowardly attack upon the free colored mechanics, saying *they* were eating the bread which should be eaten by American freemen, and swearing that they would not work with them. The feeling was, *really*, against having their labor brought into competition with that of the colored people at all; but it was too much to strike directly at the interest of the slaveholders; and, therefore proving their servility and cowardice they dealt their blows on the poor, colored freeman, and aimed to prevent *him* from serving himself, in the evening of life, with the trade with which he had served his master, during the more vigorous portion of his days. Had they succeeded in driving the black freemen out of the ship-yard, they would have determined also upon the removal of the black slaves. The feeling was very bitter toward all colored people in Baltimore, about this time (1836), and they—free and slave suffered all manner of insult and wrong.

Until a very little before I went there, white and black ship carpenters worked side by side, in the ship yards of Mr. Gardiner, Mr. Duncan, Mr. Walter Price, and Mr. Robb. Nobody seemed to see any impropriety in it. To outward seeming, all hands were well satisfied. Some of the blacks were first rate workmen, and were given jobs requiring highest skill. All at once, however, the white carpenters knocked off, and swore that they would no longer work on the same stage with free Negroes. Taking advantage of the heavy contract resting upon Mr. Gardiner, to have the war vessels for Mexico ready to launch in July, and of the difficulty of getting other hands at that season of the year, they swore they would not strike another blow for him, unless he would discharge his free colored workmen.

Now, although this movement did not extend to me, *in form*, it did reach me, *in fact*. The spirit which it awakened was one of malice and bitterness, toward colored people *generally*, and I suffered with the rest, and suffered severely. My fellow apprentices very soon began to feel it to be degrading to work with me. They began to put on high looks, and to talk contemptuously and maliciously of *"the Niggers;"* saying, that "they would take the country," that "they ought to be killed." Encouraged by the cowardly workmen, who, knowing me to be a slave, made no issue with Mr. Gardiner about my being there, these young men did their utmost to make it impossible for me to stay. They seldom called me to do any thing, without coupling the call with a curse, and Edward North, the biggest in every thing, rascality included, ventured to strike me, whereupon I picked him up, and threw him into the dock. Whenever any of them struck me, I struck back again, regardless of consequences. I could manage any of them *singly*, and, while I could keep them from combining, I succeeded very well. In the conflict which ended my stay at Mr. Gardiner's, I was beset by four of them at once— Ned North, Ned Hays, Bill Stewart, and Tom Humphreys. Two of them were as large as myself, and they came near killing me, in broad day light. The attack was made suddenly, and simultaneously. One came in front, armed with a brick; there was one at each side, and one behind, and they closed up around me. I was struck on all sides; and, while I was attending to those in front, I received a blow on my head, from behind, dealt with a heavy hand-spike. I was completely stunned by the blow, and fell, heavily, on the ground, among the timbers. Taking advantage of my fall, they rushed upon me, and began to pound me with their fists. I let them lay on, for a while, after I came to myself, with a view of gaining strength. They did me little damage, so far; but, finally, getting tired of that sport, I gave a sudden surge, and, despite their weight, I rose to my hands and knees. Just as I did this, one of their number (I know not which) planted a blow with his boot in my left eye, which, for a time, seemed to have burst my eyeball. When they saw my eye completely closed, my face covered with blood, and I staggering under the stunning blows they had given me, they left me. As soon as I gathered sufficient strength, I picked up the hand-spike, and, madly enough, attempted to pursue them; but here the carpenters interfered, and compelled me to give up my frenzied pursuit. It was impossible to stand against so many.

Dear reader, you can hardly believe the statement, but it is true, and, therefore, I write it down: not fewer than fifty white men stood by, and saw this brutal and shameless outrage committed, and not a man of them all interposed a single word of mercy. There were four against one, and that one's face was beaten and battered most horribly, and no one said, "that is enough;" but some cried out, "Kill him—kill him—kill the d—d nigger! knock his brains out—he struck a white person." I mention this inhuman outcry, to show the character of the men, and the spirit of the times, at Gardiner's ship yard, and, indeed, in Baltimore generally, in 1836. As I look back to this period, I am almost amazed that I was not murdered outright, in that ship yard, so murderous was the spirit which prevailed there. On two occasions, while there, I came near losing my life. I was driving bolts in the hold, through the keelson, with Hays. In its course, the bolt bent. Hays cursed me, and said that it was my blow which bent the bolt. I denied this, and charged it upon him. In a fit of rage he seized an adze, and darted toward me. I met him with a maul, and parried his blow, or I should have then lost my life. A son of old Tom Lanman (the latter's double murder I have elsewhere charged upon him), in the spirit of his miserable father, made an assault upon me, but the blow with his maul missed me. After the united assault of North, Stewart, Hays and Humphreys, finding that the carpenters were as bitter toward me as the apprentices, and that the latter were probably set on by the former, I found my only chances for life was in flight. I succeeded in getting away, without an additional blow. To strike a white man, was death, by Lynch law, in Gardiner's ship yard; nor was there much of any other law toward colored people, at that time, in any other part of Maryland. The whole sentiment of Baltimore was murderous.

After making my escape from the ship yard, I went straight home, and related the story of the outrage to Master Hugh Auld; and it is due to him to say, that his conduct—though he was not a religious man—was every way more humane than that of his brother, Thomas, when I went to the latter in a somewhat similar plight, from the hands of *"Brother Edward Covey."* He listened attentively to my narration of the circumstances leading to the ruffianly outrage, and gave many proofs of his strong indignation at what was done. Hugh was a rough, but manly-hearted fellow, and, at this time, his best nature showed itself.

The heart of my once almost over-kind mistress, Sophia, was again melted in pity toward me. My puffed-out eye, and my scarred and blood-covered face, moved the dear lady to tears. She kindly drew a chair by me, and with friendly, consoling words, she took water, and washed the blood from my face. No mother's hand could have been more tender than hers. She bound up my head, and covered my wounded eye with a lean piece of fresh beef. It was almost compensation for the murderous assault, and my suffering, that it furnished and occasion for the manifestation, once more, of the orignally(sic) characteristic kindness of my mistress. Her affectionate heart was not yet dead, though much hardened by time and by circumstances.

As for Master Hugh's part, as I have said, he was furious about it; and he gave expression to his fury in the usual forms of speech in that locality. He poured curses on the heads of the whole ship yard company, and swore that he would have satisfaction for the outrage. His indignation was really strong and healthy; but, unfortunately, it resulted from the thought that his rights of property, in my person, had not been respected, more than from any sense of the outrage committed on me *as a man*. I inferred as much as this, from the fact that he could, himself, beat and mangle when it suited him to do so. Bent on having satisfaction, as he said, just as soon as I got a little the better of my bruises, Master Hugh took me to Esquire Watson's office, on Bond street, Fell's Point, with a view to procuring the arrest of those who had assaulted me. He related the outrage to the magistrate, as I had related it to him, and seemed to expect that a warrant would, at once, be issued for the arrest of the lawless ruffians.

Mr. Watson heard it all, and instead of drawing up his warrant, he inquired.—

"Mr. Auld, who saw this assault of which you speak?"

"It was done, sir, in the presence of a ship yard full of hands."

"Sir," said Watson, "I am sorry, but I cannot move in this matter except upon the oath of white witnesses."

"But here's the boy; look at his head and face," said the excited Master Hugh; "*they* show *what* has been done."

But Watson insisted that he was not authorized to do anything, unless *white* witnesses of the transaction would come forward, and testify to what had taken place. He could issue no warrant on my word, against white persons; and, if I had been killed in the presence of a *thousand blacks*, their testimony, combined would have been insufficient to arrest a single murderer. Master Hugh, for once, was compelled to say, that this state of things was *too bad;* and he left the office of the magistrate, disgusted.

Of course, it was impossible to get any white man to testify against my assailants. The carpenters saw what was done; but the actors were but the agents of their malice, and only what the carpenters sanctioned. They had cried, with one accord, *"Kill the nigger!" "Kill the nigger!"* Even those who may have pitied me, if any such were among them, lacked the moral courage to come and volunteer their evidence. The slightest manifestation of sympathy or justice toward a person of color, was denounced as abolitionism; and the name of abolitionist, subjected its bearer to frightful liabilities. "D—n *abolitionists,"* and *"Kill the niggers,"* were the watch-words of the foul-mouthed ruffians of those days. Nothing was done, and probably there would not have been any thing done, had I been killed in the affray. The laws and the morals of the Christian city of Baltimore, afforded no protection to the sable denizens of that city.

Master Hugh, on finding he could get no redress for the cruel wrong, withdrew me from the employment of Mr. Gardiner, and took me into his own family, Mrs. Auld kindly taking care of me, and dressing my wounds, until they were healed, and I was ready to go again to work.

While I was on the Eastern Shore, Master Hugh had met with reverses, which overthrew his business; and he had given up ship building in his own yard, on the City Block, and was now acting as foreman of Mr. Walter Price. The best he could now do for me, was to take me into Mr. Price's yard, and afford me the facilities there, for completing the trade which I had began to learn at Gardiner's. Here I rapidly became expert in the use of my calking tools; and, in the course of a single year, I was able to command the highest wages paid to journeymen calkers in Baltimore.

The reader will observe that I was now of some pecuniary value to my master. During the busy season, I was bringing six and seven dollars per week. I have, sometimes, brought him as much as nine dollars a week, for the wages were a dollar and a half per day.

After learning to calk, I sought my own employment, made my own contracts, and collected my own earnings; giving Master Hugh no trouble in any part of the transactions to which I was a party.

Here, then, were better days for the Eastern Shore *slave*. I was now free from the vexatious assalts(sic) of the apprentices at Mr. Gardiner's; and free from the perils of plantation life, and once more in a favorable condition to increase my little stock of education, which had been at a dead stand since my removal from Baltimore. I had, on the Eastern Shore, been only a teacher, when in company with other slaves, but now there were colored persons who could instruct me. Many of the young calkers could read, write and cipher. Some of them had high notions about mental improvement; and the free ones, on Fell's Point, organized what they called the *"East Baltimore Mental Improvement Society."* To this society, notwithstanding it was intended that only free persons should attach themselves, I was admitted, and was, several times, assigned a prominent part in its debates. I owe much to the society of these young men.

The reader already knows enough of the *ill* effects of good treatment on a slave, to anticipate what was now the case in my improved condition. It was not long before I began to show signs of disquiet with slavery, and to look around for means to get out of that condition by the shortest route. I was living among *free men;* and was, in all respects, equal to them by nature and by attainments. *Why should I be a slave?* There was *no* reason why I should be the thrall of any man.

Besides, I was now getting—as I have said—a dollar and fifty cents per day. I contracted for it, worked for it, earned it, collected it; it was paid to me, and it was *rightfully* my own; and yet, upon every returning Saturday night, this money— my own hard earnings, every cent of it—was demanded of me, and taken from me by Master Hugh. He did not earn it; he had no hand in earning it; why, then, should he have it? I owed him nothing. He had given me no schooling, and I had received from him only my food and raiment; and for these, my services were supposed to pay, from the first. The right to take my earnings, was the right of the robber. He had the power to compel me to give him the fruits of my labor, and this power was his only right in the case. I became more and more dissatisfied with this state of things; and, in so becoming, I only gave proof of the same human nature which every reader of this chapter in my life—slaveholder, or nonslaveholder—is conscious of possessing.

To make a contented slave, you must make a thoughtless one. It is necessary to darken his moral and mental vision, and, as far as possible, to annihilate his power of reason. He must be able to detect no inconsistencies in slavery. The man that takes his earnings, must be able to convince him that he has a perfect right to do so. It must not depend upon mere force; the slave must know no Higher Law than his master's will. The whole relationship must not only demonstrate, to his mind, its necessity, but its absolute rightfulness. If there be one crevice through which a single drop can fall, it will certainly rust off the slave's chain.

CHAPTER XXI

My Escape from Slavery

CLOSING INCIDENTS OF "MY LIFE AS A SLAVE"—REASONS WHY FULL PARTICULARS OF THE MANNER OF MY ESCAPE WILL NOT BE GIVEN—CRAFTINESS AND MALICE OF SLAVEHOLDERS—SUSPICION OF AIDING A SLAVE'S ESCAPE ABOUT AS DANGEROUS AS POSITIVE EVIDENCE—WANT OF WISDOM SHOWN IN PUBLISHING DETAILS OF THE ESCAPE OF THE FUGITIVES—PUBLISHED ACCOUNTS REACH THE MASTERS, NOT THE SLAVES—SLAVEHOLDERS STIMULATED TO GREATER WATCHFULNESS—MY CONDITION—DISCONTENT—SUSPICIONS IMPLIED BY MASTER HUGH'S MANNER, WHEN RECEIVING MY WAGES—HIS OCCASIONAL GENEROSITY!—DIFFICULTIES IN THE WAY OF ESCAPE—EVERY AVENUE GUARDED—PLAN TO OBTAIN MONEY—I AM ALLOWED TO HIRE MY TIME—A GLEAM OF HOPE—ATTENDS CAMP-MEETING, WITHOUT PERMISSION—ANGER OF MASTER HUGH THEREAT—THE RESULT—MY PLANS OF ESCAPE ACCELERATED THERBY—THE DAY FOR MY DEPARTURE FIXED—HARASSED BY DOUBTS AND FEARS—PAINFUL THOUGHTS OF SEPARATION FROM FRIENDS—THE ATTEMPT MADE—ITS SUCCESS.

I will now make the kind reader acquainted with the closing incidents of my "Life as a Slave," having already trenched upon the limit allotted to my "Life as a Freeman." Before, however, proceeding with this narration, it is, perhaps, proper that I should frankly state, in advance, my intention to withhold a part of the(sic) connected with my escape from slavery. There are reasons for this suppression, which I trust the reader will deem altogether valid. It may be easily conceived, that a full and complete statement of all facts pertaining to the flight of a bondman, might implicate and embarrass some who may have, wittingly or unwittingly, assisted him; and no one can wish me to involve any man or woman who has befriended me, even in the liability of embarrassment or trouble.

Keen is the scent of the slaveholder; like the fangs of the rattlesnake, his malice retains its poison long; and, although it is now nearly seventeen years since I made my escape, it is well to be careful, in dealing with the circumstances relating to it. Were I to give but a shadowy outline of the process adopted, with characteristic aptitude, the crafty and malicious among the slaveholders might, possibly, hit upon the track I pursued, and involve some one in suspicion which, in a slave state, is about as bad as positive evidence. The colored man, there, must not only shun evil, but shun the very *appearance* of evil, or be condemned as a criminal. A slaveholding community has a peculiar taste for ferreting out offenses against the slave system, justice there being more sensitive in its regard for the peculiar rights of this system, than for any other interest or institution. By stringing together a train of events and circumstances, even if I were not very explicit, the means of escape might be ascertained, and, possibly, those means be rendered, thereafter, no longer available to the liberty-seeking children of bondage I have left behind me. No antislavery man can wish me to do anything favoring such results, and no slaveholding reader has any right to expect the impartment of such information.

While, therefore, it would afford me pleasure, and perhaps would materially add to the interest of my story, were I at liberty to gratify a curiosity which I know to exist in the minds of many, as to the manner of my escape, I must deprive myself of this pleasure, and the curious of the gratification, which such a statement of facts would afford. I would allow myself to suffer under the greatest imputations that evil minded men might suggest, rather than exculpate myself by explanation, and thereby run the hazards of closing the slightest avenue by which a brother in suffering might clear himself of the chains and fetters of slavery.

The practice of publishing every new invention by which a slave is known to have escaped from slavery, has neither wisdom nor necessity to sustain it. Had not Henry Box Brown and his friends attracted slaveholding attention to the manner of his escape, we might have had a thousand *Box Browns* per annum. The singularly original plan adopted by William and Ellen Crafts, perished with the first using, because every slaveholder in the land was apprised of it. The *salt water slave* who hung in the guards of a steamer, being washed three days and three nights—like another Jonah—by the waves of the sea, has, by the publicity given to the circumstance, set a spy on the guards of every steamer departing from southern ports.

I have never approved of the very public manner, in which some of our western friends have conducted what *they* call the "*Under-ground Railroad*," but which, I think, by their open declarations, has been made, most emphatically, the "*Upper*-ground Railroad." Its stations are far better known to the slaveholders than to the slaves. I honor those good men and women for their noble daring, in willingly subjecting themselves to persecution, by openly avowing their participation in the escape of slaves; nevertheless, the good resulting from such avowals, is of a very questionable character. It may kindle an enthusiasm, very pleasant to inhale; but that is of no practical benefit to themselves, nor to the slaves escaping. Nothing is more evident, than that such disclosures are a positive evil to the slaves remaining, and seeking to escape. In publishing such accounts, the anti-slavery man addresses the slaveholder, *not the slave;* he stimulates the former to greater watchfulness, and adds to his facilities for capturing his slave. We owe something to the slaves, south of Mason and Dixon's line, as well as to those north of it; and, in discharging the duty of aiding the latter, on their way to freedom, we should be careful to do nothing which would be likely to hinder the former, in making their escape from slavery. Such is my detestation of slavery, that I would keep the merciless slaveholder profoundly ignorant of the means of flight adopted by the slave. He should be left to imagine himself surrounded by myriads of invisible tormentors, ever ready to snatch, from his infernal grasp, his trembling prey. In pursuing his victim, let him be left to feel his way in the dark; let shades of darkness, commensurate with his crime, shut every ray of light from his pathway; and let him be made to feel, that, at every step he takes, with the hellish purpose of reducing a brother man to slavery, he is running the frightful risk of having his hot brains dashed out by an invisible hand.

But, enough of this. I will now proceed to the statement of those facts, connected with my escape, for which I am alone responsible, and for which no one can be made to suffer but myself.

My condition in the year (1838) of my escape, was, comparatively, a free and easy one, so far, at least, as the wants of the physical man were concerned; but the reader will bear in mind, that my troubles from the beginning, have been less physical than mental, and he will thus be prepared to find, after what is narrated in the previous chapters, that slave life was adding nothing to its charms for me, as I grew older, and became better acquainted with it. The practice, from week to week, of openly robbing me of all my earnings, kept the nature and character of slavery constantly before me. I could be robbed by *indirection,* but this was *too* open and barefaced to be endured. I could see no reason why I should, at the end of each week, pour the reward of my honest toil into the purse of any man. The thought itself vexed me, and the manner in which Master Hugh received my wages, vexed me more than the original wrong. Carefully counting the money and rolling it out, dollar by dollar, he would look me in the face, as if he would search my heart as well as my pocket, and reproachfully ask me, *"Is that all?"*—implying that I had, perhaps, kept back part of my wages; or, if not so, the demand was made, possibly, to make me feel, that, after all, I was an "unprofitable servant." Draining me of the last cent of my hard earnings, he would, however, occasionally—when I brought home an extra large sum—dole out to me a sixpence or a shilling, with a view, perhaps, of kindling up my gratitude; but this practice had the opposite effect—it was an admission of *my right to the whole sum.* The fact, that he gave me any part of my wages, was proof that he suspected that I had a right *to the whole of them.* I always felt uncomfortable, after having received anything in this way, for I feared that the giving me a few cents, might, possibly, ease his conscience, and make him feel himself a pretty honorable robber, after all!

Held to a strict account, and kept under a close watch—the old suspicion of my running away not having been entirely removed—escape from slavery, even in Baltimore, was very difficult. The railroad from Baltimore to Philadelphia was under regulations so stringent, that even *free* colored travelers were almost excluded. They must have *free* papers; they must be measured and carefully examined, before they were allowed to enter the cars; they only went in the day time, even when so examined. The steamboats were under regulations equally stringent. All the great turnpikes, leading northward, were beset with kidnappers, a class of men who watched the newspapers for advertisements for runaway slaves, making their living by the accursed reward of slave hunting.

My discontent grew upon me, and I was on the look-out for means of escape. With money, I could easily have managed the matter, and, therefore, I hit upon the plan of soliciting the privilege of hiring my time. It is quite common, in Baltimore, to allow slaves this privilege, and it is the practice, also, in New Orleans. A slave who is considered trustworthy, can, by paying his master a definite sum regularly, at the end of each week, dispose of his time as he likes. It so happened that I was not in very good odor, and I was far from being a trustworthy slave. Nevertheless, I watched my opportunity when Master Thomas came to Baltimore (for I was still his property, Hugh only acted as his agent) in the spring of 1838, to purchase his spring supply of goods, and applied to him, directly, for the much-coveted privilege of hiring my time. This request Master Thomas unhesitatingly refused to grant; and he charged me, with some sternness, with inventing this stratagem to make my escape. He told me, "I could go *nowhere* but he could catch me; and, in the event of my running away, I might be assured he should spare no pains in his efforts to recapture me." He recounted, with a good deal of eloquence, the many kind offices he had done me, and exhorted me to be contented and obedient. "Lay out no plans for the future," said he. "If you behave yourself properly, I will take care of you." Now, kind and considerate as this offer was, it failed to soothe me into repose. In spite of Master Thomas, and, I may say, in spite of myself, also, I continued to think, and worse still, to think almost exclusively about the injustice and wickedness of slavery. No effort of mine or of his could silence this trouble-giving thought, or change my purpose to run away.

About two months after applying to Master Thomas for the privilege of hiring my time, I applied to Master Hugh for the same liberty, supposing him to be unacquainted with the fact that I had made a similar application to Master Thomas, and had been refused. My boldness in making this request, fairly astounded him at the first. He gazed at me in amazement. But I had many good reasons for pressing the matter; and, after listening to them awhile, he did not absolutely refuse, but told me he would think of it. Here, then, was a gleam of hope. Once master of my own time, I felt sure that I could make, over and above my obligation to him, a dollar or two every week. Some slaves have made enough, in this way, to purchase their freedom. It is a sharp spur to industry; and some of the most enterprising colored men in Baltimore hire themselves in this way. After mature reflection—as I must suppose it was Master Hugh granted me the privilege in question, on the following terms: I was to be allowed all my time; to make all bargains for work; to find my own employment, and to collect my own wages; and, in return for this liberty, I was required, or obliged, to pay him three dollars at the end of each week, and to board and clothe myself, and buy my own calking tools. A failure in any of these particulars would put an end to my privilege. This was a hard bargain. The wear and tear of clothing, the losing and breaking of tools, and the expense of board, made it necessary for me to earn at least six dollars per week, to keep even with the world. All who are acquainted with calking, know how uncertain and irregular that employment is. It can be done to advantage only in dry weather, for it is useless to put wet oakum into a seam. Rain or shine, however, work or no work, at the end of each week the money must be forthcoming.

Master Hugh seemed to be very much pleased, for a time, with this arrangement; and well he might be, for it was decidedly in his favor. It relieved him of all anxiety concerning me. His money was sure. He had armed my love of liberty with a lash and a driver, far more efficient than any I had before known; and, while he derived all the benefits of slaveholding by the arrangement, without its evils, I endured all the evils of being a slave, and yet suffered all the care and anxiety of a responsible freeman. "Nevertheless," thought I, "it is a valuable privilege another step in my career toward freedom." It was something even to be permitted to stagger under the disadvantages of liberty, and I was determined to hold on to the newly gained footing, by all proper industry. I was ready to work by night as well as by day; and being in the enjoyment of excellent health, I was able not only to meet my current expenses, but also to lay by a small sum at the end of each week. All went on thus, from the month of May till August; then—for reasons which will become apparent as I proceed—my much valued liberty was wrested from me.

During the week previous to this (to me) calamitous event, I had made arrangements with a few young friends, to accompany them, on Saturday night, to a camp-meeting, held about twelve miles from Baltimore. On the evening of our intended start for the camp-ground, something occurred in the ship yard where I was at work, which detained me unusually late, and compelled me either to disappoint my young friends, or to neglect carrying my weekly dues to Master

Hugh. Knowing that I had the money, and could hand it to him on another day, I decided to go to camp-meeting, and to pay him the three dollars, for the past week, on my return. Once on the camp-ground, I was induced to remain one day longer than I had intended, when I left home. But, as soon as I returned, I went straight to his house on Fell street, to hand him his (my) money. Unhappily, the fatal mistake had been committed. I found him exceedingly angry. He exhibited all the signs of apprehension and wrath, which a slaveholder may be surmised to exhibit on the supposed escape of a favorite slave. "You rascal! I have a great mind to give you a severe whipping. How dare you go out of the city without first asking and obtaining my permission?" "Sir," said I, "I hired my time and paid you the price you asked for it. I did not know that it was any part of the bargain that I should ask you when or where I should go."

"You did not know, you rascal! You are bound to show yourself here every Saturday night." After reflecting, a few moments, he became somewhat cooled down; but, evidently greatly troubled, he said, "Now, you scoundrel! you have done for yourself; you shall hire your time no longer. The next thing I shall hear of, will be your running away. Bring home your tools and your clothes, at once. I'll teach you how to go off in this way."

Thus ended my partial freedom. I could hire my time no longer; and I obeyed my master's orders at once. The little taste of liberty which I had had—although as the reader will have seen, it was far from being unalloyed—by no means enhanced my contentment with slavery. Punished thus by Master Hugh, it was now my turn to punish him. "Since," thought I, "you *will* make a slave of me, I will await your orders in all things;" and, instead of going to look for work on Monday morning, as I had formerly done, I remained at home during the entire week, without the performance of a single stroke of work. Saturday night came, and he called upon me, as usual, for my wages. I, of course, told him I had done no work, and had no wages. Here we were at the point of coming to blows. His wrath had been accumulating during the whole week; for he evidently saw that I was making no effort to get work, but was most aggravatingly awaiting his orders, in all things. As I look back to this behavior of mine, I scarcely know what possessed me, thus to trifle with those who had such unlimited power to bless or to blast me. Master Hugh raved and swore his determination to *"get hold of me;"* but, wisely for *him,* and happily for *me,* his wrath only employed those very harmless, impalpable missiles, which roll from a limber tongue. In my desperation, I had fully made up my mind to measure strength with Master Hugh, in case he should undertake to execute his threats. I am glad there was no necessity for this; for resistance to him could not have ended so happily for me, as it did in the case of Covey. He was not a man to be safely resisted by a slave; and I freely own, that in my conduct toward him, in this instance, there was more folly than wisdom. Master Hugh closed his reproofs, by telling me that, hereafter, I need give myself no uneasiness about getting work; that he "would, himself, see to getting work for me, and enough of it, at that." This threat I confess had some terror in it; and, on thinking the matter over, during the Sunday, I resolved, not only to save him the trouble of getting me work, but that, upon the third day of September, I would attempt to make my escape from slavery. The refusal to allow me to hire my time, therefore, hastened the period of flight. I had three weeks, now, in which to prepare for my journey.

Once resolved, I felt a certain degree of repose, and on Monday, instead of waiting for Master Hugh to seek employment for me, I was up by break of day, and off to the ship yard of Mr. Butler, on the City Block, near the draw-bridge. I was a favorite with Mr. B., and, young as I was, I had served as his foreman on the float stage, at calking. Of course, I easily obtained work, and, at the end of the week—which by the way was exceedingly fine I brought Master Hugh nearly nine dollars. The effect of this mark of returning good sense, on my part, was excellent. He was very much pleased; he took the money, commended me, and told me I might have done the same thing the week before. It is a blessed thing that the tyrant may not always know the thoughts and purposes of his victim. Master Hugh little knew what my plans were. The going to camp-meeting without asking his permission—the insolent answers made to his reproaches— the sulky deportment the week after being deprived of the privilege of hiring my time—had awakened in him the suspicion that I might be cherishing disloyal purposes. My object, therefore, in working steadily, was to remove suspicion, and in this I succeeded admirably. He probably thought I was never better satisfied with my condition, than at the very time I was planning my escape. The second week passed, and again I carried him my full week's wages—*nine dollars;* and so well pleased was he, that he gave me TWENTY-FIVE CENTS! and "bade me make good use of it!" I told him I would, for one of the uses to which I meant to put it, was to pay my fare on the underground railroad.

Things without went on as usual; but I was passing through the same internal excitement and anxiety which I had experienced two years and a half before. The failure, in that instance, was not calculated to increase my confidence in the success of this, my second attempt; and I knew that a second failure could not leave me where my first did—I must either get to the *far north,* or be sent to the *far south.* Besides the exercise of mind from this state of facts, I had the painful sensation of being about to separate from a circle of honest and warm hearted friends, in Baltimore. The thought of such a separation, where the hope of ever meeting again is excluded, and where there can be no correspondence, is very painful. It is my opinion, that thousands would escape from slavery who now remain there, but for the strong cords of affection that bind them to their families, relatives and friends. The daughter is hindered from escaping, by the love she bears her mother, and the father, by the love he bears his children;

and so, to the end of the chapter. I had no relations in Baltimore, and I saw no probability of ever living in the neighborhood of sisters and brothers; but the thought of leaving my friends, was among the strongest obstacles to my running away. The last two days of the week—Friday and Saturday—were spent mostly in collecting my things together, for my journey. Having worked four days that week, for my master, I handed him six dollars, on Saturday night. I seldom spent my Sundays at home; and, for fear that something might be discovered in my conduct, I kept up my custom, and absented myself all day. On Monday, the third day of September, 1838, in accordance with my resolution, I bade farewell to the city of Baltimore, and to that slavery which had been my abhorrence from childhood.

How I got away—in what direction I traveled—whether by land or by water; whether with or without assistance—must, for reasons already mentioned, remain unexplained.

LIFE AS A FREEMAN

CHAPTER XXII

Liberty Attained

TRANSITION FROM SLAVERY TO FREEDOM—A WANDERER IN NEW YORK—
FEELINGS ON REACHING THAT CITY—AN OLD ACQUAINTANCE MET—
UNFAVORABLE IMPRESSIONS—LONELINESS AND INSECURITY—APOLOGY
FOR SLAVES WHO RETURN TO THEIR MASTERS—COMPELLED TO TELL
MY CONDITION—SUCCORED BY A SAILOR—DAVID RUGGLES—THE
UNDERGROUND RAILROAD—MARRIAGE—BAGGAGE TAKEN FROM ME—
KINDNESS OF NATHAN JOHNSON—MY CHANGE OF NAME—DARK NOTIONS
OF NORTHERN CIVILIZATION—THE CONTRAST—COLORED PEOPLE IN
NEW BEDFORD—AN INCIDENT ILLUSTRATING THEIR SPIRIT—A COMMON
LABORER—DENIED WORK AT MY TRADE—THE FIRST WINTER AT THE
NORTH—REPULSE AT THE DOORS OF THE CHURCH—SANCTIFIED HATE—
THE *Liberator* AND ITS EDITOR.

There is no necessity for any extended notice of the incidents of this part of my
life. There is nothing very striking or peculiar about my career as a freeman,
when viewed apart from my life as a slave. The relation subsisting between my
early experience and that which I am now about to narrate, is, perhaps, my best
apology for adding another chapter to this book.

Disappearing from the kind reader, in a flying cloud or balloon (pardon the
figure), driven by the wind, and knowing not where I should land—whether in
slavery or in freedom—it is proper that I should remove, at once, all anxiety,
by frankly making known where I alighted. The flight was a bold and perilous
one; but here I am, in the great city of New York, safe and sound, without loss of
blood or bone. In less than a week after leaving Baltimore, I was walking amid
the hurrying throng, and gazing upon the dazzling wonders of Broadway. The
dreams of my childhood and the purposes of my manhood were now fulfilled.
A free state around me, and a free earth under my feet! What a moment was
this to me! A whole year was pressed into a single day. A new world burst upon
my agitated vision. I have often been asked, by kind friends to whom I have

told my story, how I felt when first I found myself beyond the limits of slavery; and I must say here, as I have often said to them, there is scarcely anything about which I could not give a more satisfactory answer. It was a moment of joyous excitement, which no words can describe. In a letter to a friend, written soon after reaching New York. I said I felt as one might be supposed to feel, on escaping from a den of hungry lions. But, in a moment like that, sensations are too intense and too rapid for words. Anguish and grief, like darkness and rain, may be described, but joy and gladness, like the rainbow of promise, defy alike the pen and pencil.

For ten or fifteen years I had been dragging a heavy chain, with a huge block attached to it, cumbering my every motion. I had felt myself doomed to drag this chain and this block through life. All efforts, before, to separate myself from the hateful encumbrance, had only seemed to rivet me the more firmly to it. Baffled and discouraged at times, I had asked myself the question, May not this, after all, be God's work? May He not, for wise ends, have doomed me to this lot? A contest had been going on in my mind for years, between the clear consciousness of right and the plausible errors of superstition; between the wisdom of manly courage, and the foolish weakness of timidity. The contest was now ended; the chain was severed; God and right stood vindicated. I was A FREEMAN, and the voice of peace and joy thrilled my heart.

Free and joyous, however, as I was, joy was not the only sensation I experienced. It was like the quick blaze, beautiful at the first, but which subsiding, leaves the building charred and desolate. I was soon taught that I was still in an enemy's land. A sense of loneliness and insecurity oppressed me sadly. I had been but a few hours in New York, before I was met in the streets by a fugitive slave, well known to me, and the information I got from him respecting New York, did nothing to lessen my apprehension of danger. The fugitive in question was "Allender's Jake," in Baltimore; but, said he, I am "WILLIAM DIXON," in New York! I knew Jake well, and knew when Tolly Allender and Mr. Price (for the latter employed Master Hugh as his foreman, in his shipyard on Fell's Point) made an attempt to recapture Jake, and failed. Jake told me all about his circumstances, and how narrowly he escaped being taken back to slavery; that the city was now full of southerners, returning from the springs; that the black people in New York were not to be trusted; that there were hired men on the lookout for fugitives from slavery, and who, for a few dollars, would betray me into the hands of the slave-catchers; that I must trust no man with my secret; that I must not think of going either on the wharves to work, or to a boarding-house to board; and, worse still, this same Jake told me it was not in his power to help me. He seemed, even while cautioning me, to be fearing lest, after all, I might be a party to a second attempt to recapture him. Under the inspiration of this thought, I must suppose it was, he gave signs of a wish to get rid of me, and soon left me his whitewash brush in hand—as he said, for his work. He was soon lost to sight among the throng, and I was alone again, an easy prey to the kidnappers, if any should happen to be on my track.

New York, seventeen years ago, was less a place of safety for a runaway slave than now, and all know how unsafe it now is, under the new fugitive slave bill. I was much troubled. I had very little money enough to buy me a few loaves of bread, but not enough to pay board, outside a lumber yard. I saw the wisdom of keeping away from the ship yards, for if Master Hugh pursued me, he would naturally expect to find me looking for work among the calkers. For a time, every door seemed closed against me. A sense of my loneliness and helplessness crept over me, and covered me with something bordering on despair. In the midst of thousands of my fellowmen, and yet a perfect stranger! In the midst of human brothers, and yet more fearful of them than of hungry wolves! I was without home, without friends, without work, without money, and without any definite knowledge of which way to go, or where to look for succor.

Some apology can easily be made for the few slaves who have, after making good their escape, turned back to slavery, preferring the actual rule of their masters, to the life of loneliness, apprehension, hunger, and anxiety, which meets them on their first arrival in a free state. It is difficult for a freeman to enter into the feelings of such fugitives. He cannot see things in the same light with the slave, because he does not, and cannot, look from the same point from which the slave does. "Why do you tremble," he says to the slave "you are in a free state;" but the difficulty is, in realizing that he is in a free state, the slave might reply. A freeman cannot understand why the slave-master's shadow is bigger, to the slave, than the might and majesty of a free state; but when he reflects that the slave knows more about the slavery of his master than he does of the might and majesty of the free state, he has the explanation. The slave has been all his life learning the power of his master—being trained to dread his approach—and only a few hours learning the power of the state. The master is to him a stern and flinty reality, but the state is little more than a dream. He has been accustomed to regard every white man as the friend of his master, and every colored man as more or less under the control of his master's friends—the white people. It takes stout nerves to stand up, in such circumstances. A man, homeless, shelterless, breadless, friendless, and moneyless, is not in a condition to assume a very proud or joyous tone; and in just this condition was I, while wandering about the streets of New York city and lodging, at least one night, among the barrels on one of its wharves. I was not only free from slavery, but I was free from home, as well. The reader will easily see that I had something more than the simple fact of being free to think of, in this extremity.

I kept my secret as long as I could, and at last was forced to go in search of an honest man—a man sufficiently *human* not to betray me into the hands of slave-catchers. I was not a bad reader of the human face, nor long in selecting the right man, when once compelled to disclose the facts of my condition to some one.

I found my man in the person of one who said his name was Stewart. He was a sailor, warm-hearted and generous, and he listened to my story with a brother's interest. I told him I was running for my freedom—knew not where to go—money almost gone—was hungry—thought it unsafe to go the shipyards for work, and needed a friend. Stewart promptly put me in the way of getting out of my trouble. He took me to his house, and went in search of the late David Ruggles, who was then the secretary of the New York Vigilance Committee, and a very active man in all anti-slavery works. Once in the hands of Mr. Ruggles, I was comparatively safe. I was hidden with Mr. Ruggles several days. In the meantime, my intended wife, Anna, came on from Baltimore—to whom I had written, informing her of my safe arrival at New York—and, in the presence of Mrs. Mitchell and Mr. Ruggles, we were married, by Rev. James W. C. Pennington.

Mr. Ruggles* was the first officer on the under-ground railroad with whom I met after reaching the north, and, indeed, the first of whom I ever heard anything. Learning that I was a calker by trade, he promptly decided that New Bedford was the proper place to send me. "Many ships," said he, "are there fitted out for the whaling business, and you may there find work at your trade, and make a good living." Thus, in one fortnight after my flight from Maryland, I was safe in New Bedford, regularly entered upon the exercise of the rights, responsibilities, and duties of a freeman.

I may mention a little circumstance which annoyed me on reaching New Bedford. I had not a cent of money, and lacked two dollars toward paying our fare from Newport, and our baggage not very costly—was taken by the stage driver, and held until I could raise the money to redeem it. This difficulty was soon surmounted. Mr. Nathan Johnson, to whom we had a line from Mr. Ruggles, not only received us kindly and hospitably, but, on being informed about our baggage, promptly loaned me two dollars with which to redeem my little property. I shall ever be deeply grateful, both to Mr. and Mrs. Nathan Johnson, for the lively interest they were pleased to take in me, in this hour of my extremest need. They not only gave myself and wife bread and shelter, but

---

* He was a whole-souled man, fully imbued with a love of his afflicted and hunted people, and took pleasure in being to me, as was his wont, "Eyes to the blind, and legs to the lame." This brave and devoted man suffered much from the persecutions common to all who have been prominent benefactors. He at last became blind, and needed a friend to guide him, even as he had been a guide to others. Even in his blindness, he exhibited his manly character. In search of health, he became a physician. When hope of gaining is(sic) own was gone, he had hope for others. Believing in hydropathy, he established, at Northampton, Massachusetts, a large "*Water Cure*," and became one of the most successful of all engaged in that mode of treatment.

taught us how to begin to secure those benefits for ourselves. Long may they live, and may blessings attend them in this life and in that which is to come!

Once initiated into the new life of freedom, and assured by Mr. Johnson that New Bedford was a safe place, the comparatively unimportant matter, as to what should be my name, came up for considertion(sic). It was necessary to have a name in my new relations. The name given me by my beloved mother was no less pretentious than "Frederick Augustus Washington Bailey." I had, however, before leaving Maryland, dispensed with the *Augustus Washington*, and retained the name *Frederick Bailey*. Between Baltimore and New Bedford, however, I had several different names, the better to avoid being overhauled by the hunters, which I had good reason to believe would be put on my track. Among honest men an honest man may well be content with one name, and to acknowledge it at all times and in all places; but toward fugitives, Americans are not honest. When I arrived at New Bedford, my name was Johnson; and finding that the Johnson family in New Bedford were already quite numerous— sufficiently so to produce some confusion in attempts to distinguish one from another—there was the more reason for making another change in my name. In fact, "Johnson" had been assumed by nearly every slave who had arrived in New Bedford from Maryland, and this, much to the annoyance of the original "Johnsons" (of whom there were many) in that place. Mine host, unwilling to have another of his own name added to the community in this unauthorized way, after I spent a night and a day at his house, gave me my present name. He had been reading the "Lady of the Lake," and was pleased to regard me as a suitable person to wear this, one of Scotland's many famous names. Considering the noble hospitality and manly character of Nathan Johnson, I have felt that he, better than I, illustrated the virtues of the great Scottish chief. Sure I am, that had any slave-catcher entered his domicile, with a view to molest any one of his household, he would have shown himself like him of the "stalwart hand."

The reader will be amused at my ignorance, when I tell the notions I had of the state of northern wealth, enterprise, and civilization. Of wealth and refinement, I supposed the north had none. My *Columbian Orator*, which was almost my only book, had not done much to enlighten me concerning northern society. The impressions I had received were all wide of the truth. New Bedford, especially, took me by surprise, in the solid wealth and grandeur there exhibited. I had formed my notions respecting the social condition of the free states, by what I had seen and known of free, white, non-slaveholding people in the slave states. Regarding slavery as the basis of wealth, I fancied that no people could become very wealthy without slavery. A free white man, holding no slaves, in the country, I had known to be the most ignorant and poverty-stricken of men, and the laughing stock even of slaves themselves—called generally by them, in derision, *"poor white trash."* Like the non-slaveholders at the south, in holding no slaves, I suppose the northern people like them, also, in poverty and degradation. Judge, then, of my amazement and joy, when I found—as I did find—the very laboring population of New Bedford living in better houses, more elegantly furnished—surrounded by more comfort and refinement—than a majority of the slaveholders on the Eastern Shore of Maryland. There was my friend, Mr. Johnson, himself a colored man (who at the south would have been regarded as a proper marketable commodity), who lived in a better house—dined at a richer board—was the owner of more books—the reader of more newspapers—was more conversant with the political and social condition of this nation and the world—than nine-tenths of all the slaveholders of Talbot county, Maryland. Yet Mr. Johnson was a working man, and his hands were hardened by honest toil. Here, then, was something for observation and study. Whence the difference? The explanation was soon furnished, in the superiority of mind over simple brute force. Many pages might be given to the contrast, and in explanation of its causes. But an incident or two will suffice to show the reader as to how the mystery gradually vanished before me.

My first afternoon, on reaching New Bedford, was spent in visiting the wharves and viewing the shipping. The sight of the broad brim and the plain, Quaker dress, which met me at every turn, greatly increased my sense of freedom and security. "I am among the Quakers," thought I, "and am safe." Lying at the wharves and riding in the stream, were full-rigged ships of finest model, ready to start on whaling voyages. Upon the right and the left, I was walled in by large granite-fronted warehouses, crowded with the good things of this world. On the wharves, I saw industry without bustle, labor without noise, and heavy toil without the whip. There was no loud singing, as in southern ports, where ships are loading or unloading—no loud cursing or swearing—but everything went on as smoothly as the works of a well adjusted machine. How different was all this from the nosily fierce and clumsily absurd manner of labor-life in Baltimore and St. Michael's! One of the first incidents which illustrated the superior mental character of northern labor over that of the south, was the manner of unloading a ship's cargo of oil. In a southern port, twenty or thirty hands would have been employed to do what five or six did here, with the aid of a single ox attached to the end of a fall. Main strength, unassisted by skill, is slavery's method of labor. An old ox, worth eighty dollars, was doing, in New Bedford, what would have required fifteen thousand dollars worth of human bones and muscles to have performed in a southern port. I found that everything was done here with a scrupulous regard to economy, both in regard to men and things, time and strength. The maid servant, instead of spending at least a tenth part of her time in bringing and carrying water, as in Baltimore, had the pump at her elbow. The wood was dry, and snugly piled away for winter. Woodhouses, in-door pumps, sinks, drains, self-shutting gates, washing machines, pounding barrels, were all new things, and told me that I was among a thoughtful and sensible people. To the ship-repairing dock I went, and saw the same wise prudence. The carpenters struck where they aimed, and the calkers wasted no blows in idle flourishes of the mallet. I learned that men went from New Bedford to Baltimore, and bought old ships, and brought them here to repair, and made them better and more valuable than they ever were before. Men talked here of going whaling on a four *years'* voyage with more coolness than sailors where I came from talked of going a four *months'* voyage.

I now find that I could have landed in no part of the United States, where I should have found a more striking and gratifying contrast to the condition of the free people of color in Baltimore, than I found here in New Bedford. No colored man is really free in a slaveholding state. He wears the badge of bondage while nominally free, and is often subjected to hardships to which the slave is a stranger; but here in New Bedford, it was my good fortune to see a pretty near approach to freedom on the part of the colored people. I was taken all aback when Mr. Johnson—who lost no time in making me acquainted with the fact—told me that there was nothing in the constitution of Massachusetts to prevent a colored man from holding any office in the state. There, in New Bedford, the black man's children—although anti-slavery was then far from popular—went to school side by side with the white children, and apparently without objection from any quarter. To make me at home, Mr. Johnson assured me that no slaveholder could take a slave from New Bedford; that there were men there who would lay down their lives, before such an outrage could be perpetrated. The colored people themselves were of the best metal, and would fight for liberty to the death.

Soon after my arrival in New Bedford, I was told the following story, which was said to illustrate the spirit of the colored people in that goodly town: A colored man and a fugitive slave happened to have a little quarrel, and the former was heard to threaten the latter with informing his master of his whereabouts. As soon as this threat became known, a notice was read from the desk of what was then the only colored church in the place, stating that business of importance was to be then and there transacted. Special measures had been taken to secure the attendance of the would-be Judas, and had proved successful. Accordingly, at the hour appointed, the people came, and the betrayer also. All the usual formalities of public meetings were scrupulously gone through, even to the offering prayer for Divine direction in the duties of the occasion. The president himself performed this part of the ceremony, and I was told that he was unusually fervent. Yet, at the close of his prayer, the old man (one of the numerous family of Johnsons) rose from his knees, deliberately surveyed his audience, and then said, in a tone of solemn resolution, *"Well, friends, we have got him here, and I would now recommend that you young men should just take him outside the door and kill him.*" With this, a large body of the congregation, who well understood the business they had come there to transact, made a rush at the villain, and doubtless would have killed him, had he not availed himself of an open sash, and made good his escape. He has never shown his head in New Bedford since that time. This little incident is perfectly characteristic of the spirit of the colored people in New Bedford. A slave could not be taken from that town seventeen years ago, any more than he could be so taken away now. The reason is, that the colored people in that city are educated up to the point of fighting for their freedom, as well as speaking for it.

Once assured of my safety in New Bedford, I put on the habiliments of a common laborer, and went on the wharf in search of work. I had no notion of living on the honest and generous sympathy of my colored brother, Johnson, or that of the abolitionists. My cry was like that of Hood's laborer, "Oh! only give me work." Happily for me, I was not long in searching. I found employment, the third day after my arrival in New Bedford, in stowing a sloop with a load of oil for the New York market. It was new, hard, and dirty work, even for a calker, but I went at it with a glad heart and a willing hand. I was now my own master—a tremendous fact—and the rapturous excitement with which I seized the job, may not easily be understood, except by some one with an experience like mine. The thoughts—"I can work! I can work for a living; I am not afraid of work; I have no Master Hugh to rob me of my earnings"—placed me in a state of independence, beyond seeking friendship or support of any man. That day's work I considered the real starting point of something like a new existence. Having finished this job and got my pay for the same, I went next in pursuit of a job at calking. It so happened that Mr. Rodney French, late mayor of the city of New Bedford, had a ship fitting out for sea, and to which there was a large job of calking and coppering to be done. I applied to that noblehearted man for employment, and he promptly told me to go to work; but going on the float-stage for the purpose, I was informed that every white man would leave the ship if I struck a blow upon her. "Well, well," thought I, "this is a hardship, but yet not a very serious one for me." The difference between the wages of a calker and that of a common day laborer, was an hundred per cent in favor of the former; but then I was free, and free to work, though not at my trade. I now prepared myself to do anything which came to hand in the way of turning an honest penny; sawed wood—dug cellars—shoveled coal—swept chimneys with Uncle Lucas Debuty—rolled oil casks on the wharves—helped to load and unload vessels—worked in Ricketson's candle works—in Richmond's brass foundery, and elsewhere; and thus supported myself and family for three years.

The first winter was unusually severe, in consequence of the high prices of food; but even during that winter we probably suffered less than many who had been free all their lives. During the hardest of the winter, I hired out for nine dolars(sic) a month; and out of this rented two rooms for nine dollars per quarter, and supplied my wife—who was unable to work—with food and some necessary articles of furniture. We were closely pinched to bring our wants within our means; but the jail stood over the way, and I had a wholesome dread of the consequences of running in debt. This winter past, and I was up with the times—got plenty of work—got well paid for it—and felt that I had not done a foolish thing to leave Master Hugh and Master Thomas. I was now living in a new world, and was wide awake to its advantages. I early began to attend the meetings of the colored people of New Bedford, and to take part in them. I was somewhat amazed to see colored men drawing up resolutions and offering them for consideration. Several colored young men of New Bedford, at that period, gave promise of great usefulness. They were educated, and possessed what seemed to me, at the time, very superior talents. Some of them have been cut down by death, and others have removed to different parts of the world, and some remain there now, and justify, in their present activities, my early impressions of them.

Among my first concerns on reaching New Bedford, was to become united with the church, for I had never given up, in reality, my religious faith. I had become lukewarm and in a backslidden state, but I was still convinced that it was my duty to join the Methodist church. I was not then aware of the powerful influence of that religious body in favor of the enslavement of my race, nor did I see how the northern churches could be responsible for the conduct of southern churches; neither did I fully understand how it could be my duty to remain separate from the church, because bad men were connected with it. The slaveholding church, with its Coveys, Weedens, Aulds, and Hopkins, I could see through at once, but I could not see how Elm Street church, in New Bedford, could be regarded as sanctioning the Christianity of these characters in the church at St. Michael's. I therefore resolved to join the Methodist church in New Bedford, and to enjoy the spiritual advantage of public worship. The minister of the Elm Street Methodist church, was the Rev. Mr. Bonney; and although I was not allowed a seat in the body of the house, and was proscribed on account of my color, regarding this proscription simply as an accommodation of the uncoverted congregation who had not yet been won to Christ and his brotherhood, I was willing thus to be proscribed, lest sinners should be driven away form the saving power of the gospel. Once converted, I thought they would be sure to treat me as a man and a brother. "Surely," thought I, "these Christian people have none of this feeling against color. They, at least, have renounced this unholy feeling." Judge, then, dear reader, of my astonishment and mortification, when I found, as soon I did find, all my charitable assumptions at fault.

An opportunity was soon afforded me for ascertaining the exact position of Elm Street church on that subject. I had a chance of seeing the religious part of the congregation by themselves; and although they disowned, in effect, their black brothers and sisters, before the world, I did think that where none but the saints were assembled, and no offense could be given to the wicked, and the gospel could not be "blamed," they would certainly recognize us as children of the same Father, and heirs of the same salvation, on equal terms with themselves.

The occasion to which I refer, was the sacrament of the Lord's Supper, that most sacred and most solemn of all the ordinances of the Christian church. Mr. Bonney had preached a very solemn and searching discourse, which really proved him to be acquainted with the inmost secerts(sic) of the human heart. At the close of his discourse, the congregation was dismissed, and the church remained to partake of the sacrament. I remained to see, as I thought, this holy sacrament celebrated in the spirit of its great Founder.

There were only about a half dozen colored members attached to the Elm Street church, at this time. After the congregation was dismissed, these descended from the gallery, and took a seat against the wall most distant from the altar. Brother Bonney was very animated, and sung very sweetly, "Salvation 'tis a joyful sound," and soon began to administer the sacrament. I was anxious to observe the bearing of the colored members, and the result was most humiliating. During the whole ceremony, they looked like sheep without a shepherd. The white members went forward to the altar by the bench full; and when it was evident that all the whites had been served with the bread and wine, Brother Bonney—pious Brother Bonney—after a long pause, as if inquiring whether all the whites members had been served, and fully assuring himself on that important point, then raised his voice to an unnatural pitch, and looking to the corner where his black sheep seemed penned, beckoned with his hand, exclaiming, "Come forward, colored friends! come forward! You, too, have an interest in the blood of Christ. God is no respecter of persons. Come forward, and take this holy sacrament to your comfort." The colored members poor, slavish souls went forward, as invited. I went out, and have never been in that church since, although I honestly went there with a view to joining that body. I found it impossible to respect the religious profession of any who were under the dominion of this wicked prejudice, and I could not, therefore, feel that in joining them, I was joining a Christian church, at all. I tried other churches in New Bedford, with the same result, and finally, I attached myself to a small body of colored Methodists, known as the Zion Methodists. Favored with the affection and confidence of the members of this humble communion, I was soon made a classleader and a local preacher among them. Many seasons of peace and joy I experienced among them, the remembrance of which is still precious, although I could not see it to be my duty to remain with that body, when I found that it consented to the same spirit which held my brethren in chains.

In four or five months after reaching New Bedford, there came a young man to me, with a copy of the *Liberator*, the paper edited by WILLIAM LLOYD GARRISON, and published by ISAAC KNAPP, and asked me to subscribe for it. I told him I had but just escaped from slavery, and was of course very poor, and remarked further, that I was unable to pay for it then; the agent, however, very willingly took me as a subscriber, and appeared to be much pleased with securing my name to his list. From this time I was brought in contact with the mind of William Lloyd Garrison. His paper took its place with me next to the bible.

The *Liberator* was a paper after my own heart. It detested slavery exposed hypocrisy and wickedness in high places—made no truce with the traffickers in the bodies and souls of men; it preached human brotherhood, denounced oppression, and, with all the solemnity of God's word, demanded the complete emancipation of my race. I not only liked—I *loved* this paper, and its editor. He seemed a match for all the oponents(sic) of emancipation, whether they spoke in the name of the law, or the gospel. His words were few, full of holy fire, and straight to the point. Learning to love him, through his paper, I was prepared to be pleased with his presence. Something of a hero worshiper, by nature, here was one, on first sight, to excite my love and reverence.

Seventeen years ago, few men possessed a more heavenly countenance than William Lloyd Garrison, and few men evinced a more genuine or a more exalted piety. The bible was his text book—held sacred, as the word of the Eternal Father—sinless perfection—complete submission to insults and injuries—literal obedience to the injunction, if smitten on one side to turn the other also. Not only was Sunday a Sabbath, but all days were Sabbaths, and to be kept holy. All sectarism false and mischievous—the regenerated, throughout the world, members of one body, and the HEAD Christ Jesus. Prejudice against color was rebellion against God. Of all men beneath the sky, the slaves, because most neglected and despised, were nearest and dearest to his great heart. Those ministers who defended slavery from the bible, were of their "father the devil"; and those churches which fellowshiped slaveholders as Christians, were synagogues of Satan, and our nation was a nation of liars. Never loud or noisy—calm and serene as a summer sky, and as pure. "You are the man, the Moses, raised up by God, to deliver his modern Israel from bondage," was the spontaneous feeling of my heart, as I sat away back in the hall and listened to his mighty words; mighty in truth—mighty in their simple earnestness.

I had not long been a reader of the *Liberator*, and listener to its editor, before I got a clear apprehension of the principles of the anti-slavery movement. I had already the spirit of the movement, and only needed to understand its principles and measures. These I got from the *Liberator*, and from those who believed in that paper. My acquaintance with the movement increased my hope for the ultimate freedom of my race, and I united with it from a sense of delight, as well as duty.

Every week the *Liberator* came, and every week I made myself master of its contents. All the anti-slavery meetings held in New Bedford I promptly attended, my heart burning at every true utterance against the slave system, and every rebuke of its friends and supporters. Thus passed the first three years of my residence in New Bedford. I had not then dreamed of the posibility(sic) of my becoming a public advocate of the cause so deeply imbedded in my heart. It was enough for me to listen—to receive and applaud the great words of others, and only whisper in private, among the white laborers on the wharves, and elsewhere, the truths which burned in my breast.

CHAPTER XXIII

Introduced to the Abolitionists

In the summer of 1841, a grand anti-slavery convention was held in Nantucket, under the auspices of Mr. Garrison and his friends. Until now, I had taken no holiday since my escape from slavery. Having worked very hard that spring and summer, in Richmond's brass foundery—sometimes working all night as well as all day—and needing a day or two of rest, I attended this convention, never supposing that I should take part in the proceedings. Indeed, I was not aware that any one connected with the convention even so much as knew my name. I was, however, quite mistaken. Mr. William C. Coffin, a prominent abolitionst(sic) in those days of trial, had heard me speaking to my colored friends, in the little school house on Second street, New Bedford, where we worshiped. He sought me out in the crowd, and invited me to say a few words to the convention. Thus sought out, and thus invited, I was induced to speak out the feelings inspired by the occasion, and the fresh recollection of the scenes through which I had passed as a slave. My speech on this occasion is about the only one I ever made, of which I do not remember a single connected sentence. It was with the utmost difficulty that I could stand erect, or that I could command and articulate two words without hesitation and stammering. I trembled in every limb. I am not sure that my embarrassment was not the most effective part of my speech, if speech it could be called. At any rate, this is about the only part of my performance that I now distinctly remember. But excited and convulsed as I was, the audience, though remarkably quiet before, became as much excited as myself. Mr. Garrison followed me, taking me as his text; and now, whether I had made an eloquent speech in behalf of freedom or not, his was one never to be forgotten by those who heard it. Those who had heard Mr. Garrison oftenest, and had known him longest, were astonished. It was an effort of unequaled power, sweeping down, like a very tornado, every opposing barrier, whether of sentiment or opinion. For a moment, he possessed that almost fabulous inspiration, often referred to but seldom attained, in which a public meeting is transformed, as it were, into a single individuality—the orator wielding a thousand heads and hearts at once, and by the simple majesty of his all controlling thought, converting his hearers into the express image of his own soul. That night there were at least one thousand Garrisonians in Nantucket! A(sic) the close of this great meeting, I was duly waited on by Mr. John A. Collins—then the general agent of the Massachusetts anti-slavery society—and urgently solicited by him to become an agent of that society, and to publicly advocate its anti-slavery principles. I was reluctant to take the proffered position. I had not been quite three years from slavery—was honestly distrustful of my ability—wished to be excused; publicity exposed me to discovery and arrest by my master; and other objections came up, but Mr. Collins was not to be put off, and I finally consented to go out for three months, for I supposed that I should have got to the end of my story and my usefulness, in that length of time.

Here opened upon me a new life a life for which I had had no preparation. I was a "graduate from the peculiar institution," Mr. Collins used to say, when introducing me, *with my diploma written on my back!* The three years of my freedom had been spent in the hard school of adversity. My hands had been furnished by nature with something like a solid leather coating, and I had bravely marked out for myself a life of rough labor, suited to the hardness of my hands, as a means of supporting myself and rearing my children.

Now what shall I say of this fourteen years' experience as a public advocate of the cause of my enslaved brothers and sisters? The time is but as a speck, yet large enough to justify a pause for retrospection—and a pause it must only be.

Young, ardent, and hopeful, I entered upon this new life in the full gush of unsuspecting enthusiasm. The cause was good; the men engaged in it were good; the means to attain its triumph, good; Heaven's blessing must attend all, and freedom must soon be given to the pining millions under a ruthless bondage. My whole heart went with the holy cause, and my most fervent prayer to the Almighty Disposer of the hearts of men, were continually offered for its early triumph. "Who or what," thought I, "can withstand a cause so good, so holy, so indescribably glorious. The God of Israel is with us. The might of the Eternal is on our side. Now let but the truth be spoken, and a nation will start forth at the sound!" In this enthusiastic spirit, I dropped into the ranks of freedom's friends, and went forth to the battle. For a time I was made to forget that my skin was dark and my hair crisped. For a time I regretted that I could not have shared the hardships and dangers endured by the earlier workers for the slave's release. I soon, however, found that my enthusiasm had been extravagant; that hardships and dangers were not yet passed; and that the life now before me, had shadows as well as sunbeams.

Among the first duties assigned me, on entering the ranks, was to travel, in company with Mr. George Foster, to secure subscribers to the *Anti-slavery Standard* and the *Liberator*. With him I traveled and lectured through the eastern counties of Massachusetts. Much interest was awakened—large meetings assembled. Many came, no doubt, from curiosity to hear what a Negro could say in his own cause. I was generally introduced as a *"chattel"*— a *"thing"*—a piece of southern *"property"*—the chairman assuring the audience that *it* could speak. Fugitive slaves, at that time, were not so plentiful as now; and as a fugitive slave lecturer, I had the advantage of being a *"brand new fact"*—the first one out. Up to that time, a colored man was deemed a fool who confessed himself a runaway slave, not only because of the danger to which he exposed himself of being retaken, but because it was a confession of a very *low* origin! Some of my colored friends in New Bedford thought very badly of my wisdom for thus exposing and degrading myself. The only precaution I took, at the beginning, to prevent Master Thomas from knowing where I was, and what I was about, was the withholding my former name, my master's name, and the name of the state and county from which I came. During the first three or four months, my speeches were almost exclusively made up of narrations of my own personal experience as a slave. "Let us have the facts," said the people. So also said Friend George Foster, who always wished to pin me down to my simple narrative. "Give us the facts," said Collins, "we will take care of the philosophy." Just here arose some embarrassment. It was impossible for me to repeat the same old story month after month, and to keep up my interest in it. It was new to the people, it is true, but it was an old story to me; and to go through with it night after night, was a task altogether too mechanical for my nature. "Tell your story, Frederick," would whisper my then revered friend, William Lloyd Garrison, as I stepped upon the platform. I could not always obey, for I was now reading and thinking. New views of the subject were presented to my mind. It did not entirely satisfy me to *narrate* wrongs; I felt like *denouncing* them. I could not always curb my moral indignation for the perpetrators of slaveholding villainy, long enough for a circumstantial statement of the facts which I felt almost everybody must know. Besides, I was growing, and needed room. "People won't believe you ever was a slave, Frederick, if you keep on this way," said Friend Foster. "Be yourself," said Collins, "and tell your story." It was said to me, "Better have a *little* of the plantation manner of speech than not; 'tis not best that you seem too learned." These excellent friends were actuated by the best of motives, and were not altogether wrong in their advice; and still I must speak just the word that seemed to *me* the word to be spoken *by* me.

At last the apprehended trouble came. People doubted if I had ever been a slave. They said I did not talk like a slave, look like a slave, nor act like a slave, and that they believed I had never been south of Mason and Dixon's line. "He don't tell us where he came from—what his master's name was—how he got away—nor the story of his experience. Besides, he is educated, and is, in this, a contradiction of all the facts we have concerning the ignorance of the slaves." Thus, I was in a pretty fair way to be denounced as an impostor. The committee of the Massachusetts anti-slavery society knew all the facts in my case, and agreed with me in the prudence of keeping them private. They, therefore, never doubted my being a genuine fugitive; but going down the aisles of the churches in which I spoke, and hearing the free spoken Yankees saying, repeatedly, *"He's never been a slave, I'll warrant ye,"* I resolved to dispel all doubt, at no distant day, by such a revelation of facts as could not be made by any other than a genuine fugitive.

In a little less than four years, therefore, after becoming a public lecturer, I was induced to write out the leading facts connected with my experience in slavery, giving names of persons, places, and dates—thus putting it in the power of any who doubted, to ascertain the truth or falsehood of my story of being a fugitive slave. This statement soon became known in Maryland, and I had reason to believe that an effort would be made to recapture me.

It is not probable that any open attempt to secure me as a slave could have succeeded, further than the obtainment, by my master, of the money value of my bones and sinews. Fortunately for me, in the four years of my labors in the abolition cause, I had gained many friends, who would have suffered themselves to be taxed to almost any extent to save me from slavery. It was felt that I had committed the double offense of running away, and exposing the secrets and crimes of slavery and slaveholders. There was a double motive for seeking my reenslavement—avarice and vengeance; and while, as I have said, there was little probability of successful recapture, if attempted openly, I was constantly in danger of being spirited away, at a moment when my friends could render me no assistance. In traveling about from place to place—often alone I was much exposed to this sort of attack. Any one cherishing the design to betray me, could easily do so, by simply tracing my whereabouts through the anti-slavery journals, for my meetings and movements were promptly made known in advance. My true friends, Mr. Garrison and Mr. Phillips, had no faith in the power of Massachusetts to protect me in my right to liberty. Public sentiment and the law, in their opinion, would hand me over to the tormentors. Mr. Phillips, especially, considered me in danger, and said, when I showed him the manuscript of my story, if in my place, he would throw it into the fire. Thus, the reader will observe, the settling of one difficulty only opened the way for another; and that though I had reached a free state, and had attained position for public usefulness, I ws(sic) still tormented with the liability of losing my liberty. How this liability was dispelled, will be related, with other incidents, in the next chapter.

CHAPTER XXIV

Twenty-One Months in Great Britain

The allotments of Providence, when coupled with trouble and anxiety, often conceal from finite vision the wisdom and goodness in which they are sent; and, frequently, what seemed a harsh and invidious dispensation, is converted by after experience into a happy and beneficial arrangement. Thus, the painful liability to be returned again to slavery, which haunted me by day, and troubled my dreams by night, proved to be a necessary step in the path of knowledge and usefulness. The writing of my pamphlet, in the spring of 1845, endangered my liberty, and led me to seek a refuge from republican slavery in monarchical England. A rude, uncultivated fugitive slave was driven, by stern necessity, to that country to which young American gentlemen go to increase their stock of knowledge, to seek pleasure, to have their rough, democratic manners softened by contact with English aristocratic refinement. On applying for a passage to England, on board the "Cambria", of the Cunard line, my friend, James N. Buffum, of Lynn, Massachusetts, was informed that I could not be received on board as a cabin passenger. American prejudice against color triumphed over British liberality and civilization, and erected a color test and condition for crossing the sea in the cabin of a British vessel. The insult was keenly felt by my white friends, but to me, it was common, expected, and therefore, a thing of no great consequence, whether I went in the cabin or in the steerage. Moreover, I felt that if I could not go into the first cabin, first-cabin passengers could come into the second cabin, and the result justified my anticipations to the fullest extent. Indeed, I soon found myself an object of more general interest than I wished to be; and so far from being degraded by being placed in the second cabin, that part of the ship became the scene of as much pleasure and refinement, during the voyage, as the cabin itself. The Hutchinson Family, celebrated vocalists—fellow-passengers—often came to my rude forecastle deck, and sung their sweetest songs, enlivening the place with eloquent music, as well as spirited conversation, during the voyage. In two days after leaving Boston, one part of the ship was about as free to me as another. My fellow-passengers not only visited me, but invited me to visit them, on the saloon deck. My visits there, however, were but seldom. I preferred to live within my privileges, and keep upon my own premises. I found this quite as much in accordance with good policy, as with my own feelings. The effect was, that with the majority of the passengers, all color distinctions were flung to the winds, and I found myself treated with every mark of respect, from the beginning to the end of the voyage, except in a single instance; and in that, I came near being mobbed, for complying with an invitation given me by the passengers, and the captain of the "Cambria," to deliver a lecture on slavery. Our New Orleans and Georgia passengers were pleased to regard my lecture as an insult offered to them, and swore I should not speak. They went so far as to threaten to throw me overboard, and but for the firmness of Captain Judkins, probably would have (under the inspiration of *slavery* and *brandy*) attempted to put their threats into execution. I have no space to describe this scene, although its tragic and comic peculiarities are well worth describing. An end was put to the *melee*, by the captain's calling the ship's company to put the salt water mobocrats in irons. At this determined order, the gentlemen of the lash scampered, and for the rest of the voyage conducted themselves very decorously.

This incident of the voyage, in two days after landing at Liverpool, brought me at once before the British public, and that by no act of my own. The gentlemen so promptly snubbed in their meditated violence, flew to the press to justify their conduct, and to denounce me as a worthless and insolent Negro. This course was even less wise than the conduct it was intended to sustain; for, besides awakening something like a national interest in me, and securing me an audience, it brought out counter statements, and threw the blame upon themselves, which they had sought to fasten upon me and the gallant captain of the ship.

Some notion may be formed of the difference in my feelings and circumstances, while abroad, from the following extract from one of a series of letters addressed by me to Mr. Garrison, and published in the *Liberator*. It was written on the first day of January, 1846:

MY DEAR FRIEND GARRISON: Up to this time, I have given no direct expression of the views, feelings, and opinions which I have formed, respecting the character and condition of the people of this land. I have refrained thus, purposely. I wish to speak advisedly, and in order to do this, I have waited till, I trust, experience has brought my opinions to an intelligent maturity. I have been thus careful, not because I think what I say will have much effect in shaping the opinions of the world, but because whatever of influence I may possess, whether little or much, I wish it to go in the right direction, and according to truth. I hardly need say that, in speaking of Ireland, I shall be influenced by no prejudices in favor of America. I think my circumstances all forbid that. I have no end to serve, no creed to uphold, no government to defend; and as to nation, I belong to none. I have no protection at home, or resting-place abroad. The land of my birth welcomes me to her shores only as a slave, and spurns with contempt the idea of treating me differently; so that I am an outcast from the society of my childhood, and an outlaw in the land of my birth. "I am a stranger with thee, and a sojourner, as all my fathers were." That men should be patriotic, is to me perfectly natural; and as a philosophical fact, I am able to give it an *intellectual* recognition. But no further can I go. If ever I had any patriotism, or any capacity for the feeling, it was whipped out of me long since, by the lash of the American soul-drivers.

In thinking of America, I sometimes find myself admiring her bright blue sky, her grand old woods, her fertile fields, her beautiful rivers, her mighty lakes, and star-crowned mountains. But my rapture is soon checked, my joy is soon turned to mourning. When I remember that all is cursed with the infernal spirit of slaveholding, robbery, and wrong; when I remember that with the waters of her noblest rivers, the tears of my brethren are borne to the ocean, disregarded and forgotten, and that her most fertile fields drink daily of the warm blood of my outraged sisters; I am filled with unutterable loathing, and led to reproach myself that anything could fall from my lips in praise of such a land. America will not allow her children to love her. She seems bent on compelling those who would be her warmest friends, to be her worst enemies. May God give her repentance, before it is too late, is the ardent prayer of my heart. I will continue to pray, labor, and wait, believing that she cannot always be insensible to the dictates of justice, or deaf to the voice of humanity.

My opportunities for learning the character and condition of the people of this land have been very great. I have traveled almost from the Hill of Howth to the Giant's Causeway, and from the Giant's Causway, to Cape Clear. During these travels, I have met with much in the chara@@ and condition of the people to approve, and much to condemn; much that @@thrilled me with pleasure, and very much that has filled me with pain. I @@ @@t, in this letter, attempt to give any description of those scenes which have given me pain. This I will do hereafter. I have enough, and more than your subscribers will be disposed to read at one time, of the bright side of the picture. I can truly say, I have spent some of the happiest moments of my life since landing in this country. I seem to have undergone a transformation. I live a new life. The warm and generous cooperation extended to me by the friends of my despised race; the prompt and liberal manner with which the press has rendered me its aid; the glorious enthusiasm with which thousands have flocked to hear the cruel wrongs of my down-trodden and long-enslaved fellow-countrymen portrayed; the deep sympathy for the slave, and the strong abhorrence of the slaveholder, everywhere evinced; the cordiality with which members and ministers of various religious bodies, and of various shades of religious opinion, have embraced me, and lent me their aid; the kind of hospitality constantly proffered to me by persons of the highest rank in society; the spirit of freedom that seems to animate all with whom I come in contact, and the entire absence of everything that looked like prejudice against me, on account of the color of my skin—contrasted so strongly with my long and bitter experience in the United States, that I look with wonder and amazement on the transition. In the southern part of the United States, I was a slave, thought of and spoken of as property; in the language of the LAW, "*held, taken, reputed, and adjudged to be a chattel in the hands of my owners and possessors, and their executors, administrators, and assigns, to all intents, constructions, and purposes whatsoever.*" (Brev. Digest, 224). In the northern states, a fugitive slave, liable to be hunted at any moment, like a felon, and to be hurled into the terrible jaws of slavery—doomed by an inveterate prejudice against color to insult and outrage on every hand (Massachusetts out of the question)—denied the privileges and courtesies common to others in the use of the most humble means of conveyance—shut out from the cabins on steamboats—refused admission to respectable hotels—caricatured, scorned, scoffed, mocked, and maltreated with impunity by any one (no matter how black his heart), so he has a white skin. But now behold the change! Eleven days and a half gone, and I have crossed three thousand miles of the perilous deep. Instead of a democratic government, I am under a monarchical government. Instead of the bright, blue sky of America, I am covered with the soft, grey fog of the Emerald Isle. I breathe, and lo! the chattel becomes a man. I gaze around in vain for one who will question my equal humanity, claim me as his slave, or offer me an insult. I employ a cab—I am seated beside white people—I reach the hotel—I enter the same door—I am shown into the same parlor—I dine at the same table and no one is offended. No delicate nose grows deformed in my presence. I find no difficulty here in obtaining admission into any place of worship, instruction, or amusement, on equal terms with people as white as any I ever saw in the United States. I meet nothing to remind me of my complexion. I find myself regarded and treated at every turn with the kindness and deference paid to white people. When I go to church, I am met by no upturned nose and scornful lip to tell me, "*We don't allow niggers in here!*"

I remember, about two years ago, there was in Boston, near the south-west corner of Boston Common, a menagerie. I had long desired to see such a collection as I understood was being exhibited there. Never having had an opportunity while a slave, I resolved to seize this, my first, since my escape. I went, and as I approached the entrance to gain admission, I was met and told by the door-keeper, in a harsh and contemptuous tone, "*We don't allow niggers in here.*" I also remember attending a revival meeting in the Rev. Henry Jackson's meeting-house, at New Bedford, and going up the broad aisle to find a seat, I was met by a good deacon, who told me, in a pious tone, "*We don't allow niggers in here!*" Soon after my arrival in New Bedford, from the south, I had a strong desire to attend the Lyceum, but was told, "*They don't allow niggers in here!*" While passing from New York to Boston, on the steamer Massachusetts, on the night of the 9th of December, 1843, when chilled almost through with the cold, I went into the cabin to get a little warm. I was soon touched upon the shoulder, and told, "*We don't allow niggers in here!*" On arriving in Boston, from an anti-slavery tour, hungry and tired, I went into an eating-house, near my friend, Mr. Campbell's to get some refreshments. I was met by a lad in a white apron, "*We don't allow niggers in here!*" A week or two before leaving the United States, I had a meeting appointed at Weymouth, the home of that glorious band of true abolitionists, the Weston family, and others. On attempting to take a seat in the omnibus to that place, I was told by the driver (and I never shall forget his fiendish hate). "*I don't allow niggers in here!*" Thank heaven for the respite I now enjoy! I had been in Dublin but a few days, when a gentleman of great respectability kindly offered to conduct me through all the public buildings of that beautiful city; and a little afterward, I found myself dining with the lord mayor of Dublin. What a pity there was not some American democratic Christian at the door of his splendid mansion, to bark out at my approach, "*They don't allow niggers in here!*" The truth is, the people here know nothing of the republican Negro hate prevalent in our glorious land. They measure and esteem men according to their moral and intellectual worth, and not according to the color of their skin. Whatever may be said of the aristocracies here, there is none based on the color of a man's skin. This species of aristocracy belongs preeminently to "the land of the free, and the home of the brave." I have never found it abroad, in any but Americans. It sticks to them wherever they go. They find it almost as hard to get rid of, as to get rid of their skins.

The second day after my arrival at Liverpool, in company with my friend, Buffum, and several other friends, I went to Eaton Hall, the residence of the Marquis of Westminster, one of the most splendid buildings in England. On approaching the door, I found several of our American passengers, who came out with us in the "Cambria," waiting for admission, as but one party was allowed in the house at a time. We all had to wait till the company within came out. And of all the faces, expressive of chagrin, those of the Americans were preeminent. They looked as sour as vinegar, and as bitter as gall, when they found I was to be admitted on equal terms with themselves. When the door was opened, I walked in, on an equal footing with my white fellow-citizens, and from all I could see, I had as much attention paid me by the servants that showed us through the house, as any with a paler skin. As I walked through the building, the statuary did not fall down, the pictures did not leap from their places, the doors did not refuse to open, and the servants did not say, "*We don't allow niggers in here!*"

A happy new-year to you, and all the friends of freedom.

My time and labors, while abroad were divided between England, Ireland, Scotland, and Wales. Upon this experience alone, I might write a book twice the size of this, *My Bondage and My Freedom*. I visited and lectured in nearly all the large towns and cities in the United Kingdom, and enjoyed many favorable opportunities for observation and information. But books on England are abundant, and the public may, therefore, dismiss any fear that I am meditating another infliction in that line; though, in truth, I should like much to write a book on those countries, if for nothing else, to make grateful mention of the many dear friends, whose benevolent actions toward me are ineffaceably stamped upon my memory, and warmly treasured in my heart. To these friends I owe my freedom in the United States. On their own motion, without any solicitation from me (Mrs. Henry Richardson, a clever lady, remarkable for her devotion to every good work, taking the lead), they raised a fund sufficient to purchase my freedom, and actually paid it over, and placed the papers* of my manumission

---

* The following is a copy of these curious papers, both of my transfer from Thomas to Hugh Auld, and from Hugh to myself:

"Know all men by these Presents, That I, Thomas Auld, of Talbot county, and state of Maryland, for and in consideration of the sum of one hundred dollars, current money, to me paid by Hugh Auld, of the city of Baltimore, in the said state, at and before the sealing and delivery of these presents, the receipt whereof, I, the said Thomas Auld, do hereby acknowledge, have granted, bargained, and sold, and by these presents do grant, bargain, and sell unto the said Hugh Auld, his executors, administrators, and assigns, ONE NEGRO MAN, by the name of FREDERICK BAILY, or DOUGLASS, as he callls(sic) himself—he is now about twenty-eight years of age—to have and to hold the said negro man for life. And I, the said Thomas Auld, for myself my heirs, executors, and administrators, all and singular, the said FREDERICK BAILY *alias* DOUGLASS, unto the said Hugh Auld, his executors, administrators, and assigns against me, the said Thomas Auld, my executors, and administrators, and against ali and every other person or persons whatsoever, shall and will warrant and forever defend by these presents. In witness whereof, I set my hand and seal, this thirteenth day of November, eighteen hundred and forty-six.

THOMAS AULD

"Signed, sealed, and delivered in presence of Wrightson Jones.
"JOHN C. LEAS.

The authenticity of this bill of sale is attested by N. Harrington, a justice of the peace of the state of Maryland, and for the county of Talbot, dated same day as above.

in my hands, before they would tolerate the idea of my returning to this, my native country. To this commercial transaction I owe my exemption from the democratic operation of the Fugitive Slave Bill of 1850. But for this, I might at any time become a victim of this most cruel and scandalous enactment, and be doomed to end my life, as I began it, a slave. The sum paid for my freedom was one hundred and fifty pounds sterling.

Some of my uncompromising anti-slavery friends in this country failed to see the wisdom of this arrangement, and were not pleased that I consented to it, even by my silence. They thought it a violation of anti-slavery principles—conceding a right of property in man—and a wasteful expenditure of money. On the other hand, viewing it simply in the light of a ransom, or as money extorted by a robber, and my liberty of more value than one hundred and fifty pounds sterling, I could not see either a violation of the laws of morality, or those of economy, in the transaction.

It is true, I was not in the possession of my claimants, and could have easily remained in England, for the same friends who had so generously purchased my freedom, would have assisted me in establishing myself in that country. To this, however, I could not consent. I felt that I had a duty to perform—and that was, to labor and suffer with the oppressed in my native land. Considering, therefore, all the circumstances—the fugitive slave bill included—I think the very best thing was done in letting Master Hugh have the hundred and fifty pounds sterling, and leaving me free to return to my appropriate field of labor. Had I been a private person, having no other relations or duties than those of a personal and family nature, I should never have consented to the payment of so large a sum for the privilege of living securely under our glorious republican form of government. I could have remained in England, or have gone to some other country; and perhaps I could even have lived unobserved in this. But to this I could not consent. I had already become somewhat notorious, and withal quite as unpopular as notorious; and I was, therefore, much exposed to arrest and recapture.

"To all whom it may concern: Be it known, that I, Hugh Auld, of the city of Baltimore, in Baltimore county, in the state of Maryland, for divers good causes and considerations, me thereunto moving, have released from slavery, liberated, manumitted, and set free, and by these presents do hereby release from slavery, liberate, manumit, and set free, MY NEGRO MAN, named FREDERICK BAILY, otherwise called DOUGLASS, being of the age of twenty-eight years, or thereabouts, and able to work and gain a sufficient livelihood and maintenance; and him the said negro man named FREDERICK BAILY, otherwise called FREDERICK DOUGLASS, I do declare to be henceforth free, manumitted, and discharged from all manner of servitude to me, my executors, and administrators forever.

"In witness whereof, I, the said Hugh Auld, have hereunto set my hand and seal the fifth of December, in the year one thousand eight hundred and forty-six.

Hugh Auld

"Sealed and delivered in presence of T. Hanson Belt.
"JAMES N. S. T. WRIGHT"

The main object to which my labors in Great Britain were directed, was the concentration of the moral and religious sentiment of its people against American slavery. England is often charged with having established slavery in the United States, and if there were no other justification than this, for appealing to her people to lend their moral aid for the abolition of slavery, I should be justified. My speeches in Great Britain were wholly extemporaneous, and I may not always have been so guarded in my expressions, as I otherwise should have been. I was ten years younger then than now, and only seven years from slavery. I cannot give the reader a better idea of the nature of my discourses, than by republishing one of them, delivered in Finsbury chapel, London, to an audience of about two thousand persons, and which was published in the *London Universe*, at the time.*

Those in the United States who may regard this speech as being harsh in its spirit and unjust in its statements, because delivered before an audience supposed to be anti-republican in their principles and feelings, may view the matter differently, when they learn that the case supposed did not exist. It so happened that the great mass of the people in England who attended and patronized my anti-slavery meetings, were, in truth, about as good republicans as the mass of Americans, and with this decided advantage over the latter— they are lovers of republicanism for all men, for black men as well as for white men. They are the people who sympathize with Louis Kossuth and Mazzini, and with the oppressed and enslaved, of every color and nation, the world over. They constitute the democratic element in British politics, and are as much opposed to the union of church and state as we, in America, are to such an union. At the meeting where this speech was delivered, Joseph Sturge—a world-wide philanthropist, and a member of the society of Friends—presided, and addressed the meeting. George William Alexander, another Friend, who has spent more than an Ameriacn(sic) fortune in promoting the anti-slavery cause in different sections of the world, was on the platform; and also Dr. Campbell (now of the *British Banner*) who combines all the humane tenderness of Melanchthon, with the directness and boldness of Luther. He is in the very front ranks of non-conformists, and looks with no unfriendly eye upon America. George Thompson, too, was there; and America will yet own that he did a true man's work in relighting the rapidly dying-out fire of true republicanism in the American heart, and be ashamed of the treatment he met at her hands. Coming generations in this country will applaud the spirit of this much abused republican friend of freedom. There were others of note seated on the platform, who would gladly ingraft upon English institutions all that is purely republican in the institutions of America. Nothing, therefore, must be set down against this

---

* See Appendix to this volume, page 317.

speech on the score that it was delivered in the presence of those who cannot appreciate the many excellent things belonging to our system of government, and with a view to stir up prejudice against republican institutions.

Again, let it also be remembered—for it is the simple truth—that neither in this speech, nor in any other which I delivered in England, did I ever allow myself to address Englishmen as against Americans. I took my stand on the high ground of human brotherhood, and spoke to Englishmen as men, in behalf of men. Slavery is a crime, not against Englishmen, but against God, and all the members of the human family; and it belongs to the whole human family to seek its suppression. In a letter to Mr. Greeley, of the New York Tribune, written while abroad, I said:

I am, nevertheless aware that the wisdom of exposing the sins of one nation in the ear of another, has been seriously questioned by good and clear-sighted people, both on this and on your side of the Atlantic. And the thought is not without weight on my own mind. I am satisfied that there are many evils which can be best removed by confining our efforts to the immediate locality where such evils exist. This, however, is by no means the case with the system of slavery. It is such a giant sin—such a monstrous aggregation of iniquity—so hardening to the human heart—so destructive to the moral sense, and so well calculated to beget a character, in every one around it, favorable to its own continuance,— that I feel not only at liberty, but abundantly justified, in appealing to the whole world to aid in its removal.

But, even if I had—as has been often charged—labored to bring American institutions generally into disrepute, and had not confined my labors strictly within the limits of humanity and morality, I should not have been without illustrious examples to support me. Driven into semi-exile by civil and barbarous laws, and by a system which cannot be thought of without a shudder, I was fully justified in turning, if possible, the tide of the moral universe against the heaven-daring outrage.

Four circumstances greatly assisted me in getting the question of American slavery before the British public. First, the mob on board the "Cambria," already referred to, which was a sort of national announcement of my arrival in England. Secondly, the highly reprehensible course pursued by the Free Church of Scotland, in soliciting, receiving, and retaining money in its sustentation fund for supporting the gospel in Scotland, which was evidently the ill-gotten gain of slaveholders and slave-traders. Third, the great Evangelical Alliance—or rather the attempt to form such an alliance, which should include slaveholders of a certain description—added immensely to the interest felt in the slavery question. About the same time, there was the World's Temperance Convention, where I had the misfortune to come in collision with sundry American doctors of divinity—Dr. Cox among the number—with whom I had a small controversy.

It has happened to me—as it has happened to most other men engaged in a good cause—often to be more indebted to my enemies than to my own skill or to the assistance of my friends, for whatever success has attended my labors. Great surprise was expressed by American newspapers, north and south, during my stay in Great Britain, that a person so illiterate and insignificant as myself could awaken an interest so marked in England. These papers were not the only parties surprised. I was myself not far behind them in surprise. But the very contempt and scorn, the systematic and extravagant disparagement of which I was the object, served, perhaps, to magnify my few merits, and to render me of some account, whether deserving or not. A man is sometimes made great, by the greatness of the abuse a portion of mankind may think proper to heap upon him. Whether I was of as much consequence as the English papers made me out to be, or not, it was easily seen, in England, that I could not be the ignorant and worthless creature, some of the American papers would have them believe I was. Men, in their senses, do not take bowie-knives to kill mosquitoes, nor pistols to shoot flies; and the American passengers who thought proper to get up a mob to silence me, on board the "Cambria," took the most effective method of telling the British public that I had something to say.

But to the second circumstance, namely, the position of the Free Church of Scotland, with the great Doctors Chalmers, Cunningham, and Candlish at its head. That church, with its leaders, put it out of the power of the Scotch people to ask the old question, which we in the north have often most wickedly asked— "*What have we to do with slavery?*" That church had taken the price of blood into its treasury, with which to build *free* churches, and to pay *free* church ministers for preaching the gospel; and, worse still, when honest John Murray, of Bowlien Bay—now gone to his reward in heaven—with William Smeal, Andrew Paton, Frederick Card, and other sterling anti-slavery men in Glasgow, denounced the transaction as disgraceful and shocking to the religious sentiment of Scotland, this church, through its leading divines, instead of repenting and seeking to mend the mistake into which it had fallen, made it a flagrant sin, by undertaking to defend, in the name of God and the bible, the principle not only of taking the money of slave-dealers to build churches, but of holding fellowship with the holders and traffickers in human flesh. This, the reader will see, brought up the whole question of slavery, and opened the way to its full discussion, without any agency of mine. I have never seen a people more deeply moved than were the people of Scotland, on this very question. Public meeting succeeded public meeting. Speech after speech, pamphlet after pamphlet, editorial after editorial, sermon after sermon, soon lashed the conscientious Scotch people into a perfect *furore.* "SEND BACK THE MONEY!" was indignantly cried out, from Greenock to Edinburgh, and from Edinburgh to Aberdeen. George Thompson, of London, Henry C. Wright, of the United States, James N. Buffum, of Lynn,

Massachusetts, and myself were on the anti-slavery side; and Doctors Chalmers, Cunningham, and Candlish on the other. In a conflict where the latter could have had even the show of right, the truth, in our hands as against them, must have been driven to the wall; and while I believe we were able to carry the conscience of the country against the action of the Free Church, the battle, it must be confessed, was a hard-fought one. Abler defenders of the doctrine of fellowshiping slaveholders as christians, have not been met with. In defending this doctrine, it was necessary to deny that slavery is a sin. If driven from this position, they were compelled to deny that slaveholders were responsible for the sin; and if driven from both these positions, they must deny that it is a sin in such a sense, and that slaveholders are sinners in such a sense, as to make it wrong, in the circumstances in which they were placed, to recognize them as Christians. Dr. Cunningham was the most powerful debater on the slavery side of the question; Mr. Thompson was the ablest on the anti-slavery side. A scene occurred between these two men, a parallel to which I think I never witnessed before, and I know I never have since. The scene was caused by a single exclamation on the part of Mr. Thompson.

The general assembly of the Free Church was in progress at Cannon Mills, Edinburgh. The building would hold about twenty-five hundred persons; and on this occasion it was densely packed, notice having been given that Doctors Cunningham and Candlish would speak, that day, in defense of the relations of the Free Church of Scotland to slavery in America. Messrs. Thompson, Buffum, myself, and a few anti-slavery friends, attended, but sat at such a distance, and in such a position, that, perhaps we were not observed from the platform. The excitement was intense, having been greatly increased by a series of meetings held by Messrs. Thompson, Wright, Buffum, and myself, in the most splendid hall in that most beautiful city, just previous to the meetings of the general assembly. "SEND BACK THE MONEY!" stared at us from every street corner; "SEND BACK THE MONEY!" in large capitals, adorned the broad flags of the pavement; "SEND BACK THE MONEY!" was the chorus of the popular street songs; "SEND BACK THE MONEY!" was the heading of leading editorials in the daily newspapers. This day, at Cannon Mills, the great doctors of the church were to give an answer to this loud and stern demand. Men of all parties and all sects were most eager to hear. Something great was expected. The occasion was great, the men great, and great speeches were expected from them.

In addition to the outside pressure upon Doctors Cunningham and Candlish, there was wavering in their own ranks. The conscience of the church itself was not at ease. A dissatisfaction with the position of the church touching slavery, was sensibly manifest among the members, and something must be done to counteract this untoward influence. The great Dr. Chalmers was in feeble health, at the time. His most potent eloquence could not now be summoned to Cannon Mills, as formerly. He whose voice was able to rend asunder and dash down the granite walls of the established church of Scotland, and to lead a host in solemn procession from it, as from a doomed city, was now old and enfeebled. Besides, he had said his word on this very question; and his word had not silenced the clamor without, nor stilled the anxious heavings within. The occasion was momentous, and felt to be so. The church was in a perilous condition. A change of some sort must take place in her condition, or she must go to pieces. To stand where she did, was impossible. The whole weight of the matter fell on Cunningham and Candlish. No shoulders in the church were broader than theirs; and I must say, badly as I detest the principles laid down and defended by them, I was compelled to acknowledge the vast mental endowments of the men. Cunningham rose; and his rising was the signal for almost tumultous applause. You will say this was scarcely in keeping with the solemnity of the occasion, but to me it served to increase its grandeur and gravity. The applause, though tumultuous, was not joyous. It seemed to me, as it thundered up from the vast audience, like the fall of an immense shaft, flung from shoulders already galled by its crushing weight. It was like saying, "Doctor, we have borne this burden long enough, and willingly fling it upon you. Since it was you who brought it upon us, take it now, and do what you will with it, for we are too weary to bear it. ["no close"].

Doctor Cunningham proceeded with his speech, abounding in logic, learning, and eloquence, and apparently bearing down all opposition; but at the moment—the fatal moment—when he was just bringing all his arguments to a point, and that point being, that neither Jesus Christ nor his holy apostles regarded slaveholding as a sin, George Thompson, in a clear, sonorous, but rebuking voice, broke the deep stillness of the audience, exclaiming, HEAR! HEAR! HEAR! The effect of this simple and common exclamation is almost incredible. It was as if a granite wall had been suddenly flung up against the advancing current of a mighty river. For a moment, speaker and audience were brought to a dead silence. Both the doctor and his hearers seemed appalled by the audacity, as well as the fitness of the rebuke. At length a shout went up to the cry of "*Put him out!*" Happily, no one attempted to execute this cowardly order, and the doctor proceeded with his discourse. Not, however, as before, did the learned doctor proceed. The exclamation of Thompson must have reechoed itself a thousand times in his memory, during the remainder of his speech, for the doctor never recovered from the blow.

The deed was done, however; the pillars of the church—*the proud, Free Church of Scotland*—were committed and the humility of repentance was absent. The Free Church held on to the blood-stained money, and continued to justify itself in its position—and of course to apologize for slavery—and does so till this day. She lost a glorious opportunity for giving her voice, her vote, and her example to the cause of humanity; and to-day she is staggering under the curse of the enslaved, whose blood is in her skirts. The people of Scotland are, to this day, deeply grieved at the course pursued by the Free Church, and would hail, as a relief from a deep and blighting shame, the "sending back the money" to the slaveholders from whom it was gathered.

One good result followed the conduct of the Free Church; it furnished an occasion for making the people of Scotland thoroughly acquainted with the character of slavery, and for arraying against the system the moral and religious sentiment of that country. Therefore, while we did not succeed in accomplishing the specific object of our mission, namely—procure the sending back of the money—we were amply justified by the good which really did result from our labors.

Next comes the Evangelical Alliance. This was an attempt to form a union of all evangelical Christians throughout the world. Sixty or seventy American divines attended, and some of them went there merely to weave a world-wide garment with which to clothe evangelical slaveholders. Foremost among these divines, was the Rev. Samuel Hanson Cox, moderator of the New School Presbyterian General Assembly. He and his friends spared no pains to secure a platform broad enough to hold American slaveholders, and in this partly succeeded. But the question of slavery is too large a question to be finally disposed of, even by the Evangelical Alliance. We appealed from the judgment of the Alliance, to the judgment of the people of Great Britain, and with the happiest effect. This controversy with the Alliance might be made the subject of extended remark, but I must forbear, except to say, that this effort to shield the Christian character of slaveholders greatly served to open a way to the British ear for anti-slavery discussion, and that it was well improved.

The fourth and last circumstance that assisted me in getting before the British public, was an attempt on the part of certain doctors of divinity to silence me on the platform of the World's Temperance Convention. Here I was brought into point blank collison with Rev. Dr. Cox, who made me the subject not only of bitter remark in the convention, but also of a long denunciatory letter published in the New York Evangelist and other American papers. I replied to the doctor as well as I could, and was successful in getting a respectful hearing before the British public, who are by nature and practice ardent lovers of fair play, especially in a conflict between the weak and the strong.

Thus did circumstances favor me, and favor the cause of which I strove to be the advocate. After such distinguished notice, the public in both countries was compelled to attach some importance to my labors. By the very ill usage I received at the hands of Dr. Cox and his party, by the mob on board the "Cambria," by the attacks made upon me in the American newspapers, and by the aspersions cast upon me through the organs of the Free Church of Scotland,

I became one of that class of men, who, for the moment, at least, "have greatness forced upon them." People became the more anxious to hear for themselves, and to judge for themselves, of the truth which I had to unfold. While, therefore, it is by no means easy for a stranger to get fairly before the British public, it was my lot to accomplish it in the easiest manner possible.

Having continued in Great Britain and Ireland nearly two years, and being about to return to America—not as I left it, a slave, but a freeman—leading friends of the cause of emancipation in that country intimated their intention to make me a testimonial, not only on grounds of personal regard to myself, but also to the cause to which they were so ardently devoted. How far any such thing could have succeeded, I do not know; but many reasons led me to prefer that my friends should simply give me the means of obtaining a printing press and printing materials, to enable me to start a paper, devoted to the interests of my enslaved and oppressed people. I told them that perhaps the greatest hinderance to the adoption of abolition principles by the people of the United States, was the low estimate, everywhere in that country, placed upon the Negro, as a man; that because of his assumed natural inferiority, people reconciled themselves to his enslavement and oppression, as things inevitable, if not desirable. The grand thing to be done, therefore, was to change the estimation in which the colored people of the United States were held; to remove the prejudice which depreciated and depressed them; to prove them worthy of a higher consideration; to disprove their alleged inferiority, and demonstrate their capacity for a more exalted civilization than slavery and prejudice had assigned to them. I further stated, that, in my judgment, a tolerably well conducted press, in the hands of persons of the despised race, by calling out the mental energies of the race itself; by making them acquainted with their own latent powers; by enkindling among them the hope that for them there is a future; by developing their moral power; by combining and reflecting their talents—would prove a most powerful means of removing prejudice, and of awakening an interest in them. I further informed them—and at that time the statement was true—that there was not, in the United States, a single newspaper regularly published by the colored people; that many attempts had been made to establish such papers; but that, up to that time, they had all failed. These views I laid before my friends. The result was, nearly two thousand five hundred dollars were speedily raised toward starting my paper. For this prompt and generous assistance, rendered upon my bare suggestion, without any personal efforts on my part, I shall never cease to feel deeply grateful; and the thought of fulfilling the noble expectations of the dear friends who gave me this evidence of their confidence, will never cease to be a motive for persevering exertion.

Proposing to leave England, and turning my face toward America, in the spring of 1847, I was met, on the threshold, with something which painfully reminded me of the kind of life which awaited me in my native land. For the first time in the many months spent abroad, I was met with proscription on account of my color. A few weeks before departing from England, while in London, I was careful to purchase a ticket, and secure a berth for returning home, in the "Cambria"—the steamer in which I left the United States—paying therefor the round sum of forty pounds and nineteen shillings sterling. This was first cabin fare. But on going aboard the Cambria, I found that the Liverpool agent had ordered my berth to be given to another, and had forbidden my entering the saloon! This contemptible conduct met with stern rebuke from the British press. For, upon the point of leaving England, I took occasion to expose the disgusting tyranny, in the columns of the London *Times*. That journal, and other leading journals throughout the United Kingdom, held up the outrage to unmitigated condemnation. So good an opportunity for calling out a full expression of British sentiment on the subject, had not before occurred, and it was most fully embraced. The result was, that Mr. Cunard came out in a letter to the public journals, assuring them of his regret at the outrage, and promising that the like should never occur again on board his steamers; and the like, we believe, has never since occurred on board the steamships of the Cunard line.

It is not very pleasant to be made the subject of such insults; but if all such necessarily resulted as this one did, I should be very happy to bear, patiently, many more than I have borne, of the same sort. Albeit, the lash of proscription, to a man accustomed to equal social position, even for a time, as I was, has a sting for the soul hardly less severe than that which bites the flesh and draws the blood from the back of the plantation slave. It was rather hard, after having enjoyed nearly two years of equal social privileges in England, often dining with gentlemen of great literary, social, political, and religious eminence never, during the whole time, having met with a single word, look, or gesture, which gave me the slightest reason to think my color was an offense to anybody—now to be cooped up in the stern of the "Cambria," and denied the right to enter the saloon, lest my dark presence should be deemed an offense to some of my democratic fellow-passengers. The reader will easily imagine what must have been my feelings.

CHAPTER XXV

Various Incidents

NEWSPAPER ENTERPRISE—UNEXPECTED OPPOSITION—THE OBJECTIONS TO IT—THEIR PLAUSIBILITY ADMITTED—MOTIVES FOR COMING TO ROCHESTER—DISCIPLE OF MR. GARRISON—CHANGE OF OPINION—CAUSES LEADING TO IT—THE CONSEQUENCES OF THE CHANGE—PREJUDICE AGAINST COLOR—AMUSING CONDESCENSION—"JIM CROW CARS"—COLLISIONS WITH CONDUCTORS AND BRAKEMEN—TRAINS ORDERED NOT TO STOP AT LYNN—AMUSING DOMESTIC SCENE—SEPARATE TABLES FOR MASTER AND MAN—PREJUDICE UNNATURAL—ILLUSTRATIONS—IN HIGH COMPANY—ELEVATION OF THE FREE PEOPLE OF COLOR—PLEDGE FOR THE FUTURE.

I have now given the reader an imperfect sketch of nine years' experience in freedom—three years as a common laborer on the wharves of New Bedford, four years as a lecturer in New England, and two years of semi-exile in Great Britain and Ireland. A single ray of light remains to be flung upon my life during the last eight years, and my story will be done.

A trial awaited me on my return from England to the United States, for which I was but very imperfectly prepared. My plans for my then future usefulness as an anti-slavery advocate were all settled. My friends in England had resolved to raise a given sum to purchase for me a press and printing materials; and I already saw myself wielding my pen, as well as my voice, in the great work of renovating the public mind, and building up a public sentiment which should, at least, send slavery and oppression to the grave, and restore to "liberty and the pursuit of happiness" the people with whom I had suffered, both as a slave and as a freeman. Intimation had reached my friends in Boston of what I intended to do, before my arrival, and I was prepared to find them favorably disposed toward my much cherished enterprise. In this I was mistaken. I found them very earnestly opposed to the idea of my starting a paper, and for several reasons. First, the paper was not needed; secondly, it would interfere with my usefulness as a lecturer; thirdly, I was better fitted to speak than to write; fourthly, the paper could not succeed. This opposition, from a quarter so highly esteemed, and to which I had been accustomed to look for advice and direction, caused me not only to hesitate, but inclined me to abandon the enterprise. All previous attempts to establish such a journal having failed, I felt that probably I should but add another to the list of failures, and thus contribute another proof of the mental and moral deficiencies of my race. Very much that was said to me in respect to my imperfect literary acquirements, I felt to be most painfully true. The unsuccessful projectors of all the previous colored newspapers were my superiors in point of education, and if they failed, how could I hope for success? Yet I did hope for success, and persisted in the undertaking. Some of my English friends greatly encouraged me to go forward, and I shall never cease to be grateful for their words of cheer and generous deeds.

I can easily pardon those who have denounced me as ambitious and presumptuous, in view of my persistence in this enterprise. I was but nine years from slavery. In point of mental experience, I was but nine years old. That one, in such circumstances, should aspire to establish a printing press, among an educated people, might well be considered, if not ambitious, quite silly. My American friends looked at me with astonishment! "A wood-sawyer" offering himself to the public as an editor! A slave, brought up in the very depths of ignorance, assuming to instruct the highly civilized people of the north in the principles of liberty, justice, and humanity! The thing looked absurd. Nevertheless, I persevered. I felt that the want of education, great as it was, could be overcome by study, and that knowledge would come by experience; and further (which was perhaps the most controlling consideration). I thought that an intelligent public, knowing my early history, would easily pardon a large share of the deficiencies which I was sure that my paper would exhibit. The most distressing thing, however, was the offense which I was about to give my Boston friends, by what seemed to them a reckless disregard of their sage advice. I am not sure that I was not under the influence of something like a slavish adoration of my Boston friends, and I labored hard to convince them of the wisdom of my undertaking, but without success. Indeed, I never expect to succeed, although time has answered all their original objections. The paper has been successful. It is a large sheet, costing eighty dollars per week—has three thousand subscribers—has been published regularly nearly eight years—and bids fair to stand eight years longer. At any rate, the eight years to come are as full of promise as were the eight that are past.

It is not to be concealed, however, that the maintenance of such a journal, under the circumstances, has been a work of much difficulty; and could all the perplexity, anxiety, and trouble attending it, have been clearly foreseen, I might have shrunk from the undertaking. As it is, I rejoice in having engaged in the enterprise, and count it joy to have been able to suffer, in many ways, for its success, and for the success of the cause to which it has been faithfully devoted. I look upon the time, money, and labor bestowed upon it, as being amply rewarded, in the development of my own mental and moral energies, and in the corresponding development of my deeply injured and oppressed people.

From motives of peace, instead of issuing my paper in Boston, among my New England friends, I came to Rochester, western New York, among strangers, where the circulation of my paper could not interfere with the local circulation of the *Liberator* and the *Standard;* for at that time I was, on the anti-slavery question, a faithful disciple of William Lloyd Garrison, and fully committed to his doctrine touching the pro-slavery character of the constitution of the United States, and the *non-voting principle,* of which he is the known and distinguished advocate. With Mr. Garrison, I held it to be the first duty of the non-slaveholding states to dissolve the union with the slaveholding states; and hence my cry, like his, was, "No union with slaveholders." With these views, I came into western New York; and during the first four years of my labor here, I advocated them with pen and tongue, according to the best of my ability.

About four years ago, upon a reconsideration of the whole subject, I became convinced that there was no necessity for dissolving the "union between the northern and southern states;" that to seek this dissolution was no part of my duty as an abolitionist; that to abstain from voting, was to refuse to exercise a legitimate and powerful means for abolishing slavery; and that the constitution of the United States not only contained no guarantees in favor of slavery, but, on the contrary, it is, in its letter and spirit, an anti-slavery instrument, demanding the abolition of slavery as a condition of its own existence, as the supreme law of the land.

Here was a radical change in my opinions, and in the action logically resulting from that change. To those with whom I had been in agreement and in sympathy, I was now in opposition. What they held to be a great and important truth, I now looked upon as a dangerous error. A very painful, and yet a very natural, thing now happened. Those who could not see any honest reasons for changing their views, as I had done, could not easily see any such reasons for my change, and the common punishment of apostates was mine.

The opinions first entertained were naturally derived and honestly entertained, and I trust that my present opinions have the same claims to respect. Brought directly, when I escaped from slavery, into contact with a class of abolitionists regarding the constitution as a slaveholding instrument, and finding their views supported by the united and entire history of every department of the government, it is not strange that I assumed the constitution to be just what their interpretation made it. I was bound, not only by their superior knowledge, to take their opinions as the true ones, in respect to the subject, but also because I had no means of showing their unsoundness. But for the responsibility of conducting a public journal, and the necessity imposed upon me of meeting opposite views from abolitionists in this state, I should in all probability have remained as firm in my disunion views as any other disciple of William Lloyd Garrison.

My new circumstances compelled me to re-think the whole subject, and to study, with some care, not only the just and proper rules of legal interpretation, but the origin, design, nature, rights, powers, and duties of civil government, and also the relations which human beings sustain to it. By such a course of thought and reading, I was conducted to the conclusion that the constitution of the United States—inaugurated "to form a more perfect union, establish justice, insure domestic tranquillity, provide for the common defense, promote the general welfare, and secure the blessing of liberty"—could not well have been designed at the same time to maintain and perpetuate a system of rapine and murder, like slavery; especially, as not one word can be found in the constitution to authorize such a belief. Then, again, if the declared purposes of an instrument are to govern the meaning of all its parts and details, as they clearly should, the constitution of our country is our warrant for the abolition of slavery in every state in the American Union. I mean, however, not to argue, but simply to state my views. It would require very many pages of a volume like this, to set forth the arguments demonstrating the unconstitutionality and the complete illegality of slavery in our land; and as my experience, and not my arguments, is within the scope and contemplation of this volume, I omit the latter and proceed with the former.

I will now ask the kind reader to go back a little in my story, while I bring up a thread left behind for convenience sake, but which, small as it is, cannot be properly omitted altogether; and that thread is American prejudice against color, and its varied illustrations in my own experience.

When I first went among the abolitionists of New England, and began to travel, I found this prejudice very strong and very annoying. The abolitionists themselves were not entirely free from it, and I could see that they were nobly struggling against it. In their eagerness, sometimes, to show their contempt for the feeling, they proved that they had not entirely recovered from it; often illustrating the saying, in their conduct, that a man may "stand up so straight as to lean backward." When it was said to me, "Mr. Douglass, I will walk to meeting with you; I am not afraid of a black man," I could not help thinking— seeing nothing very frightful in my appearance—"And why should you be?" The children at the north had all been educated to believe that if they were bad, the old *black* man—not the old *devil*—would get them; and it was evidence of some courage, for any so educated to get the better of their fears.

The custom of providing separate cars for the accommodation of colored travelers, was established on nearly all the railroads of New England, a dozen years ago. Regarding this custom as fostering the spirit of caste, I made it a rule to seat myself in the cars for the accommodation of passengers generally. Thus seated, I was sure to be called upon to betake myself to the *"Jim Crow car."* Refusing to obey, I was often dragged out of my seat, beaten, and severely bruised, by conductors and brakemen. Attempting to start from Lynn, one day, for Newburyport, on the Eastern railroad, I went, as my custom was, into one of the best railroad carriages on the road. The seats were very luxuriant and beautiful. I was soon waited upon by the conductor, and ordered out; whereupon I demanded the reason for my invidious removal. After a good deal of parleying, I was told that it was because I was black. This I denied, and appealed to the company to sustain my denial; but they were evidently unwilling to commit themselves, on a point so delicate, and requiring such nice powers of discrimination, for they remained as dumb as death. I was soon waited on by half a dozen fellows of the baser sort (just such as would volunteer to take a bull-dog out of a meeting-house in time of public worship), and told that I must move out of that seat, and if I did not, they would drag me out. I refused to move, and they clutched me, head, neck, and shoulders. But, in anticipation of the stretching to which I was about to be subjected, I had interwoven myself among the seats. In dragging me out, on this occasion, it must have cost the company twenty-five or thirty dollars, for I tore up seats and all. So great was the excitement in Lynn, on the subject, that the superintendent, Mr. Stephen A. Chase, ordered the trains to run through Lynn without stopping, while I remained in that town; and this ridiculous farce was enacted. For several days the trains went dashing through Lynn without stopping. At the same time that they excluded a free colored man from their cars, this same company allowed slaves, in company with their masters and mistresses, to ride unmolested.

After many battles with the railroad conductors, and being roughly handled in not a few instances, proscription was at last abandoned; and the "Jim Crow car"—set up for the degradation of colored people—is nowhere found in New England. This result was not brought about without the intervention of the people, and the threatened enactment of a law compelling railroad companies to respect the rights of travelers. Hon. Charles Francis Adams performed signal service in the Massachusetts legislature, in bringing this reformation; and to him the colored citizens of that state are deeply indebted.

Although often annoyed, and sometimes outraged, by this prejudice against color, I am indebted to it for many passages of quiet amusement. A half-cured subject of it is sometimes driven into awkward straits, especially if he happens to get a genuine specimen of the race into his house.

In the summer of 1843, I was traveling and lecturing, in company with William A. White, Esq., through the state of Indiana. Anti-slavery friends were not very abundant in Indiana, at that time, and beds were not more plentiful than friends. We often slept out, in preference to sleeping in the houses, at some points. At the close of one of our meetings, we were invited home with a kindly-disposed old farmer, who, in the generous enthusiasm of the moment, seemed to have forgotten that he had but one spare bed, and that his guests were an ill-matched pair. All went on pretty well, till near bed time, when signs of uneasiness began to show themselves, among the unsophisticated sons and daughters. White is remarkably fine looking, and very evidently a born gentleman; the idea of putting us in the same bed was hardly to be tolerated; and yet, there we were, and but the one bed for us, and that, by the way, was in the same room occupied by the other members of the family. White, as well as I, perceived the difficulty, for yonder slept the old folks, there the sons, and a little farther along slept the daughters; and but one other bed remained. Who should have this bed, was the puzzling question. There was some whispering between the old folks, some confused looks among the young, as the time for going to bed approached. After witnessing the confusion as long as I liked, I relieved the kindly-disposed family by playfully saying, "Friend White, having got entirely rid of my prejudice against color, I think, as a proof of it, I must allow you to sleep with me to-night." White kept up the joke, by seeming to esteem himself the favored party, and thus the difficulty was removed. If we went to a hotel, and called for dinner, the landlord was sure to set one table for White and another for me, always taking him to be master, and me the servant. Large eyes were generally made when the order was given to remove the dishes from my table to that of White's. In those days, it was thought strange that a white man and a colored man could dine peaceably at the same table, and in some parts the strangeness of such a sight has not entirely subsided.

Some people will have it that there is a natural, an inherent, and an invincible repugnance in the breast of the white race toward dark-colored people; and some very intelligent colored men think that their proscription is owing solely to the color which nature has given them. They hold that they are rated according to their color, and that it is impossible for white people ever to look upon dark races of men, or men belonging to the African race, with other than feelings of aversion. My experience, both serious and mirthful, combats this conclusion. Leaving out of sight, for a moment, grave facts, to this point, I will state one or two, which illustrate a very interesting feature of American character as well as American prejudice. Riding from Boston to Albany, a few years ago, I found myself in a large car, well filled with passengers. The seat next to me was about the only vacant one. At every stopping place we took in new passengers, all of whom, on reaching the seat next to me, cast a disdainful glance upon it, and passed to another car, leaving me in the full enjoyment of a hole form. For a time, I did not know but that my riding there was prejudicial to the interest of the railroad company. A circumstance occurred, however, which gave me an elevated position at once. Among the passengers on this train was Gov. George N. Briggs. I was not acquainted with him, and had no idea that I was known to him, however, I was, for upon observing me, the governor left his place, and making his way toward me, respectfully asked the privilege of a seat by my side; and upon introducing himself, we entered into a conversation very pleasant and instructive to me. The despised seat now became honored. His excellency had removed all the prejudice against sitting by the side of a Negro; and upon his leaving it, as he did, on reaching Pittsfield, there were at least one dozen applicants for the place. The governor had, without changing my skin a single shade, made the place respectable which before was despicable.

A similar incident happened to me once on the Boston and New Bedford railroad, and the leading party to it has since been governor of the state of Massachusetts. I allude to Col. John Henry Clifford. Lest the reader may fancy I am aiming to elevate myself, by claiming too much intimacy with great men, I must state that my only acquaintance with Col. Clifford was formed while I was *his hired servant*, during the first winter of my escape from slavery. I owe it him to say, that in that relation I found him always kind and gentlemanly. But to the incident. I entered a car at Boston, for New Bedford, which, with the exception of a single seat was full, and found I must occupy this, or stand up, during the journey. Having no mind to do this, I stepped up to the man having the next seat, and who had a few parcels on the seat, and gently asked leave to take a seat by his side. My fellow-passenger gave me a look made up of reproach and indignation, and asked me why I should come to that particular seat. I assured him, in the gentlest manner, that of all others this was the seat for me. Finding that I was actually about to sit down, he sang out, "O! stop, stop! and let me get out!" Suiting the action to the word, up the agitated man got, and sauntered to the other end of the car, and was compelled to stand for most of the way thereafter. Halfway to New Bedford, or more, Col. Clifford, recognizing me, left his seat, and not having seen me before since I had ceased to wait on him (in everything except hard arguments against his pro-slavery position), apparently forgetful of his rank, manifested, in greeting me, something of the feeling of an old friend. This demonstration was not lost on the gentleman whose dignity I had, an hour before, most seriously offended. Col. Clifford was known to be about the most aristocratic gentleman in Bristol county; and it was evidently thought that I must be somebody, else I should not have been thus noticed, by a person so distinguished. Sure enough, after Col. Clifford left me, I found myself surrounded with friends; and among the number, my offended friend stood nearest, and with an apology for his rudeness, which I could not resist, although it was one of the lamest ever offered. With such facts as these before me—and I have many of them—I am inclined to think that pride and fashion have much to do with the treatment commonly extended to colored people in the United States. I once heard a very plain man say (and he was cross-eyed, and awkwardly flung together in other respects) that he should be a handsome man when public opinion shall be changed.

Since I have been editing and publishing a journal devoted to the cause of liberty and progress, I have had my mind more directed to the condition and circumstances of the free colored people than when I was the agent of an abolition society. The result has been a corresponding change in the disposition of my time and labors. I have felt it to be a part of my mission—under a gracious Providence to impress my sable brothers in this country with the conviction that, notwithstanding the ten thousand discouragements and the powerful hinderances, which beset their existence in this country—notwithstanding the blood-written history of Africa, and her children, from whom we have descended, or the clouds and darkness (whose stillness and gloom are made only more awful by wrathful thunder and lightning) now overshadowing them—progress is yet possible, and bright skies shall yet shine upon their pathway; and that "Ethiopia shall yet reach forth her hand unto God."

Believing that one of the best means of emancipating the slaves of the south is to improve and elevate the character of the free colored people of the north I shall labor in the future, as I have labored in the past, to promote the moral, social, religious, and intellectual elevation of the free colored people; never forgetting my own humble orgin(sic), nor refusing, while Heaven lends me ability, to use my voice, my pen, or my vote, to advocate the great and primary work of the universal and unconditional emancipation of my entire race.

APPENDIX

RECEPTION SPEECH[*].

At Finsbury Chapel, Moorfields, England, May 12, 1846

Mr. Douglass rose amid loud cheers, and said: I feel exceedingly glad of the opportunity now afforded me of presenting the claims of my brethren in bonds in the United States, to so many in London and from various parts of Britain, who have assembled here on the present occasion. I have nothing to commend me to your consideration in the way of learning, nothing in the way of education, to entitle me to your attention; and you are aware that slavery is a very bad school for rearing teachers of morality and religion. Twenty-one years of my life have been spent in slavery—personal slavery—surrounded by degrading influences, such as can exist nowhere beyond the pale of slavery; and it will not be strange, if under such circumstances, I should betray, in what I have to say to you, a deficiency of that refinement which is seldom or ever found, except among persons that have experienced superior advantages to those which I have enjoyed. But I will take it for granted that you know something about the degrading influences of slavery, and that you will not expect great things from me this evening, but simply such facts as I may be able to advance immediately in connection with my own experience of slavery.

Now, what is this system of slavery? This is the subject of my lecture this evening—what is the character of this institution? I am about to answer the inquiry, what is American slavery? I do this the more readily, since I have found persons in this country who have identified the term slavery with that which I think it is not, and in some instances, I have feared, in so doing, have rather (unwittingly, I know) detracted much from the horror with which the term slavery is contemplated. It is common in this country to distinguish every bad

---

[*] Mr. Douglass' published speeches alone, would fill two volumes of the size of this. Our space will only permit the insertion of the extracts which follow; and which, for originality of thought, beauty and force of expression, and for impassioned, indignatory eloquence, have seldom been equaled.

thing by the name of slavery. Intemperance is slavery; to be deprived of the right to vote is slavery, says one; to have to work hard is slavery, says another; and I do not know but that if we should let them go on, they would say that to eat when we are hungry, to walk when we desire to have exercise, or to minister to our necessities, or have necessities at all, is slavery. I do not wish for a moment to detract from the horror with which the evil of intemperance is contemplated—not at all; nor do I wish to throw the slightest obstruction in the way of any political freedom that any class of persons in this country may desire to obtain. But I am here to say that I think the term slavery is sometimes abused by identifying it with that which it is not. Slavery in the United States is the granting of that power by which one man exercises and enforces a right of property in the body and soul of another. The condition of a slave is simply that of the brute beast. He is a piece of property—a marketable commodity, in the language of the law, to be bought or sold at the will and caprice of the master who claims him to be his property; he is spoken of, thought of, and treated as property. His own good, his conscience, his intellect, his affections, are all set aside by the master. The will and the wishes of the master are the law of the slave. He is as much a piece of property as a horse. If he is fed, he is fed because he is property. If he is clothed, it is with a view to the increase of his value as property. Whatever of comfort is necessary to him for his body or soul that is inconsistent with his being property, is carefully wrested from him, not only by public opinion, but by the law of the country. He is carefully deprived of everything that tends in the slightest degree to detract from his value as property. He is deprived of education. God has given him an intellect; the slaveholder declares it shall not be cultivated. If his moral perception leads him in a course contrary to his value as property, the slaveholder declares he shall not exercise it. The marriage institution cannot exist among slaves, and one-sixth of the population of democratic America is denied its privileges by the law of the land. What is to be thought of a nation boasting of its liberty, boasting of its humanity, boasting of its Christianity, boasting of its love of justice and purity, and yet having within its own borders three millions of persons denied by law the right of marriage?—what must be the condition of that people? I need not lift up the veil by giving you any experience of my own. Every one that can put two ideas together, must see the most fearful results from such a state of things as I have just mentioned. If any of these three millions find for themselves companions, and prove themselves honest, upright, virtuous persons to each other, yet in these cases—few as I am bound to confess they are—the virtuous live in constant apprehension of being torn asunder by the merciless men-stealers that claim them as their property. This is American slavery; no marriage—no education— the light of the gospel shut out from the dark mind of the bondman—and he forbidden by law to learn to read. If a mother shall teach her children to read, the law in Louisiana proclaims that she may be hanged by the neck. If the father attempt to give his son a knowledge of letters, he may be punished by the whip in one instance, and in another be killed, at the discretion of the court. Three millions of people shut out from the light of knowledge! It is easy for you to conceive the evil that must result from such a state of things.

I now come to the physical evils of slavery. I do not wish to dwell at length upon these, but it seems right to speak of them, not so much to influence your minds on this question, as to let the slaveholders of America know that the curtain which conceals their crimes is being lifted abroad; that we are opening the dark cell, and leading the people into the horrible recesses of what they are pleased to call their domestic institution. We want them to know that a knowledge of their whippings, their scourgings, their brandings, their chainings, is not confined to their plantations, but that some Negro of theirs has broken loose from his chains—has burst through the dark incrustation of slavery, and is now exposing their deeds of deep damnation to the gaze of the christian people of England.

The slaveholders resort to all kinds of cruelty. If I were disposed, I have matter enough to interest you on this question for five or six evenings, but I will not dwell at length upon these cruelties. Suffice it to say, that all of the peculiar modes of torture that were resorted to in the West India islands, are resorted to, I believe, even more frequently, in the United States of America. Starvation, the bloody whip, the chain, the gag, the thumb-screw, cat-hauling, the cat-o'-nine-tails, the dungeon, the blood-hound, are all in requisition to keep the slave in his condition as a slave in the United States. If any one has a doubt upon this point, I would ask him to read the chapter on slavery in Dickens's *Notes on America*. If any man has a doubt upon it, I have here the "testimony of a thousand witnesses," which I can give at any length, all going to prove the truth of my statement. The blood-hound is regularly trained in the United States, and advertisements are to be found in the southern papers of the Union, from persons advertising themselves as blood-hound trainers, and offering to hunt down slaves at fifteen dollars a piece, recommending their hounds as the fleetest in the neighborhood, never known to fail. Advertisements are from time to time inserted, stating that slaves have escaped with iron collars about their necks, with bands of iron about their feet, marked with the lash, branded with red-hot irons, the initials of their master's name burned into their flesh; and the masters advertise the fact of their being thus branded with their own signature, thereby proving to the world, that, however damning it may appear to non-slavers, such practices are not regarded discreditable among the slaveholders themselves. Why, I believe if a man should brand his horse in this country—burn the initials of his name into any of his cattle, and publish the ferocious deed here—that the united execrations of Christians in

Britain would descend upon him. Yet in the United States, human beings are thus branded. As Whittier says—

> ... Our countrymen in chains,
> The whip on woman's shrinking flesh,
> Our soil yet reddening with the stains
> Caught from her scourgings warm and fresh.

The slave-dealer boldly publishes his infamous acts to the world. Of all things that have been said of slavery to which exception has been taken by slaveholders, this, the charge of cruelty, stands foremost, and yet there is no charge capable of clearer demonstration, than that of the most barbarous inhumanity on the part of the slaveholders toward their slaves. And all this is necessary; it is necessary to resort to these cruelties, in order to *make the slave a slave*, and to *keep him a slave*. Why, my experience all goes to prove the truth of what you will call a marvelous proposition, that the better you treat a slave, the more you destroy his value *as a slave*, and enhance the probability of his eluding the grasp of the slaveholder; the more kindly you treat him, the more wretched you make him, while you keep him in the condition of a slave. My experience, I say, confirms the truth of this proposition. When I was treated exceedingly ill; when my back was being scourged daily; when I was whipped within an inch of my life—*life* was all I cared for. "Spare my life," was my continual prayer. When I was looking for the blow about to be inflicted upon my head, I was not thinking of my liberty; it was my life. But, as soon as the blow was not to be feared, then came the longing for liberty. If a slave has a bad master, his ambition is to get a better; when he gets a better, he aspires to have the best; and when he gets the best, he aspires to be his own master. But the slave must be brutalized to keep him as a slave. The slaveholder feels this necessity. I admit this necessity. If it be right to hold slaves at all, it is right to hold them in the only way in which they can be held; and this can be done only by shutting out the light of education from their minds, and brutalizing their persons. The whip, the chain, the gag, the thumb-screw, the blood-hound, the stocks, and all the other bloody paraphernalia of the slave system, are indispensably necessary to the relation of master and slave. The slave must be subjected to these, or he ceases to be a slave. Let him know that the whip is burned; that the fetters have been turned to some useful and profitable employment; that the chain is no longer for his limbs; that the blood-hound is no longer to be put upon his track; that his master's authority over him is no longer to be enforced by taking his life—and immediately he walks out from the house of bondage and asserts his freedom as a man. The slaveholder finds it necessary to have these implements to keep the slave in bondage; finds it necessary to be able to say, "Unless you do so and so; unless you do as I bid you—I will take away your life!"

Some of the most awful scenes of cruelty are constantly taking place in the middle states of the Union. We have in those states what are called the slave-breeding states. Allow me to speak plainly. Although it is harrowing to your feelings, it is necessary that the facts of the case should be stated. We have in the United States slave-breeding states. The very state from which the minister from our court to yours comes, is one of these states—Maryland, where men, women, and children are reared for the market, just as horses, sheep, and swine are raised for the market. Slave-rearing is there looked upon as a legitimate trade; the law sanctions it, public opinion upholds it, the church does not condemn it. It goes on in all its bloody horrors, sustained by the auctioneer's block. If you would see the cruelties of this system, hear the following narrative. Not long since the following scene occurred. A slave-woman and a slaveman had united themselves as man and wife in the absence of any law to protect them as man and wife. They had lived together by the permission, not by right, of their master, and they had reared a family. The master found it expedient, and for his interest, to sell them. He did not ask them their wishes in regard to the matter at all; they were not consulted. The man and woman were brought to the auctioneer's block, under the sound of the hammer. The cry was raised, "Here goes; who bids cash?" Think of it—a man and wife to be sold! The woman was placed on the auctioneer's block; her limbs, as is customary, were brutally exposed to the purchasers, who examined her with all the freedom with which they would examine a horse. There stood the husband, powerless; no right to his wife; the master's right preeminent. She was sold. He was next brought to the auctioneer's block. His eyes followed his wife in the distance; and he looked beseechingly, imploringly, to the man that had bought his wife, to buy him also. But he was at length bid off to another person. He was about to be separated forever from her he loved. No word of his, no work of his, could save him from this separation. He asked permission of his new master to go and take the hand of his wife at parting. It was denied him. In the agony of his soul he rushed from the man who had just bought him, that he might take a farewell of his wife; but his way was obstructed, he was struck over the head with a loaded whip, and was held for a moment; but his agony was too great. When he was let go, he fell a corpse at the feet of his master. His heart was broken. Such scenes are the everyday fruits of American slavery. Some two years since, the Hon. Seth. M. Gates, an anti-slavery gentleman of the state of New York, a representative in the congress of the United States, told me he saw with his own eyes the following circumstances. In the national District of Columbia, over which the star-spangled emblem is constantly waving, where orators are ever holding forth on the subject of American liberty, American democracy, American republicanism, there are two slave prisons. When going across a bridge, leading to one of these prisons, he saw a young woman run out, bare-footed and bare-headed, and with very little clothing on. She was running with all speed to the bridge he was approaching. His eye was fixed upon her, and he stopped to see what was the matter. He had not paused long before he saw three men run out after her. He now knew what the nature of the case was; a slave escaping from her chains—a young woman, a sister—escaping from the bondage in which she had been held. She made her way to the bridge, but had not reached, ere from the Virginia side there came two slaveholders. As soon as they saw them, her pursuers called out, "Stop her!" True to their Virginian instincts, they came to the rescue of their brother kidnappers, across the bridge. The poor girl now saw that there was no chance for her. It was a trying time. She knew if she went back, she must be a slave forever—she must be dragged down to the scenes of pollution which the slaveholders continually provide for most of the poor, sinking, wretched young women, whom they call their property. She formed her resolution; and just as those who were about to take her, were going to put hands upon her, to drag her back, she leaped over the balustrades of the bridge, and down she went to rise no more. She chose death, rather than to go back into the hands of those christian slaveholders from whom she had escaped.

Can it be possible that such things as these exist in the United States? Are not these the exceptions? Are any such scenes as this general? Are not such deeds condemned by the law and denounced by public opinion? Let me read to you a few of the laws of the slaveholding states of America. I think no better exposure of slavery can be made than is made by the laws of the states in which slavery exists. I prefer reading the laws to making any statement in confirmation of what I have said myself; for the slaveholders cannot object to this testimony, since it is the calm, the cool, the deliberate enactment of their wisest heads, of their most clear-sighted, their own constituted representatives. "If more than seven slaves together are found in any road without a white person, twenty lashes a piece; for visiting a plantation without a written pass, ten lashes; for letting loose a boat from where it is made fast, thirty-nine lashes for the first offense; and for the second, shall have cut off from his head one ear; for keeping or carrying a club, thirty-nine lashes; for having any article for sale, without a ticket from his master, ten lashes; for traveling in any other than the most usual and accustomed road, when going alone to any place, forty lashes; for traveling in the night without a pass, forty lashes." I am afraid you do not understand the awful character of these lashes. You must bring it before your mind. A human being in a perfect state of nudity, tied hand and foot to a stake, and a strong man standing behind with a heavy whip, knotted at the end, each blow cutting into the flesh, and leaving the warm blood dripping to the feet; and for these trifles. "For being found in another person's negro-quarters, forty lashes; for hunting with dogs in the woods, thirty lashes; for being on horseback without the written permission of his master, twenty-five lashes; for riding or going abroad in the night, or riding horses in the day time, without leave, a slave may be whipped, cropped, or branded in the cheek with the letter R. or otherwise punished, such punishment not extending to life, or so as to render him unfit for labor." The laws referred to, may be found by consulting *Brevard's Digest; Haywood's Manual; Virginia Revised Code; Prince's Digest; Missouri Laws; Mississippi Revised Code.* A man, for going to visit his brethren, without the permission of his master—and in many instances he may not have that permission; his master, from caprice or other reasons, may not be willing to allow it—may be caught on his way, dragged to a post, the branding-iron heated, and the name of his master or the letter R branded into his cheek or on his forehead. They treat slaves thus, on the principle that they must punish for light offenses, in order to prevent the commission of larger ones. I wish you to mark that in the single state of Virginia there are seventy-one crimes for which a colored man may be executed; while there are only three of these crimes, which, when committed by a white man, will subject him to that punishment. There are many of these crimes which if the white man did not commit, he would be regarded as a scoundrel and a coward. In the state of Maryland, there is a law to this effect: that if a slave shall strike his master, he may be hanged, his head severed from his body, his body quartered, and his head and quarters set up in the most prominent places in the neighborhood. If a colored woman, in the defense of her own virtue, in defense of her own person, should shield herself from the brutal attacks of her tyrannical master, or make the slightest resistance, she may be killed on the spot. No law whatever will bring the guilty man to justice for the crime.

But you will ask me, can these things be possible in a land professing Christianity? Yes, they are so; and this is not the worst. No; a darker feature is yet to be presented than the mere existence of these facts. I have to inform you that the religion of the southern states, at this time, is the great supporter, the great sanctioner of the bloody atrocities to which I have referred. While America is printing tracts and bibles; sending missionaries abroad to convert the heathen; expending her money in various ways for the promotion of the gospel in foreign lands—the slave not only lies forgotten, uncared for, but is trampled under foot by the very churches of the land. What have we in America? Why, we have slavery made part of the religion of the land. Yes, the pulpit there stands up as the great defender of this cursed *institution*, as it is called. Ministers of religion come forward and torture the hallowed pages of inspired wisdom to sanction the bloody deed. They stand forth as the foremost, the strongest defenders of this "institution." As a proof of this, I need not do more than state the general fact, that slavery has existed under the droppings of the sanctuary of the south for the last two hundred years, and there has not been any war between the *religion* and the *slavery* of the south. Whips, chains, gags, and thumb-screws have all lain under the droppings of the sanctuary, and instead of rusting from off the limbs of the bondman, those droppings have served to preserve them in all their strength. Instead of preaching the gospel against this tyranny, rebuke, and wrong, ministers of religion have sought, by all and every means, to throw in the back-ground whatever in the bible could be construed into opposition to slavery, and to bring forward that which they could torture into its support. This I conceive to be the darkest feature of slavery, and the most difficult to attack, because it is identified with religion, and exposes those who denounce it to the charge of infidelity. Yes, those with whom I have been laboring, namely, the old organization anti-slavery society of America, have been again and again stigmatized as infidels, and for what reason? Why, solely in consequence of the faithfulness of their attacks upon the slaveholding religion of the southern states, and the northern religion that sympathizes with it. I have found it difficult to speak on this matter without persons coming forward and saying, "Douglass, are you not afraid of injuring the cause of Christ? You do not desire to do so, we know; but are you not undermining religion?" This has been said to me again and again, even since I came to this country, but I cannot be induced to leave off these exposures. I love the religion of our blessed Savior. I love that religion that comes from above, in the "wisdom of God," which is first pure, then peaceable, gentle, and easy to be entreated, full of mercy and good fruits, without partiality and without hypocrisy. I love that religion that sends its votaries to bind up the wounds of him that has fallen among thieves. I love that religion that makes it the duty of its disciples to visit the father less and the widow in their affliction. I love that religion that is based upon the glorious principle, of love to God and love to man; which makes its followers do unto others as they themselves would be done by. If you demand liberty to yourself, it says, grant it to your neighbors. If you claim a right to think for yourself, it says, allow your neighbors the same right. If you claim to act for yourself, it says, allow your neighbors the same right. It is because I love this religion that I hate the slaveholding, the woman-whipping, the mind-darkening, the soul-destroying religion that exists in the southern states of America. It is because I regard the one as good, and pure, and holy, that I cannot but regard the other as bad, corrupt, and wicked. Loving the one I must hate the other; holding to the one I must reject the other.

I may be asked, why I am so anxious to bring this subject before the British public—why I do not confine my efforts to the United States? My answer is, first, that slavery is the common enemy of mankind, and all mankind should be made acquainted with its abominable character. My next answer is, that the slave is a man, and, as such, is entitled to your sympathy as a brother. All the feelings, all the susceptibilities, all the capacities, which you have, he has. He is a part of the human family. He has been the prey—the common prey—of Christendom for the last three hundred years, and it is but right, it is but just, it is but proper, that his wrongs should be known throughout the world. I have another reason for bringing this matter before the British public, and it is this: slavery is a system of wrong, so blinding to all around, so hardening to the heart, so corrupting to the morals, so deleterious to religion, so sapping to all the principles of justice in its immediate vicinity, that the community surrounding it lack the moral stamina necessary to its removal. It is a system of such gigantic evil, so strong, so overwhelming in its power, that no one nation is equal to its removal. It requires the humanity of Christianity, the morality of the world to remove it. Hence, I call upon the people of Britain to look at this matter, and to exert the influence I am about to show they possess, for the removal of slavery from America. I can appeal to them, as strongly by their regard for the slaveholder as for the slave, to labor in this cause. I am here, because you have an influence on America that no other nation can have. You have been drawn together by the power of steam to a marvelous extent; the distance between London and Boston is now reduced to some twelve or fourteen days, so that the denunciations against slavery, uttered in London this week, may be heard in a fortnight in the streets of Boston, and reverberating amidst the hills of Massachusetts. There is nothing said here against slavery that will not be recorded in the United States. I am here, also, because the slaveholders do not want me to be here; they would rather that I were not here. I have adopted a maxim laid down by Napoleon, never to occupy ground which the enemy would like me to occupy. The slaveholders would much rather have me, if I will denounce slavery, denounce it in the northern states, where their friends and supporters are, who will stand by and mob me for denouncing it. They feel something as the man felt, when he uttered his prayer, in which he made out a most horrible case for himself, and one of his neighbors touched him and said, "My friend, I always had the opinion of you that you have now expressed for yourself—that you are a very great sinner." Coming from himself, it was all very well, but coming from a stranger it was rather cutting. The slaveholders felt that when slavery was denounced among themselves, it was not so bad; but let one of the slaves get loose, let him summon the people of Britain, and make known to them the conduct of the slaveholders toward their slaves, and it cuts them to the quick, and produces a sensation such as would be produced by nothing else. The power I exert now is something like the power that is exerted by the man at the end of the lever; my influence now is just in proportion to the distance that I am from the United States. My exposure of slavery abroad will tell more upon the hearts and consciences of slaveholders, than if I was attacking them in America; for almost every paper that I now receive from the United States, comes teeming with statements about this fugitive Negro, calling him a "glib-tongued scoundrel," and saying that he is running out against the institutions and people of America. I deny the charge that I am saying a word against the institutions of America, or the people, as such. What I have to say is against slavery and slaveholders. I feel at liberty to speak on this subject. I have on my back the marks of the lash; I have four sisters and one brother now under the galling chain. I feel it my duty to cry aloud and spare not. I am not averse to having the good opinion of my fellow creatures. I am not averse to being kindly regarded by all men; but I am bound, even at the hazard of making a large class of religionists in this country hate me, oppose me, and malign me as they have done—I am bound by the prayers, and tears, and entreaties of three millions of kneeling bondsmen, to have no compromise with men who are in any shape or form connected with the slaveholders of America. I expose slavery in this country, because to expose it is to kill it. Slavery is one of those monsters of darkness to whom the light of truth is death. Expose slavery, and it dies. Light is to slavery what the heat of the sun is to the root of a tree; it must die under it. All the slaveholder asks of me is silence. He does not ask me to go abroad and preach *in favor* of slavery; he does not ask any one to do that. He would not say that slavery is a good thing, but the best under the circumstances. The slaveholders want total darkness on the subject. They want the hatchway shut down, that the monster may crawl in his den of darkness, crushing human hopes and happiness, destroying the bondman at will, and having no one to reprove or rebuke him. Slavery shrinks from the light; it hateth the light, neither cometh to the light, lest its deeds should be reproved. To tear off the mask from this abominable system, to expose it to the light of heaven, aye, to the heat of the sun, that it may burn and wither it out of existence, is my object in coming to this country. I want the slaveholder surrounded, as by a wall of anti-slavery fire, so that he may see the condemnation of himself and his system glaring down in letters of light. I want him to feel that he has no sympathy in England, Scotland, or Ireland; that he has none in Canada, none in Mexico, none among the poor wild Indians; that the voice of the civilized, aye, and savage world is against him. I would have condemnation blaze down upon him in every direction, till, stunned and overwhelmed with shame and confusion, he is compelled to let go the grasp he holds upon the persons of his victims, and restore them to their long-lost rights.

Dr. Campbell's Reply

From Rev. Dr. Campbell's brilliant reply we extract the following: FREDERICK DOUGLASS, "the beast of burden," the portion of "goods and chattels," the representative of three millions of men, has been raised up! Shall I say the *man?* If there is a man on earth, he is a man. My blood boiled within me when I heard his address tonight, and thought that he had left behind him three millions of such men.

We must see more of this man; we must have more of this man. One would have taken a voyage round the globe some forty years back—especially since the introduction of steam—to have heard such an exposure of slavery from the lips of a slave. It will be an era in the individual history of the present assembly. Our children—our boys and girls—I have tonight seen the delightful sympathy of their hearts evinced by their heaving breasts, while their eyes sparkled with wonder and admiration, that this black man—this slave—had so much logic, so much wit, so much fancy, so much eloquence. He was something more than a man, according to their little notions. Then, I say, we must hear him again. We have got a purpose to accomplish. He has appealed to the pulpit of England. The English pulpit is with him. He has appealed to the press of England; the press of England is conducted by English hearts, and that press will do him justice. About ten days hence, and his second master, who may well prize "such a piece of goods," will have the pleasure of reading his burning words, and his first master will bless himself that he has got quit of him. We have to create public opinion, or rather, not to create it, for it is created already; but we have to foster it; and when tonight I heard those magnificent words—the words of Curran, by which my heart, from boyhood, has ofttimes been deeply moved—I rejoice to think that they embody an instinct of an Englishman's nature. I heard, with inexpressible delight, how they told on this mighty mass of the citizens of the metropolis.

Britain has now no slaves; we can therefore talk to the other nations now, as we could not have talked a dozen years ago. I want the whole of the London ministry to meet Douglass. For as his appeal is to England, and throughout England, I should rejoice in the idea of churchmen and dissenters merging all sectional distinctions in this cause. Let us have a public breakfast. Let the ministers meet him; let them hear him; let them grasp his hand; and let him enlist their sympathies on behalf of the slave. Let him inspire them with abhorrence of the man-stealer—the slaveholder. No slaveholding American shall ever my cross my door. No slaveholding or slavery-supporting minister shall ever pollute my pulpit. While I have a tongue to speak, or a hand to write, I will, to the utmost of my power, oppose these slaveholding men. We must have Douglass amongst us to aid in fostering public opinion.

The great conflict with slavery must now take place in America; and while they are adding other slave states to the Union, our business is to step forward and help the abolitionists there. It is a pleasing circumstance that such a body of men has risen in America, and whilst we hurl our thunders against her slavers, let us make a distinction between those who advocate slavery and those who oppose it. George Thompson has been there. This man, Frederick Douglass, has been there, and has been compelled to flee. I wish, when he first set foot on our shores, he had made a solemn vow, and said, "Now that I am free, and in the sanctuary of freedom, I will never return till I have seen the emancipation of my country completed." He wants to surround these men, the slaveholders, as by a wall of fire; and he himself may do much toward kindling it. Let him travel over the island—east, west, north, and south—everywhere diffusing knowledge and awakening principle, till the whole nation become a body of petitioners to America. He will, he must, do it. He must for a season make England his home. He must send for his wife. He must send for his children. I want to see the sons and daughters of such a sire. We, too, must do something for him and them worthy of the English name. I do not like the idea of a man of such mental dimensions, such moral courage, and all but incomparable talent, having his own small wants, and the wants of a distant wife and children, supplied by the poor profits of his publication, the sketch of his life. Let the pamphlet be bought by tens of thousands. But we will do something more for him, shall we not?

It only remains that we pass a resolution of thanks to Frederick Douglass, the slave that was, the man that is! He that was covered with chains, and that is now being covered with glory, and whom we will send back a gentleman.

LETTER TO HIS OLD MASTER.*.

To My Old Master, Thomas Auld

SIR—The long and intimate, though by no means friendly, relation which unhappily subsisted between you and myself, leads me to hope that you will easily account for the great liberty which I now take in addressing you in this open and public manner. The same fact may remove any disagreeable surprise which you may experience on again finding your name coupled with mine, in any other way than in an advertisement, accurately describing my person, and offering a large sum for my arrest. In thus dragging you again before the public, I am aware that I shall subject myself to no inconsiderable amount of censure. I shall probably be charged with an unwarrantable, if not a wanton and reckless disregard of the rights and properties of private life. There are those north as well as south who entertain a much higher respect for rights which are merely conventional, than they do for rights which are personal and essential. Not a few there are in our country, who, while they have no scruples against robbing the laborer of the hard earned results of his patient industry, will be shocked by the extremely indelicate manner of bringing your name before the public. Believing this to be the case, and wishing to meet every reasonable or plausible objection to my conduct, I will frankly state the ground upon which I justfy(sic) myself in this instance, as well as on former occasions when I have thought proper to mention your name in public. All will agree that a man guilty of theft, robbery, or murder, has forfeited the right to concealment and private life; that the community have a right to subject such persons to the most complete exposure. However much they may desire retirement, and aim to conceal themselves and their movements from the popular gaze, the public have a right to ferret them out, and bring their conduct before the proper tribunals of the country for investigation. Sir, you will undoubtedly make the proper application of these generally admitted principles, and will easily see the light in which you are regarded by me; I will not therefore manifest ill temper, by calling you hard

---

* It is not often that chattels address their owners. The following letter is unique; and probably the only specimen of the kind extant. It was written while in England.

names. I know you to be a man of some intelligence, and can readily determine the precise estimate which I entertain of your character. I may therefore indulge in language which may seem to others indirect and ambiguous, and yet be quite well understood by yourself.

I have selected this day on which to address you, because it is the anniversary of my emancipation; and knowing no better way, I am led to this as the best mode of celebrating that truly important events. Just ten years ago this beautiful September morning, yon bright sun beheld me a slave—a poor degraded chattel—trembling at the sound of your voice, lamenting that I was a man, and wishing myself a brute. The hopes which I had treasured up for weeks of a safe and successful escape from your grasp, were powerfully confronted at this last hour by dark clouds of doubt and fear, making my person shake and my bosom to heave with the heavy contest between hope and fear. I have no words to describe to you the deep agony of soul which I experienced on that never-to-be-forgotten morning—for I left by daylight. I was making a leap in the dark. The probabilities, so far as I could by reason determine them, were stoutly against the undertaking. The preliminaries and precautions I had adopted previously, all worked badly. I was like one going to war without weapons—ten chances of defeat to one of victory. One in whom I had confided, and one who had promised me assistance, appalled by fear at the trial hour, deserted me, thus leaving the responsibility of success or failure solely with myself. You, sir, can never know my feelings. As I look back to them, I can scarcely realize that I have passed through a scene so trying. Trying, however, as they were, and gloomy as was the prospect, thanks be to the Most High, who is ever the God of the oppressed, at the moment which was to determine my whole earthly career, His grace was sufficient; my mind was made up. I embraced the golden opportunity, took the morning tide at the flood, and a free man, young, active, and strong, is the result.

I have often thought I should like to explain to you the grounds upon which I have justified myself in running away from you. I am almost ashamed to do so now, for by this time you may have discovered them yourself. I will, however, glance at them. When yet but a child about six years old, I imbibed the determination to run away. The very first mental effort that I now remember on my part, was an attempt to solve the mystery—why am I a slave? and with this question my youthful mind was troubled for many days, pressing upon me more heavily at times than others. When I saw the slave-driver whip a slave-woman, cut the blood out of her neck, and heard her piteous cries, I went away into the corner of the fence, wept and pondered over the mystery. I had, through some medium, I know not what, got some idea of God, the Creator of all mankind, the black and the white, and that he had made the blacks to serve the whites as slaves. How he could do this and be *good*, I could not tell. I was not satisfied with this theory, which made God responsible for slavery, for it pained me greatly, and I have wept over it long and often. At one time, your first wife, Mrs. Lucretia, heard me sighing and saw me shedding tears, and asked of me the matter, but I was afraid to tell her. I was puzzled with this question, till one night while sitting in the kitchen, I heard some of the old slaves talking of their parents having been stolen from Africa by white men, and were sold here as slaves. The whole mystery was solved at once. Very soon after this, my Aunt Jinny and Uncle Noah ran away, and the great noise made about it by your father-in-law, made me for the first time acquainted with the fact, that there were free states as well as slave states. From that time, I resolved that I would some day run away. The morality of the act I dispose of as follows: I am myself; you are yourself; we are two distinct persons, equal persons. What you are, I am. You are a man, and so am I. God created both, and made us separate beings. I am not by nature bond to you, or you to me. Nature does not make your existence depend upon me, or mine to depend upon yours. I cannot walk upon your legs, or you upon mine. I cannot breathe for you, or you for me; I must breathe for myself, and you for yourself. We are distinct persons, and are each equally provided with faculties necessary to our individual existence. In leaving you, I took nothing but what belonged to me, and in no way lessened your means for obtaining an *honest* living. Your faculties remained yours, and mine became useful to their rightful owner. I therefore see no wrong in any part of the transaction. It is true, I went off secretly; but that was more your fault than mine. Had I let you into the secret, you would have defeated the enterprise entirely; but for this, I should have been really glad to have made you acquainted with my intentions to leave.

You may perhaps want to know how I like my present condition. I am free to say, I greatly prefer it to that which I occupied in Maryland. I am, however, by no means prejudiced against the state as such. Its geography, climate, fertility, and products, are such as to make it a very desirable abode for any man; and but for the existence of slavery there, it is not impossible that I might again take up my abode in that state. It is not that I love Maryland less, but freedom more. You will be surprised to learn that people at the north labor under the strange delusion that if the slaves were emancipated at the south, they would flock to the north. So far from this being the case, in that event, you would see many old and familiar faces back again to the south. The fact is, there are few here who would not return to the south in the event of emancipation. We want to live in the land of our birth, and to lay our bones by the side of our fathers; and nothing short of an intense love of personal freedom keeps us from the south. For the sake of this, most of us would live on a crust of bread and a cup of cold water.

Since I left you, I have had a rich experience. I have occupied stations which I never dreamed of when a slave. Three out of the ten years since I left you, I spent as a common laborer on the wharves of New Bedford, Massachusetts. It was there I earned my first free dollar. It was mine. I could spend it as I pleased. I could buy hams or herring with it, without asking any odds of anybody. That was a precious dollar to me. You remember when I used to make seven, or eight, or even nine dollars a week in Baltimore, you would take every cent of it from me every Saturday night, saying that I belonged to you, and my earnings also. I never liked this conduct on your part—to say the best, I thought it a little mean. I would not have served you so. But let that pass. I was a little awkward about counting money in New England fashion when I first landed in New Bedford. I came near betraying myself several times. I caught myself saying phip, for fourpence; and at one time a man actually charged me with being a runaway, whereupon I was silly enough to become one by running away from him, for I was greatly afraid he might adopt measures to get me again into slavery, a condition I then dreaded more than death.

I soon learned, however, to count money, as well as to make it, and got on swimmingly. I married soon after leaving you; in fact, I was engaged to be married before I left you; and instead of finding my companion a burden, she was truly a helpmate. She went to live at service, and I to work on the wharf, and though we toiled hard the first winter, we never lived more happily. After remaining in New Bedford for three years, I met with William Lloyd Garrison, a person of whom you have *possibly* heard, as he is pretty generally known among slaveholders. He put it into my head that I might make myself serviceable to the cause of the slave, by devoting a portion of my time to telling my own sorrows, and those of other slaves, which had come under my observation. This was the commencement of a higher state of existence than any to which I had ever aspired. I was thrown into society the most pure, enlightened, and benevolent, that the country affords. Among these I have never forgotten you, but have invariably made you the topic of conversation—thus giving you all the notoriety I could do. I need not tell you that the opinion formed of you in these circles is far from being favorable. They have little respect for your honesty, and less for your religion.

But I was going on to relate to you something of my interesting experience. I had not long enjoyed the excellent society to which I have referred, before the light of its excellence exerted a beneficial influence on my mind and heart. Much of my early dislike of white persons was removed, and their manners, habits, and customs, so entirely unlike what I had been used to in the kitchen-quarters on the plantations of the south, fairly charmed me, and gave me a strong disrelish for the coarse and degrading customs of my former condition. I therefore made an effort so to improve my mind and deportment, as to be somewhat fitted to the station to which I seemed almost providentially called. The transition from degradation to respectability was indeed great, and to get from one to the other without carrying some marks of one's former condition, is truly a difficult matter. I would not have you think that I am now entirely clear of all plantation peculiarities, but my friends here, while they entertain the strongest dislike to them, regard me with that charity to which my past life somewhat entitles me, so that my condition in this respect is exceedingly pleasant. So far as my domestic affairs are concerned, I can boast of as comfortable a dwelling as your own. I have an industrious and neat companion, and four dear children—the oldest a girl of nine years, and three fine boys, the oldest eight, the next six, and the youngest four years old. The three oldest are now going regularly to school—two can read and write, and the other can spell, with tolerable correctness, words of two syllables. Dear fellows! they are all in comfortable beds, and are sound asleep, perfectly secure under my own roof. There are no slaveholders here to rend my heart by snatching them from my arms, or blast a mother's dearest hopes by tearing them from her bosom. These dear children are ours—not to work up into rice, sugar, and tobacco, but to watch over, regard, and protect, and to rear them up in the nurture and admonition of the gospel—to train them up in the paths of wisdom and virtue, and, as far as we can, to make them useful to the world and to themselves. Oh! sir, a slaveholder never appears to me so completely an agent of hell, as when I think of and look upon my dear children. It is then that my feelings rise above my control. I meant to have said more with respect to my own prosperity and happiness, but thoughts and feelings which this recital has quickened, unfit me to proceed further in that direction. The grim horrors of slavery rise in all their ghastly terror before me; the wails of millions pierce my heart and chill my blood. I remember the chain, the gag, the bloody whip; the death-like gloom overshadowing the broken spirit of the fettered bondman; the appalling liability of his being torn away from wife and children, and sold like a beast in the market. Say not that this is a picture of fancy. You well know that I wear stripes on my back, inflicted by your direction; and that you, while we were brothers in the same church, caused this right hand, with which I am now penning this letter, to be closely tied to my left, and my person dragged, at the pistol's mouth, fifteen miles, from the Bay Side to Easton, to be sold like a beast in the market, for the alleged crime of intending to escape from your possession. All this, and more, you remember, and know to be perfectly true, not only of yourself, but of nearly all of the slaveholders around you.

At this moment, you are probably the guilty holder of at least three of my own dear sisters, and my only brother, in bondage. These you regard as your property. They are recorded on your ledger, or perhaps have been sold to human flesh-mongers, with a view to filling our own ever-hungry purse. Sir, I desire to know how and where these dear sisters are. Have you sold them? or are they still in your possession? What has become of them? are they living or dead? And my dear old grandmother, whom you turned out like an old horse to die in the woods—is she still alive? Write and let me know all about them. If my grandmother be still alive, she is of no service to you, for by this time she must be nearly eighty years old—too old to be cared for by one to whom she has ceased to be of service; send her to me at Rochester, or bring her to Philadelphia, and it shall be the crowning happiness of my life to take care of her in her old age. Oh! she was to me a mother and a father, so far as hard toil for my comfort could make her such. Send me my grandmother! that I may watch over and take care of her in her old age. And my sisters—let me know all about them. I would write to them, and learn all I want to know of them, without disturbing you in any way, but that, through your unrighteous conduct, they have been entirely deprived of the power to read and write. You have kept them in utter ignorance, and have therefore robbed them of the sweet enjoyments of writing or receiving letters from absent friends and relatives. Your wickedness and cruelty, committed in this respect on your fellow-creatures, are greater than all the stripes you have laid upon my back or theirs. It is an outrage upon the soul, a war upon the immortal spirit, and one for which you must give account at the bar of our common Father and Creator.

The responsibility which you have assumed in this regard is truly awful, and how you could stagger under it these many years is marvelous. Your mind must have become darkened, your heart hardened, your conscience seared and petrified, or you would have long since thrown off the accursed load, and sought relief at the hands of a sin-forgiving God. How, let me ask, would you look upon me, were I, some dark night, in company with a band of hardened villains, to enter the precincts of your elegant dwelling, and seize the person of your own lovely daughter, Amanda, and carry her off from your family, friends, and all the loved ones of her youth—make her my slave—compel her to work, and I take her wages—place her name on my ledger as property—disregard her personal rights—fetter the powers of her immortal soul by denying her the right and privilege of learning to read and write—feed her coarsely—clothe her scantily, and whip her on the naked back occasionally; more, and still more horrible, leave her unprotected—a degraded victim to the brutal lust of fiendish overseers, who would pollute, blight, and blast her fair soul—rob her of all dignity—destroy her virtue, and annihilate in her person all the graces that adorn the character of virtuous womanhood? I ask, how would you regard me, if such were my conduct? Oh! the vocabulary of the damned would not afford a word sufficiently infernal to express your idea of my God-provoking wickedness. Yet, sir, your treatment of my beloved sisters is in all essential points precisely like the case I have now supposed. Damning as would be such a deed on my part, it would be no more so than that which you have committed against me and my sisters.

I will now bring this letter to a close; you shall hear from me again unless you let me hear from you. I intend to make use of you as a weapon with which to assail the system of slavery—as a means of concentrating public attention on the system, and deepening the horror of trafficking in the souls and bodies of men. I shall make use of you as a means of exposing the character of the American church and clergy—and as a means of bringing this guilty nation, with yourself, to repentance. In doing this, I entertain no malice toward you personally. There is no roof under which you would be more safe than mine, and there is nothing in my house which you might need for your comfort, which I would not readily grant. Indeed, I should esteem it a privilege to set you an example as to how mankind ought to treat each other.

I am your fellow-man, but not your slave.

THE NATURE OF SLAVERY.

Extract from a Lecture on Slavery, at Rochester, December 1, 1850

More than twenty years of my life were consumed in a state of slavery. My childhood was environed by the baneful peculiarities of the slave system. I grew up to manhood in the presence of this hydra headed monster—not as a master—not as an idle spectator—not as the guest of the slaveholder—but as A SLAVE, eating the bread and drinking the cup of slavery with the most degraded of my brother-bondmen, and sharing with them all the painful conditions of their wretched lot. In consideration of these facts, I feel that I have a right to speak, and to speak *strongly*. Yet, my friends, I feel bound to speak truly.

Goading as have been the cruelties to which I have been subjected—bitter as have been the trials through which I have passed—exasperating as have been, and still are, the indignities offered to my manhood—I find in them no excuse for the slightest departure from truth in dealing with any branch of this subject.

First of all, I will state, as well as I can, the legal and social relation of master and slave. A master is one—to speak in the vocabulary of the southern states—who claims and exercises a right of property in the person of a fellow-man. This he does with the force of the law and the sanction of southern religion. The law gives the master absolute power over the slave. He may work him, flog him, hire him out, sell him, and, in certain contingencies, *kill* him, with perfect impunity. The slave is a human being, divested of all rights—reduced to the level of a brute—a mere "chattel" in the eye of the law—placed beyond the circle of human brotherhood—cut off from his kind—his name, which the "recording angel" may have enrolled in heaven, among the blest, is impiously inserted in a *master's ledger*, with horses, sheep, and swine. In law, the slave has no wife, no children, no country, and no home. He can own nothing, possess nothing, acquire nothing, but what must belong to another. To eat the fruit of his own toil, to clothe his person with the work of his own hands, is considered stealing. He toils that another may reap the fruit; he is industrious that another may live in idleness; he eats unbolted meal that another may eat the bread of fine flour; he labors in chains at home, under a burning sun and biting lash, that another may ride in ease and splendor abroad; he lives in ignorance that another may be educated; he is abused that another may be exalted; he rests his toil-worn limbs on the cold, damp ground that another may repose on the softest pillow; he is clad in coarse and tattered raiment that another may be arrayed in purple and fine linen; he is sheltered only by the wretched hovel that a master may dwell in a magnificent mansion; and to this condition he is bound down as by an arm of iron.

From this monstrous relation there springs an unceasing stream of most revolting cruelties. The very accompaniments of the slave system stamp it as the offspring of hell itself. To ensure good behavior, the slaveholder relies on the whip; to induce proper humility, he relies on the whip; to rebuke what he is pleased to term insolence, he relies on the whip; to supply the place of wages as an incentive to toil, he relies on the whip; to bind down the spirit of the slave, to imbrute and destroy his manhood, he relies on the whip, the chain, the gag, the thumb-screw, the pillory, the bowie knife the pistol, and the blood-hound. These are the necessary and unvarying accompaniments of the system. Wherever slavery is found, these horrid instruments are also found. Whether on the coast of Africa, among the savage tribes, or in South Carolina, among the refined and civilized, slavery is the same, and its accompaniments one and the same. It makes no difference whether the slaveholder worships the God of the Christians, or is a follower of Mahomet, he is the minister of the same cruelty, and the author of the same misery. *Slavery* is always *slavery;* always the same foul, haggard, and damning scourge, whether found in the eastern or in the western hemisphere.

There is a still deeper shade to be given to this picture. The physical cruelties are indeed sufficiently harassing and revolting; but they are as a few grains of sand on the sea shore, or a few drops of water in the great ocean, compared with the stupendous wrongs which it inflicts upon the mental, moral, and religious nature of its hapless victims. It is only when we contemplate the slave as a moral and intellectual being, that we can adequately comprehend the unparalleled enormity of slavery, and the intense criminality of the slaveholder. I have said that the slave was a man. "What a piece of work is man! How noble in reason! How infinite in faculties! In form and moving how express and admirable! In action how like an angel! In apprehension how like a God! The beauty of the world! The paragon of animals!"

The slave is a man, "the image of God," but "a little lower than the angels;" possessing a soul, eternal and indestructible; capable of endless happiness, or immeasurable woe; a creature of hopes and fears, of affections and passions, of joys and sorrows, and he is endowed with those mysterious powers by which man soars above the things of time and sense, and grasps, with undying tenacity, the elevating and sublimely glorious idea of a God. It is *such* a being that is smitten and blasted. The first work of slavery is to mar and deface those characteristics of its victims which distinguish *men* from *things*, and *persons* from *property*. Its first aim is to destroy all sense of high moral and religious responsibility. It reduces man to a mere machine. It cuts him off from his Maker, it hides from him the laws of God, and leaves him to grope his way from time to eternity in the dark, under the arbitrary and despotic control of a frail, depraved, and sinful fellow-man. As the serpent-charmer of India is compelled to extract the deadly teeth of his venomous prey before he is able to handle him with impunity, so the slaveholder must strike down the conscience of the slave before he can obtain the entire mastery over his victim.

It is, then, the first business of the enslaver of men to blunt, deaden, and destroy the central principle of human responsibility. Conscience is, to the individual soul, and to society, what the law of gravitation is to the universe. It holds society together; it is the basis of all trust and confidence; it is the pillar of all moral rectitude. Without it, suspicion would take the place of trust; vice would be more than a match for virtue; men would prey upon each other, like the wild beasts of the desert; and earth would become a *hell*.

Nor is slavery more adverse to the conscience than it is to the mind. This is shown by the fact, that in every state of the American Union, where slavery exists, except the state of Kentucky, there are laws absolutely prohibitory of education among the slaves. The crime of teaching a slave to read is punishable with severe fines and imprisonment, and, in some instances, with *death itself.*

Nor are the laws respecting this matter a dead letter. Cases may occur in which they are disregarded, and a few instances may be found where slaves may have learned to read; but such are isolated cases, and only prove the rule. The great mass of slaveholders look upon education among the slaves as utterly subversive of the slave system. I well remember when my mistress first announced to my master that she had discovered that I could read. His face colored at once with surprise and chagrin. He said that "I was ruined, and my value as a slave destroyed; that a slave should know nothing but to obey his master; that to give a negro an inch would lead him to take an ell; that having learned how to read, I would soon want to know how to write; and that by-and-by I would be running away." I think my audience will bear witness to the correctness of this philosophy, and to the literal fulfillment of this prophecy.

It is perfectly well understood at the south, that to educate a slave is to make him discontened(sic) with slavery, and to invest him with a power which shall open to him the treasures of freedom; and since the object of the slaveholder is to maintain complete authority over his slave, his constant vigilance is exercised to prevent everything which militates against, or endangers, the stability of his authority. Education being among the menacing influences, and, perhaps, the most dangerous, is, therefore, the most cautiously guarded against.

It is true that we do not often hear of the enforcement of the law, punishing as a crime the teaching of slaves to read, but this is not because of a want of disposition to enforce it. The true reason or explanation of the matter is this: there is the greatest unanimity of opinion among the white population in the south in favor of the policy of keeping the slave in ignorance. There is, perhaps, another reason why the law against education is so seldom violated. The slave is too poor to be able to offer a temptation sufficiently strong to induce a white man to violate it; and it is not to be supposed that in a community where the moral and religious sentiment is in favor of slavery, many martyrs will be found sacrificing their liberty and lives by violating those prohibitory enactments.

As a general rule, then, darkness reigns over the abodes of the enslaved, and "how great is that darkness!"

We are sometimes told of the contentment of the slaves, and are entertained with vivid pictures of their happiness. We are told that they often dance and sing; that their masters frequently give them wherewith to make merry; in fine, that they have little of which to complain. I admit that the slave does sometimes sing, dance, and appear to be merry. But what does this prove? It only proves to my mind, that though slavery is armed with a thousand stings, it is not able entirely to kill the elastic spirit of the bondman. That spirit will rise and walk abroad, despite of whips and chains, and extract from the cup of nature occasional drops of joy and gladness. No thanks to the slaveholder, nor to slavery, that the vivacious captive may sometimes dance in his chains; his very mirth in such circumstances stands before God as an accusing angel against his enslaver.

It is often said, by the opponents of the anti-slavery cause, that the condition of the people of Ireland is more deplorable than that of the American slaves. Far be it from me to underrate the sufferings of the Irish people. They have been long oppressed; and the same heart that prompts me to plead the cause of the American bondman, makes it impossible for me not to sympathize with the oppressed of all lands. Yet I must say that there is no analogy between the two cases. The Irishman is poor, but he is not a slave. He may be in rags, but he is not a slave. He is still the master of his own body, and can say with the poet, "The hand of Douglass is his own." "The world is all before him, where to choose;" and poor as may be my opinion of the British parliament, I cannot believe that it will ever sink to such a depth of infamy as to pass a law for the recapture of fugitive Irishmen! The shame and scandal of kidnapping will long remain wholly monopolized by the American congress. The Irishman has not only the liberty to emigrate from his country, but he has liberty at home. He can write, and speak, and cooperate for the attainment of his rights and the redress of his wrongs.

The multitude can assemble upon all the green hills and fertile plains of the Emerald Isle; they can pour out their grievances, and proclaim their wants without molestation; and the press, that "swift-winged messenger," can bear the tidings of their doings to the extreme bounds of the civilized world. They have their "Conciliation Hall," on the banks of the Liffey, their reform clubs, and their newspapers; they pass resolutions, send forth addresses, and enjoy the right of petition. But how is it with the American slave? Where may he assemble? Where is his Conciliation Hall? Where are his newspapers? Where is his right of petition? Where is his freedom of speech? his liberty of the press? and his right of locomotion? He is said to be happy; happy men can speak. But ask the slave what is his condition—what his state of mind—what he thinks of enslavement? and you had as well address your inquiries to the *silent dead*. There comes no *voice* from the enslaved. We are left to gather his feelings by imagining what ours would be, were our souls in his soul's stead.

If there were no other fact descriptive of slavery, than that the slave is dumb, this alone would be sufficient to mark the slave system as a grand aggregation of human horrors.

Most who are present, will have observed that leading men in this country have been putting forth their skill to secure quiet to the nation. A system of measures to promote this object was adopted a few months ago in congress. The result of those measures is known. Instead of quiet, they have produced alarm; instead of peace, they have brought us war; and so it must ever be.

While this nation is guilty of the enslavement of three millions of innocent men and women, it is as idle to think of having a sound and lasting peace, as it is to think there is no God to take cognizance of the affairs of men. There can be no peace to the wicked while slavery continues in the land. It will be condemned; and while it is condemned there will be agitation. Nature must cease to be nature; men must become monsters; humanity must be transformed; Christianity must be exterminated; all ideas of justice and the laws of eternal goodness must be utterly blotted out from the human soul—ere a system so foul and infernal can escape condemnation, or this guilty republic can have a sound, enduring peace.

INHUMANITY OF SLAVERY.

Extract from A Lecture on Slavery, at Rochester, December 8, 1850

The relation of master and slave has been called patriarchal, and only second in benignity and tenderness to that of the parent and child. This representation is doubtless believed by many northern people; and this may account, in part, for the lack of interest which we find among persons whom we are bound to believe to be honest and humane. What, then, are the facts? Here I will not quote my own experience in slavery; for this you might call one-sided testimony. I will not cite the declarations of abolitionists; for these you might pronounce exaggerations. I will not rely upon advertisements cut from newspapers; for these you might call isolated cases. But I will refer you to the laws adopted by the legislatures of the slave states. I give you such evidence, because it cannot be invalidated nor denied. I hold in my hand sundry extracts from the slave codes of our country, from which I will quote. * * *

Now, if the foregoing be an indication of kindness, *what is cruelty*? If this be parental affection, *what is bitter malignity*? A more atrocious and blood-thirsty string of laws could not well be conceived of. And yet I am bound to say that they fall short of indicating the horrible cruelties constantly practiced in the slave states.

I admit that there are individual slaveholders less cruel and barbarous than is allowed by law; but these form the exception. The majority of slaveholders find it necessary, to insure obedience, at times, to avail themselves of the utmost extent of the law, and many go beyond it. If kindness were the rule, we should not see advertisements filling the columns of almost every southern newspaper, offering large rewards for fugitive slaves, and describing them as being branded with irons, loaded with chains, and scarred by the whip. One of the most telling testimonies against the pretended kindness of slaveholders, is the fact that uncounted numbers of fugitives are now inhabiting the Dismal Swamp, preferring the untamed wilderness to their cultivated homes—choosing rather to encounter hunger and thirst, and to roam with the wild beasts of the forest, running the hazard of being hunted and shot down, than to submit to the authority of *kind* masters.

I tell you, my friends, humanity is never driven to such an unnatural course of life, without great wrong. The slave finds more of the milk of human kindness in the bosom of the savage Indian, than in the heart of his *Christian* master. He leaves the man of the *bible*, and takes refuge with the man of the *tomahawk*. He rushes from the praying slaveholder into the paws of the bear. He quits the homes of men for the haunts of wolves. He prefers to encounter a life of trial, however bitter, or death, however terrible, to dragging out his existence under the dominion of these *kind* masters.

The apologists for slavery often speak of the abuses of slavery; and they tell us that they are as much opposed to those abuses as we are; and that they would go as far to correct those abuses and to ameliorate the condition of the slave as anybody. The answer to that view is, that slavery is itself an abuse; that it lives by abuse; and dies by the absence of abuse. Grant that slavery is right; grant that the relations of master and slave may innocently exist; and there is not a single outrage which was ever committed against the slave but what finds an apology in the very necessity of the case. As we said by a slaveholder (the Rev. A. G. Few) to the Methodist conference, "If the relation be right, the means to maintain it are also right;" for without those means slavery could not exist. Remove the dreadful scourge—the plaited thong—the galling fetter—the accursed chain—and let the slaveholder rely solely upon moral and religious power, by which to secure obedience to his orders, and how long do you suppose a slave would remain on his plantation? The case only needs to be stated; it carries its own refutation with it.

Absolute and arbitrary power can never be maintained by one man over the body and soul of another man, without brutal chastisement and enormous cruelty.

To talk of *kindness* entering into a relation in which one party is robbed of wife, of children, of his hard earnings, of home, of friends, of society, of knowledge, and of all that makes this life desirable, is most absurd, wicked, and preposterous.

I have shown that slavery is wicked—wicked, in that it violates the great law of liberty, written on every human heart—wicked, in that it violates the first command of the decalogue—wicked, in that it fosters the most disgusting licentiousness—wicked, in that it mars and defaces the image of God by cruel and barbarous inflictions—wicked, in that it contravenes the laws of eternal justice, and tramples in the dust all the humane and heavenly precepts of the New Testament.

The evils resulting from this huge system of iniquity are not confined to the states south of Mason and Dixon's line. Its noxious influence can easily be traced throughout our northern borders. It comes even as far north as the state of New York. Traces of it may be seen even in Rochester; and travelers have told me it casts its gloomy shadows across the lake, approaching the very shores of Queen Victoria's dominions.

The presence of slavery may be explained by—as it is the explanation of—the mobocratic violence which lately disgraced New York, and which still more recently disgraced the city of Boston. These violent demonstrations, these outrageous invasions of human rights, faintly indicate the presence and power of slavery here. It is a significant fact, that while meetings for almost any purpose under heaven may be held unmolested in the city of Boston, that in the same city, a meeting cannot be peaceably held for the purpose of preaching the doctrine of the American Declaration of Independence, "that all men are created equal." The pestiferous breath of slavery taints the whole moral atmosphere of the north, and enervates the moral energies of the whole people.

The moment a foreigner ventures upon our soil, and utters a natural repugnance to oppression, that moment he is made to feel that there is little sympathy in this land for him. If he were greeted with smiles before, he meets with frowns now; and it shall go well with him if he be not subjected to that peculiarly fining method of showing fealty to slavery, the assaults of a mob.

Now, will any man tell me that such a state of things is natural, and that such conduct on the part of the people of the north, springs from a consciousness of rectitude? No! every fibre of the human heart unites in detestation of tyranny, and it is only when the human mind has become familiarized with slavery, is accustomed to its injustice, and corrupted by its selfishness, that it fails to record its abhorrence of slavery, and does not exult in the triumphs of liberty.

The northern people have been long connected with slavery; they have been linked to a decaying corpse, which has destroyed the moral health. The union of the government; the union of the north and south, in the political parties; the union in the religious organizations of the land, have all served to deaden the moral sense of the northern people, and to impregnate them with sentiments and ideas forever in conflict with what as a nation we call *genius of American institutions*. Rightly viewed, this is an alarming fact, and ought to rally all that is pure, just, and holy in one determined effort to crush the monster of corruption, and to scatter "its guilty profits" to the winds. In a high moral sense, as well as in a national sense, the whole American people are responsible for slavery, and must share, in its guilt and shame, with the most obdurate men-stealers of the south.

While slavery exists, and the union of these states endures, every American citizen must bear the chagrin of hearing his country branded before the world as a nation of liars and hypocrites; and behold his cherished flag pointed at with the utmost scorn and derision. Even now an American *abroad* is pointed out in the crowd, as coming from a land where men gain their fortunes by "the blood of souls," from a land of slave markets, of blood-hounds, and slave-hunters; and, in some circles, such a man is shunned altogether, as a moral pest. Is it not time, then, for every American to awake, and inquire into his duty with respect to this subject?

Wendell Phillips—the eloquent New England orator—on his return from Europe, in 1842, said, "As I stood upon the shores of Genoa, and saw floating on the placid waters of the Mediterranean, the beautiful American war ship Ohio, with her masts tapering proportionately aloft, and an eastern sun reflecting her noble form upon the sparkling waters, attracting the gaze of the multitude, my first impulse was of pride, to think myself an American; but when I thought that the first time that gallant ship would gird on her gorgeous apparel, and wake from beneath her sides her dormant thunders, it would be in defense of the African slave trade, I blushed in utter *shame* for my country."

Let me say again, *slavery is alike the sin and the shame of the American people;* it is a blot upon the American name, and the only national reproach which need make an American hang his head in shame, in the presence of monarchical governments.

With this gigantic evil in the land, we are constantly told to look *at home;* if we say ought against crowned heads, we are pointed to our enslaved millions; if we talk of sending missionaries and bibles abroad, we are pointed to three millions now lying in worse than heathen darkness; if we express a word of sympathy for Kossuth and his Hungarian fugitive brethren, we are pointed to that horrible and hell-black enactment, "the fugitive slave bill."

Slavery blunts the edge of all our rebukes of tyranny abroad—the criticisms that we make upon other nations, only call forth ridicule, contempt, and scorn. In a word, we are made a reproach and a by-word to a mocking earth, and we must continue to be so made, so long as slavery continues to pollute our soil.

We have heard much of late of the virtue of patriotism, the love of country, &c., and this sentiment, so natural and so strong, has been impiously appealed to, by all the powers of human selfishness, to cherish the viper which is stinging our national life away. In its name, we have been called upon to deepen our infamy before the world, to rivet the fetter more firmly on the limbs of the enslaved, and to become utterly insensible to the voice of human woe that is wafted to us on every southern gale. We have been called upon, in its name, to desecrate our whole land by the footprints of slave-hunters, and even to engage ourselves in the horrible business of kidnapping.

I, too, would invoke the spirit of patriotism; not in a narrow and restricted sense, but, I trust, with a broad and manly signification; not to cover up our national sins, but to inspire us with sincere repentance; not to hide our shame from the the(sic) world's gaze, but utterly to abolish the cause of that shame; not to explain away our gross inconsistencies as a nation, but to remove the hateful, jarring, and incongruous elements from the land; not to sustain an egregious wrong, but to unite all our energies in the grand effort to remedy that wrong.

I would invoke the spirit of patriotism, in the name of the law of the living God, natural and revealed, and in the full belief that "righteousness exalteth a nation, while sin is a reproach to any people." "He that walketh righteously, and speaketh uprightly; he that despiseth the gain of oppressions, that shaketh his hands from the holding of bribes, he shall dwell on high, his place of defense shall be the munitions of rocks, bread shall be given him, his water shall be sure."

We have not only heard much lately of patriotism, and of its aid being invoked on the side of slavery and injustice, but the very prosperity of this people has been called in to deafen them to the voice of duty, and to lead them onward in the pathway of sin. Thus has the blessing of God been converted into a curse. In the spirit of genuine patriotism, I warn the American people, by all that is just and honorable, to BEWARE!

I warn them that, strong, proud, and prosperous though we be, there is a power above us that can "bring down high looks; at the breath of whose mouth our wealth may take wings; and before whom every knee shall bow;" and who can tell how soon the avenging angel may pass over our land, and the sable bondmen now in chains, may become the instruments of our nation's chastisement! Without appealing to any higher feeling, I would warn the American people, and the American government, to be wise in their day and generation. I exhort them to remember the history of other nations; and I remind them that America cannot always sit "as a queen," in peace and repose; that prouder and stronger governments than this have been shattered by the bolts of a just God; that the time may come when those they now despise and hate, may be needed; when those whom they now compel by oppression to be enemies, may be wanted as friends. What has been, may be again. There is a point beyond which human endurance cannot go. The crushed worm may yet turn under the heel of the oppressor. I warn them, then, with all solemnity, and in the name of retributive justice, *to look to their ways;* for in an evil hour, those sable arms that have, for the last two centuries, been engaged in cultivating and adorning the fair fields of our country, may yet become the instruments of terror, desolation, and death, throughout our borders.

It was the sage of the Old Dominion that said—while speaking of the possibility of a conflict between the slaves and the slaveholders—"God has no attribute that could take sides with the oppressor in such a contest. I tremble for my country when I reflect that God *is just,* and that his justice cannot sleep forever." Such is the warning voice of Thomas Jefferson; and every day's experience since its utterance until now, confirms its wisdom, and commends its truth.

WHAT TO THE SLAVE
IS THE FOURTH OF JULY?

Extract from an Oration, at Rochester, July 5, 1852

Fellow-Citizens—Pardon me, and allow me to ask, why am I called upon to speak here to-day? What have I, or those I represent, to do with your national independence? Are the great principles of political freedom and of natural justice, embodied in that Declaration of Independence, extended to us? and am I, therefore, called upon to bring our humble offering to the national altar, and to confess the benefits, and express devout gratitude for the blessings, resulting from your independence to us?

Would to God, both for your sakes and ours, that an affirmative answer could be truthfully returned to these questions! Then would my task be light, and my burden easy and delightful. For who is there so cold that a nation's sympathy could not warm him? Who so obdurate and dead to the claims of gratitude, that would not thankfully acknowledge such priceless benefits? Who so stolid and selfish, that would not give his voice to swell the hallelujahs of a nation's jubilee, when the chains of servitude had been torn from his limbs? I am not that man. In a case like that, the dumb might eloquently speak, and the "lame man leap as an hart."

But, such is not the state of the case. I say it with a sad sense of the disparity between us. I am not included within the pale of this glorious anniversary! Your high independence only reveals the immeasurable distance between us. The blessings in which you this day rejoice, are not enjoyed in common. The rich inheritance of justice, liberty, prosperity, and independence, bequeathed by your fathers, is shared by you, not by me. The sunlight that brought life and healing to you, has brought stripes and death to me. This Fourth of July is *yours*, not mine. You may rejoice, I must mourn. To drag a man in fetters into the grand illuminated temple of liberty, and call upon him to join you in joyous anthems, were inhuman mockery and sacrilegious irony. Do you mean, citizens, to mock me, by asking me to speak to-day? If so, there is a parallel to your conduct. And let me warn you that it is dangerous to copy the example of a nation whose crimes, towering up to heaven, were thrown down by the breath of the Almighty, burying that nation in irrecoverable ruin! I can to-day take up the plaintive lament of a peeled and woe-smitten people.

"By the rivers of Babylon, there we sat down. Yea! we wept when we remembered Zion. We hanged our harps upon the willows in the midst thereof. For there, they that carried us away captive, required of us a song; and they who wasted us required of us mirth, saying, Sing us one of the songs of Zion. How can we sing the Lord's song in a strange land? If I forget thee, O Jerusalem, let my right hand forget her cunning. If I do not remember thee, let my tongue cleave to the roof of my mouth."

Fellow-citizens, above your national, tumultous joy, I hear the mournful wail of millions, whose chains, heavy and grievous yesterday, are to-day rendered more intolerable by the jubilant shouts that reach them. If I do forget, if I do not faithfully remember those bleeding children of sorrow this day, "may my right hand forget her cunning, and may my tongue cleave to the roof of my mouth!" To forget them, to pass lightly over their wrongs, and to chime in with the popular theme, would be treason most scandalous and shocking, and would make me a reproach before God and the world. My subject, then, fellow-citizens, is AMERICAN SLAVERY. I shall see this day and its popular characteristics from the slave's point of view. Standing there, identified with the American bondman, making his wrongs mine, I do not hesitate to declare, with all my soul, that the character and conduct of this nation never looked blacker to me than on this Fourth of July. Whether we turn to the declarations of the past, or to the professions of the present, the conduct of the nation seems equally hideous and revolting. America is false to the past, false to the present, and solemnly binds herself to be false to the future. Standing with God and the crushed and bleeding slave on this occasion, I will, in the name of humanity which is outraged, in the name of liberty which is fettered, in the name of the constitution and the bible, which are disregarded and trampled upon, dare to call in question and to denounce, with all the emphasis I can command, everything that serves to perpetuate slavery—the great sin and shame of America! "I will not equivocate; I will not excuse;" I will use the severest language I can command; and yet not one word shall escape me that any man, whose judgment is not blinded by prejudice, or who is not at heart a slaveholder, shall not confess to be right and just.

But I fancy I hear some one of my audience say, it is just in this circumstance that you and your brother abolitionists fail to make a favorable impression on the public mind. Would you argue more, and denounce less, would you persuade more and rebuke less, your cause would be much more likely to succeed. But, I submit, where all is plain there is nothing to be argued. What point in the anti-slavery creed would you have me argue? On what branch of the subject do the people of this country need light? Must I undertake to prove that the slave is a man? That point is conceded already. Nobody doubts it. The slaveholders themselves acknowledge it in the enactment of laws for their government. They acknowledge it when they punish disobedience on the part of the slave. There are seventy-two crimes in the state of Virginia, which, if committed by a black man (no matter how ignorant he be), subject him to the punishment of death; while only two of these same crimes will subject a white man to the like punishment. What is this but the acknowledgement that the slave is a moral, intellectual, and responsible being. The manhood of the slave is conceded. It is admitted in the fact that southern statute books are covered with enactments forbidding, under severe fines and penalties, the teaching of the slave to read or write. When you can point to any such laws, in reference to the beasts of the field, then I may consent to argue the manhood of the slave. When the dogs in your streets, when the fowls of the air, when the cattle on your hills, when the fish of the sea, and the reptiles that crawl, shall be unable to distinguish the slave from a brute, then will I argue with you that the slave is a man!

For the present, it is enough to affirm the equal manhood of the Negro race. Is it not astonishing that, while we are plowing, planting, and reaping, using all kinds of mechanical tools, erecting houses, constructing bridges, building ships, working in metals of brass, iron, copper, silver, and gold; that, while we are reading, writing, and cyphering, acting as clerks, merchants, and secretaries, having among us lawyers, doctors, ministers, poets, authors, editors, orators, and teachers; that, while we are engaged in all manner of enterprises common to other men—digging gold in California, capturing the whale in the Pacific, feeding sheep and cattle on the hillside, living, moving, acting, thinking, planning, living in families as husbands, wives, and children, and, above all, confessing and worshiping the Christian's God, and looking hopefully for life and immortality beyond the grave—we are called upon to prove that we are men!

Would you have me argue that man is entitled to liberty? that he is the rightful owner of his own body? You have already declared it. Must I argue the wrongfulness of slavery? Is that a question for republicans? Is it to be settled by the rules of logic and argumentation, as a matter beset with great difficulty, involving a doubtful application of the principle of justice, hard to be understood? How should I look to-day in the presence of Americans, dividing and subdividing a discourse, to show that men have a natural right to freedom, speaking of it relatively and positively, negatively and affirmatively? To do so, would be to make myself ridiculous, and to offer an insult to your understanding. There is not a man beneath the canopy of heaven that does not know that slavery is wrong for *him*.

What! am I to argue that it is wrong to make men brutes, to rob them of their liberty, to work them without wages, to keep them ignorant of their relations to their fellow-men, to beat them with sticks, to flay their flesh with the lash, to load their limbs with irons, to hunt them with dogs, to sell them at auction, to sunder their families, to knock out their teeth, to burn their flesh, to starve them into obedience and submission to their masters? Must I argue that a system, thus marked with blood and stained with pollution, is wrong? No; I will not. I have better employment for my time and strength than such arguments would imply.

What, then, remains to be argued? Is it that slavery is not divine; that God did not establish it; that our doctors of divinity are mistaken? There is blasphemy in the thought. That which is inhuman cannot be divine. Who can reason on such a proposition! They that can, may! I cannot. The time for such argument is past.

At a time like this, scorching irony, not convincing argument, is needed. Oh! had I the ability, and could I reach the nation's ear, I would to-day pour out a fiery stream of biting ridicule, blasting reproach, withering sarcasm, and stern rebuke. For it is not light that is needed, but fire; it is not the gentle shower, but thunder. We need the storm, the whirlwind, and the earthquake. The feeling of the nation must be quickened; the conscience of the nation must be roused; the propriety of the nation must be startled; the hypocrisy of the nation must be exposed; and its crimes against God and man must be proclaimed and denounced.

What to the American slave is your Fourth of July? I answer, a day that reveals to him, more than all other days in the year, the gross injustice and cruelty to which he is the constant victim. To him, your celebration is a sham; your boasted liberty, an unholy license; your national greatness, swelling vanity; your sounds of rejoicing are empty and heartless; your denunciations of tyrants, brass-fronted impudence; your shouts of liberty and equality, hollow mockery; your prayers and hymns, your sermons and thanksgivings, with all your religious parade and solemnity, are to him mere bombast, fraud, deception, impiety, and hypocrisy—a thin veil to cover up crimes which would disgrace a nation of savages. There is not a nation on the earth guilty of practices more shocking and bloody, than are the people of these United States, at this very hour.

Go where you may, search where you will, roam through all the monarchies and despotisms of the old world, travel through South America, search out every abuse, and when you have found the last, lay your facts by the side of the every-day practices of this nation, and you will say with me, that, for revolting barbarity and shameless hypocrisy, America reigns without a rival.

THE INTERNAL SLAVE TRADE.

Extract from an Oration, at Rochester, July 5, 1852

Take the American slave trade, which, we are told by the papers, is especially prosperous just now. Ex-senator Benton tells us that the price of men was never higher than now. He mentions the fact to show that slavery is in no danger. This trade is one of the peculiarities of American institutions. It is carried on in all the large towns and cities in one-half of this confederacy; and millions are pocketed every year by dealers in this horrid traffic. In several states this trade is a chief source of wealth. It is called (in contradistinction to the foreign slave trade) *"the internal slave trade."* It is, probably, called so, too, in order to divert from it the horror with which the foreign slave trade is contemplated. That trade has long since been denounced by this government as piracy. It has been denounced with burning words, from the high places of the nation, as an execrable traffic. To arrest it, to put an end to it, this nation keeps a squadron, at immense cost, on the coast of Africa. Everywhere in this country, it is safe to speak of this foreign slave trade as a most inhuman traffic, opposed alike to the laws of God and of man. The duty to extirpate and destroy it is admitted even by our *doctors of divinity.* In order to put an end to it, some of these last have consented that their colored brethren (nominally free) should leave this country, and establish themselves on the western coast of Africa. It is, however, a notable fact, that, while so much execration is poured out by Americans, upon those engaged in the foreign slave trade, the men engaged in the slave trade between the states pass without condemnation, and their business is deemed honorable.

Behold the practical operation of this internal slave trade—the American slave trade sustained by American politics and American religion! Here you will see men and women reared like swine for the market. You know what is a swine-drover? I will show you a man-drover. They inhabit all our southern states. They perambulate the country, and crowd the highways of the nation with droves of human stock. You will see one of these human-flesh-jobbers, armed with pistol, whip, and bowie-knife, driving a company of a hundred men, women, and children, from the Potomac to the slave market at New Orleans. These wretched people are to be sold singly, or in lots, to suit purchasers. They are food for the cotton-field and the deadly sugar-mill. Mark the sad procession as it moves wearily along, and the inhuman wretch who drives them. Hear his savage yells and his blood-chilling oaths, as he hurries on his affrighted captives. There, see the old man, with locks thinned and gray. Cast one glance, if you please, upon that young mother, whose shoulders are bare to the scorching sun, her briny tears falling on the brow of the babe in her arms. See, too, that girl of thirteen, weeping, yes, weeping, as she thinks of the mother from whom she has been torn. The drove moves tardily. Heat and sorrow have nearly consumed their strength. Suddenly you hear a quick snap, like the discharge of a rifle; the fetters clank, and the chain rattles simultaneously; your ears are saluted with a scream that seems to have torn its way to the center of your soul. The crack you heard was the sound of the slave whip; the scream you heard was from the woman you saw with the babe. Her speed had faltered under the weight of her child and her chains; that gash on her shoulder tells her to move on. Follow this drove to New Orleans. Attend the auction; see men examined like horses; see the forms of women rudely and brutally exposed to the shocking gaze of American slave-buyers. See this drove sold and separated forever; and never forget the deep, sad sobs that arose from that scattered multitude. Tell me, citizens, where, under the sun, can you witness a spectacle more fiendish and shocking. Yet this is but a glance at the American slave trade, as it exists at this moment, in the ruling part of the United States.

I was born amid such sights and scenes. To me the American slave trade is a terrible reality. When a child, my soul was often pierced with a sense of its horrors. I lived on Philpot street, Fell's Point, Baltimore, and have watched from the wharves the slave ships in the basin, anchored from the shore, with their cargoes of human flesh, waiting for favorable winds to waft them down the Chesapeake. There was, at that time, a grand slave mart kept at the head of Pratt street, by Austin Woldfolk. His agents were sent into every town and county in Maryland, announcing their arrival through the papers, and on flaming hand-bills, headed, "cash for negroes." These men were generally well dressed, and very captivating in their manners; ever ready to drink, to treat, and to gamble. The fate of many a slave has depended upon the turn of a single card; and many a child has been snatched from the arms of its mothers by bargains arranged in a state of brutal drunkenness.

The flesh-mongers gather up their victims by dozens, and drive them, chained, to the general depot at Baltimore. When a sufficient number have been collected here, a ship is chartered, for the purpose of conveying the forlorn crew to Mobile or to New Orleans. From the slave-prison to the ship, they are usually driven in the darkness of night; for since the anti-slavery agitation a certain caution is observed.

In the deep, still darkness of midnight, I have been often aroused by the dead, heavy footsteps and the piteous cries of the chained gangs that passed our door. The anguish of my boyish heart was intense; and I was often consoled, when speaking to my mistress in the morning, to hear her say that the custom was very wicked; that she hated to hear the rattle of the chains, and the heart-rending cries. I was glad to find one who sympathized with me in my horror.

Fellow citizens, this murderous traffic is to-day in active operation in this boasted republic. In the solitude of my spirit, I see clouds of dust raised on the highways of the south; I see the bleeding footsteps; I hear the doleful wail of fettered humanity, on the way to the slave markets, where the victims are to be sold like horses, sheep, and swine, knocked off to the highest bidder. There I see the tenderest ties ruthlessly broken, to gratify the lust, caprice, and rapacity of the buyers and sellers of men. My soul sickens at the sight.

> Is this the land your fathers loved?
> The freedom which they toiled to win?
> Is this the earth whereon they moved?
> Are these the graves they slumber in?

But a still more inhuman, disgraceful, and scandalous state of things remains to be presented. By an act of the American congress, not yet two years old, slavery has been nationalized in its most horrible and revolting form. By that act, Mason and Dixon's line has been obliterated; New York has become as Virginia; and the power to hold, hunt, and sell men, women, and children as slaves, remains no longer a mere state institution, but is now an institution of the whole United States. The power is coextensive with the star-spangled banner and American christianity. Where these go, may also go the merciless slave-hunter. Where these are, man is not sacred. He is a bird for the sportsman's gun. By that most foul and fiendish of all human decrees, the liberty and person of every man are put in peril. Your broad republican domain is a hunting-ground for *men*. Not for thieves and robbers, enemies of society, merely, but for men guilty of no crime. Your law-makers have commanded all good citizens to engage in this hellish sport. Your president, your secretary of state, your lords, nobles, and ecclesiastics, enforce as a duty you owe to your free and glorious country and to your God, that you do this accursed thing. Not fewer than forty Americans have within the past two years been hunted down, and without a moment's warning, hurried away in chains, and consigned to slavery and excruciating torture. Some of these have had wives and children dependent on them for bread; but of this no account was made. The right of the hunter to his prey, stands superior to the right of marriage, and to *all* rights in this republic, the rights of God included! For black men there are neither law, justice, humanity, nor religion. The fugitive slave law makes MERCY TO THEM A CRIME; and bribes the judge who tries them. An American judge GETS TEN DOLLARS FOR EVERY VICTIM HE CONSIGNS to slavery, and five, when he fails to do so. The oath of an(sic) two villains is sufficient, under this hell-black enactment, to send the most pious and exemplary black man into the remorseless jaws of slavery! His own testimony is nothing. He can bring no witnesses for himself. The minister of American justice is bound by the law to hear but *one side*, and that side is the side of the oppressor. Let this damning fact be perpetually told. Let it be thundered around the world, that, in tyrant-killing, king hating, people-loving, democratic, Christian America, the seats of justice are filled with judges, who hold their office under an open and palpable *bribe*, and are bound, in deciding in the case of a man's liberty, *to hear only his accusers!*

In glaring violation of justice, in shameless disregard of the forms of administering law, in cunning arrangement to entrap the defenseless, and in diabolical intent, this fugitive slave law stands alone in the annals of tyrannical legislation. I doubt if there be another nation on the globe having the brass and the baseness to put such a law on the statute-book. If any man in this assembly thinks differently from me in this matter, and feels able to disprove my statements, I will gladly confront him at any suitable time and place he may select.

THE SLAVERY PARTY.

Extract from a Speech Delivered before the A. A. S. Society, in New York, May, 1853

Sir, it is evident that there is in this country a purely slavery party—a party which exists for no other earthly purpose but to promote the interests of slavery. The presence of this party is felt everywhere in the republic. It is known by no particular name, and has assumed no definite shape; but its branches reach far and wide in the church and in the state. This shapeless and nameless party is not intangible in other and more important respects. That party, sir, has determined upon a fixed, definite, and comprehensive policy toward the whole colored population of the United States. What that policy is, it becomes us as abolitionists, and especially does it become the colored people themselves, to consider and to understand fully. We ought to know who our enemies are, where they are, and what are their objects and measures. Well, sir, here is my version of it—not original with me—but mine because I hold it to be true.

I understand this policy to comprehend five cardinal objects. They are these: 1st. The complete suppression of all anti-slavery discussion. 2d. The expatriation of the entire free people of color from the United States. 3d. The unending perpetuation of slavery in this republic. 4th. The nationalization of slavery to the extent of making slavery respected in every state of the Union. 5th. The extension of slavery over Mexico and the entire South American states.

Sir, these objects are forcibly presented to us in the stern logic of passing events; in the facts which are and have been passing around us during the last three years. The country has been and is now dividing on these grand issues. In their magnitude, these issues cast all others into the shade, depriving them of all life and vitality. Old party ties are broken. Like is finding its like on either side of these great issues, and the great battle is at hand. For the present, the best representative of the slavery party in politics is the democratic party. Its great head for the present is President Pierce, whose boast it was, before his election, that his whole life had been consistent with the interests of slavery, that he is above reproach on that score. In his inaugural address, he reassures the south on this point. Well, the head of the slave power being in power, it is natural that the pro slavery elements should cluster around the administration, and this is rapidly being done. A fraternization is going on. The stringent protectionists and the free-traders strike hands. The supporters of Fillmore are becoming the supporters of Pierce. The silver-gray whig shakes hands with the hunker democrat; the former only differing from the latter in name. They are of one heart, one mind, and the union is natural and perhaps inevitable. Both hate Negroes; both hate progress; both hate the "higher law;" both hate William H. Seward; both hate the free democratic party; and upon this hateful basis they are forming a union of hatred. "Pilate and Herod are thus made friends." Even the central organ of the whig party is extending its beggar hand for a morsel from the table of slavery democracy, and when spurned from the feast by the more deserving, it pockets the insult; when kicked on one side it turns the other, and preseveres in its importunities. The fact is, that paper comprehends the demands of the times; it understands the age and its issues; it wisely sees that slavery and freedom are the great antagonistic forces in the country, and it goes to its own side. Silver grays and hunkers all understand this. They are, therefore, rapidly sinking all other questions to nothing, compared with the increasing demands of slavery. They are collecting, arranging, and consolidating their forces for the accomplishment of their appointed work.

The keystone to the arch of this grand union of the slavery party of the United States, is the compromise of 1850. In that compromise we have all the objects of our slaveholding policy specified. It is, sir, favorable to this view of the designs of the slave power, that both the whig and the democratic party bent lower, sunk deeper, and strained harder, in their conventions, preparatory to the late presidential election, to meet the demands of the slavery party than at any previous time in their history. Never did parties come before the northern people with propositions of such undisguised contempt for the moral sentiment and the religious ideas of that people. They virtually asked them to unite in a war upon free speech, and upon conscience, and to drive the Almighty presence from the councils of the nation. Resting their platforms upon the fugitive slave bill, they boldly asked the people for political power to execute the horrible and hell-black provisions of that bill. The history of that election reveals, with great clearness, the extent to which slavery has shot its leprous distillment through the life-blood of the nation. The party most thoroughly opposed to the cause of justice and humanity, triumphed; while the party suspected of a leaning toward liberty, was overwhelmingly defeated, some say annihilated.

But here is a still more important fact, illustrating the designs of the slave power. It is a fact full of meaning, that no sooner did the democratic slavery party come into power, than a system of legislation was presented to the legislatures of the northern states, designed to put the states in harmony with the fugitive slave law, and the malignant bearing of the national government toward the colored inhabitants of the country. This whole movement on the part of the states, bears the evidence of having one origin, emanating from one head, and urged forward by one power. It was simultaneous, uniform, and general, and looked to one end. It was intended to put thorns under feet already bleeding; to crush a people already bowed down; to enslave a people already but half free; in a word, it was intended to discourage, dishearten, and drive the free colored people out of the country. In looking at the recent black law of Illinois, one is struck dumb with its enormity. It would seem that the men who enacted that law, had not only banished from their minds all sense of justice, but all sense of shame. It coolly proposes to sell the bodies and souls of the blacks to increase the intelligence and refinement of the whites; to rob every black stranger who ventures among them, to increase their literary fund.

While this is going on in the states, a pro-slavery, political board of health is established at Washington. Senators Hale, Chase, and Sumner are robbed of a part of their senatorial dignity and consequence as representing sovereign states, because they have refused to be inoculated with the slavery virus. Among the services which a senator is expected by his state to perform, are many that can only be done efficiently on committees; and, in saying to these honorable senators, you shall not serve on the committees of this body, the slavery party took the responsibility of robbing and insulting the states that sent them. It is an attempt at Washington to decide for the states who shall be sent to the senate. Sir, it strikes me that this aggression on the part of the slave power did not meet at the hands of the proscribed senators the rebuke which we had a right to expect would be administered. It seems to me that an opportunity was lost, that the great principle of senatorial equality was left undefended, at a time when its vindication was sternly demanded. But it is not to the purpose of my present statement to criticise the conduct of our friends. I am persuaded that much ought to be left to the discretion of anti slavery men in congress, and charges of recreancy should never be made but on the most sufficient grounds. For, of all the places in the world where an anti-slavery man needs the confidence and encouragement of friends, I take Washington to be that place.

Let me now call attention to the social influences which are operating and cooperating with the slavery party of the country, designed to contribute to one or all of the grand objects aimed at by that party. We see here the black man attacked in his vital interests; prejudice and hate are excited against him; enmity is stirred up between him and other laborers. The Irish people, warm-hearted, generous, and sympathizing with the oppressed everywhere, when they stand upon their own green island, are instantly taught, on arriving in this Christian country, to hate and despise the colored people. They are taught to believe that we eat the bread which of right belongs to them. The cruel lie is told the Irish, that our adversity is essential to their prosperity. Sir, the Irish-American will find out his mistake one day. He will find that in assuming our avocation he also has assumed our degradation. But for the present we are sufferers. The old employments by which we have heretofore gained our livelihood, are gradually, and it may be inevitably, passing into other hands. Every hour sees us elbowed out of some employment to make room perhaps for some newly-arrived emigrants, whose hunger and color are thought to give them a title to especial favor. White men are becoming house-servants, cooks, and stewards, common laborers, and flunkeys to our gentry, and, for aught I see, they adjust themselves to their stations with all becoming obsequiousness. This fact proves that if we cannot rise to the whites, the whites can fall to us. Now, sir, look once more. While the colored people are thus elbowed out of employment; while the enmity of emigrants is being excited against us; while state after state enacts laws against us; while we are hunted down, like wild game, and oppressed with a general feeling of insecurity—the American colonization society—that old offender against the best interests and slanderer of the colored people—awakens to new life, and vigorously presses its scheme upon the consideration of the people and the government. New papers are started—some for the north and some for the south—and each in its tone adapting itself to its latitude. Government, state and national, is called upon for appropriations to enable the society to send us out of the country by steam! They want steamers to carry letters and Negroes to Africa. Evidently, this society looks upon our "extremity as its opportunity," and we may expect that it will use the occasion well. They do not deplore, but glory, in our misfortunes.

But, sir, I must hasten. I have thus briefly given my view of one aspect of the present condition and future prospects of the colored people of the United States. And what I have said is far from encouraging to my afflicted people. I have seen the cloud gather upon the sable brows of some who hear me. I confess the case looks black enough. Sir, I am not a hopeful man. I think I am apt even to undercalculate the benefits of the future. Yet, sir, in this seemingly desperate case, I do not despair for my people. There is a bright side to almost every picture of this kind; and ours is no exception to the general rule. If the influences against us are strong, those for us are also strong. To the inquiry, will our enemies prevail in the execution of their designs. In my God and in my soul, I believe they *will not*. Let us look at the first object sought for by the slavery party of the country, viz: the suppression of anti slavery discussion. They desire to suppress discussion on this subject, with a view to the peace of the slaveholder and the security of slavery. Now, sir, neither the principle nor the subordinate objects here declared, can be at all gained by the slave power, and for this reason: It involves the proposition to padlock the lips of the whites, in order to secure the fetters on the limbs of the blacks. The right of speech, precious and priceless, *cannot, will not*, be surrendered to slavery. Its suppression is asked for, as I have said, to give peace and security to slaveholders. Sir, that thing cannot be done. God has interposed an insuperable obstacle to any such result. "There can be *no peace*, saith my God, to the wicked." Suppose it were possible to put down this discussion, what would it avail the guilty slaveholder, pillowed as he is upon heaving bosoms of ruined souls? He could not have a peaceful spirit. If every anti-slavery tongue in the nation were silent—every anti-slavery organization dissolved—every anti-slavery press demolished—every anti slavery periodical, paper, book, pamphlet, or what not, were searched out, gathered, deliberately burned to ashes, and their ashes given to the four winds of heaven, still, still the slaveholder could have *"no peace."* In every pulsation of his heart, in every throb of his life, in every glance of his eye, in the breeze that soothes, and in the thunder that startles, would be waked up an accuser, whose cause is, "Thou art, verily, guilty concerning thy brother."

THE ANTI-SLAVERY MOVEMENT.

Extracts from a Lecture before Various Anti-Slavery Bodies, in the Winter of 1855

A grand movement on the part of mankind, in any direction, or for any purpose, moral or political, is an interesting fact, fit and proper to be studied. It is such, not only for those who eagerly participate in it, but also for those who stand aloof from it—even for those by whom it is opposed. I take the anti-slavery movement to be such an one, and a movement as sublime and glorious in its character, as it is holy and beneficent in the ends it aims to accomplish. At this moment, I deem it safe to say, it is properly engrossing more minds in this country than any other subject now before the American people. The late John C. Calhoun—one of the mightiest men that ever stood up in the American senate—did not deem it beneath him; and he probably studied it as deeply, though not as honestly, as Gerrit Smith, or William Lloyd Garrison. He evinced the greatest familiarity with the subject; and the greatest efforts of his last years in the senate had direct reference to this movement. His eagle eye watched every new development connected with it; and he was ever prompt to inform the south of every important step in its progress. He never allowed himself to make light of it; but always spoke of it and treated it as a matter of grave import; and in this he showed himself a master of the mental, moral, and religious constitution of human society. Daniel Webster, too, in the better days of his life, before he gave his assent to the fugitive slave bill, and trampled upon all his earlier and better convictions—when his eye was yet single—he clearly comprehended the nature of the elements involved in this movement; and in his own majestic eloquence, warned the south, and the country, to have a care how they attempted to put it down. He is an illustration that it is easier to give, than to take, good advice. To these two men—the greatest men to whom the nation has yet given birth—may be traced the two great facts of the present—the south triumphant, and the north humbled. Their names may stand thus—Calhoun and domination—Webster and degradation. Yet again. If to the enemies of liberty this subject is one of engrossing interest, vastly more so should it be such to freedom's friends. The latter, it leads to the gates of all valuable knowledge—philanthropic, ethical, and religious; for it brings them to the study of man, wonderfully and fearfully made—the proper study of man through all time—the open book, in which are the records of time and eternity.

Of the existence and power of the anti-slavery movement, as a fact, you need no evidence. The nation has seen its face, and felt the controlling pressure of its hand. You have seen it moving in all directions, and in all weathers, and in all places, appearing most where desired least, and pressing hardest where most resisted. No place is exempt. The quiet prayer meeting, and the stormy halls of national debate, share its presence alike. It is a common intruder, and of course has the name of being ungentlemanly. Brethren who had long sung, in the most affectionate fervor, and with the greatest sense of security,

> Together let us sweetly live—together let us die,

have been suddenly and violently separated by it, and ranged in hostile attitude toward each other. The Methodist, one of the most powerful religious organizations of this country, has been rent asunder, and its strongest bolts of denominational brotherhood started at a single surge. It has changed the tone of the northern pulpit, and modified that of the press. A celebrated divine, who, four years ago, was for flinging his own mother, or brother, into the remorseless jaws of the monster slavery, lest he should swallow up the Union, now recognizes anti-slavery as a characteristic of future civilization. Signs and wonders follow this movement; and the fact just stated is one of them. Party ties are loosened by it; and men are compelled to take sides for or against it, whether they will or not. Come from where he may, or come for what he may, he is compelled to show his hand. What is this mighty force? What is its history? and what is its destiny? Is it ancient or modern, transient or permanent? Has it turned aside, like a stranger and a sojourner, to tarry for a night? or has it come to rest with us forever? Excellent chances are here for speculation; and some of them are quite profound. We might, for instance, proceed to inquire not only into the philosophy of the anti-slavery movement, but into the philosophy of the law, in obedience to which that movement started into existence. We might demand to know what is that law or power, which, at different times, disposes the minds of men to this or that particular object—now for peace, and now for war— now for freedom, and now for slavery; but this profound question I leave to the abolitionists of the superior class to answer. The speculations which must precede such answer, would afford, perhaps, about the same satisfaction as the learned theories which have rained down upon the world, from time to time, as to the origin of evil. I shall, therefore, avoid water in which I cannot swim, and deal with anti-slavery as a fact, like any other fact in the history of mankind, capable of being described and understood, both as to its internal forces, and its external phases and relations.

[After an eloquent, a full, and highly interesting exposition of the nature, character, and history of the anti-slavery movement, from the insertion of which want of space precludes us, he concluded in the following happy manner.]

Present organizations may perish, but the cause will go on. That cause has a life, distinct and independent of the organizations patched up from time to time to carry it forward. Looked at, apart from the bones and sinews and body, it is a thing immortal. It is the very essence of justice, liberty, and love. The moral life of human society, it cannot die while conscience, honor, and humanity remain. If but one be filled with it, the cause lives. Its incarnation in any one individual man, leaves the whole world a priesthood, occupying the highest moral eminence even that of disinterested benevolence. Whoso has ascended his height, and has the grace to stand there, has the world at his feet, and is the world's teacher, as of divine right. He may set in judgment on the age, upon the civilization of the age, and upon the religion of the age; for he has a test, a sure and certain test, by which to try all institutions, and to measure all men. I say, he may do this, but this is not the chief business for which he is qualified. The great work to which he is called is not that of judgment. Like the Prince of Peace, he may say, if I judge, I judge righteous judgment; still mainly, like him, he may say, this is not his work. The man who has thoroughly embraced the principles of justice, love, and liberty, like the true preacher of Christianity, is less anxious to reproach the world of its sins, than to win it to repentance. His great work on earth is to exemplify, and to illustrate, and to ingraft those principles upon the living and practical understandings of all men within the reach of his influence. This is his work; long or short his years, many or few his adherents, powerful or weak his instrumentalities, through good report, or through bad report, this is his work. It is to snatch from the bosom of nature the latent facts of each individual man's experience, and with steady hand to hold them up fresh and glowing, enforcing, with all his power, their acknowledgment and practical adoption. If there be but *one* such man in the land, no matter what becomes of abolition societies and parties, there will be an anti-slavery cause, and an anti-slavery movement. Fortunately for that cause, and fortunately for him by whom it is espoused, it requires no extraordinary amount of talent to preach it or to receive it when preached. The grand secret of its power is, that each of its principles is easily rendered appreciable to the faculty of reason in man, and that the most unenlightened conscience has no difficulty in deciding on which side to register its testimony. It can call its preachers from among the fishermen, and raise them to power. In every human breast, it has an advocate which can be silent only when the heart is dead. It comes home to every man's understanding, and appeals directly to every man's conscience. A man that does not recognize and approve for himself the rights and privileges contended for, in behalf of the American slave, has not yet been found. In whatever else men may differ, they are alike in the apprehension of their natural and personal rights. The difference between abolitionists and those by whom they are opposed, is not as to principles. All are agreed in respect to these. The manner of applying them is the point of difference.

The slaveholder himself, the daily robber of his equal brother, discourses eloquently as to the excellency of justice, and the man who employs a brutal driver to flay the flesh of his negroes, is not offended when kindness and humanity are commended. Every time the abolitionist speaks of justice, the anti-abolitionist assents says, yes, I wish the world were filled with a disposition to render to every man what is rightfully due him; I should then get what is due me. That's right; let us have justice. By all means, let us have justice. Every time the abolitionist speaks in honor of human liberty, he touches a chord in the heart of the anti-abolitionist, which responds in harmonious vibrations. Liberty—yes, that is evidently my right, and let him beware who attempts to invade or abridge that right. Every time he speaks of love, of human brotherhood, and the reciprocal duties of man and man, the anti-abolitionist assents—says, yes, all right—all true—we cannot have such ideas too often, or too fully expressed. So he says, and so he feels, and only shows thereby that he is a man as well as an anti-abolitionist. You have only to keep out of sight the manner of applying your principles, to get them endorsed every time. Contemplating himself, he sees truth with absolute clearness and distinctness. He only blunders when asked to lose sight of himself. In his own cause he can beat a Boston lawyer, but he is dumb when asked to plead the cause of others. He knows very well whatsoever he would have done unto himself, but is quite in doubt as to having the same thing done unto others. It is just here, that lions spring up in the path of duty, and the battle once fought in heaven is refought on the earth. So it is, so hath it ever been, and so must it ever be, when the claims of justice and mercy make their demand at the door of human selfishness. Nevertheless, there is that within which ever pleads for the right and the just.

In conclusion, I have taken a sober view of the present anti-slavery movement. I am sober, but not hopeless. There is no denying, for it is everywhere admitted, that the anti-slavery question is the great moral and social question now before the American people. A state of things has gradually been developed, by which that question has become the first thing in order. It must be met. Herein is my hope. The great idea of impartial liberty is now fairly before the American people. Anti-slavery is no longer a thing to be prevented. The time for prevention is past. This is great gain. When the movement was younger and weaker—when it wrought in a Boston garret to human apprehension, it might have been silently put out of the way. Things are different now. It has grown too large—its friends are too numerous—its facilities too abundant—its ramifications too extended—its power too omnipotent, to be snuffed out by the contingencies of infancy. A thousand strong men might be struck down, and its ranks still be invincible. One flash from the heart-supplied intellect of Harriet Beecher Stowe could light a million camp fires in front of the embattled host of slavery, which not all the waters of the Mississippi, mingled as they are with blood, could extinguish. The present will be looked to by after coming generations, as the age of anti-slavery literature—when supply on the gallop could not keep pace with the ever growing demand—when a picture of a Negro on the cover was a help to the sale of a book—when conservative lyceums and other American literary associations began first to select their orators for distinguished occasions from the ranks of the previously despised abolitionists. If the anti-slavery movement shall fail now, it will not be from outward opposition, but from inward decay. Its auxiliaries are everywhere. Scholars, authors, orators, poets, and statesmen give it their aid. The most brilliant of American poets volunteer in its service. Whittier speaks in burning verse to more than thirty thousand, in the National Era. Your own Longfellow whispers, in every hour of trial and disappointment, "labor and wait." James Russell Lowell is reminding us that "men are more than institutions." Pierpont cheers the heart of the pilgrim in search of liberty, by singing the praises of "the north star." Bryant, too, is with us; and though chained to the car of party, and dragged on amidst a whirl of political excitement, he snatches a moment for letting drop a smiling verse of sympathy for the man in chains. The poets are with us. It would seem almost absurd to say it, considering the use that has been made of them, that we have allies in the Ethiopian songs; those songs that constitute our national music, and without which we have no national music. They are heart songs, and the finest feelings of human nature are expressed in them. "Lucy Neal," "Old Kentucky Home," and "Uncle Ned," can make the heart sad as well as merry, and can call forth a tear as well as a smile. They awaken the sympathies for the slave, in which antislavery principles take root, grow, and flourish. In addition to authors, poets, and scholars at home, the moral sense of the civilized world is with us. England, France, and Germany, the three great lights of modern civilization, are with us, and every American traveler learns to regret the existence of slavery in his country. The growth of intelligence, the influence of commerce, steam, wind, and lightning are our allies. It would be easy to amplify this summary, and to swell the vast conglomeration of our material forces; but there is a deeper and truer method of measuring the power of our cause, and of comprehending its vitality. This is to be found in its accordance with the best elements of human nature. It is beyond the power of slavery to annihilate affinities recognized and established by the Almighty. The slave is bound to mankind by the powerful and inextricable net-work of human brotherhood. His voice is the voice of a man, and his cry is the cry of a man in distress, and man must cease to be man before he can become insensible to that cry. It is the righteous of the cause—the humanity of the cause—which constitutes its potency. As one genuine bankbill is worth more than a thousand counterfeits, so is one man, with right on his side, worth more than a thousand in the wrong. "One may chase a thousand, and put ten thousand to flight." It is, therefore, upon the goodness of our cause, more than upon all other auxiliaries, that we depend for its final triumph.

Another source of congratulations is the fact that, amid all the efforts made by the church, the government, and the people at large, to stay the onward progress of this movement, its course has been onward, steady, straight, unshaken, and unchecked from the beginning. Slavery has gained victories large and numerous; but never as against this movement—against a temporizing policy, and against northern timidity, the slave power has been victorious; but against the spread and prevalence in the country, of a spirit of resistance to its aggression, and of sentiments favorable to its entire overthrow, it has yet accomplished nothing. Every measure, yet devised and executed, having for its object the suppression of anti-slavery, has been as idle and fruitless as pouring oil to extinguish fire. A general rejoicing took place on the passage of "the compromise measures" of 1850. Those measures were called peace measures, and were afterward termed by both the great parties of the country, as well as by leading statesmen, a final settlement of the whole question of slavery; but experience has laughed to scorn the wisdom of pro-slavery statesmen; and their final settlement of agitation seems to be the final revival, on a broader and grander scale than ever before, of the question which they vainly attempted to suppress forever. The fugitive slave bill has especially been of positive service to the anti-slavery movement. It has illustrated before all the people the horrible character of slavery toward the slave, in hunting him down in a free state, and tearing him away from wife and children, thus setting its claims higher than marriage or parental claims. It has revealed the arrogant and overbearing spirit of the slave states toward the free states; despising their principles—shocking their feelings of humanity, not only by bringing before them the abominations of slavery, but by attempting to make them parties to the crime. It has called into exercise among the colored people, the hunted ones, a spirit of manly resistance well calculated to surround them with a bulwark of sympathy and respect hitherto unknown. For men are always disposed to respect and defend rights, when the victims of oppression stand up manfully for themselves.

There is another element of power added to the anti-slavery movement, of great importance; it is the conviction, becoming every day more general and universal, that slavery must be abolished at the south, or it will demoralize and destroy liberty at the north. It is the nature of slavery to beget a state of things all around it favorable to its own continuance. This fact, connected with the system of bondage, is beginning to be more fully realized. The slave-holder is not satisfied to associate with men in the church or in the state, unless he can thereby stain them with the blood of his slaves. To be a slave-holder is to be a propagandist from necessity; for slavery can only live by keeping down the under-growth morality which nature supplies. Every new-born white babe comes armed from the Eternal presence, to make war on slavery. The heart of pity, which would melt in due time over the brutal chastisements it sees inflicted on the helpless, must be hardened. And this work goes on every day in the year, and every hour in the day.

What is done at home is being done also abroad here in the north. And even now the question may be asked, have we at this moment a single free state in the Union? The alarm at this point will become more general. The slave power must go on in its career of exactions. Give, give, will be its cry, till the timidity which concedes shall give place to courage, which shall resist. Such is the voice of experience, such has been the past, such is the present, and such will be that future, which, so sure as man is man, will come. Here I leave the subject; and I leave off where I began, consoling myself and congratulating the friends of freedom upon the fact that the anti-slavery cause is not a new thing under the sun; not some moral delusion which a few years' experience may dispel. It has appeared among men in all ages, and summoned its advocates from all ranks. Its foundations are laid in the deepest and holiest convictions, and from whatever soul the demon, selfishness, is expelled, there will this cause take up its abode. Old as the everlasting hills; immovable as the throne of God; and certain as the purposes of eternal power, against all hinderances, and against all delays, and despite all the mutations of human instrumentalities, it is the faith of my soul, that this anti-slavery cause will triumph.

Made in the USA
Monee, IL
07 July 2026